THE PROGRESS OF AFRO-AMERICAN WOMEN

THE PROGRESS OF AFRO-AMERICAN WOMEN

A SELECTED BIBLIOGRAPHY AND RESOURCE GUIDE

Compiled by Janet L. Sims
Foreword by Bettye Thomas

Greenwood Press
Westport, Connecticut • London, England

Library of Congress Cataloging in Publication Data

Sims, Janet, 1945-
The progress of Afro-American women.

Includes index.
1. Afro-American women—Bibliography. I. Title.
Z1361.N39S52 [E185.86] 016.973'04'96073 79-8948
ISBN 0-313-22083-2 lib. bdg.

Library of Congress Catalog Card Number: 79-8948
ISBN: 0-313-22083-2

First published in 1980

Greenwood Press
A division of Congressional Information Service, Inc.
51 Riverside Avenue, Westport, Connecticut 06880

Printed in the United States of America

10 9 8 7 6 5 4 3 2 1

To the
Sims family
and to Ray

CONTENTS

FOREWORD

Less than a decade ago women's history was viewed as an exotic area of historical inquiry, unworthy of the attention of serious scholars. A survey of theses and dissertations written prior to 1965 reveals little historical research on women. A survey of scholarly journals and books published prior to 1965 reveals this same trend. Research and publication trends generally reflect public interest and societal attitudes. Historically, women have been considered inferior. Their lives and contributions have not been viewed as significant enough to record, and often their organizational and individual records have not been preserved in major repositories. Clearly, women have been the victims of scholarly neglect. Black women, possessing a double minority status, have received even less scholarly consideration.

As a result of the civil rights and feminist movements, women's history has become a legitimate area of scholarly endeavor. The national conventions of major historical associations, university and college curricula, private and public foundation grants lists, newspaper articles, media programs, scholarly and popular journals and magazines are all beginning to reflect the growing concern for the preservation, identification, research and writing of women's history. Archives and libraries now are inundated by requests for primary and secondary sources pertaining to women. Unfortunately, the demand for these resources has preceded the development of adequate research materials and tools. Many repositories are just beginning to include in their card catalogues specific categories identifying holdings related to women's history. Finding aids and bibliographies gradually are coming into existence for researchers interested in women's history.

The major obstacle confronting scholars researching the history of black women in America is the lack of identifiable, readily accessible sources. Apart from a few collections located in repositories, such as the Moorland-Spingarn

Research Center, the Atlanta University Trevor Arnett Library, the Arthur and Elizabeth Schlesinger Library, and the National Archives for Black Women's History, the papers of black women and black women's organizations are still in private hands, moldering in attics, basements, and garages. The records of the National Council of Negro Women, located at the National Archives for Black Women's History, and the records of the Alpha Kappa Alpha Sorority, located at the Moorland-Spingarn Research Center, are the only manuscript collections of national black women's organizations currently in repositories. The papers of major black female leaders, writers, performers, and artists, for the most part, are unavailable to scholars. In many cases, the records have not even been located. The major and most valuable sources of information pertaining to black women, black newspapers and periodicals, are virtually unexplored.

There are several published documentary histories of black women in America, but there is no comprehensive, scholarly monograph that documents the history of the black women's club movements, the status and role of the black women in the black community and in the larger society, the literary and artistic accomplishments of black women and numerous other aspects of the life, history, existence and thought of this group of Americans. There are a number of bibliographies that identify sources relevant to the Afro-American experience and a few that relate specifically to black women. Most of these bibliographies have been short, topical bibliographical essays published in journals and other periodicals. Most of the book-length bibliographies have reference only published books and have not utilized the varied and rich source materials found in black periodical and newspaper sources.

The Progress of Afro-American Women: A Selected Bibliography & Resource Guide is an important work because it is the most comprehensive publication of nineteenth- and twentieth-century sources pertaining to black women. It cites materials from major black publications, master's theses, and doctoral dissertations and includes subject categories that have not appeared previously in published bibliographies. This is a selective bibliography and includes a variety of topics. The contributions and the work of Afro-American women in the armed services and defense movement, the suffrage movement, the women's rights and feminist movement, the church, and the family as well as their involvement in sports, in community organizations, in politics, in law and law enforcement, and in medicine are documented in this work.

This is not a definitive work; however, it is a most significant beginning. This publication should encourage funding agencies, scholars, libraries, and others who are concerned about the research and writing of Afro-American history to identify and collect records that are in private hands and to develop meaningful guides and indexes to these underutilized sources. Black newspapers and periodicals are important not only because they contain a wealth of information but also because they provide an Afro-centric view of black life. The majority of articles and news items in the nineteenth- and twentieth-century black press were written by black people. These sources provide rare insights into the black psyche and black life. It is for these reasons that this bibliography is a refreshing and important work. We look forward to the publication of additional works that explore and tap the extensive reservoir of source materials created by black Americans and that provide scholars with new research topics to expand our knowledge of black people.

Bettye C. Thomas, Ph.D.
Director of Historical Development
The National Council of Negro Women

ACKNOWLEDGMENTS

This work would not have been possible without the help and encouragement of many people, all of whom I cannot list individually. I must give special thanks to the staff of the Moorland-Spingarn Research Center and to the staffs of the libraries I visited or wrote for assistance.

I wish to thank Dr. Michael R. Winston, Dr. Dorothy B. Porter, Dr. Lenwood G. Davis, and Professor Sharon Harley for their critical analyses and suggestions.

I wish to thank Jeane Brooks, Virginia Brown, and Linda Pearce for their help in typing and editing my work.

I especially wish to thank Dr. Bettye Thomas for writing the foreword and for sharing her invaluable knowledge on the Afro-American woman.

Finally, I owe a special debt of gratitude to my family for their support and patience.

INTRODUCTION

The Afro-American woman! Her role in American society has rarely been emphasized. Traditionally, she has been viewed negatively. Her contributions to the fight for freedom, the economic front, the literary world, public life, and to education have not been accurately documented. Her personal health and beauty, her self-image, and her relationship to the black man have been minimized. Through it all, the Afro-American woman has survived and remained a stabilizing force for her family, her community, and society.

Today, many universities are conducting courses, scholarly research, and conferences on Afro-American women. Many universities and organizations are beginning to open archives on Afro-American women.

This subject bibliography includes nineteenth- and twentieth-century materials on the Afro-American Woman. It covers all aspects of her life, from slavery to her participation in the women's rights movement. The slave narratives give some insight into how the Afro-American woman acted and reacted to her bondage. The doctoral dissertations and masters theses are unique resources that have been neglected. The audiovisual aids lists materials that have not been widely published.

Although this bibliography is quite comprehensive, there are still omissions, and much research still needs to be done. The newspapers of both the nineteenth- and twentieth-centuries, which contain a wealth of information, have yet to be exhausted. There is little information on the Afro-American woman's contribution to the sciences.

This is the first major bibliography on the Afro-American woman covering all subject areas, since Lenwood Davis published an annotated bibliography on *The Black Woman In American Society*, in 1975. Another excellent bibliography is Ora Williams' *American Black Women In The Arts and Sciences,* 1973 and 1978.

This bibliography should help put into proper perspective the tremendous impact the Afro-American woman has made on our society and should encourage more scholarly research on the Afro-American woman, past, present, and future.

Janet L. Sims
Moorland-Spingarn Research Center
Howard University

THE PROGRESS OF AFRO-AMERICAN WOMEN

ARMED SERVICES AND DEFENSE WORK

Armed Services and Defense Work

1
"African-American Women War Workers." The African. Vol. 2, August, 1943, pp. 10-11.

2
"Aid of Colored Women." New York Post. 22 October, 1918.

3
"Air Force Now Recruits Negro Women Mechanics." Norfolk Journal And Guide. 26 December, 1942.

4
"Air Force Used Women Mechanics." East Tennessee News. 17 December, 1942.

5
"Air Force's Education Expert." Ebony. Vol. 25, November, 1969, pp. 88-91.

6
Anderson, Mary. "Negro Women On The Production Front." Opportunity. Vol. 21, April, 1943, pp. 37-38.

7
"Army Court Convicts 4 Negro Wacs of Disobeying Superior." Washington Post. 21 March, 1945, pp. 4.

8
"Army's First Female Dental Intern Completes Studies." Jet. Vol. 47, October 3, 1974, pp. 18.

9
"Automobile Corps of Negro Women Organized." New York Herald. 30 October, 1918.

10
Baker, Joseph V. "To A Brown Lady." The Brown American. Vol. 5, Fall, 1943, editorial page.

11
Beale, Bessie Bernell. "A Study of The Food Habits and Practices of A Selected Group of Women War Workers In Washington, D.C." Master's Thesis, Howard University, 1945, 56p.

12
Berkley, Charles C. "War Work - A Challenge to Negro Womanpower." Opportunity. Vol. 21, April, 1943, pp. 58-59.

13
"Black Females With The Armed Forces," in Black Armed Forces Officers, 1736-1971, edited by Jesse J. Jackson. Hampton, Virginia: Jesse J. Jackson, 1971, 170p., pp. 129-156.

14
"Black Woman In Court Martial Over Corn Row." Jet. Vol. 47, February 20, 1975, pp. 19.

15
"Black Women In War Production," in America's Working Women, edited by Rosalyn Baxandall, Linda Gordon and Susan Reverby. New York: Random House, 1976, 399p., pp. 285-287.

16
Blood, Kathryn. "Heroines On The Home Front." Pulse. Vol. 1, September, 1943, pp. 15, 27.

17
__________. "Maybe We Can't Carry Rifles -" Service Above And Beyond The Call of Duty." Pulse. Vol. 2, August, 1944, pp. 26-27.

18
__________. "Now It's Woman's Work: "Okay, Soldier, I'll Take Over!" Pulse. Vol. 1, November, 1943, pp. 22-23.

19
__________. "Women Warriors." Pulse. Vol. 1, December, 1943, pp. 20-21.

20
Booker, Simeon. "Navy Trains First Black Woman Pilot." Jet. Vol. 47, November 28, 1974, pp. 20-24.

21
Bowles, Eva D. "Negro Women And The War." The Southern Workman. Vol. 47, September, 1918, pp. 425-426.

22
Brown, Jean Collier. "The Negro Woman Worker." The Aframerican Woman's Journal. Vol. 2, Summer/Fall, 1941, pp. 18-25

23
"Brown Women Making History As American Plane Pilots." Black Dispatch. 23 January, 1943.

24
Candee, Beatrice. "Women In Defense Industry." Opportunity. Vol. 21, April, 1943, pp. 46-49, 86-87.

25
Caproel, Joan. "Big Welcome In Britain for Negro WACS." P. M. 14 February, 1945.

26
Carr, Polly. "The Saga of Ma Sanders." Ebony, Vol. 3, August, 1948, pp. 43.

27
"Clark, Ida Coker. "Negro Woman Worker, What Now?" Opportunity. Vol. 22, April/June, 1944, pp. 84-85, 93.

28
Coggs, Pauline R. "Community War Challenges To Negro Women." The Aframerican Woman's Journal. Vol. 3, Summer, 1943, pp. 8-9.

29
"Colored Girl In Canadian WAC Unit." Service. Vol. 8, June, 1944, pp. 7.

30
"Colored Red Cross Women Are Working Earnestly In Cause." Pittsburgh Leader. 29 March, 1918.

31
"Colored Secretaries for Y.M.C.A." New York Post. 25 April, 1919.

32
"Colored WAAC Units With D. C. Officers Arrive in Arizona." Washington Star. 1 December, 1942.

33
"Colored Women And War Industries." Jersey City Journal. 2 August, 1918.

34
"Deborah Gannett, Heroine Of The Fourth Massachusetts Regiment," in Black Patroits Of The American Revolution: 1775-1783, by James A. Bullock. Princeton: Carolingian Press, 1969, 31p., pp. 23-24.

35
DeMar, George E. "Negro Woman Are American Workers, Too." Opportunity. Vol. 21, April, 1943, pp. 41-43, 77.

36
"Doling Out Gear." Headlines. Vol. 1, March, 1945, pp. 31.

37
"The Drill Sergeant Is A Lady." Ebony. Vol. 27, December, 1973, pp. 84-89.

38
"Employment and Placement of Women in National Defense Industries." The Aframerican Woman's Journal. Vol. 2, Summer/Fall, 1941, pp. 6-9.

39
"Encouragement From The Lieutenant." Headlines. Vol. 1, March, 1945, pp. 30.

40
"First WACs Overseas." Headlines. Vol. 1, March, 1945, pp. 33.

41
"First Waves Win Praise." Headlines. Vol. 1, February, 1945, pp. 18.

42
Foster, G. Allen. "The Woman Who Saved The Union Navy." Ebony. Vol. 19, July, 1964, pp. 48-50, 52, 54-55.

43
"Getting Established." Headlines. Vol. 1, March, 1945, pp. 31.

44
"Gold Star Mothers Help War Effort." Headlines and Pictures. Vol. 2, July, 1945, pp. 7.

45
Granger, Lester B. "Women Are Vital To Victory." Opportunity. Vol. 21, April, 1943, pp. 36.

46
Gregory, Chester W. "The Black Woman In War Work, 1941-1945." Northwest Journal of African and Black American Studies. Vol. 2, Winter, 1974, pp. 21-26.

47
Gregory, George, Jr. "Wartime Guidance For Tomorrow's Citizens." Opportunity. Vol. 21, April, 1943, pp. 70-71, 90-91.

48
Hampton, Elizabeth C. "Negro Women and The WAAC." Opportunity. Vol. 21, April, 1943, pp. 54-55, 93.

49
"Harriet Tubman's Petition, 1898," in *A Documentary History of The Negro People In The United States, Vol. 1*, edited by Herbert Aptheker. New York: Citadel Press, 1951, 942p., pp. 781

50
Harris, Delolah Turner. "A Challenge To Negro Women." *Opportunity.* Vol. 21, April, 1943, pp. 72, 95.

51
"Hazel Johnson Becomes 1st Black Woman General." *Jet*. Vol. 56, June 21, 1979, pp. 18.

52
Height, Dorothy I. "Negro Women In Civilian Defense Work." *The Aframerican Woman's Journal*. Vol. 2, Winter, 1941-1942, pp. 9, 12.

53
Hicks, James L. "Negro WACs Barred From Overseas Stations By Top General's Orders." *Call and Post.* 20 July, 1946.

54
Holbrook, Stewart H. "The First American WAC." *The Negro Digest*. Vol. 3, November, 1944, pp. 39-43.

55
Holt, Bryan D. "Miss Mines Is First Black Woman Midshipman." *Key News*. 29 July, 1976, pp. 1.

56
"Howard Grad Is Female ROTC Teacher at FAMU." *Jet*. Vol. 47, November 14, 1974, pp. 19.

57
"Howe Will Train Colored Women For New War Work." *Memphis Commercial Appeal*. 24 August, 1918.

58
Hudson, Roy. *Post-War Jobs For Veterans, Negroes, Women*. New York: Workers Library, 1944, 24p.

59
Hunton, Addie. *Two Colored Women With The American Expeditionary Forces*. New York: Eagle Press, 1920, 256p.

60
"Ill. Names 1st Black Woman to Merchant Marines." *Jet*. Vol. 50, April 1, 1976, pp. 42.

61
"In Step! For America's Victory-To-Be." *Pulse*. Vol. 1, September, 1943, pp. 28-29.

62
"Ind. Woman First Air Force Cadet." Philadelphia Independent. 23 July, 1949.

63
Jasper, John. "Biggest Hoax In The Revolutionary War." The Afro American Magazine Section. October 21-25, 1975, pp. 1.

64
Jeffries, LeRoy W. "Step Up, Lady - Want A War Job?" Opportunity. Vol. 21, April, 1943, pp. 39-40, 91.

65
"Joan Bynum Is Navy's First Black Female Captain." Jet. Vol. 55, November 23, 1978, pp. 5.

66
Johnson, Jesse J. Black Women In The Armed Forces, 1942-1974: A Pictorial History. Hampton, Virginia: Hampton Institute, 1974, 110p.

67
Johnson, Patrice. "Cadet Benjamin Tries Her Wings." Encore. Vol. 6, January 3, 1977, pp. 17-18.

68
Johnson-Roundtree, Dovey. "Out Of The Service Into New Careers." Opportunity. Vol. 25, April/June, 1947, pp. 83-84, 126-127.

69
Jollies, Naomi. "Four Negro Wacs Convicted - NAACP Leader Calls It Fair." New York Post. 21 March, 1945.

70
Jones, Caroline R. "Black Women In The Army: Where The Jobs Are." The Crisis. Vol. 82, May, 1975, pp. 175-177.

71
________________. "Making A Career Out of The Military." Encore. Vol. 4, June 23/July 4, 1975, pp. 76.

72
King, Anita. "Masquerade Of A Decade." Essence. Vol. 4, May, 1973, pp. 6.

73
"Leader of Men." Jet. Vol. 46, August 1, 1974, pp. 21.

74
Lewis, Nellie W. "Negro Women Volunteers - Jacksonville, Florida: Something For Them To Do." The Aframerican Woman's Journal. Vol. 3, Summer, 1943, pp. 16-17.

75
"Local Women End WAC Basic Study." Philadelphia Independent.

3 January, 1943, pp. 6.

76
Macy, J. Noel. "Negro Women In The WAC." Opportunity. Vol. 23, Winter, 1945, pp. 14.

77
"Many Women Replace Men." Black Dispatch. 10 April, 1943.

78
McFadden, Ina M. "Women Answer America's Call." Pulse. Vol. 1, February, 1943, pp. 4.

79.
McPhee, Mary. "The Colonel Is A Lady." Sepia. Vol. 21, June, 1972, pp. 30-32, 34, 36.

80
"Military," in Black Women Makers of History: A Portrait, by George F. Jackson. Sacramento: Fong & Fong, 1977, 289p., pp. 279-283.

81
Miller, Frieda S. "Negro Women Workers." Opportunity. Vol. 23, Fall, 1945, pp. 207-208.

82
"Miss Mary Williams To Accompany War Widows." Tuskegee Messenger. Vol. 7, April 11-25, 1931, pp. 4.

83
"More Varied Jobs Offered WAAC;s." Oklahoma Eagle. 20 March, 1943.

84
"Mother Is A Sergeant." Ebony. Vol. 29, October, 1974, pp. 156-158, 160-161.

85
"Motor Corps of Negro Women." New York Post. 31 October, 1918.

86
"Mrs. Mabel K. Staupers Named To New State Commission." Opportunity. Vol. 20, November, 1942, pp. 340.

87
"Mrs. Maudelle Bousfield Appointed To Women's Policy Committee." Opprotunity. Vol. 20, September, 1942, pp. 281.

88
"Navy First." Headlines. Vol. 1, January, 1945, pp. 28.

89
"Navy Gets Its First Black Woman in Medical Corps." Jet. Vol. 48, May 29, 1975, pp. 24.

90
"Negro Volunteers of The American Women's Volunteer Services." The Aframerican Woman's Journal. Vol. 3, Summer, 1943, pp. 11-12.

91
"Negro Woman Best Welder at Shipyard." Louisiana Weekly. 1 May, 1943.

92
"The Negro Woman Looks At National Defense." The Missionary Recorder. Vol. 33, May, 1941, pp. 1.

93
"Negro Women Bridge Manpower Gap." Service. Vol. 10, September, 1945, pp. 13.

94
"Negro Women Busy." Richmond Journal. 5 April, 1918.

95
"Negro Women Give Valiant Aid To Country On The European Battlefields." New York Telegram. 19 March, 1919.

96
"Negro Women Going To France." New York Post. 20 March, 1918.

97
"Negro Women In Skilled Defense Jobs." Monthly Labor Review. Vol. 57, November, 1943, pp. 953

"Negro Women In Skilled Defense Jobs." Service. Vol. 7, April, 1943, pp. 23.

98
"Negro Women In The USO." The Aframerican Woman's Jorunal. Vol. 3, Summer, 1943, pp. 14-15.

99
"Negro Women In The War Effort." Service. Vol. 8, April, 1944, pp. 13, 31.

100
"The Negro Woman in War Work," in Women In Defense Work During World War II - An Analysis Of The Labor Problem and Women's Rights, by Chester W. Gregory. New York: Exposition Press, 1974, 243p., pp. 140-151.

101
"Negro Women Employed For First Time By Washington Navy Yard." Opportunity. Vol. 21, April, 1943, pp. 79.

102
"Negro Women To Get Curtis Wright's Help." Philadelphia Tribune. 19 October, 1942.

103
"New England Woman First Honored." *Pulse*. Vol. 2, December, 1944, pp. 10.

104
"New York National Guard Gets First Black Woman." *Jet*. Vol. 45, October 11, 1973, pp. 38.

105
"Objective Obtained." *Headlines and Pictures*. Vol. 1, April, 1945, pp. 15.

106
Pitts, Lucia M. *One Negro WAC's Story*. Los Angeles: Lucia Mae Pitts, 1968, 22p.

107
"Plan Women's Land Army." *Pulse*. Vol. 1, June, 1943, pp. 18.

108
Porter, Dorothy B. "Negro Women In Our Wars." *The Negro History Bulletin.* Vol. 7, June, 1944, pp. 195-196.

109
"Pretty Petty Officer Is Navy Electronics Expert." *Jet*. Vol. 49, December 18, 1975, pp. 33.

110
"Q M Skipper." *Headlines.* Vol. 1, March, 1945, pp. 18.

111
Qualey, J. S. "Negro WACs Get Year For Defying Orders." *P.M.* 21 March, 1945, pp. 10.

112
"Race Woman Top Welder At Brooklyn Yard." *Philadelphia Independent*. 21 March, 1943.

113
"Race Women Employed In Washington Navy Yard." *The Sepia Socialite*. 27 February, 1943.

114
"Recent Releases on 'The Negro Woman In National Defense'." *The Aframerican Woman's Journal*. Vol. 2, Summer/Fall, 1941, pp. 32.

115
Rice, C. W. "Women Must Prepare To Take Men's Jobs." *Service*. Vol. 7, January, 1943, pp. 8-9.

116
Robinson, Rosa. "Women Who Remain At Home." *Service*. Vol. 7, November, 1943, pp. 25.

117
Rosenberg, Anna M. "Womanpower And The War." Opportunity. Vol. 21, April, 1943, pp. 35-36.

118
Sawyer, Annabel. "The Negro Woman in National Defense." The Aframerican Woman's Journal. Vol. 2, Summer/Fall, 1941, pp. 2-5.

119
"Segregation for WAVES, Even in New York City." Afro American. 4 November, 1944.

120
"Seven Hundred Negro Women Now in Air Force." Jet. Vol. 2, June 12, 1952, pp. 9.

121
"She Runs The Reels." Headlines. Vol. 1, March, 1945, pp. 18.

122
"Ship Shape: Josephine Delores Rosa Is The First Negro WAVE to Get Sea-Going Duty." Our World. Vol. 9, February, 1954, pp. 58, 60-61.

123
Smith, Mary. "Black Women in Uniform." Sacramento Observer. 1 June, 1972, pp. D-18.

124
"So That's A Parachute..." Headlines. Vol. 1, March, 1945, pp. 30.

125
Taylor, Susie King. Reminiscences of My Life With The 33rd United States Colored Troops. Boston: Susie King Taylor, 1902, 82p.

126
"They Also Serve." The Brown American. Vol. 5, Summer, 1943, pp. 12.

127
"To Train Women in War Plant." Norfolk Journal And Guide. 19 December, 1942.

128
Treadwell, Mattie E. The Woman's Army Corps. Washington, D. C.: U. S. Department of the Army, 1954, 841p.

129
U. S. Department of Labor, Women's Bureau. Negro Women War Workers. Washington, D. C.: G. P. O., 1945, 23p.

130
"The WAAC - The Girl Who Wouldn't Be Left Behind." The Afra-

merican Woman's Journal. Vol. 3, #1 & 2, 1942, pp. 7.

131
"WAAC's Cure For Narrow Nationalism." Norfolk Journal and Guide. 21 November, 1942.

132
"WAAC's Open Ranks to Colored Applicants." Philadelphia Tribune. 3 October, 1942.

133
"WAC At Work." Headlines. Vol. 1, March, 1945, pp. 17.

134
"WAC Promoted." Headlines. Vol. 1, November, 1944, pp. 24.

135
"WAC Swears Menial Duties Goes To Negroes." P.M. 20 March, 1945.

136
"WAC Technicians." Service. Vol. 8, March, 1944, pp. 8.

137
"WACs Left Intact." Headlines and Pictures. Vol. 2, August, 1945, pp. 31.

138
"WACs Meet Jim Crow." Headlines." Vol. 1, February, 1945, pp. 11.

139
WACs Released, Back To Work." Headlines and Pictures. Vol. 1, May, 1945, pp. 10.

140
Watson, Florence Peters. "A Negro Woman Looks At War." The Brown American. Vol. 4, May, 1941, pp. 21.

141
"Wave Head, Race Women Hold Confab." Chicago Defender. 31 July, 1944.

142
"Wave Officers." Headlines. Vol. 1, January, 1945, pp. 29.

143
Williams, Mary E. "Negro War Mothers Journey to France." Tuskegee Messenger. Vol. 7, December, 1931, pp. 4, 11.

144
"Woman General." Sacramento Observer Magazine. Vol. 16, June 14-20, 1979, pp. F-3.

145
"Woman Given Promotion in War Factory." Black Dispatch. 28

November, 1942.

146
"Woman's Saving Touch In Wartime Or In Peace." Pulse. Vol. 2, June, 1944, pp. 12.

147
"Woman's Work Is Never Done." Service. Vol. 7, December, 1943, pp. 16.

148
"Women At War." The Brown American. Vol. 5, Summer, 1943, pp. 3-7, 12, 15.

149
"The Women Behind The Men Behind The Guns." The African. Vol. 2, May, 1943, pp. 10-11.

150
"Women In The Army." Service. Vol. 7, October, 1942, pp. 14.

151
"Women In The Service Academies." Ebony. Vol. 32, November, 1976, pp. 31-34, 36, 38.

152
"Women In Uniform." Ebony. Vol. 18, December, 1962, pp. 62-67.

153
"Women In The War Effort." Service. Vol. 9, May, 1945, pp. 32.

154
"Women 'Take Over' In Army Zone Abroad." Chicago Defender. 17 April, 1948, pp. 13.

155
"Women Who Can Work In Defense Industries." Service. Vol. 5, December, 1940, pp. 30-31.

156
"Women Work In D. C. Shipyards." Oklahoma Eagle. 27 February, 1943.

157
"The Women's Army for National Defense." The Aframerican Woman's Journal. Vol. 3, Summer, 1943, pp. 13-14.

158
"Women's Land Army Planned; Regional Conferences Held." Opportunity. Vol. 21, July, 1943, pp. 141-142.

159
"Work Opportunities for Negro Women In The National Defense Program." The Aframerican Woman's Journal. Vol. 2, Summer/Fall, 1941, pp. 9-11.

160
Yearwood, Ruby Bryant. "Women Volunteers Unite To Serve." Opportunity. Vol. 21, April, 1943, pp. 60-62, 88-89.

161.
"Yesterday In Negro History." Jet. Vol. 4, July 23, 1953, pp. 10.

THE ARTS

Art

162
Andrews, Benny. "New Colors, Old Canvass." Encore. Vol. 4, June 23/July 4, 1975, pp. 64-66.

163
Biggers, John Thomas. "The Negro Woman In American Life And Education: A Mural Presentation." Doctoral Dissertation, Pennsylvania State University, 1954.

164
Bims, Hamilton. "A Sculptress Looks at Martin Luther King." Ebony. Vol. 28, April, 1973, pp. 95-96, 98, 100, 102, 104.

165
Catlett, Elizabeth. Painting, Sculpture And Prints Of The Negro Woman, December 1947 - January, 1948. Washington, D. C.: Barnett Aden Gallery, 4p.

166
"Elizabeth Prophet, Sculptor." The Crisis. Vol. 36, December, 1929, pp. 407, 427, 429.

167
An Exhibition of Black Women Artists, May 5-17, 1975. Santa Barbara: University of California, Committee For Black Culture, 1975, 41p.

168
Hayes, Tritobia M. "Black Female Sculptors, 1950-1970." Master's Thesis, Howard University, 1970, 146p.

169
Hoover, Velma J. "Meta Vaux Warrick Fuller: Her Life And Art." The Negro History Bulletin. Vol. 40, March/April, 1977, pp. 678-681.

170
"Inspiring And Talented Young Women Exhibit Art In Plaster And Bronze." Norfolk Journal And Guide. 30 May, 1925, pp. 7.

171
"Interview With A Young Sculptress," in The Black West: A Documentary and Pictorial History, by William L. Katz. New York: Anchor Books, 1973, 336p., pp. 46-47.

172
Jefferson, Margo. "Make Miracles From Leftovers: Black Women In The Arts," in Woman In The Year 2000, edited by Maggie Tripp. New York: Arbor House Publishing Company, 1974, 302p., pp. 46-49.

173
Johnson, Channing D. "Betye Saar's 'Hoodoo' World of Art." Essence. Vol. 6, March, 1976, pp. 84-85.

174
Klaw, Barbara. "She Made Art Pay." The Negro Digest. Vol. 4, December, 1945, pp. 35-36.

175
Marr, Warren, II. "Alma Thomas: May Crisis Cover Artist." The Crisis. Vol. 77, May, 1970, pp. 192-193.

176
McKenzie, Marjorie. "In Fifty Years, Women Move Forward In Arts and Professions." Pittsburgh Courier. 27 January, 1951, pp. 20.

177
Morrison, Allan. "Women In The Arts." Ebony. Vol. 21, August, 1966, pp. 90-94.

178
Pierre-Noel, Lois Jones. "Black Women In The Visual Arts." Black Arts Review. Vol. 2, July/August, 1979, pp. 4-5, 10.

179
_______________________. "Black Women In The Visual Arts: A Comparative Study." New Directions. Vol. 3, April, 1976, pp. 12-20.

180
_______________________. "Laura Wheeler Waring: Portarit Painter." The Aframerican Woman's Journal. Winter, 1947, pp. 25.

181
"Poetess In Stone." Headlines And Pictures. Vol. 2, May, 1946, pp. 41-42.

182
"Poetry and Sculpture," in Black Women Makers of History: A

Portrait, by George F. Jackson. Sacramento: Fong & Fong, 1977, 289p., pp. 200-206.

183
"Prominent Richmond Artist." Norfolk Journal And Guide. 20. June, 1925, pp. 1.

184
"Ruth Brall's Sculptured Portraits of Distinguished American Negroes." The Crisis. Vol. 56, April, 1949, pp. 112-113.

185
"A Sculptor." The Crisis. Vol. 15, January, 1918, pp. 133.

186
"Sculptured Reality." Essence. Vol. 3, July, 1972, pp. 50-51

187
"Selected Portraits From The Great Beautiful Black Women Collection." The Negro History Bulletin. Vol. 42, January February/March, 1979, pp. 13-14.

188
"Selects Commercial Art For Career." Norfolk Journal And Guide. 5 November, 1927, pp. 1.

189
"She Designs For Friendship." Pulse. Vol. 5, September, 1947 pp. 28.

190
Thomas, A. A. "Virginia Honors Its Winners of Harmon Awards." Norfolk Journal And Guide. 15 January, 1927, pp. 1.

191
"Traveling Exhibitions on Black Women." Black Collegian. Vol 9, May/June, 1979, pp. 58.

192
Trescott, Jacqueline. "Sculptor Selma Burke: A Life of Art, For Art." Washington Post. 17 March, 1975, pp. B-1.

193
"Woman Artist." The Crisis. Vol. 39, August, 1932, pp. 259.

194
"Woman's Exchange Art Circle." Norfolk Journal And Guide. 7 July, 1917, pp. 5.

195
"Works of Negro Sculptress On Exhibit." Norfolk Journal And Guide. 24 March, 1917, pp. 6.

Dance

196
"Amii Tells Why Dancing Is Good For Black Girls." Jet. Vol. 56, August 9, 1979, pp. 22.

197
"Are Night Club Dancers Getting Younger?" Jet. Vol. 7, November 18, 1954, pp. 60-62.

198
"Chicago Dancer With Women's Minstrels." New York Age. 15 April, 1922, pp. 8.

199
"Chicago Women's Minstrels In Brooklyn Performance." New York Age. 29 April, 1922, pp. 5.

200
"Cotton Club Girls." Ebony. Vol. 4, April, 1949, pp. 34-38.

201
"Dancers Go Dramatic." Ebony. Vol. 24, September, 1969, pp. 38.

202
"The Dunham Dancers." Our World. Vol. 1, July, 1946, pp. 38.

203
"Europe's Dancing Doll." Ebony. Vol. 7, September, 1952, pp. 60-64, 66.

204
"Girls Make Hit In Minstrelsy." New York Age. 1 July, 1922, pp. 1, 6.

205
"Girls Minstrel Show To Be Charity Benefit." New York Age. 3 June, 1922, pp. 6.

206
"Girls Minstrels To Appear For Charity." New York Age. 24 June, 1922, pp. 1.

207
"Love Life of Chorus Girls." Jet. Vol. 3, May 21, 1953, pp. 33-38.

208
"Must Chorus Girls Be Playgirls." Jet. Vol. 2, August 21, 1952, pp. 32-37.

209
"Outdoor Chorus Girls." Jet. Vol. 8, July 21, 1955, pp. 58-60.

210
"Why Girls Become Shake Dancers." Jet. Vol. 4, October 29,

153, pp. 32-37.

Music

211
Asklund, Gunnar. "Preparing For An Operatic Career." Etude. Vol. 72, February, 1954, pp. 15-16.

212
Cavin, Susan. "Missing Women: On The Voodoo Trail To Jazz." Journal of Jazz Studies. Vol. 3, Fall, 1975, pp. 4-27.

213
"Classic Blues: Mamie Smith, Bessie Smith, Ma Rainey, Ida Cox, Bertha "Chippie" Hill," in The World of Soul, by Arnold Shaw. New York: Cowles Book Company, 1970, 306p., pp. 33-43.

214
"Colored Girl Wins Coveted Julliard Alumni Voice Scholarship." Tuskegee Messenger. Vol. 7, December, 1931, pp. 9.

215
"Concert Artists, Classic and Jive." Pulse. Vol. 6, April, 1948, pp. 17.

216
Daughtry, Willia Estelle. "Sissieretta Jones: A Study of The Negro's Contribution To Nineteenth Century American Concert And Theatrical Life." Doctoral Dissertation. Syracuse University, 1968, 257p.

217
DeLerma, Dominique-Rene. "Black Women Composers." Black Arts Review. Vol. 2, July/August, 1979, pp. 8.

218
"Diahann Carroll And Female Singers Take The Lead," in To Find An Image, by James Murray. New York: Bobbs-Merrill, 1973, 205p., pp. 36-41.

219
Eagleson, Oran and Lillian E. Taylor. "Study of Chord Perference In A Group Of Negro College Women." Journal of Experimental Psychology. Vol. 26, June, 1940, pp. 619-621.

220
"First Famous Negro Opera Singer Dies." Jet. Vol. 33, December 21, 1967, pp. 55.

221
"Ga. Soprano Is First Negro Girl at La Scala." Jet. Vol. 3, February 26, 1953, pp. 52.

222
Green, Mildred Denby. "A Study of The Lives And Works Of Five

Black Women Composers In America." Doctoral Dissertation, The University of Oklahoma, 1975, 331p.

223
Harrison, Daphne Duval. "Black Women In The Blues Tradition," in The Afro American Woman: Struggles And Images, edited by Sharon Harley and Rosalyn Terborg-Penn. New YOrk: Kennikat Press, 1978, 137p., pp. 58-73.

224
Hopkins, Pauline E. "Famous Women of The Negro Race - Phenomenal Vocalists." The Colored American Magazine. Vol. 4, November, 1901, pp. 45-53.

225
"In Retrospect: Black Prima Donnas Of The Nineteenth Century." The Black Perspective In Music. Vol. 7, Spring, 1979, pp. 95-106.

226
Jackson, Irene V. "Afro-American Women in Music: Focus On Roberta Martin, 1907-1969." Feeling The Spirit. Vol. 5, #4, 1978, pp. 2-9.

227
"The Jazz Singers: Billie Holiday, Ella Fitzgerald, Sarah Vaughan, Carmen McRae, Nancy Wilson," in The World of Soul, by Arnold Shaw. New York: Cowles Book Company, Inc., 1970, 306p., pp. 49-60.

228
"Last Of The Brownskin Mamas." Ebony. Vol. 8, November, 1952, pp. 49-50.

229
McIntosh, India. "Harlem Prodigy." The Negro Digest. Vol. 2, September, 1944, pp. 67-68.

230
"Music." Encore. Vol. 4, June 23/July 4, 1975, pp. 54-55.

231
"Opera's Most Promising Negro Voice." Jet. Vol. 4, October 8, 1953, pp. 60-62.

232
"The Pianist Who Captured Paris." Jet. Vol. 4, December 10, 1953, pp. 58-59.

233
"Queens of The Juke Boxes." Jet. Vol. 3, March 26, 1953, pp. 56-61.

234
Reagon Bernice. "The Lady Street Singer." Southern Exposure. Vol. 2, Spring/Summer, 1974, pp. 38-41.

235
Ryder, Georgia A. "Black Women in Song: Some Socio-Cultural Images." The Negro History Bulletin. Vol. 39, May, 1976, pp. 601-603.

236
Shapiro, Samuel. "Black Women And The Blues: The Social Content of Bessie Smith's Music." Northwest Journal of African and Black American Studies. Vol. 2, Winter, 1974, pp. 11-19.

237
"She Sings Along With Mitch." Ebony. Vol. 17, March, 1962, pp. 40-42, 44-46.

238
Stewart-Baxter, Derrick. Ma Rainey And The Classic Blues Singers. New York: Stein & Day, 1970, 112p.

239
"Why Girl Bands Don't Click." Jet. Vol. 5, February 11, 1954, pp. 60-62.

240
"When Malindy Sings," in Beautiful, Also, Are The Souls Of My Black Sisters: A History of The Black Woman In America, by Jeanne Noble. New Jersey: Prentice-Hall, Inc., 1978, 353p., pp. 209-287.

241
"Woman Composer, 27, Gets Guggenheim Fellowship." Jet. Vol. 6, May, 27, 1954, pp. 62.

AUDIOVISUAL MATERIALS

Cartoons

242
"70 Soul Secrets of Sapphire"
Carolyn Jetter Greene
Sapphire Publishing Company

Motion Pictures And Film Strips

243
"Angela Davis: Portriat Of A Revolutionary"
Yolande DuLuart
60 min.

244
"Aretha Franklin; Soul Singer"
McGraw-Hill
25 min.
1968

245
"Autobiography of Miss Jane Pittman"
Learning Corporation of America
110 min.
1974

246
"Billie Holiday Story"
Third World

247
"Black Woman"
Indiana University
52 min.
1971

248
"Chains of Slavery - Harriet Tubman"
Encyclopedia Britannica Education Corp.
1969

249
"Dr. Mary McLeod Bethune
Film Associates
1967

250
"Fannie Lou Hamer"
Rediscovery Productions
10 min.
1970

251
"Felicia"
Anti Defamation League
12½ min.
1965

252
"Gwendolyn Brooks"
Indiana University
30 min.
1967

253
"Gwendolyn Brooks"
NET
30 min.
1967

254
"Harriet Tubman"
Society For Visual Education

255
"Harriet Tubman And The Underground Railroad"
McGraw-Hill
54 min.
1964

256
"I Am Somebody"
McGraw-Hill
28 min.
1970

257
"The Lady In The Lincoln Memorial"
New York Times Company Teaching Resources
18 min

258
"Leading American Negroes"
Society For Visual Education

259
"Marian Anderson"
LES/MUS
30 min.

260
"Marian Anderson - Contralto"
Mills
26 min.
1953

261
"Negro History And Culture Series - The Family and Socialization"
Audio-Video Duplication Center
30 min.

262
"No Handouts For Mrs. Hedgepeth"
North Carolina Fund
27 min.

263
"Patricia Harris"
McGraw-Hill

264
"Roberta Flack"
Indiana University
30 min
1971

265
"Shirley Chisholm"
McGraw-Hill

266
"Shirley Chisholm: Elect One Of Your Own"
Doubleday
1969

267
"To Be Young, Gifted, and Black"
University of California
90 min.

268
"Veronica"
Jason Films
27 min.
1969

Records and Video-Recordings

Records:

269
"Angela Davis; Soul And Soledad"
Flying Dutchman

270
"Bessie Smith: The World's Greatest Blues Singer"
Columbia Records

271
"Coretta Scott King Reads From _My Life With Martin Luther King, Jr._"
Caedon

272
"Coretta Scott King, Free At Last: His Truth Is Marching On"
Caedon

273
"My Life With Martin Luther King, Jr."
Caedon

274
"Lorraine Handsberry On Her Art And The Black Experience"
Caedon

275
"Lorraine Hansberry Speaks Out: Art And The Black Experience"
Caedon

276
"Marian Anderson"
Eye Gate House

277
"Mary McLeod Bethune"
Eye Gate House

278
"The Negro Woman"
Folkways Records

279
"Poetry of Maya Angelou"
GWP Records

280
"Poetry of The Black Man"
United Artists

281
"To Be Young, Gifted, And Black"
Caedon

282
"Vinnie Burrows"
Listening Library, Inc.

283
"Women In Literature - Lorraine Hansberry: Raisin In The Sun"
Caedon

284
"Women In Literature - Gwendolyn Brooks Reading Her Poetry"
Caedon

Video-Recordings

285
"Accomplished Women"
Films, Inc.

286
"Angela Davis: A Closer Look"
WNET - TV

287
"Black High School Girls
Martha Stuart Communications

288
"New Images For Black Women"
WNET - TV

289
"This Is The Home of Mrs. Levant Graham"
New Thing Art and Architecture Center

Tapes

Audio:

290
"The Role of The Black Woman In America"
Pacifica Tape Library
50 min.

291
"A Salute To Ella Baker"
Pacifica Tape Library
60 min.

Cassettes:

292
"The Changing Role of Black Women In Africa and America"
Film, Inc.

293
"Kathleen Cleaver On Black Panther Politics and The Feminist Movement"
Pacifica Tape Library
34 min.

294
"Nikki Giovanni Reads Re:Creation"
Broadside

295
"The Rocks Cry Out"
Broadside

296
"Vinnie Burrows"
Production Listening Library, Inc.

Video:

297
"The Role Of The Black Woman In America"
Pacifica
50 min.

BIBLIOGRAPHIES

298
"Bibliography On Negro Nursing." National Negro Health News. Vol. 6, April/June, 1939, pp. 26-27.

299
Bickner, Mei Liang. Women At Work: An Annotated Bibliography, 2 Vols. Los Angeles: University of California, Manpower Research Center, Institute of Industrial Relations, 1974, 1977, 800p.

300
Brown, Barbara, Deborah A. McDonald and Arnell J. Marshall. The Contemporary Black Woman In Africa And America: A Selected Bibliography Of Books And Periodical Articles Published From 1960-1975. Washington, D. C.: Howard University, Founders Library, 1975, 55p.

301
Cole, Johnneta B. "Black Women In America, An Annotated Bibliography." Black Scholar. Vol. 3, December, 1971, pp. 42-53

302
Davis, Lenwood G. The Black Family In The United States: A Selected Bibliography of Annotated Books, Articles And Dissertations on Black Families In America. Westport, Connecticut: Greenwood Press, 1978, 132p.

303
__________. The Black Family In Urban Areas Of The United States. Monticello, Illinois: Council of Planning Librarians, 1973, 60p.

304
__________. "The Black Woman In America: Autobiographical And Biographical Materials." Northwest Journal of African And Black American Studies. Vol. 2, Winter, 1974, pp. 27-29.

305
Davis, Lenwood G. The Black Woman In American Society: A Selected, Annotated Bibliography. Boston: G. K. Hall, 1975, 200p.

306
______________. Black Women In The Cities, 1872-1972; A Bibliography Of Published Works Of Black Women In Cities In The United States. Monticello, Illinois: Council of Planning Librarians, 1972, 53p.

307
Enabulele, Arlene B. and Dionne J. Jones. A Resource Guide On Black Women In The United States. Washington, D. C.: Howard University, Institute For Urban Affairs and Research, 1978, 107p.

308
Jackson, Jacquelyne Johnson. "A Partial Bibliography On Or Related To Black Women." Journal of Social and Behavioral Sciences. Vol. 21, Winter, 1975, pp. 90-135.

309
Klotman, Phyllis R. Black Family And The Black Woman: A Bibliography. Indiana: Indiana University Library, 1972, 107p.

310
Leffall, Dolores C. and Janet L. Sims. "Mary McLeod Bethune - The Educator; Also Including A Selected Annotated Bibliography." Journal of Negro Education. Vol. 45, Summer, 1976, pp. 342-359.

311
Loff, Jon N. "Gwendolyn Brooks: A Bibliography." CLA Journal. Vol. 17, September, 1973, pp. 21-32.

312
Marzolf, Marion, Ramona R. Rush and Darlene Stern. "The Literature Of Women In Journalism History." Journalism History. Vol. 1, Winter, 1974-1975, pp. 117-128.

313
"Negro Women," in A Bibliography of The Negro In Africa And America, by Monroe N. Work. New York: Argosy-Antiquarian Ltd., 1928, 698p., pp. 504-507.

314
Porter, Dorothy B. "Selected Writings By Negro Women." Women's Education. Vol. 7, December, 1968, pp. 4-5.

315
Psychological Perspectives On Black Women: A Selected Bibliography of Recent Citations. Washington, D. C.: Committee on Black Women's Concerns, American Psychological Association, August, 1977, 10p.

316
Reddick, L. D. "A Select Bibliography For The Exhibit of 'The Contribution of Negro Women To American Civilization'." Journal of the National Association of College Women. #18, 1941, pp. 61-63.

317
Sims, Janet L. Black Women - A Selected Bibliography. Washington, D. C.: Howard University, Moorland-Spingarn Research Center, 1976, 18p.

318
_____________. Black Women In The Employment Sector. Monticello, Illinois: Vance Bibliographies, 1979, 28p.

319
Stroman, Carolyn Alma. "Toward A Sociology Of The Black Family: A Bibliographic Essay." Master's Thesis. Atlanta University, 1973, 60p.

320
Terbourg-Penn, Rosalyn M. "The Historical Treatment of Afro-Americans In The Woman's Movement, 1900-1920; A Bibliographical Essay." A Current Bibliography On African Affairs. Vol. 7, Summer, 1974, pp. 245-259.

321
Truesdell, Marilyn R. Black Women In Religion: A Bibliography. n.p., n.p., Fall, 1975, 19p.

322
Wilcox, Preston. Women And Race; Bibliography. New York: Afram Associates, 1969, 4p.

323
Wilkinson, Doris Y. "Toward A Positive Frame of Reference For Analysis of Black Families: A Selected Bibliography." Journal of Marriage And The Family. Vol. 40, November, 1978, pp. 707-708.

324
Williams, Ora. American Black Women In The Arts And Social Sciences: A Bibliographic Survey. New Jersey: Scarecrow Press, 1973, 1976, 141p.

325
_____________. "A Bibliography of Works Written By American Black Women." CLA Journal. Vol. 15, March, 1972, pp. 354-377.

326
_____________. "Works By And About Alice (Moore Dunbar-Nelson): A Bibliography." CLA Journal. Vol. 19, March, 1976, pp. 322-326.

BIOGRAPHIES—FICTION

Hemings, Sally

327
Chase-Riboud, Barbara. Sally Hemings: A Novel. New York: Viking Press, 1979, 346p.

Meriwether, Louise

328
Meriwether, Louise. Daddy Was A Number Runner. New Jersey: Prentice-Hall, 1970, 208p.

Pittman, Jane

329
Gaines, Ernest J. The Autobiography of Miss Jane Pittman. New York: Dial Press, 1971, 245p.

Prince, Lucy Terry

330
Katz, Bernard and Jonathan Katz. Black Woman: A Fictionalized Biography of Lucy Terry Prince. New York: Pantheon, 1973, 269p.

Tubman, Harriet

331
Heidish, Marcy. A Woman Called Moses: A Novel Based On The Life of Harriet Tubman. Boston: Houghton-Mifflin, 1976, 270p.

BIOGRAPHIES AND AUTOBIOGRAPHIES

Anderson, Marian

332
Albus, Harry James. The 'Deep River' Girl; The Life Of Marian Anderson In Story Form. Grand Rapids, Michigan: W. B. Erdmans Publishing Co., 1949, 85p.

333
Anderson, Marian. My Lord What A Morning, An Autobiography. New York: Viking Press, 1969, 312p.

334
Newman, Shirlee P. Marian Anderson: Lady From Philadelphia. New York: Westminster Press, 1965, 175p.

335
Piquion, Rene. Marian Anderson. Port-au-Prince: Henry Deschamps, n.d., 13p.

336
Stevenson, Janet. Singing For The World: Marian Anderson. Chicago: Encyclopedia Britannica Press, 1963, 189p.

337
Tobias, Tobi. Marian Anderson. New York: Crowell, 1972, 40p.

338
Vehanen, Kosti. Marian Anderson: A Portrait. New York: McGraw Hill, 1941, 270p.

Anderson, Rosa Claudette

339
Anderson, Rosa Claudette. River, Face Homeward: An Afro American In Ghana. New York: Exposition Press, 1966, 121p.

Angelou, Maya

340
Angelou, Maya. Gather Together In My Name. New York: Random House, 1974, 181p.

341
__________. I Know Why The Caged Bird Sings. New York: Random House, 1969, 281p.

342
__________. Oh Pray My Wings Are Gonna Fit Me Well. New York: Random House, 1975, 67p.

343
__________. Singin' And Swingin' And Gettin' Merry Like Christmas. New York: Random House, 1976, 269p.

Bailey, Pearl

344
Bailey, Pearl. The Raw Pearl. New York: Harcourt, Brace and World, 1968, 206p.

345
__________. Talking To Myself. New York: Harcourt, Brace and World, 1971, 233p.

Baker, Josephine

346
Baker, Josephine and Jo Bouillon. Josephine. New York: Harper & Row, 1977, 302p.

Barlow, Leila Mae

347
Barlow, Leila Mae. Across The Years, Memoirs. Montgomery: Paragon, 1959, 84p.

Barnett, Ida B. Wells

348
Duster, Alfreda M., ed. Crusade For Justice: The Autobiography of Ida B. Wells. Chicago: University of Chicago Press, 1970, 434p.

349
Thompson, Mildred. "Ida B. Wells-Barnett: An Exploratory Study Of An American Black Woman, 1893-1930." Doctoral Dissertation, George Washington University, 1979, 268p.

Bass, Charlotta A.

350
Bass, Charlotta A. Forty Years: Memoirs From The Pages Of A

Newspaper. Los Angeles: C. A. Bass, 1960, 198p.

Bates, Daisy

351
Bates, Daisy. The Long Shadow of Little Rock: A Memoir. New York: McKay, 1962, 234p.

Beckett, Catherine S. Campbell

352
Coppin, Levi Jenkins, ed. In Memoriam: Catherine S. Campbell Beckett. n.p., 1888, 109p.

Bethune, Mary McLeod

353
Carruth, Ella K. She Wanted To Read: The Story of Mary McLeod Bethune. New York: Abingdon Press, 1966, 80p.

354
Dees, Jesse W. The College Built On Prayer: Mary McLeod Bethune. Daytona Beach: Bethune-Cookman College, 1963, 78p.

355
Flemming, Sheila Yvette. "Mary McLeod Bethune And The National Youth Administration." Master's Thesis, Atlanta University, 1972, 41p.

356
Greenfield, Eloise. Mary McLeod Bethune. New York: Crowell, 1977, 32p.

357
Holt, Rackham. Mary McLeod Bethune: A Biography. New York: Doubleday, 1964, 306p.

358
Peare, Catherine O. Mary McLeod Bethune. New York: Vanguard Press, 1951, 219p.

359
Radford, Ruby Lorraine. Mary McLeod Bethune. New York: Putnam, 1973, 61p.

360
Sterne, Emma Gelders. Mary McLeod Bethune. New York: Knopf, 1957, 268p.

Bragg, Nellie G.

361
Bragg, George F. Tribute To Mrs. Nellie G. Bragg. Baltimore: St. James Church, September 19, 1937, 7p.

Brooks, Gwendolyn

362
Brooks, Gwendolyn. Report From Part One. Detroit: Broadside Press, 1972, 215p.

Brown, Charlotte Hawkins

363
Marteena, Constance H. The Lengthening Shadow Of A Woman: A Woman: A Biography Of Charlotte Hawkins Brown. New York: Exposition Press, 1977, 135p.

Brown, Clara

364
Bruyn, Dathleen. Aunt Clara Brown; Story Of A Black Pioneer. Colorado: Pruett Publishing Company, 1970, 206p.

Brown, Hallie Quinn

365
McFarlin, Annjennette Sophie. "Hallie Quinn Brown - Black Woman Elocutionist: 1845 (?) - 1949." Doctoral Dissertation, Washington State University, 1975, 190p.

Browne, Rose Butler

366
Browne, Rose Butler. Love My Children: An Autobiography. New York: Meredith Press, 1969, 245p.

Burroughs, Nannie Helen

367
Pickens, William. Nannie Burroughs And The School Of The Three B's. New York: William Pickens, 1921, 43p.

Carwell, Lucy

368
Ladd, Elizabeth. Some Account Of Lucy Carwell, A Woman Of Colour, Who Departed This Life On The 25th of The 3rd Month, 1824 - Aged 39 Years. Philadelphia: Benjamin & Thomas Kite, 1824, 4p.

Caution, Sarah Estelle

369
Reid, Harriet Edwards. Sarah Estelle Caution, A Tribute. Boston: Spaulding-Moss Company, 1935, 29p.

Chisholm, Shirley

370
Brownmiller, Susan. Shirley Chisholm: A Biography. New York: Doubleday, 1971, 141p.

371
Chisholm, Shirley. The Good Fight. New York: Harper & Row, 1973, 206p.

372
________________. Unbought And Unbossed. Boston: Houghton-Mifflin, 1970, 177p.

373
Haskins, James. Fighting Shirley Chisholm. New York: Dial Press, 1975, 211p.

374
Hicks, Nancy. The Honorable Shirley Chisholm, Congresswoman From Brooklyn. New York: Lion Books, 1971, 118p.

Clark, Septima

375
Clark, Septima. Echo In My Soul. New York: Dutton, 1962, 243p.

Cole, Natalie

376
Jacobs, Linda. Natalie Cole: Star Child. St. Paul, Minnesota: EMC Corporation, 1977, 38p.

Cooper, Anna Julia

377
Cooper, Anna J. The Third Step. n.p., n.p., n.d., 44p.

378
________________. A Voice From The South By A Black Woman Of The South. Xenia, Ohio: Aldrine Printing House, 1892, 304p.

Coppin, Fannie Jackson

379
Coppin, Fannie Jackson. Reminiscences of School Life, And Hints On Teaching. Philadelphia: A. M. E. Book Concern, 1913, 191p.

Cotton, Ella Earls

380
Cotton, Ella Earls. A Spark For My People: The Sociological Autobiography Of A Negro Teacher. New York: Exposition Press, 1954, 288p.

Dandridge, Dorothy

381
Dandridge, Dorothy and Earl Conrad. Everything And Nothing: The Dorothy Dandridge Tragedy. New York: Abelard-Schuman Ltd., 1970, 215p.

382
Mills, Earl. Dorothy Dandridge: A Portrait In Black. California: Holloway House, 1970, 248p.

Davis, Angela

383
Aptheker, Bettina. The Morning Breaks: The Trial of Angela Davis. New York: International Publishers, 1975, 284p.

384
Davis, Angela. Angela Davis: An Autobiography. New York: Random House, 1974, 400p.

385
________ and Bettina Aptheker. If They Come In The Morning: Voices of Resistance. New York: The Third Press, 1971, 281p.

386
Finke, Blythe F. Angela Davis: Traitor or Martyr Of The Freedom Of Expression. New York: SamHar Press, 1972, 28p.

387
Major, Reginald. Justice In The Round; The Trial of Angela Davis. New York: The Third Press, 1973, 314p.

388
Nadelson, Regina. Who Is Angela Davis? The Biography Of A Revolutionary. New York: Peter H. Wyden, 1972, 208p.

389
Parker, J. A. Angela Davis: The Making Of A Revolutionary. New York: Arlington House, 1973, 272p.

390
Smith, Nelda J. From Where I Sat. New York: Vantage Press, 1973, 246p.

391
Timothy, Mary. Jury Woman. Palo Alto, California: Emty Press, 1974, 307p.

Day, Helen Caldwell

392
Day, Helen Caldwell. Color Ebony. New York: Sheed & Ward, 1951 182p.

Derricotte, Juliette

393
Cuthbert, Marion. Juliett Derricotte. New York: Woman's Press, 1933, 55p.

Dubois, Silvia

394
Larison, C. W. Silvia Dubois (Now 116 Years Old); A Biography Of The Slave Who Whipt Her Mistress And Gained Her Freedom. New York: Negro Universities Press, 1883, 1969, 124p.

Dunham, Katherine

395
Biemiller, Ruth. Dance: The Story of Katherine Dunham. New York: Doubleday, 1969, 144p.

396
Buckle, Richard. Katherine Dunham, Her Dancers, Singers, Musicians. London: Ballett Publications, 1949, 79p.

397
Dunham, Katherine. Katherine Dunham's Journey To The Accompong. New York: Holt & Company, 1946, 162p.

398
________________. A Touch Of Innocence. New York: Harcourt, Brace & Company, 1959, 312p.

Dunnigan, Alice A.

399
Dunnigan, Alice A. A Black Woman's Experience - From Schoolhouse To White House. Philadelphia: Dorrance & Company, 1974, 673p.

Elaw, Zilpha

400
Elaw, Zilpha. Memoirs Of The Life, Religious Expereince, Ministerial Travels And Labours Of Mrs. Zilpha Elaw: An American Female Of Color. London: Elaw Zilpha, 1846, 172p.

Eldridge, Elleanor

401
McDougall, Frances Harriet (Whipple). Elleanor's Second Book. Providence: B. T. Albro, 1839, 128p.

402
____________________________________. Memoirs Of Elleanor Eldridge. Providence: B. T. Albro, 1845, 127p.

Everett, Syble Ethel Byrd

403
Everett, Syble Ethel Byrd. Adventures With Life: An Autobiography Of A Distinguished Negro Citizen. Boston: Meador Publishing Company, 1945, 182p.

Evers, Myrlie

404
Evers, Myrlie. For Us The Living. New York: Doubleday, 1967, 378p.

Flack, Roberta

405
Morse, Charles. Roberta Flack. Chicago: Childrens Press, 1974, 31p.

Foote, Julia

406
Foote, Julia. A Brand Plucked From The Fire: An Autobiographical Sketch. Cleveland: W. F. Schneider, 1879, 124p.

Freeman, Elizabeth

407
Felton, Harold W. Mumbet: The Story of Elizabeth Freeman. New York: Dodd, Mead, 1970, 63p.

Gannett, Deborah Sampson

408
Felton, Harold W. Deborah Sampson, Soldier Of The Revolution. New York: Dodd, Mead, 1976, 111p.

409
McGovern, Ann. The Secret Soldier: The Story of Deborah Sampson. New York: Four Winds Press, 1975, 62p.

Gibson, Althea

410
Gibson, Althea. I Always Wanted To Be Somebody. New York: Harper & Row, 1958, 176p.

411
__________. So Much To Live For. New York: Putnam, 1968, 160p.

Giovanni, Nikki

412
Giovanni, Nikki. Gemini: An Extented Autobiographical Statement On My First Twenty-Five Years Of Being A Black Poet. New York: Bobbs-Merrill, 1972, 149p.

Goodwin, Ruby Berkley

413
Goodwin, Ruby. It's Good To Be Black. New York: Doubleday, 1953, 256p.

Greenfield, Elizabeth Taylor

414
The Black Swan At Home And Abroad; Or, A Biographical Sketch Of Miss Elizabeth Taylor Greenfield, The American Vocalist. Philadelphia: W. S. Young, 1855, 64p.

Griffin, Edna L.

415
Bronson, Helen Kitchen. Let There Be Life, The Contemporary Account Of Edna L. Griffin. Pasadena: M. S. Sen, 1947, 135p.

Grimke, Charlotte Forten

416
Billington, Ray Allen, ed. The Journal of Charlotte Forten: A Free Negro In The Slave Era. New York: Dryden Press, 1953, 246p.

417
Douty, Esther M. Charlotte Forten: Free Black Teacher. Champaign, Illinois: Garrard, 1971, 144p.

418
Longworth, Polly I. Charlotte Forten, Black And Free. New York: Crowell, 1970, 248p.

Guffy, Ossie

419
Guffy, Ossie. Ossie: The Autobiography Of A Black Woman. New York: W. W. Norton, 1971, 224p.

Hackley, E. Azalia.

420
Davenport, M. Marguerite. Azalia: The Life Of Madame E. Azalia Hackley. Boston: Chapman & Grimes, Inc., 1947, 196p.

Hamer, Fannie Lou

421
Jordan, June. Fannie Lou Hamer. New York: Crowell, 1972, 39p.

Hansberry, Lorraine

422
Hansberry, Lorraine. To Be Young, Gifted, And Black. New Jersey: Prentice-Hall, 1969, 266p.

Harper, Frances Ella Watkins

423
Daniel, Theodora Williams. "The Poems of Frances E. W. Harper, Edited With A Biographical And Critical Introduction And

Critical Introduction And Bibliography." Master's Thesis, Howard University, 1937, 257p.

424
Greer, Beatrice Tatum. "A Study of The Life and Works of Mrs. Frances Ellen Watkins Harper." Master's Thesis. Hampton Institute, 1952, 100p.

Hedgeman, Anna

425
Hedgeman, Anna Arnold. The Trumpet Sound: A Memoir of Negro Leadership. New York: Holt, Rinehart & Winston, 1964, 202p.

Hicks, Estelle Belle

426
Hicks, Estelle Bell. The Golden Apples: Memoirs Of A Retired Teacher. New York: Exposition Press, 1958, 75p.

Holiday, Billie

427
Chilton, John. Billie's Blues: The Billie Holiday Story, 1933-1959. New York: Stein & Day, 1975, 264p.

428
Holiday, Billie. Lady Sings The Blues. New York: Doubleday, 1956, 250p.

Hope, Lugenia Burns

429
Beard, Annie R. "Mrs. John Hope, Black Community Builder In Atlanta, Georgia, 1900-1936." Master's Thesis. Atlanta University, 1975, 45p.

Horne, Lena

430
Horne, Lena and Carlton Moss. In Person, Lena Horne. New York: Greenberg, 1950, 240p.

431
__________ and Richard Schickel. Lena. New York: Doubleday, 1965, 300p.

Hurston, Zora Neale

432
Hemenway, Robert E. Zora Neale Hurston: A Literary Biography. Chicago: University of Illinois Press, 1977, 371p.

433
Hurston, Zora Neale. Dust Tracks On A Road. New York: Arno Press, 1942, 1969, 294p.

Jackson, Mahalia

434
Goreau, Laurraine. Just Mahalia, Baby. Texas: Word Books, 1975, 611p.

435
Jackson, Jesse. Make A Joyful Noise Unto The Lord: The Life Of Mahalia Jackson, Queen Of Gospel Singers. New York: Dell, 1975, 126p.

436
Jackson, Mahalia and Evan McLeod Whylie. Movin' On Up. New York: Hawthorne Books, 1966, 212p.

437
McDearmon, Kay. Mahalia: Gospel Singer. New York: Dodd, Mead, 1976, 45p.

Jordan, Barbara

438
Bryant, Ira B. Barbara Charline Jordan: From The Ghetto To The Capitol. Houston: D. Armstrong Company, Inc., 1977, 105p.

439
Haskins, James. Barbara Jordan. New York: Dial Press, 1977, 215p.

440
Jacobs, Linda. Barbara Jordan: Keeping Faith. St. Paul, Minnesota: EMC Corp., 1978, 39p.

441
Jordan, Barbara and Shelby Hearon. Barbara Jordan: A Self-Portrait. New York: Doubleday, 1979, 269p.

Keckley, Elizabeth

442
Keckley, Elizabeth. Behind The Scenes: Or Thirty Years A Slave And Four Years In The White House. New York: G. W. Carleton, 1868, 371p.

King, Coretta Scott

443
King, Coretta Scott. My Life With Martin Luther King, Jr. New York: Holt, Rinehart & Winston, 1969, 372p.

444
Patterson, Lillie. Coretta Scott King. Champaign, Illinois: Garrard, 1977, 96p.

445
Taylor, Paula. Coretta Scott King, A Woman of Peace. Chicago:

Childrens Press, 1974, 31p.

446
Vivian, Octavia B. Coretta: The Story of Mrs. Martin Luther King, Jr. Philadelphia: Fortress Press, 1970, 111p.

Kitt, Eartha

447
Kitt, Eartha. Alone With Me: A New Autobiography. Chicago: H. Regnery Company, 1976, 276p.

448
__________. Thursday's Child. New York: Duell, Sloan & Pearce, Inc., 1956, 250.

Lee, Helen

449
Lee, Helen Jackson. Nigger In The Window: Autobiography Of A Black Woman. New York: Doubleday, 1978,

Lee, Jarena

450
Lee, Jarena. The Life And Religious Experiences of Jarena Lee, A Coloured Lady, Giving An Account of Her Call To Preach The Gospel. Philadelphia: Jarena Lee, 1836, 24p.

Lee, Reba

451
Lee, Reba (pseud.). I Passed For White. New York: Longmans, Green, 1955, 274p.

Little, Joan

452
Reston, James, Jr. The Innocence of Joan Little: A Southern Mystery. New York: Times Books, 340p.

McCollum, Ruby.

453
Huie, William Bradford. Ruby McCollum: Woman In The Swannee Jail. New York: Dutton Press, 1956, 249p.

Moody, Ann

454
Moody, Ann. Coming Of Age In Mississippi. New York: Dial Press, 1968, 348p.

Moore, Martha Edith Bannister

455
Moore, Martha Edith Bannister. Unmasked: The Story Of My Life

On Both Sides Of The Race Barrier. New York: Expostion Press, 1964, 106p.

Morton, Lena Beatrice

456
Morton, Lena Beatrice. My First Sixty Years: Passion And Wisdom. New York: Philosophical Library, 1965, 175p.

Murray, Pauli

457
Murray, Pauli. Proud Shoes: The Story Of An American Family. New York: Harper & Row, 1956, 276p; 1978, 280p.

Parks, Lillian Rogers

458
Parks, Lillian Rogers. My Thirty Years Backstairs At The White House. New York: Fleet Publishing Company, 1961, 346p.

459
____________ and Frances Spatz Leighton. It Was Fun Working At The White House. New York: Fleet Publishing Company, 1969, 208p.

Parks, Rosa

460
Greenfield, Eloise. Rosa Parks. New York: Crowell, 1973, 32p.

Patterson, Katheryn M.

461
Patterson, Katheryn M. No Time For Tears. Chicago: Johnson Publishing Company, 1965, 109p.

Peake, Mary S.

462
Lockwood, Lewis C. Mary S. Peake, The Colored Teacher At Fortress Monroe. Boston: American Tract Society, 1863, 64p.

Pittman, Portia M. Washington

463
Hill, Roy L. Booker T's Child: The Life And Times Of Portia Marshall Washington Pittman. New Jersey: McDaniel Press, 1974, 90p.

464
Stewart, Ruth Ann. Portia: The Life Of Portia Washington Pittman. New York: Anchor Press, 1977, 154p.

Pleasant, Mary Ellen (Mammy)

465
Holdredge, Helen O'Connell. Mammy Pleasant. New York: Putnam, 1953, 311p.

466
___________________________. Mammy Pleasant's Partner. New York: Putnam, 1954, 300p.

Price, Leontyne

467
Lyon, Hugh Lee. Leontyne Price: Highlights Of A Prima Donna. New York: Vantage Press, 1973, 218p.

Prince, Nancy

468
Prince, Nancy. A Narrative Of Life And Travels of Nancy Prince. Boston: Nancy Prince, 1856, 89p.

Ross, Diana

469
Eldred, Patricia Mulronney. Diana Ross. Chicago: Childrens Press, 1975, 31p.

Rudloph, Wilma

470
Rudolph, Wilma and Bud Greenspan. Wilma. New York: New American Library, 1977, 172p.

Sams, Jessie Bennett

471
Sams, Jessie Bennett. White Mother. New York: McGraw Hill, 1957, 241p.

Schuyler, Phillippa Duke

472
Schuyler, Phillippa Duke. Adventures In Black And White. New York: Robert Speller & Sons, 1960, 302p.

Smith, Amanda

473
Cadbury, M. A. The Life Of Amanda Smith. Birmingham: Cornish Brothers, 1916, 84p.

474
Smith, Amanda. An Autobiography; The Story Of The Lord's Dealings With Mrs. Amanda Smith, The Colored Evangelist. Chicago: Meyer & Brothers, 1893, 506p.

475
Taylor, Marshall W. The Life Travels, Labors, and Helpers Of Mrs. Amanda Smith, The Famous Negro Missionary Evangelist. Cincinnati: Cranston & Stone, 1888, 63p.

Smith, Bessie

476
Albertson, Chris. Bessie. New York: Stein & Day, 1927, 253p.

477
Bessie Smith, Empress Of The Blues. New York: W. Kane, 1975, 143p.

478
Moore, Carman. Somebody's Angel Child: The Story of Bessie Smith. New York: Crowell, 1969, 121p.

479
Oliver, Paul. Bessie Smith. New York: A. S. Barnes, 1961, 83p.

Spencer, Anne

480
Greene, J. Lee. Time's Unfading Garden: Ann Spencer's Life And Poetry. Baton Rouge: Louisiana State University Press, 1977, 204p.

Stewart, Maria W.

481
Stewart, Maria W. Meditations From The Pen of Mrs. Maria W. Stewart. Washington: Lloyd Garrison & Knapp, 1879, 82p.

Stewart, Rebecca

482
Stewart, Theophilus Gould. Memoir of Mrs. Rebecca Stewart. Philadelphia: A. M. E. Church, 1877, 3p.

Tarry, Ellen

483
Tarry, Ellen. The Third Door: The Autobiography Of An American Negro Woman. New York: McKay, 1955, 304p.

Taylor, Susie King

484
Booker, Simeon. Susie King Taylor, Civil War Nurse. New York: McGraw Hill, 1969, 127p.

Terrell, Mary Church

485
Desselle, Frances. "The Life And Contributions Of Mary Church

Terrell." Master's Thesis. Howard University, 1974, 187p.

486
Shepperd, Gladys Byram. Mary Church Terrell: Respectable Person. Baltimore: Human Relations Press, 1959, 125p.

487
Terrell, Mary Church. A Colored Woman In A White World. Washington, D. C.: Randsdell Publishing Company, 1940, 437p.

Thompson, Era Bell

488
Thompson, Era Bell. American Daughter. Chicago: University of Chicago Press, 1946, 299p.

Towne, Laura Matilda

489
Towne, Laura Matilda. Letters And Diary Of Laura M. Towne; Written From The Sea Islands Of South Carolina, 1862-1884. New York: Negro Universities Press, 1912, 1969, 310p.

Truth, Sojourner

490
Bernard, Jacqueline. Journey Toward Freedom: The Story of Sojourner Truth. New York: Norton, 1967, 265p.

491
Fauset, Arthur H. Sojourner Truth: God's Faithful Pilgrim. Chapel Hill: University of North Carolina Press, 1938, 187p.

492
Gilbert, Olive. Narrative Of Sojourner Truth. Chicago: Johnson Publishing Company, 1970, 240p.

493
Graves, Zena Orphelia. "Sojourner Truth: A Study In Personality And Culture." Master's Thesis. Fisk University, 1943, 91p.

494
May, Julian. Sojourner Truth: Freedom-Fighter. Chicago: Childrens Press, 1973, 39p.

495
Ortiz, Victoria. Sojourner Turth, A Self-Made Woman. Philadelphia: Lippincott, 1974, 157p.

496
Pauli, Hertha Ernestine. Her Name Was Sojourner Truth. New York: Appleton-Century Crofts, 1962, 250p.

497
Peterson, Helen Stone. Sojourner Truth, Fearless Crusader. Champaign, Illinois: Garrard, 1972, 96p.

Tubman, Harriet

498
Bradford, Sarah Elizabeth. Harriet: The Moses Of Her People. New York: Corinth Books, 1961, 149p.

499
Conrad, Earl. Harriet Tubman: Negro Soldier And Abolitionist. New York: International Press, 1942, 47p.

500
Epstein, Sam and Beryl Epstein. Harriet Tubman: Guide To Freedom. Champaign, Illinois: Garrard, 1968, 96p.

501
Grant, Matthew G. Harriet Tubman: Black Liberator. Chicago: Childrens Press, 1974, 29p.

502
Lawrence, Jacob. Harriet And The Promised Land. New York: Windmill Books, 1968, 1 vol.

503
McGovern, Ann. Runaway Slave: The Story Of Harriet Tubman. New York: Four Winds Press, 1965, 1 vol.

504
Palmer, Gertrude Edna (Mary Eusebius, Sister, S. M.). "Harriet Tubman: Moses Of The American Negro." Master's Thesis. St. John's University, 1946, 129p.

505
Petry, Ann. Harriet Tubman: Conductor Of the Underground Railroad. New York: Crowell, 1955, 247p.

506
Sterling, Dorothy. Freedom Train: The Story Of Harriet Tubman. New York: Doubleday, 1954, 191p.

507
Winders, Gertrude Hecker. Harriet Tubman: Freedom Girl. New York: Bobbs-Merrill, 1969, 200p.

Turnor, Mae Caesar

508
Turnor, Mae Caesar. Memory Lane In My Southern World. New York: Vantage Press, 1968, 136p.

Walker, Maggie Lena

509
Bankett, Lelia W. A Testimonial Of Love Tendered Mrs. Maggie L. Walker,...Twenty-five Years Of Service. Richmond: St. Luke Press, 1925, 60p.

510
Dabney, Wendell Phillip. Maggie L. Walker And The I. O. Saint Luke: The Woman And Her Work. Cincinnati: Dabney, 1927, 137p.

Waring, Laura Wheeler

511
In Memoriam, Laura Wheeler Waring, 1887-1948: An Exhibit Of Paintings, May and June, 1949. Washington, D. C.: Howard University, Gallery of Art, 1949.

Waters, Ethel

512
Knaack, Twila. Ethel Waters: I Touched A Sparrow. Waco, Texas: World Books, 1978, 128p.

513
Waters, Ethel. His Eye Is On The Sparrow: An Autobiography. New York: Doubleday, 1951, 278p.

Wheatley, Phillis

514
Borland, Kathryn K. and Helen R. Speicher. Phillis Wheatley: Young Colonial Poet. New York: Bobbs-Merrill, 1968, 200p.

515
Deane, Charles, ed. Letters Of Phillis Wheatley: The Negro Slave Poet Of Boston. Boston: n.p., 1864, 19p.

516
Graham, Shirley. The Story Of Phillis Wheatley. New York: Messner, 1949, 176p.

517
Heartman, Charles F. Phillis Wheatley (Phillis Peters): A Critical Attempt And Bibliography Of Her Writings. New York: Charles F. Heartman, 1915, 44p.

518
Robinson, William H. Phillis Wheatley In The Black American Beginnings. Detroit: Broadside Press, 1975, 95p.

Williams, Rose Berthenia Clay

519
Williams, Rose Berthenia Clay. Black And White Orange: An

Autobiography. New York: Vantage Press, 1961, 135p.

Workman, Willie Mae (Cartwright)

520
Kytle, Elizabeth L. Willie Mae. New York: Knopf, 1958, 243p.

Wright, Charlotte Crogman

521
Wright, Charlotte Crogman. Beneath The Southern Cross: The Story Of An American Bishop's Wife In South Africa. New York: Exposition Press, 1955, 184p.

COLLECTED BIOGRAPHIES

522
"Autobiographies Of Black Women: Ida Wells, Maya Angelou, Anne Moody," in Black Autobiography In America, by Stephen Butterfield. Amherst: University of Massachusetts Press, 1974, 303p., pp. 201-217.

523
Beckles, Frances N. 20 Black Women: A Profile Of Contemporary Black Maryland Women. Baltimore: Gateway Press, 1978, 146p.

524
Brawley, Banjamin G. Women Of Achievement. Chicago: Woman's American Baptist Home Mission Society, 1919, 92p.

525
Brown, Hallie Quinn. Homespun Heroines And Other Women Of Distinction. Xenia, Ohio: Aldine Publishing Company, 1926, 248p.

526
Burt, Olive W. Black Women Of Valor. New York: Messner, 1974.

527
Cherry, Gwendolyn. Portraits In Color: The Lives Of Negro Women. New York: Pageant Press, 1962, 224p.

528
Daniel, Sadie I. Women Builders. Washington, D. C.: Associated Publishers, 1970, 308p.

529
Hale, Sarah J. Woman's Record; Or, Sketches Of All Distinguished Women, From The Creation To A. D. 1854. New York: Harper & Brothers, 1869, 912p.

530
Haviland, Laura A. Woman's Life Work: Labors And Experiences. Miami: Mnemosyne Publishing Company, 1887, 554p.

531
Jones, Hettie. Big Star Fallin' Mama; Five Women In Black Music. New York: Viking Press, 1974, 150p.

532
Majors, Monroe A. Noted Negro Women, Their Triumphs And Activities. Chicago: Conohue & Henneberry, 1893, 365p.

533
National Council of Negro Women. Contributions of Black Women To Minnesota History. St. Paul: Mason Publishing Company, 1977, 118p.

534
"Nine Profiles of Black Womanhood." Ebony. Vol. 32, August, 1977, pp. 69-70, 72-74, 76-78.

535
North Carolina Negro Library Association. Achivements Of Afro-American Women Of The Twentieth Century; A Checklist. Greensboro: North Carolina Negro Library Association, 1949.

536
Our Famous Women. Hartford: The Hartford Publishing Company, 1888, 715p.

537
Scruggs, Lawson A. Women Of Distinction: Remarkable In Works And Invincible In Character. Raleigh, N. C.: L. A. Scruggs, 1893, 382p.

538
Sillen, Samuel. Women Against Slavery. New York: Masses & Mainstream, 1955, 102p.

539
Sterling, Dorothy. Black Foremothers: Three Lives. New York: Feminist Press, 1979, 167p.

540
Stewarton. The Female Revolutionary Plutarch, Containing Biographical, Historical, And Revolutionary Sketches, Characters, And Anecdotes. London: J. & W. Smith, 1806, 424p.

541
"A Symphony In Action, 1939." The Aframerican Woman's Journal. Vol. 1, Spring, 1940, pp. 10-18.

542
"A Symphony In Action, 1940." The Aframerican Woman's Journal. Vol. 1, Summer/Fall, 1940, pp. 19-28.

543
"These Days Black Women Are Singing Strong." Vogue. Vol. 153, May, 1969, pp. 169-173.

544
Willard, Frances E. A Woman Of The Century, Fourteen Hundred-Seventy Biographical Sketches Accompanied By Portraits Of Leading American Women In All Walks Of Life. Detroit: Gale Research Company, 1967, 812p.

545
Wright, Richardson. Forgotten Ladies; Nine Portraits From The American Family Album. Philadelphia: Lippincott, 1928, 307p.

ECONOMIC CONDITIONS

546
Alexander, Sadie T. M. "Negro Women In Our Economic Life." Opportunity. Vol. 8, July, 1930, pp. 201-203.

547
Anderson, Mary. "Economic Problems of Negro Women Discussed." Tuskegee Messenger. Vol. 7, April 11, 1931, pp. 5.

548
"Black Spending Influenced By Women." Sacramento Observer. 1 June, 1972, pp. D-11.

549
"Black Women's World: Money Woes." Sacramento Observer. 1 June, 1972, pp. D-11.

550
Brown, Jean Collier. "The Economic Status of Negro Women." The Southern Workman. Vol. 60, October, 1931, pp. 428-437.

551
"Chicago Hearings Focus On Women In Poverty." Jet. Vol. 46, July 4, 1974, pp. 8.

552
Curran, Barbara W. "Getting By With A Little Help From My Friends: Informal Networks Among Older Black And White Urban Women Below The Poverty Line." Doctoral Dissertation, University of Arizona, 1978, 186p.

553
Daly, Frederica Y. "To Be Black, Poor, Female And Old." Freedomways. Vol. 16, 4th quarter, 1976, pp. 222-229.

554
Gossett, Ruth. "Economics of Black Widowhood." Journal of Afro American Issues. Vol. 3, Summer/Fall, 1975, pp. 309-315.

555
Haney, C. Allen, Robert Michielutte, Clark E. Vincent and Carl Cochrane. "Factors Associated With The Poverty of Black Women." Sociology And Social Research. Vol. 59, October, 1974, pp. 40-49.

556
Hill, Robert B. "Illusion of Black Progress." Black Scholar. Vol. 10, October, 1978, pp. 18-24.

557
____________. "Profile of The Black Aged." Sacramento Observer. 1 June, 1972, pp. D-14.

558
Jackson, Jacquelyne J. "Plight Of Older Black Women In The United States." Black Scholar. Vol. 7, April, 1976, pp. 47-55.

559
Ladner, Joyce. "Black Women In Poverty." Journal of Social And Behavorial Sciences." Vol. 20, Spring, 1974, pp. 41-51.

560
"The Long Thrust Toward Economic Equality." Ebony. Vol. 21, August, 1966, pp. 38-40, 42.

561
"More Slavery At The South." The Independent. Vol. 72, January 25, 1912, pp. 196-200.

562
Morgan, Betty. "Four Pennies To My Name: What It's Like On Welfare." Public Welfare. Vol. 37, Spring, 1979, pp. 12-22.

563
"The Negro Woman Goes To Market." The Brown American. Vol. 1, April, 1936, pp. 13.

564
"Negro Women Render Patriotic Service." Service. Vol. 7, September, 1943, pp. 28.

565
Payne, Resedu Berry. "Investigation Into The Buying Experiences of Fifth and Sixth Grade Girls At Jackson School." Master's Thesis. University of Cincinnati, 1932, 121p.

566
Porter, Sylvia. "Negro Women And Poverty." San Francisco Chronicle. 5 August, 1969.

567
Robinson, Patricia. "Poor Black Women." Community. Vol. 33, Spring, 1974, pp. 18-19.

568
Unni, V. K. "A Study Of Selected Characteristics Of Consumption, Life Style, And Social Class Concepts Among Wives of Negro Blue-Color Industrial Workers In Selected Louisiana Parishes." Doctoral Dissertation. Louisiana Tech University, 1973, 123p.

569
White, Carolyn Payne. "Southern Heights: A Study of Fifty Black Middle-Class Women in Baton Rouge, Louisiana." Master's Thesis. Fisk University, 1971, 72p.

570
Williams, Fannie B. "The Smaller Economcis." Voice Of The Negro. Vol. 1, May, 1904, pp. 184-185.

571
"The Woman And The Brotherhood." The Messenger. Vol. 8, July, 1926, pp. 209.

572
"Women And Thrift." The Southern Workman. Vol. 46, September 1, 1917, pp. 469-470.

573
"Women Can't Get Credit." Sacramento Observer. 1 June, 1972, pp. D-11.

574
"Women To The Rescue." Pulse. Vol. 1, September, 1943, pp. 22-23, 31.

575
Worford, Lucille. "A Study of Social And Economic Factors Affecting A Selected Group of Negro Women Workers In The Federal Tin Company, Baltimore, Maryland, 1948." Master's Thesis, Atlanta University, 1949, 35p.

EDUCATION

576
"Academic Preparation And Professional Status of Negroes Listed In Who's Who in American Education." Negro Education Review Review. Vol. 4, July, 1953, pp. 125-130.

577
Adams, Effie Kay. Experiences of A Fullbright Teacher. Boston: Christopher Publishing House, 1956, 215p.

578
Ademu-John, Shirley and Cassandra Edwards. "Black Coeds - Doing It Naturally." The Black Collegian. Vol. 7, May/June, 1977, pp. 16-17.

579
Amiten, Kenneth George. "A Correlational Analysis of Selected Career Development Competencies And Personality Characteristics Among Low-Income Black Women." Doctoral Dissertation, Gerogia State University, 1978, 166p.

580
Anthony, Mary. "Dean Of The School Marms." The Negro Digest. Vol. 9, May, 1951, pp. 31-32.

581
Ashley-Foster, Adabelle. "A Study Of The Relationship Between Career Maturity And Selected Characteristics Among Urban Black American High School Females." Doctoral Dissertation, Kent State University, 1978, 132p.

582
"Auburn University To Get First Black Faculty Member." Jet. Vol. 40, September 9, 1971, pp. 29.

583
Barnett, Evelyn Brooks. "Nannie Burroughs And The Education of Black Women," in The Afro American Woman: Struggles And Images, edited by Sharon Harley and Rosalyn Terborg-Penn. New York: Kennikat Press, 1978, 137p., pp. 97-108.

584
Biles, Vernicka. "An Investigation of Selected Post-Graduate Concerns of College Senior Women Student And Their Use Of Student Personnel Services." Master's Thesis, Howard University, 1972, 95p.

585
Binderman, Murray. "Factors In Desegregation Decisions of Black Mothers." Doctoral Dissertation, University of North Carolina at Chapel Hill, 1970, 215p.

586
"Black Coed Honored For Helping Job Corps Graduates." Black News Digest. April 30, 1979, pp. 2.

587
"The Black Woman In Higher Education," in Black Educators In White Colleges, edited by William Moore, Jr. and Lonnie H. Wagstaff. San Francisco: Jossey-Bass, 1974, 225p., pp. 154-177.

588
"Black Woman Named City School Board Chairwoman In Va." Jet. Vol. 42, July 27, 1972, pp. 26.

589
"Blacks And Women Continue Steady Education Gains." New York Times. 2 January, 1975, pp. 22C.

590
Blackwell, Barbara Grant. "The Advocacies And Ideological Commitments Of A Black Educator: Mary McLeod Bethune, 1875-1955." Doctoral Dissertation, University of Connecticut, 1979, 272p.

591
Blair, Dorothy Reeves. "A Study Of The Vocational Interests Of The Women Students at Clark College, 1942-1943, In Relation To The Positions Available To Negro Women In The War Program." Master's Thesis, Atlanta University, 1943, 66p.

592
Bolton, Ina Alexander. "The Problems Of Negro College Women." Doctoral Dissertation. University of Southern California, 1949, 258p.

593
Bowles, Eva D. "Opportunity For The Educated Colored Woman." Opportunity. Vol. 1, March, 1923, pp. 8-10.

594
Brindley, Fern Belle. "Social Factors Influencing Educational Aspirations of Black And White Girls." Doctoral Dissertation, Case Western Reserve University, 1970, 129p.

595
Brock-Smith, Carmen B. "A Survey Of Married Negro Female Students Enrolled In The Howard University Graduate School, 2nd Semester, 1970-1971." Master's Thesis. Howard University, 1971, 47p.

596
Brooks, Barbara Jean Roberts. "A Profile Of Black Females In Selected Administrative Positions In The Public School Systems of Flordia." Doctoral Dissertation, The University of Michigan, 1975, 184p.

597
Brown, Antoinette Mason. "An Analysis Of Homemaking Education Needs of Out-of-School Negro Girls In A Virginia Community." Master's Thesis, Ohio State University, 1939, 68p.

598
Brown, Esther R. "Home-Training Courses At Hampton." The Southern Workman. Vol. 32, September, 1903, pp. 417-421.

599
Brown, Georgia C. "Student Problems Encountered Daily By Deans of Women in Sixteen Colleges For Negroes." Master's Thesis, University of Michigan, 1944, 82p.

600
Bruce, Josephine B. "What Has Education Done For Colored Women." Voice Of The Negro. Vol. 1, July, 1904, pp. 294-298.

601
Burch, Burnice L. "Women 'Came Into Their Own' Round Turn Of The Century." The Philadelphia Tribune. 26 October, 1954.

602
Burroughs, Nannie H. Making Their Mark: Results In The Lives Of Graduates, The Yardstick By Which To Measure Values In Education. Washington, D. C.: The National Training School For Women And Girls, n.p., n.d., 21p.

603
Butcher, Beatrice. "The Evolution of Negro Women's Schools In The United States." Master's Thesis, Howard University, 1936, 70p.

604
Byrnes, Thomas Evans. "The Saint Frances' Home For Girls, Normandy, Missouri, December 31, 1947: A Study Of The Facilities And Program of The Saint Francis' Home For Girls Conducted By The Oblate Sisters of Providence At Normandy, Missouri, December 31, 1947." Master's Thesis, St. Louis University, 1948, 58p.

605
Carroll, Constance M. "Three's A Crowd: The Dilemma Of Black

Women In Higher Education," in Academic Women On The Move, edited by Alice S. Rossi and Ann Calderwood. New York: Russel Sage Foundation, 1973, 560p., pp. 173-185.

606
Chappelle, Yvonne R. "The Black Woman On The Negro College Campus." Black Scholar. Vol. 1, January/February, 1970, pp. 36-39.

607
" 'Cherchez la Femme' - Woman At Morehouse," in A Candle In The Dark: A History of Morehouse College, by Edward A. Jones. Valley Forge, Pennsylvania: Judson Press, 1967, 380p., pp. 295-296.

608
Clarke, John Henrik. "The Black Woman In Education: A Figure In World History." The Black Collegian. Vol. 5, November/December, 1974, pp. 40-41, 64-67.

609
"Colleges Offer More War Training Courses For Women." Opportunity. Vol. 21, April, 1943, pp. 79.

610
"Colored Girls Top Honor List." Norfolk Journal And Guide. 7 February, 1925, pp. 1.

611
"Colored Girls Urged to Enter High School." Philadelphia Ledger. 22 January, 1920.

612
Congehl, Irene Helen. "Withdrawal From High School Before Graduation By Negro Girls In St. Louis City." Master's Thesis, Washington University, 1946, 88p.

613
Curry, Lillian King. "A Study Of The Homemaking Activities Of The Rosenwald High School Homemaking Girls and Drop-Outs." Master's Thesis, Hampton Institute, 1950, 104p.

614
Cuthbert, Marion V. "Education And Marginality; A Study Of The Negro Woman College Graduate." Master's Thesis, Columbia University, 1942, 167p.

615
Davis, Dorothy. "She Knocks At The Door of Missouri University." The Crisis. Vol. 47, May, 1940, pp. 140.

616
Doneghy, Shirley Elsier. "A Comparative Study of Certain Personality Traits Of A Selected Group Of Negro College Women." Master's Thesis, Atlanta University, 1959, 42p.

617
Douglas, Margaret. "The Negro Woman's Role In Education." New York Age. 22 October, 1949.

618
Dove, Nannie Myrtle. "The Occupational Needs Of Negro High School Girls With Home Economics Training." Master's Thesis. Pennsylvania State University, 1939, 133p.

619
"The Edith Stern Scholarship." Tuskegee Messenger. Vol. 4, January 12, 1929, pp. 5.

620
"Education," in Black Women Makers of History: A Portrait, by George F. Jackson. Sacramento: Fong & Fong, 1977, 289p., pp. 187-199.

621
"Elizabeth D. Koontz, President-Elect 1968, N.E.A." The Negro History Bulletin. Vol. 30, December, 1967, pp. 4-5.

622
"Elizabeth Duncan Koontz - President of The National Education Association's Department of Classroom Teachers." The Negro History Bulletin. Vol. 28, December, 1964, pp. 55-56.

623
"Ex-NAACP Lawyer Named To Yale University Board." Jet. Vol. 40, July 8, 1971, pp. 44.

624
Feger, H. V. "A Girl Who Became A Great Woman." The Negro History Bulletin. Vol. 5, March, 1942, pp. 123.

625
"Female Prof. Named 1st Black to Chair Confab." Jet. Vol. 50, April 8, 1976, pp. 55.

626
"1st Black Gets Ph.D. In Speech At Penn State." Jet. Vol. 40, April 29, 1971, pp. 21.

627
"1st Black Woman To Get N. Y. Principal License Dies." Jet. Vol. 40, August 5, 1971, pp. 29.

628
"First Negro Woman Enrolled at Md. College." Jet. Vol. 4, October 1, 1953, pp. 18.

629
Fischer, Ruth. "Black, Female and Qualified," in Women On Campus: The Unfinished Liberation, edited by Change Magazine. New York: Change Magazine, 1975, 256p., pp. 160-166.

630
Fitcher, Joseph H. Negro Women Bachelors; A Comparative Exploration Of The Experiences And Expectations of College Graduates Of The Class of June, 1961. Chicago: National Opinion Research Center, 1965, 155p.

631
"Four-Fifths Female." Headlines And Pictures. Vol. 1, June, 1945, pp. 36.

632
"400 Girls Attend First Girls' Day At Tuskegee Inst." New York Age. 17 November, 1923, pp. 2.

633
Fox, Frances Juanita. "Black Women Administrators In The Denver Public Schools." Doctoral Dissertation, The University of Colorado, 1975, 167p.

634
"Georgetown Names Black Woman To Regents Board." Jet. Vol. 42, August 3, 1972, pp. 7.

635
Gilliard, Evelyn Nelson. "The Effects Of A Structured Parent Stimulation Approach Toward Education Of A Selected Group of Black Mothers." Doctoral Dissertation, Georgia State University, 1975, 173p.

636
Gilyard, Geraline Lewis. "Coping Behavior, Self-Concept And Academic Achievement of Black High School Females." Doctoral Dissertation, The University of Miami, 1975, 138p.

637
"Going Back To Get Ahead." Encore. Vol. 5, December 20, 1976, pp. 13.

638
"Girl Collegians Told To Prepare For Home And Career." Service. Vol. 12, September, 1947, pp. 11, 29.

639
Grasty, Patricia E. "Tutor, Mentor, Teacher." Encore. Vol. 4, June 23/July 4, 1975, pp. 63-64.

640
Gray, Edith Elizabeth. "The Effects of Interracial Mixing Experience And Group Membership On Student Attitudes Toward Acceptable Campus Mixing Behavior: A Study of Negro Women Students at Pennsylvania State University." Master's Thesis, Pennsylvania State University, 1968, 145p.

641
Gurin, Patricia and Carolyn Gaylord. "Educational And Occupational Goals of Men And Women At Black Colleges." Monthly Labor Review. Vol. 99, June, 1976, pp. 10-16.

642
"Hampton Young Woman Leads Class of Sixty At Fisk U." Norfolk Journal And Guide. 7 May, 1927, pp. 4.

643
Hardy, Blanche Brewster. "The Relation of Scholastic Aptitude And English Test Performance To Academic Achievement of One Hundred Freshmen Women." Master's Thesis. Fisk University, 1948, 42p.

644
Harley, Sharon. "Anna J. Cooper: A Voice For Black Women," in The Afro American Woman: Struggles And Images, by Sharon Harley and Rosalyn Terborg-Penn. New York: Kennikat Press, 137p., pp. 87-96.

645
Haskin, Frederic J. "Training For Negro Girls." Asbury Park Press. 15 July, 1913.

646
"Home Making To Be Course For Young Women." Norfolk Journal And Guide. 2 April, 1927, pp. 9.

647
Hooks, Ruthie Lee Bush. "Homemaking Activities of Girls In The Central Junior High School, Shreveport, Louisiana." Master's Thesis. Hampton Institute, 1950, 99p.

648
Hosford, Philip L. Minority Women In Research And Education: A Report Of The Dallas Conference on Expanding The Role Of Minority Women In Educational Research. Las Cruces, New Mexico: New Mexico State University, 1978, 71p.

649
Howe, F. "Sexism, Racism and The Education of Women." Today's Education. Vol. 62, May, 1973, pp. 47-48.

650
Jackson, Audrey Hudson. "The Relationship Between Personal Adjustment and Academic Achievement Manifested By Fifty Selected Negro College Women." Master's Thesis. Atlanta University, 1957, 119p.

651
James, Allee Winifred. "The Homemaking Activities Of A Selected Group of Negro Homemakers In East Texas." Master's Thesis, Kansas State University, 1939, 75p.

652
Jeffries, Henrietta Carney. "A Study of Pertinent Questions Asked By Girls At the James B. Dudley High School, Greensboro, North Carolina." Master's Thesis, Pennsylvania State University, 1950, 49p.

653
Jenkins, Beatrice E. Haddon. "Vocational Opportunities For High School Girls And Graduates Trained in Homemaking At Industrial High School, West Palm Beach, Florida." Master's Thesis, Hampton Institute, 1949, 81p.

654
Johnson, Alma. "A New Epoch For St. Philips." The Negro American. October, 1927, pp. 9.

655
Johnson, Audrey Louise. "The Perceptions And Social Characteristics Related to Occupational Mobility Of Black Women And Intraracial Assimilation of Blacks In America." Doctoral Dissertation, New School For Social Research, 1977, 241p.

656
Johnson, Gussie Brown. "An Analysis Of The Vocational Interests Of Senior High School Girls In The Negro Schools Of Oklahoma." Master's Thesis, Fisk University, 1940, 88p.

657
Jones, Anna H. "The American Colored Woman." Voice Of The Negro. Vol. 2, October, 1905, pp. 692-694.

658
Jones, David D. "The War And The Higher Education of Negro Women." Journal of Negro Education. Vol. 11, July, 1942, pp. 329-337.

659
Jones, Fannye Miles. "Homemaking Activities of Harlan County Girls Enrolled In Home Economics." Master's Thesis, Hampton Institute, 1949, 96p.

660
Kealey, Robert Joseph. "Attitudes of Female Catholic Black And Hispanic Parish Leaders And Female, Catholic White School Personnel Concepting The Utilization of Catholic Schools." Doctoral Dissertation, Fordham University, 1975, 145p.

661
Keith, Ethel Hannah. "The Home And Social Background Of The Women Students At Samuel Houston College For Negroes During 1937-1938." Master's Thesis, Kansas State College, 1938, 66p.

662
Kelly, Willie M. Aspiration of Black Female College Students. New York: Exposition Press, 1973.

663
Kennedy, Vivian Niles. "The Homemaking Needs And Activities of High School Girls In Howard Academy, Ocala, Florida."

Master's Thesis, Hampton Institute, 1949, 84p.

664
Kirke, Edmund. "Education of The Negro." North American Review. Vol. 143, November, 1886, p. 421.

665
Kittrell, F. P. "Current Problems and Programs In The Higher Education of Negro Women." Quarterly Review of Higher Education Among Negroes. Vol. 12, January, 1944, pp. 13-15.

666
Kleinpeter, Eva Bonnet. "An Investigation of Black Female College Faculty In The Twenty Largest Private Predominantly Black Colleges and Universities." Doctoral Dissertation, Kansas State University, 1975, 232p.

667
Krystall, Eric R., Neil Friedman, Glenn Howze and Edgar G. Epps. "Attitudes Toward Integregation And Black Consciousness: Southern Negro High School Seniors And Their Mothers." Phylon. Vol. 3, Summer, 1970, pp. 104-113.

668
Lane, Cecilia Scott. "The Place of Home Economics In The Curriculum For Women of Houston College For Negroes." Master's Thesis, Iowa State University, 1937, 122p.

669
Laney, Lucy C. "The Burden of The Education Colored Woman." The Southern Workman. September, 1899, pp. 341-344.

670
Larkin, Ronald Francis. "The Expectations of Black Female Teachers And White Female Teachers Toward Black Second And Third Grade Pupils, And Effects Of These Expectations On Black Pupil Gains In Reading Scores In Urban Schools." Doctoral Dissertation, Rutgers University, 1978, 116p.

671
Lemieux, Melba. "Outstanding Black Coeds of 1979." The Black Collegian. Vol.9, May/June, 1979, pp. 38.

672
Lenox, Mary Frances. "Black Women: Student Perception Of Their Contributions." Doctoral Dissertation, University of Massachusetts, 1975, 162p.

673
Lewis, Daisy L. "A Functional Adult Program for Negro Homemakers In Georgia." Master's Thesis. Atlanta University, 1949, 55p.

674
Lightfoot, Sara L. "Socialization and Education of Young Black Girls In School." Teachers College Record. Vol. 78, December, 1976, pp. 239-262.

675
"Living Conditions Among Colored Girls At Northern Colleges." National Association of College Women. April 16-18, 1925, pp. 30-31.

676
"Local College Women Who Conducted Vocational Guidance Week." Norfolk Journal And Guide. 13 June, 1925, pp. 3.

677
Lyford, Carrie A. "A Hampton Girl's Training." The Southern Workman. Vol. 49, May, 1920, pp. 209-216.

678
______________. "Home Economics for Negro Girls." The Southern Workman. Vol. 50, November, 1921, pp. 513-518.

679
Mackey, Sarah Edith. "Socioeconomic Status and The Performance on Entrance Achievement Tests of Freshmen Women From The North And South." Master's Thesis, Fisk University, 1950, 61p.

680
Madison, Stephanie C. "Black Coed-White Campus." Essence. Vol. 4, August, 1973, pp. 36-37, 68, 84.

681
"Maid Gets B.A. Degree." Jet. Vol. 40, July 1, 1971, pp. 20.

682
Malveaux, Julianne. "Black Women On White Campuses." Essence. Vol. 10, August, 1979, pp. 78-79, 102, 105-106, 109, 130.

683
Marable, June Morehead. "The Role of Women In Public School Administration As Perceived By Black Women Administrators In The Field." Doctoral Dissertation, Miami University, 1974, 251p.

684
Marshall, Lillie Mae. "Study Of The Needs of Fifth, Sixth, and Seventh Grade Girls In The Lee Street Elementary School As A Basis For A Homemaking Program In Blackshear, Georgia." Master's Thesis, Hampton Institute, 1950, 57p.

685
Mason, Vivian C. "Women In Education," in American Women: The Changing Image, edited by Beverly B. Cassara. Boston: Beacon Press, 1962, 141p., pp. 116-123.

686
"Mature Women Returning To College." Sacramento Observer. 1 June, 1972, pp. D-8.

687
McAfee, Mildred H. "The War and Higher Education of Women." Journal of Negro Education. Vol. 11, July, 1942, pp. 262-266.

688
McCamey, Delener Sue. "The Status Of Black And White Women In Central Administrative Positions In Michigan Public Schools." Doctoral Dissertation. The University of Michigan, 1976, 128p.

689
McCoy, Virgie Rhea. "Homemaking Activities That Have Implications For The Home Economics Curriculum; Out of School Activities of Tenth Grade Negro Girls Vocational Home Economics - Alabama." Master's Thesis. Tuskegee Institute, 1945, 98p.

690
McDougald, Elise Johnson." The Negro Woman Teacher And The Negro Student." The Messenger. Vol. 7, July, 1923, pp. 769-770.

691
Micklebury, Mexico Hembree. "A Study Of The Personal Problems of Freshmen and Senior College Women During A Five Year Period, 1947-1952." Master's Thesis, Atlanta University, 1958, 62p.

692
Miller, Bernice J. "Inner City Women in White Schools." Journal of Negro Education. Vol. 42, Summer, 1973, pp. 392-413.

693
Miller, Julia Rudyne. "Family Communication And Academic Achievement of Black Adolescent Females." Doctoral Dissertation, University of Maryland, 1974, 147p.

694
Minority Women And Higher Education. Washington, D. C.: Association of American Colleges, 1974, 4p.

695
Moore, Angie. "Alabama's First Jeanes Teacher." Service. Vol. 12, January, 1948, pp. 22, 34.

696
Mosley, Geneva. "A Study Of The Consistency of Vocational Choices and Interests of Black Women Graduates of A Local Liberal Arts College, 1970-1974." Doctoral Dissertation, Atlanta University, 1977, 90p.

697
Munford, Mary B. "Southern Women's Work For Education." The Southern Workman. Vol. 38, May, 1909, pp. 265-269.

698
"Names New Head of College Fund Women's Division." Jet. Vol. 39, February 11, 1971, pp. 40.

699
"NEA Honors Mrs. Koontz For Aiding Women's Rights." Jet. Vol. 43, January 4, 1973, pp. 12.

700
"Negro Teachers Association Conference." Integrated Education. Vol. 5, August/September, 1967, pp. 47.

701
"Negro Will Be Oxford's 1st Woman Ph.D. From U. S." Jet. Vol. 5, December 31, 1953, pp. 16.

702
"New Black Educator In Sacramento." Sacramento Observer. 1 June, 1972, pp. D-8.

703
"New Fields Explored." Jorunal of The National Association Of College Women. #19, 1941-1943, pp. 23-24.

704
Noble, Jeanne L. "The Negro Woman Looks At Her College Education." Doctoral Dissertation, Columbia University, 1955.

705
______________. The Negro Woman's College Education. New York: Columbia University Teachers College, 1956, 163p.

706
______________. "Negro Women Today And Their Education." Journal of Negro Education. Vol. 26, Winter, 1957, pp. 15-21.

707
"Norfolk Girl Awarded $700 Fellowship." Norfolk Journal And Guide. 17 September, 1927, pp. 1.

708
"Opportunities For Educated Colored Women." Opportunity. Vol. 1, March, 1923, pp. 8-10.

709
Parrish, Dorothy. "A Question of Survival: The Predicament Of Black Women," in We'll Do It Ourselves: Combating Sexism In Education, edited by David Rosen, Steve Werner and Barbara Yates. Lincoln, Nebraska: University of Nebraska, 1974, 321p., pp. 33-53.

710
Parsons, Cynthia. "Two Women With A Vision." Southern Education Report. Vol. 4, April, 1969. pp. 20-23.

711
Payne, Norma Joyce. "The Status of Black Women In Education Administation." Doctoral Dissertation, Atlanta University, 1975, 173p.

712
Peltier, Marie (Mary Consuella, Sister, F. H. M.). "A Catholic Philosophy of Homemaking Education For The Colored." Master's Thesis, St. John's University, 1948, 41p.

713
Perkins, Linda Marie. "Fanny Jackson Coppin And The Institute for Colored Youth: A Model of Nineteenth Century Black Female Educational and Community Leadership, 1837-1902." Doctoral Dissertation, The University of Illinois at Urbana-Champaign, 1978, 356p.

714
Peters, Iva L. "The Orientation of The Trained Woman." Journal Of The National Association of College Women. April 16-18, 1925, pp. 19.

715
Peterson, Marcella Tandy. "Status And Trends In The Promotion of Women To Secondary School Prinicpalships With Special Reference To Black Women." Doctoral Dissertation. Wayne State University, 1973, 218p.

716
Petway, Jamesetta. "Black Women And White Managers: An Action Program For Increased Strength And Influence." Doctoral Dissertation, Case Western Reserve University, 1975, 286p.

717
Pierce, Ponchita. "Problems of The Negro Woman Intellectual." Ebony. Vol. 21, August, 1966, pp. 144-149.

718
Pitman, Dorothy E. "Reactions To Desegregation: A Study of Negro Mothers." Doctoral Dissertation, University of North Carolina, 1960, 241p.

719
Poinsett, Alex. "Ruth Holloway's War On Illiteracy." Ebony. Vol. 29, September, 1974, pp. 62, 64-66, 69, 70-71.

720
____________. "Washington's New Public School Boss." Ebony. Vol. 30, January, 1974, pp. 102-104, 106.

721
Poole, Roy Raymond. "Evaluation Of A Small Group Teaching-Learning Process Design To Facilitate The Occupational Preparation of Black Undergraduate Univeristy Women." Doctoral Dissertation, The University of Oregon, 1973, 123p.

722
"Problems of Educated Women Acute In Southern States." New York Age. 22 July, 1922, pp. 7.

723
Puckett, Dorothea Emma Webb. "Educational Counseling Groups For Black Adolescent Females From A Low-Income Housing Area." Doctoral Dissertation, The University of Michigan, 1976, 160p.

724
Quint, Catherine Isabella. "The Role of American Negro Women Educators In The Growth Of The Common School." Doctoral Dissertation, Boston University, 1970, 267p.

725
Randall, Gladys M. Lowman. "A Study Of The Home Activities Of The Homemaking Girls In The Macon County Training School Montezuma, Georgia." Master's Thesis, Hampton Institute, 1951, 61p.

726
Rea, Katharine. "A Follow-Up Study of The Women Graduates From The State Colleges of Mississippi, Class of 1956." Doctoral Dissertation, The Ohio State University, 1958, 234p.

727
Read, Florence M. "The Place Of The Women's College In The Pattern of Negro Education." Opportunity. Vol. 15, September, 1937, pp. 267-270.

728
Robinson, Omelia T. "Contributions Of Black American Academic Women To American Higher Education." Doctoral Dissertation, Wayne State University, 1978, 247p.

729
Satterfield, D. I. "The Education of Afro-American Girls." American Missionary Magazine. Vol. 46, July, 1892, pp. 239-242.

730
"School Board In Kansas Town Gets 1st Black Woman." Jet. Vol. 40, May 27, 1971, pp. 46.

731
"Select N. C. Black Girl For Scandinavian Tour." Jet. Vol. 40, August 12, 1971, pp. 47.

732
Shootes, Queen Ester. "Gainful Employment of Negro Home Economics Graduates With Implications For Education Programs." Doctoral Dissertation, The University of Wisconsin, 1965, 157p.

733
Simcox, Charles Q. "The Effect of Facial Attractiveness Upon The Evaluation Of Fictitious Black And White Potential Female Dropouts By The Faculty of Selected Pennsylvania Community Colleges: A Psycholinguistic Investigation." Doctoral Dissertation, The Pennsylvania State University, 1975, 162p.

734
Sims, Annevesta Belle. "A Study of The Activities of The Homemaking Girls and Drop-outs Of Meriwether County High School, Manchester, Georgia." Master's Thesis, Hampton Institute, 1951, 76p.

735
Sizemore, Barbara. "Women School Administrators: My Experience With Discrimination," in Women's Lifes: Perspectives On Progress And Change, edited by Virginia Lee Lassier and Joyce Jennings Walstedt. Newark: University of Delaware, 1977, 245p.

736
Slowe, Lucy D. "The College Woman And Our Public Life." Journal of The National Association of College Women. April 21-23, 1927, pp. 26-28.

737
____________. "A Colored Girls Enters College - What Shall She Expect?" Opportunity. Vol. 15, September, 1937, pp. 276-279.

738
____________. "The Dormitory: A Cultural Influence." Journal of The National Association of College Women. 1931-1932, pp. 11-14.

739
____________. "Higher Education For Negro Women." Journal of Negro Education. Vol. 2, July, 1933, pp. 352.

740
Smith, Glenda Diane. "Black Women in Continuing Education: The Effects of Socio-Economic Status and Selected Communication Variables at Specific Functions Within The Innovation Decision Process, Philadelphia, 1977." Master's Thesis, Temple University, 1978, 183p.

741
Snitow, Virginia L. "I Teach Negro Girls." The Negro Digest. Vol. 1, December, 1942, pp. 27-31.

742
Snowden, E. Celine Marcus. "Occupations Opened To Home Economics Trained High School Girls, Halifax County Training School As A Basis For A Guidance Program." Master's Thesis, Hampton Institute, 1946, 68p.

743
Taylor, Annie Alford. "The Current Status of Black Women In American Higher Education Administration." Doctoral Dissertation, The Arizona State University, 1977, 156p.

744
Taylor, Estelle. "Emma Frances Grayson Merritt: Pioneer In Negro Education." The Negro History Bulletin. Vol. 38, August/September, 1975, pp. 434-435.

745
"Teacher Dismissed In Va. Is Awarded $3,500." Jet. Vol. 41, October 21, 1971, pp. 22.

746
Tefft, Lyman B. "Hartshorn Memorial College." Voice Of The Negro. Vol. 4, June, 1907, pp. 248-252.

747
Thomas, Caroline Elizabeth." A Study Of The Vocational Interests of The High School Girls At The Manning Training School." Master's Thesis, Hampton Institute, 1950, 55p.

748
Thomas, Emma Joahanne. "Career Patterns of Black Women Administrators In Historically Negro Senior Colleges and Universities." Doctoral Dissertation, Washington State University, 1976.

749
"Three Colored Girls Get Degrees At Radcliffe." Norfolk Journal And Guide. 30 June, 1917, pp. 4.

750
Thrift, Pinkie E. "Negro Girl In The Home Management House." Journal of Home Economics. Vol. 35, January, 1943, pp. 35-36.

751
"To Get An Education And To Teach My People," in Black Women In Nineteenth-Century American Life: Their Words, Their Thoughts, Their Feelings, by Bert James Loewenberg and Ruth Bogin. University Park: The Pennsylvania State University Press, 1976, 355p., pp. 281-331.

752
Tobin, McLean. A Profile Of Black Women Doctorate Holders In Black Public Colleges and Universities: 1973-1974." Doctoral Dissertation, Kansas State University, 1975, 128p.

753
"Training Negro Women As Race Leaders." New York Post. 8 December, 1919.

754
Turner, Barbara F. and Joanne Hammar McCaffrey. "Socialization

And A Career Orientation Among Black And White College Women." Journal of Vocational Behavior. Vol. 5, December, 1974, pp. 307-319.

755
"Two Colored Sisters Win Honors At High Schools In Philly." Norfolk Journal And Guide. 5 February, 1927, pp. 5.

756
"Two New York Women Win Honors At Smith." Chicago Defender. 25 June, 1921, pp. 5.

757
"University of Maryland Names Black To Top Post." Jet. Vol. 46, July 11, 1974, pp. 29.

758
U. S. Department of Labor, Women's Bureau. Fact Sheet On Educational Attainment of Nonwhite Women. Washington, D. C.: G. P. O., 1968, 2p.

759
Ware, Caroline F. "Information and Suggestions From Government Agencies On A Wartime College Program For Women." Journal of Negro Education. Vol. 12, Spring, 1943, pp. 246-250.

760
"Washington Businesswoman Elected Education Chairman." Jet. Vol. 44, May 24, 1973, pp. 7.

761
Wesley, Charles H. "A Challenge To Women." Journal of The National Association of College Women. April 16-18, 1925, pp. 10-19.

762
"West Virginia Girl Wins French Honors From Columbia Univ." New York Age. 20 October, 1923, pp. 2.

763
Williams, Edith Coleman. "Black College Women's Dignity And Leadership Quest: An Evaluation of A Program To Motivate Degree Completion." Doctoral Dissertation, Wayne State University, 1973, 242p.

764
Williams, Flora Frazier. "A Study of The Homemaking Needs Of Fifty Elementary School Girls." Master's Thesis, Hampton Institute, 1951, 39p.

765
Williams, Leonora Patton. "The Possible Contributions of Home Economics To The Development of The Men and Women Students In The Negro Junior College of Little Rock, Arkansas." Master's Thesis, Iowa State University, 1938, 183p.

766
Williams, Louise Hodge. "A Comparative Study of Home Economics Training of Three Hundred High School Girls In Brunswick, Georgia." Master's Thesis, Virginia State College, 1961, 45p.

767
Witherspoon, Lois Asaline. "A Study of The Needs For Homemaking Instruction For Girls In The Negro Elementary Schools Of Greensville County, Virginia." Master's Thesis, Hampton Institute, 1952, 49p.

768
Woman Vice President of Virginia Union Univ." Jet. Vol. 40, May 13, 1971, pp. 46.

769
"Women Head $37 Million HEW Teacher Corporation Program." Jet Vol. 42, July 27, 1972, pp. 26.

770
"Women Principals Direct Seven Norfolk Schools." Norfolk Jour-And Guide. 7 February, 1925, pp. 1.

771
"Women Who Led In Education," in Negro Builders And Heroes, by Benajmin Brawley. Chapel Hill: University of North Carolina Press, 1937, 315p., pp. 273-288.

772
Wood, Mary E. "The Impact Of The War On College Women." Journal of The National Association of College Women. #19, 1941-1943, pp. 3-5.

773
Wright, Irma Paige. "The Effect of Home Economics Training On High School Girls." Master's Thesis. Virginia State College, 1947, 38p.

774
"Young Brooklyn Girl Wins High Honors At Smith College." New York Age. 25 June, 1921, pp. 2.

EMPLOYMENT

Accounting

775
"Black Woman Elected As Detroit's Chief Auditor." Jet. Vol. 48, April, 17, 1975, pp. 14.

776
"Nation's First Black Woman CPA Honored." Jet. Vol. 54, February 23, 1978, pp. 19.

777
Thompson, Jacqueline A. "On Being Black And Female And An Accountant." MBA. Vol. 9, February, 1975, pp. 35-36, 38.

Thompson, Jacqueline A. "On Being Black And Female And An Accountant," in Women In The Organization, edited by Harold H. Frank. Philadelphia: University of Pennsylvania Press, 1977, 310p., pp. 266-270.

Airlines And Aviation

778
"Black Woman Heads Gary's Second Largest Airport." Jet. Vol. 40, September 2, 1971, pp. 15.

779
"Chicago Colored Girl Is Made Aviatrix By French." New York Age. 1 October, 1921, pp. 1.

780
"Flying Sisters." Ebony. Vol. 20, November, 1964, pp. 81-82, 84-86.

781
"Going Down." Headlines And Pictures. Vol. 2, October, 1945, pp. 33.

782
"Howard Grad Stewardess With Northwest Airline." Jet. Vol. 25, January 16, 1964, pp. 18.

783
"Jill Brown May Be First Black Woman Navy Pilot." Jet. Vol. 47, October 24, 1974, pp. 19.

784
King, Anita. "Brave Bessie: First Black Pilot. Essence. Vol. 7, May, 1976, pp. 36; June, 1976, pp. 48.

785
"Lady Plane Mechanic." Ebony. Vol. 3, January, 1948, pp. 28-31.

786
"Negress Turns Aviatrix." Philadelphia Inquirer. 26 September, 1921.

787
"Open Skies For Negro Girls." Ebony. Vol. 18, June, 1963, pp. 43-46, 48, 50.

788
Rorty, James. "The First Colored Air Hostess." The Crisis. Vol. 65, June/July, 1958, pp. 339-342.

789
"TWA Hires First Negro Air Hostess." Ebony. Vol. 14, July, 1959, pp. 37-38, 40.

Architects

790
"Architect." Norfolk Journal And Guide. 5 December, 1925, pp. 13.

791
"Black Woman 1st of 3 To Speak At Women Architects Confab In Iran." Jet. Vol. 51, November 18, 1976, pp. 19.

792
"Black Women Architects," in Black Involvement In Architecture. Washington, D. C.: Afro-American Bicentennial Corporation, 1976, pp. 12.

793
"Mrs. Architect, Norma Merrick Fairweather; First Negro Woman to Graduate From Columbia University's School of Architecture." Our World. Vol. 5, November, 1960, pp. 57-59.

Banking

794
"Black Woman Vice-President Of Bank." The Negro History Bulletin. Vol. 34, March, 1971, pp. 61.

795
"A Distinguished Business Woman." Voice Of The Negro. Vol. 2, May, 1905, pp. 304-305.

796
"Female Advances," in Negro Employment In Finance: A Study Of Racial Policies In Banking And Insurance, Vol. II, by Armand J. Theiblot, Jr. and Linda P. Fletcher. Philadelphia: University of Pennsylvania Press, 1970, 178p., pp. 37.

797
Fleming, Beatrice J. "America's First Woman Bank President." The Negro History Bulletin. Vol. 5, January, 1942, pp. 75, 95.

798
"Maggie L. Walker: First Woman Bank President." Encore. Vol. 4, May 19, 1975, pp. 5.

799
"Minority Group Members," in Women And Minorities In Banking: Shortchanged/Update, edited by Wendy C. Schwartz. New York: Praeger, 1977, 173p., pp. 21-34.

800
Simmons, Charles Willis. "Maggie Lena Walker And The Consolidated Bank And Trust Company." The Negro History Bulletin. Vol. 38, February/March, 1975, pp. 345-349.

Bar Maids

801
"Harlem Women Help Defeat Bill Against Barmaids." Jet. Vol. 3, March 19, 1953, pp. 7.

802
Richmond, Charles. "Barmaids: Unheralded Eyes And Ears Of The Community." Core. Vol. 3, Summer, 1973, pp. 48-51.

Beauty Culture

803
Adams, Frankie V. "The Negro Beautician." Service. Vol. 5, June, 1941, pp. 10-11.

804
"Appointment At Seven." The Brown American. Vol. 3, February, 1940, pp. 9-11, 16.

805
"Beaute Salon Serves Community." Service. Vol. 9, June, 1945, pp. 19-20.

806
"Beauticians' Business Down For Five Years But Up Again." Jet. Vol. 44, August 9, 1973, pp. 5.

807
"Beauticians Hold National Convention in Louisville." Jet. Vol. 46, June 27, 1974, pp. 20.

808
"Beauty, Brains And Brass." Service. Vol. 5, July, 1941, pp. 12.

809
"Beauty Culture Grads Vie with Cap And Gown Sisters." Norfolk Journal And Guide. 13 June, 1925, pp. 1.

810
"Beauty Culturist of International Repute Sponsors Nationwide Beauty Contest." Norfolk Journal And Guide. 23 May, 1925, pp. 8.

811
"Beauty Is A Business." The Brown American. Vol. 5, Winter/Spring, 1944, pp. 12-14.

812
"Beauty Salon For The Social Register." Ebony. Vol. 4, May, 1949, pp. 31-32.

813
"Beauty Show Best Yet For Culturists." Chicago Defender. 20 August, 1921, pp. 2.

814
"Black Beauticians Seek To Become United Group." Jet. Vol. 40, August 19, 1971, pp. 25.

815
Brokenburr, Robert Lee. "A Negro Woman's Success." The Southern Workman. Vol. 47, February, 1918, pp. 70-74.

816
"The C. J. Walker College Graduates Beauty Culturists." Norfolk Journal And Guide. 21 February, 1925, pp. 7.

817
DuBois, W. E. B. "A Great Woman." The Crisis. Vol. 18, July, 1919, pp. 131.

818
Engelbach, Jerry. "The Lady With The Million-Dollar Formula." Encore. Vol. 3, October, 1974, pp. 6.

819
"Enterprising And Prominent Young Norfolk Women." Norfolk Journal And Guide. 30 September, 1916, pp. 1.

820
"First Class of Local Poro Graduates." Norfolk Journal And Guide. 19 November, 1927, pp. 5.

821
Gordon, William. "A Successful Beautician." Service. Vol. 7, September, 1943, pp. 8.

822
"House of Beauty." Ebony. Vol. 1, May, 1946, pp. 25-29.

823
"Integration Comes To The Beauty Business." Ebony. Vol. 21, August, 1966, pp. 140, 142-143.

824
Jeffries, LeRoy W. "The Decay of The Beauty Parlor Industry In Harlem." Opportunity. Vol. 16, February, 1938, pp. 49-52.

825
Johnson, Mary Willie. "The Beauty Shop And The Beautician In An Urban Negro Community." Master's Thesis, Atlanta University, 1950, 50p.

826
"Lady Barbers." Jet. Vol. 4, November 19, 1953, pp. 24-28.

827
"Madam Poindexter." The Colored American Review. Vol. 1, June, 1916, pp. 246-247.

828
"Mme Anna L. Anderson Opens New Beauty Shop At 2157 Seventh Avenue." New York Age. 30 June, 1923, pp. 8.

829
"National Beauty Culturists Hold Annual Meet." Norfolk Journal And Guide. 26 September, 1925, pp. 10.

830
"Negro Hair: A Million Dollar Business." Jet. Vol. 1, February 14, 1952, pp. 48-53.

831
"Presented Beauty Culture Diploma Amidst Ceremonies." Norfolk Journal And Guide. 19 March, 1927, pp. 4.

832
"Poro Beauty School Graduates Of St. Louis, Missouri." The Negro. Vol. 1, February/March, 1944, pp. 84.

833
"Proposed Bill Is Death Kneel To Beauty Shop." Chicago Defender. 9 April, 1921, pp. 2.

834
"Purchases Beauty Parlor." Chicago Defender. 25 June, 1921, pp. 5.

835
"A Successful Beautician." Service. Vol. 9, July, 1945, pp. 20.

836
"Top Beauty Shop In Nation's Capitol." Pulse. Vol. 5, January, 1948, pp. 24.

837
U. S. Department of Labor, Women's Bureau. "Negro Beauty Shops," in Employment Conditions In Beauty Shops: A Study Of Four Cities. Washington, D. C.: G. P. O., 1935, 46p., pp. 37-46.

838
"Young Women Graduate From Poro Station." Norfolk Journal And Guide. 31 October, 1925, pp. 8.

839
"Wonderful Success of Mme. C. J. Walker: Remarkable Business Triumph of A Colored Woman." The Colored American Review. Vol. 1, March, 1916, pp. 182.

Business

840
Alpha Kappa Alpha Sorority. Women In Business. Chicago: AKA Sorority, 1970, 24p.

841
"As Six of Them See It: Black Women Executives Discuss Their Lives And Careers." Black Enterprise. Vol. 5, August, 1974, pp. 20-23, 40-41.

842
"Atlanta's Execs: Kathy Jackson." Essence. Vol. 6, March, 1976, pp. 70-73.

843
"Birmingham's Lady Tycoon." Our World. Vol. 6, July, 1951, pp. 12-13.

844.
"Black Woman Builds Successful Tool Business." Access. January/February, 1978, pp. 8, 10.

845
"Black Woman Joins Three Boards." Business Week. May 29, 1971, pp. 22

846
"Black Women In Boardrooms." Sacramento Observer - National Scene. May, 1979, pp. 5.

847
Burgen, Michele. "Women In Business: They Are Owners, Bosses,

Workers." Ebony. Vol. 32, August, 1977, pp. 122-124, 126, 128.

848
"Business." Encore. Vol. 4, June 23/July 4, 1975, pp. 72.

849
"Business And Entertainment," in Black Women Makers Of History: A Portrait, by George F. Jackson. Sacramento: Fong & Fong, 1977, 289p., pp. 207-268.

850
Calloway, L. N. "Women In Business." The Negro Woman's World. October, 1934, pp. 4.

851
"Cites Businesswoman In Congressional Record." Jet. Vol. 39, March 18, 1971, pp. 6.

852
"Colored Woman In Business." Tuskegee Messenger. Vol. 5, January 15, 1927, pp. 2.

853
"Colored Women Are Making Good In New York Commercially." New York Age. 22 September, 1923, pp. 1, 2.

854
Conyers, Jean Louise Farris. "The Negro Businesswoman In Atlanta." Master's Thesis, Atlanta University, 1967, 63p.

855
DeWitt, Karen. "Black Women In Business." Black Enterprise. Vol. 5, August, 1974, pp. 14-19.

856
Directory of Colored Business And Professional Women Of Philadelphia And Vicinity. Philadelphia: Josephine Bond Keene, 1939.

857
"Dr. Coleman In Rapid Rise As Business Woman." Chicago Defender. 16 September, 1922.

858
"Ex-Actress With An Eye For Business." Ebony. Vol. 24, March, 1969, pp. 82-84, 86, 88.

859
"Exhibit of Arts, Industries, Professions, And Business Occupations of Colored Women of Brooklyn, N. Y." The Crisis. Vol. 36, February, 1929, pp. 54.

860
"Finest Dress Shop Owned By Race Women Operated By Mmes. Carrie and Grantland." New York Age. 10 November, 1923, pp. 1, 5.

861
"First Lady of Talent Booking." Ebony. Vol. 29, June, 1974, pp. 73-74, 76-78, 80.

862
"First Negro Woman U. S. Business Advisor Named." Jet. Vol. 7, November 11, 1954, pp. 23.

863
Graham, Gladys P. "Negro Women Own N. Y. Button Works." Black Dispatch. 1 November, 1947.

864
Higgins, Chester. "Women Executive Scraps Job Testing, Revolutionizes Hiring." Jet. Vol. 29, February 24, 1966, pp. 16-21.

865
Holsey, Albon L. "Negro Women And Business." The Southern Workman. Vol. 56, August, 1927, pp. 343-349.

866
Howard, Julia C. "Negro Business Women of Atlanta." Christian Recorder. 20 April, 1911.

867
Hunter-Gault, Charlayne. "Women Executives: The New Breed." Tuesday At Home. May, 1975, pp. 4-6, 8, 15.

868
"It Happened In Our World." Our World. Vol. 6, April, 1951, pp. 12-13.

869
Jones, Michael. "Black Women And Business." Business Today. Vol. 11, Fall, 1974, pp. 35-36.

870
Miller, Ethel A. "A Successful Woman In A Man's World: Mrs. George Brown, Scranton, Pennsylvania." Opportunity. Vol. 8, July, 1930, pp. 214-215.

871
Morton, Carol A. "Black Women In Corporate America." Ebony. Vol. 30, November, 1975, pp. 106-108, 110, 112, 114.

872
"100 Women Form $1 Million Investment Club." Jet. Vol. 25, January 2, 1964, pp. 19.

873
Payne, Ethel L. "Black Women In Business: Can We Overcome The Barriers?" Contact. Vol. 5, Fall, 1974, pp. 16, 18, 66.

874
"Rarest Breed of Women: Black Businesswomen In The Executive Suites." Time. Vol. 98, November 8, 1971, pp. 102.

875
Regusters, Donald. "Women On The Move." Black Business Digest. Vol. 2, March, 1972, pp. 7-10.

876
Scott, Gil. "Women Retailers Mean Business." Black Enterprise. Vol. 9, May, 1979, pp. 43-45, 47.

877
Sims, Harold R. "The Quest For Corporate Social Responsibility: Altruism, Necessity or Opportunity?" Contact. Vol. 5, Fall, 1974, pp. 34, 39-41.

878
Taylor, Len. "Women In Business." Essence. Vol. 1, March, 1971, pp. 50-55.

879
"Top Execs In Biggest Black Business." Ebony. Vol. 32, August, 1977, pp. 132.

880
Washington, E. "Patricia Harris, Blunt New Voice In The Boardroom." Life. Vol. 71, September 24, 1971, pp. 81.

881
Waters, Kathleen Graham. "A Profile Of Black Female Office Personnel In Southwestern Athletic Conference Universities." Doctoral Dissertation, Kansas State University, 1976, 144p.

882
Williams, Fannie B. "The Women's Part In A Man's Business." Voice Of The Negro. Vol. 1, November, 1904, pp. 543-547.

883
Williams, Frances Harriett. The Business Girl Looks At The Negro World: A Study Course. New York: Women's Press, 1937, 55p.

884
"Women In Business." The Woman's National Magazine. Vol. 4, February, 1937, pp. 36-39.

885
"Women Seek Equal Changes In Business: First National Conference For Minority Businesswomen Produces Keen Insights." Commerce Today. Vol. 2, July 10, 1972, pp. 4-7.

886
"Women To Aid League." Tuskegee Messenger. Vol. 6, July 12-26, 1930, pp. 8.

Designers

887
Brown, Dorothea. "Carlyne Wormley: A Designing Woman." New Lady. Vol. 2, December, 1969, pp. 20-24.

888
Congdon, T. B., Jr. "Ann Lowe, Society's Best Kept Secret: Only Negro American Dress Designer." Saturday Evening Post. Vol. 237, December 12, 1964, pp. 74-76.

889
"Designing First Ladies." Our World. Vol. 6, February, 1951, pp. 54.

890
Hueston, Frederick. "Hats For Hollywood." The Negro Digest. Vol. 2, September, 1944, pp. 15-16.

891
"Pattern Designer Seeks Break With Chain Stores." Jet. Vol. 45, January 24, 1974, pp. 44.

892
"Prize Winning Designer." Norfolk Journal And Guide. 9 April, 1927, pp. 1.

893
"Scarf Designer." Ebony. Vol. 11, May, 1956, pp. 80.

894
Smallwood, Bill. "The Girl With The Golden Hands." The Brown American. Vol. 4, December, 1940, pp. 7, 17.

Dietetics And Food Service

895
"Appoint Woman Food Inspector In Chicago." Chicago Defender. 28 May, 1921, pp. 3.

896
"Birmingham Girl Tops In Dietetic Class." Jet. Vol. 40, September 2, 1971, pp. 29.

897
Blood, Kathryn. "The Cafeteria Worker." Service. Vol. 10, February, 1946, pp. 14-15.

898
____________. "Twenty-four Hours A Day." Pulse. Vol. 2, February, 1944, pp. 20-21.

899
Bond, Barbara. "Women Invade A Man's World." Service. Vol. 10, September, 1945, pp. 17.

900
"Commercial Dietetics Interns Visit Department of Agriculture." Service. Vol. 17, April, 1953, pp. 23.

901
"Forty Attend School For Dieticians." National Negro Health News. Vol. 14, October/December, 1946, pp. 24.

902
Graves, Patsy. "College Dietitian - Mrs. Gwendolyn C. Goldson." Service. Vol. 17, September, 1952, pp. 7-8.

903
__________. "Educational Activities Representative - Mrs. Louise R. Protho." Service. Vol. 16, July, 1952, pp. 7-8.

904
__________. "Food And Nutrition Specialist - Mrs. Bessie B. Ramseur." Service. Vol. 16, April, 1952, pp. 7-8.

905
__________. "Hospital Dietitian - Mrs. Abbie Mitchell." Service. Vol. 16, May, 1952, pp. 7-8.

906
__________. "Miss Sallie Redmond - Public Health Nutritionist." Service. Vol. 17, August, 1952, pp. 7.

907
__________. "Mrs. Blanche Boone Davis, Home Economist." Service. Vol. 16, June, 1952, pp. 21-23.

908
__________. "Mrs. Lucile H. Douthit - Director of Women's Program." Service. Vol. 17, October, 1952, pp. 10-12.

909
__________. "Myrtle Brown, Nutritionist." Service. Vol. 16, March, 1952, pp. 7-8.

910
McEnge, Fannie J. "The Hospital Dietitian." Service. Vol. 16, May, 1952, pp. 12-14.

911
"Meet Our Marian - National Culinary Association's Secretary-Treasurer." Service, Vol. 17, December, 1952, pp. 20.

912
"Marian Mason Higgins: Young - Talented - Perserving Pioneering in Dietetics." The Aframerican Woman's Journal. Winter, 1947, pp. 15.

913
"Negro Women Enrolls For Work In Local Dietetics Classes." Galveston News. 23 October, 1918.

914
"The Outlook For Women As Food Service Managers And Supervisors." Service. Vol. 17, February, 1953, pp. 23-23, 26.

915
"Pastry Specialist." Service. Vol. 10, May, 1946, pp. 17.

916
Porter, Helen Louise. "Negro Women's Opportunities For Training And Service In The Field Of Dietetics." Master's Thesis, University of Iowa, 1942, 81p.

Porter, Helen Louise. "Negro Women's Opportunities for Training And Service In The Field of Dietetics." Journal of Negro Education. Vol. 12, Winter, 1943, pp. 14-20.

917
"Tuskegee Trained Dietitian." Service. Vol. 9, December, 1944, pp. 14.

Doll Manufacturers

918
"Making Colored Dolls A Lucrative Business." New York Age. 9 December, 1922, pp. 7.

919
"Mme. Allone Expands Colored Doll Business." New York Age. 24 March, 1923, pp. 8.

920
"Myla Perkins' Living Black Dolls." Ebony. Vol. 30, January, 1975, pp. 88-90, 92, 94.

921
"New Business Buildings Add To Attractiveness of Block on Seventh Avenue." New York Age. 15 September, 1923, pp. 1.

Domestic Workers

922
Adams, Frankie V. "A Perusal of The Negro Woman Domestic Worker." Service. Vol. 5, May, 1941, pp. 10.

923
Altmeyer, A. J. "Security For Domestic Workers." Service. Vol. 11, August, 1946, pp. 34.

924
Anderson, Mary. "The Plight of Negro Domestic Labor." Journal Of Negro Education. Vol. 5, January, 1936, pp. 66-72.

925
Baker, Ella and Marvel Cooke. "The Bronx Slave Market." The Crisis. Vol. 42, November, 1935, pp. 330-331.

926
Ballard, J. C. "The Status of Household Employees." Service. Vol. 5, March, 1941, pp. 26-27.

927
Barksdale-Sloan, Edith. "WCHE: Gaining Respect For Household Workers." Essence. Vol. 5, July, 1974, pp. 34-35, 67, 69.

928
Beckley, Zoe. "Some Study Needed To Lure Girls To Kitchens." Norfolk Journal And Guide. 10 February, 1917, pp. 1.

929
Berry, Riley M. Fletcher. "The Black Mammy Memorial Institute: Southern Training School For Colored Women." Good Housekeeping. Vol. 53, October, 19-1, pp. 562-563.

930
"Better Trained Domestics Aim of 200 Negroes. "National Negro Health News. Vol. 13, October/December, 1945, pp. 22.

931
Blood, Kathryn. "Hard-Working Americans: Not WACS, Not WAVES, But - Domestic Workers." Pulse. Vol. 1, January, 1944, pp. 14-15, 35.

932
Bolden, Dorothy. "Forty-two Years A Maid Starting At Nine In Atlanta," in Nobody Speaks For Me! Self-Portraits Of American Working Class Women, edited by Nancy Seifer. New York: Simon & Schuster, 1976, 477 p., pp. 138-177.

933
Candler, Ruth. "Housework: A Job In The Process of Becoming A Profession." Service. Vol. 11, November, 1946, pp. 17.

934
"Cass Timberlane: Hollywood Calls Negro Maid 'Mrs' For First Time." Ebony. Vol. 3, November, 1947, pp. 23-24.

935
Cooper, Ester V. "The Negro Woman Domestic Worker In Relation To Trade Unionism." "Master's Thesis. Fisk University, 1940, 105p.

936
Curry, Nannie Trudy. "A Study Of Trends In Domestic Service Employment Among Negroes During The War Period, 1940-1943." Master's Thesis, Atlanta University, 1944, 51p.

937
Dejoie, Beverly Raymond. "A Study Of Negro Women In Domestic And Personal Service Employment In New Orleans, Louisiana, From 1940 to 1946." Master's Thesis, Atlanta University, 1946, 146p.

938
"Dishwasher Images," in Beautiful, Also, Are The Souls Of My Black Sisters: A History Of The Black Woman In America, by Jeanne Noble. New Jersey: Prentice Hall, 1978, 353p, pp. 75-89.

939
"Domestic Service: The Black Experience," in Women In The American Economy: A Documentary History, 1675-1929, by

W. Elliot Brownlee and Mary M. Brownlee. Connecticut: Yale University Press, 1976, 350p., pp. 243-249.

940
"Doubtful Remedies," in Domestic Service, by Lucy Maynard Salmon, New York: Macmillan Company, 1897, 307p., pp. 172-175.

941
Eastman, Wyllie. "A Million And A Half Women." Service. Vol. 4, July, 1940, pp. 13.

942
Ellis, Benson. A Socio-Economic Study of The Female Domestic Worker In Private Homes With Special Reference To New York City. New York: n.p., 1929, 101p.

943
Fisher, Mary Shattuck. "Household Employment And Human Values." Service. Vol. 5, December, 1940, pp. 28-30.

944
Gaither, Alexander Davis. "Negro Women Employed In Domestic Service In Columbus, Ohio." Master's Thesis, The Ohio State University, 1938, 65p.

945
Giovanni, Nikki. "The Silent Revolution of The Domestic Worker." Encore. Vol. 4, June 23/July 4, 1975, pp. 36.

946
Grosnenor, Verta Mae. Thursdays And Every Other Sunday Off. New York: Doubleday, 1972, 156p.

947
Hamburger, Robert. A Stranger In The House. New York: Macmillan, 1978, 168p.

948
Hamilton, Bernard. "Goodbye, Aunt Jemima; Hello, Mrs. Brown." Core. Vol. 3, Summer, 1973, pp. 13-16.

949
Haynes, Elizabeth R. "Negroes In Domestic Service In The U. S." Journal of Negro History. Vol. 8, October, 1923, pp. 384-442.

950
Hornaday, Mary. "Out Of The Kitchens." The Negro Digest. Vol. 1, November, 1942, pp. 33-34.

951
"Improving Domestic Service." Service. Vol. 11, March, 1947, pp. 8.

952
Jones, Dora. "A Self-Help Program of Household Employees." The Aframerican Woman's Journal. Vol. 2, Summer/Fall, 1941, pp. 26-29.

953
Knighten, Grace. "I Was A Lady-In-Waiting." The Negro Digest. Vol. 9, September, 1951, pp. 53-57.

954
"Maid of Hollywood." Jet. Vol. 2, September 11, 1952, pp. 62-65.

955
"Marion Cuthbert Pens Gripping Story of Negro Women Household Workers and Domestics." Black Dispatch. 13 June, 1936.

956
May, Agnes Elizabeth. "Employment of Women In Domestic And Personal Service - With Special Reference To The Negro Woman In Atlanta, Georgia." Master's Thesis, Atlanta University, 1939, 62p.

957
Moore, Louise R. "Maid In Westchester." Liberator. Vol. 7, January, 1967, pp. 18-19.

958
"Movie Maids." Ebony. Vol. 3, August, 1948, pp. 56-59.

959
Ness, Jane Van. "Training Maids For Hotel Work." Service. Vol. 7, August, 1942, pp. 20-21.

960
"Norfolk Domestics Ask Better Wages." Norfolk Journal And Guide. 6 October, 1917, pp. 1.

961
"Prefab Maid Service Is Yours For The Asking." Service. Vol. 12, October, 1947, pp. 21.

962
Reynolds, Lois A. "Sustenance Position of Texas Negro Domestic Servants In The Texas Economy." Master's Thesis. Prairie View State College, 1942, 69p.

963
Roebuck, Julian. "Domestic Service: With Particular Attention To The Negro Female Servant In The South." Master's Thesis, Duke University, 1944, 143p.

964
Russell, R. D. "Experiences of Negro High School Girls With Domestic Placement Agencies." Journal Of Negro Education. Vol. 31, Spring, 1962, pp. 172-176.

965
Searcy, L. J. "The Domestic Worker." Service. Vol. 5, June, 1941, pp. 14-15.

966
Shannon, Mary G. "An Occupational Study Of Negro Maids In Dallas." Master's Thesis, Southern Methodist University, 1941, 154p.

967
"Shirley Chisholm Leads Battle To Aid Domestics." Jet. Vol. 44, July 19, 1973, pp. 7.

968
"A Southern Domestic Worker Speaks," in A Documentary History Of The Negro People In The United States: Vol. 2, 1910-1932, edited by Herbert Aptheker. New Jersey: Citadel Press, 1973, 754p., pp. 46-53.

969
"Special Report On Negro Domestic Service In The Seventh Ward," in The Philadelphia Negro: A Social Study, by W. E. B. DuBois. Philadelphia: University of Pennsylvania, 1899, 520p., pp. 427-509.

970
Sragow, Darry A. "Taking The Mammy Out Of Housework." Sacramento Observer. 1 June, 1972, pp. D-9.

971
Travis, Sue. "The Servant Problem." The Negro. Vol. 2, October, 1944, pp. 42-45.

972
U. S. Department of Labor, Women's Bureau. Domestic Workers And Their Employment Relations. Bulletin #39. Washington, D. C.: G. P. O., 1924, 87p.

973
U. S. Department of Labor, Women's Bureau. "Negro Household Workers," in Reading List of References on Household Employment. Bulletin #138. Washington, D. C.: G. P. O., 1936, 15p., pp. 8.

974
U. S. Department of Labor, Women's Bureau. "Negro Household Workers," in Reading List of References On Household Employment. Bulletin #154. Washington, D. C.: G. P. O., 1937, 17p., pp. 10.

975
Winston, Thyra S. "Treasure Life Of A Colored Maid." American Mercury. Vol. 28, February, 1933, pp. 149-152.

Engineering

976
Clark, Yvonne Y. and Lilia A. Abron-Robinson. "Minority Women In Engineering Schools." IEEE Transactions On Education. Vol. E-18, February, 1975, pp. 34-35.

977
Seneviratne, Gamini. "Women In Engineering: What's A Nice Girl Like You..." Encore. Vol. 5, May 3, 1976, pp. 47.

978
"Tennessee State's Lady Engineer." Ebony. Vol. 19, July, 1964, pp. 75-76, 78, 80.

979
"Woman Engineer." Ebony. Vol. 17, December, 1961, pp. 87-92.

980
"Women's College Seeks Black Women Engineers." Jet. Vol. 46, June 20, 1974, pp. 21.

Farming

981
Bell, Oscar L. "Why The Negro Girl Should Study Agriculture." The Rural Messenger (Tuskegee Institute). Vol. 1, January, 1921, pp. 6.

982
Blood, Kathryn. "There's Victory In Victuals: Women Farmers." Pulse. Vol. 2, May, 1944, pp. 32-33.

983
Brown, M. M. "Black Women In Agriculture." Agricultural History. Vol. 50, January, 1976, pp. 202-212.

984
"Champion Girl Farmers of Wisconsin." Norfolk Journal And Guide. 1 January, 1917, pp. 5.

985
"Colored Farm Men And Women To Meet At Hampton Institute." New York Age. 1 June, 1923, pp. 5.

986
"Conference Held To Plan Women's Land Army." Service. Vol. 7, June/July, 1943, pp. 29.

987
Ellis, Elaine. "Women Of The Cotton Fields." The Crisis. Vol. 45, October, 1938, pp. 333-342.

988
"Farm Women Plan Housework Schedules." Tuskegee Messenger. Vol. 6, January 11, 1930, pp. 6.

989
"The First Negro Farm Women's Short Course Proved Real Success." Norfolk Journal And Guide. 15 October, 1927, pp. 1.

990
"Kittrell, Flemmie P. "The Farm Camp At Hampton Institute." Journal of The National Association of College Women. #20, 1947, pp. 20-21.

991
"The Negro Woman," in The Labor of Women In The Production of Cotton, by Ruth Alice Allen. New York: Arno Press, 1933, 1975, 285p., pp. 174-208.

992
"Negro Women Are Wanted In Gardens." Birmingham Herald. 13 June, 1918.

993
"Negro Women Wanted To Pick Cotton Crop." Memphis Commercial Appeal. 11 August, 1918.

994
"1924 Girls' Day Enthusiastically Celebrated At Tuskegee." Tuskegee Messenger. Vol. 1, October 25, 1924, pp. 2.

995
"North Carolina Forms Women's Short Course." Norfolk Journal And Guide. 30 July, 1927, pp. 8.

996
Price, Alice M. "Women Farmers." The Southern Workman. Vol. 47, December, 1918, pp. 577-581.

997
"Vanishing Farm Wife." Ebony. Vol. 21, August, 1966, pp. 76-77, 80-83.

Firefighters

998
Perry, Harmon. "Black Women Hold Their Own With Atlanta's Fire Dept." Jet. Vol. 54, June 22, 1978, pp. 22-23.

Florists

999
Carter, Elmer Anderson. "Flower Girl of Indianapolis." Opportunity. Vol. 15, April, 1937, pp. 110-112.

1000
"Lady Florist." Ebony. Vol. 4, November, 1948, pp. 51-54.

1001
"She Turned Her Avocation Into A Growing And Prosperous Business." Norfolk Journal And Guide. 30 May, 1925, pp. 9.

General Works

1002
"Abuse Of The 'Work or Fight' Slogan." New York Age. 28 September, 1918.

1003
Agnew, Patricia. "Choice: A Job Or A Baby." Evening Star. 31 December, 1971.

1004
Aldous, Joan. "Wives; Employment Status And Lower-Class Men As Husband-Fathers: Support For The Moynihan Thesis." Journal of Marriage And The Family. Vol. 31, August, 1969, pp. 469-476.

1005
Aldridge, Delores. "Black Women In The Economic Marketplace: A Battle Unfinished." Journal Of Social And Behavioral Sciences. Vol. 21, Winter, 1975, pp. 48-62.

1006
Almquist, Elizabeth. "The Disadvantaged Status of Black Women," in Woman In A Man-Made World: A Socioeconomic Handbook, edited by Nona Glazer-Malbin and Helen Y. Waehrer. Chicago: Rand McNally, 1977, 443p., pp. 335-344.

1007
________. Untangling The Effects of Race and Sex: The Disadvantaged Status of Black Women." Social Science Quarterly. Vol. 56, June, 1975, pp. 129-142.

1008
"America's Emerging Black Women." Congressional Record. Vol. 119, November 14, 1973, pp. S20353-20356.

1009
Anderson, Alvin Frederick. "An Analysis Of Job Placement Patterns of Black And Non-Black Male and Female Undergraduates at The University of Virginia and Hampton Institute." Doctoral Dissertation, University of Virginia, 1975, 127p.

1010
Aschenfelter, Orley. "Changes In Labor Market Discrimination Over Time." Journal of Human Resources. Vol. 5, Fall, 1970, pp. 403-430.

1011
Ash, Philip. "Job Satisfaction Differences Among Women of Different Ethnic Groups." Journal of Vocational Behavior. Vol. 2, October, 1972, pp. 495.

1012
Astin, Helen S. and Ann S. Bisconti. Career Plans of Black And Non-White College Graduates. Bethlehem, Pennsylvania: CPC Foundation, 1973, 15p.

1013
Axelson, Leland J. "The Working Wife: Differences In Perception Among Negro And White Males." Journal of Marriage And The Family. Vol. 32, August, 1970, pp. 457-464.

1014
"Bachelor Career Girls." Jet. Vol. 4, October 22, 1953, pp. 58-61.

1015
"Back To Slavery." The Crisis. Vol. 43, October, 1936, pp. 316-317.

1016
Baker, Sally Hielsman and Bernard Levenson. "Job Opportunities of Black And White Working-Class Women." Social Problems. Vol. 22, April, 1975, pp. 510-533.

1017
Bartel, Carole. "The Sexism Sickness / The Racism Killer." Core. Vol. 5, Winter, 1975, pp. 17-18.

1018
Beckett, Joyce O. "Working Wives: A Racial Comparison." Social Work. Vol. 21, November, 1976, pp. 463-471.

1019
Bell, Duran. "Why Participation Rates of Black And White Wives Differ." Journal of Human Resources. Vol. 9, Fall, 1974, pp. 465-479.

1020
Berg, Gene. "Boss Lady Who Makes Other Ladies Bosses." Encore. Vol. 5, October 4, 1976, pp. 14.

1021
"Birmingham's Candy Queen." Headlines And Pictures. Vol. 3, August, 1946, pp. 19-21.

1022
"Black Professional Women, Forging New Careers Despite Dual Standards And Doing Quite Well, Thank You." Black Enterprise. Vol. 2, November, 1971, pp. 35-39.

1023
"Black Slaves," in America's Working Women, by Rosalyn Baxandall, Linda Gordon and Susan Reverby. New York: Random House, 1976, 399p., pp. 30-34.

1024
"Black-White Differences In Wives' Earnings And Contribution To Family Income," in Women In The Labor Force, by James A. Sweet. New York: Seminar Press, 1973, 211p., pp. 168-198.

1025
"Black Woman Honored As Top Handicapped Employee In Federal Government." Jet. Vol. 42, May 11, 1972, pp. 14-15.

1026
"Black Woman Named To National Service Board." Jet. Vol. 47, October 31, 1974, pp. 5.

1027
"Black Women And The Labor Force." Sacramento Observer. 1 June, 1972, pp. D-9.

1028
"Black Women In Various Professions, in Black Women Makers Of History: A Portrait, by George F. Jackson. Sacramento: Fong & Fong, 1977, 289p., pp. 167-187.

1029
"Black Women Make Their Mark." Black Enterprise. Vol. 5, August, 1974, pp. 37-39.

1030
"Black Women Win Pact For $100 Million In Jobs." Jet. Vol. 54, January 12, 1978, pp. 12.

1031
Bock, E. Wilbur. "Farmer's Daughter Effect: The Case Of The Negro Female Professionals." Phylon. Vol. 30, Spring, 1969, pp. 17-26.

Bock, E. Wilbur. "Farmer's Daughter Effect: The Case Of The Negro Female Professionals," in The Professional Woman, edited by Athena Theodore. Cambridge: Schenkman Publishing Company, 1971, 769p., pp. 119-131.

1032
Bogan, Forrest A. "Work Expereince Of The Population: Spotlight On Women And Youth." Monthly Labor Review. Vol. 92, June, 1969, pp. 44-50.

1033
Bonner, Alice. "Jobs, Food Goals of Black Women's Unity Day." Washington Post. 21 April, 1975, pp. C-1.

1034
Booker, Simeon. "Black Woman Heads U.N. Security Council." Jet. Vol. 43, November 23, 1972, pp. 18.

1035
"Briefings For Federally Employed Ethnic and Racial Minority Women," in ...To Form A More Perfect Union...Justice For American Women. Report Of The National Commission Of The Observance of International Women's Year. Washington, D. C.: G. P. O., 1976, 382p., pp. 301-302.

1036
Bright, Margruetta V. "Factors Related To The Traditionally Or Innovativeness Of Career Choices In Black College Women." Master's Thesis, Howard University, 1970, 39p.

1037
"Building For Tomorrow." Pulse. Vol. 1, September, 1943, pp. 30.

1038
Burgen, Michele. "Problems of Women Bosses." Ebony. Vol. 33, November, 1977, pp. 94, 96, 98, 100.

1039
Burns, Monique L. "Serving The World." Essence. Vol. 10, July, 1979, pp. 28.

1040
"Career Expectations of Negro Women Graduates." Monthly Labor Review. Vol. 90, November, 1967, pp. 36-42.

1041
"Career Women, 1975," Essence. Vol. 5, March, 1975, pp. 32, 37, 39-40, 42, 116.

1042
"Career Women, 1976." Essence. Vol. 6, March, 1976, pp. 39-40, 43, 46.

1043
Carr, Cynthia. "Women At Work." Tuesday At Home. March, 1975, pp. 6-8.

1044
Carson, Charles. "And So Lucille Went To College." The Crisis. Vol. 42, October, 1935, pp. 299.

1045
"Census Report of The Negro." Voice Of The Negro. Vol. 1, August, 1904, pp. 304.

1046
"Changing Status of Negro Women Workers." Monthly Labor Review. Vol. 87, June, 1964, pp. 671-673.

1047
"Colored Girls In Cleveland." The Crisis. Vol. 36, December, 1929, pp. 411-412.

1048
"The Colored Woman As A Breadwinner," in Half A Man: The Status Of The Negro In New York, by Mary White Ovington. New York: Hill & Wang, 1911, 128p., pp. 76-92.

1049
"Colored Women In Postwar Era." Service. Vol. 9, April, 1945, pp. 9.

1050
Cooper, Anna J. "Colored Women As Wage-Earners." The Southern Workman. Vol. 28, July, 1899, pp. 295-298.

1051
Cuthbert, Marion. "Problems Facing Negro Young Women." Opportunity. Vol. 14, February, 1936, pp. 47-49.

1052
Denard, Jessie L. Lanier. "Some Aspects Of Women In American Labor With Emphasis On Negro Women In The South, 1940-1950." Master's Thesis, Atlanta University, 1955, 67p.

1053
Diggs, Olive M. "The Negro Woman Assesses New Horizons." The Aframerican Woman's Journal. #3, 1943, pp. 17, 22.

1054
"The Disadvantage of Being Female And Black, in The American Woman: Who Was She?, by Anne Firor Scott. New Jersey: Prentice-Hall, 1971, 182p., pp. 28-32.

1055
"The Earning and Labor Force Status of Negro Women," in Sex And The Marketplace: American Women At Work, by Juanita Kreps. Baltimore: The Johns Hopkins University Press, 1971, 117p., pp. 8-10.

1056
Edwards, Thyra J. "Let's Have More Like Mr. Sopkins." The Crisis. Vol. 42, March, 1935, pp. 72, 82.

1057
"The Employed Woman - Race," in Developing Woman's Potential, by Edwin C. Lewis. Ames, Iowa: Iowa State University Press, 1968, 389p., pp. 126-127.

1058
"Employment of Colored Women In Chicago." The Crisis. Vol. 1, January, 19-1, pp. 24-25.

1059
Epstein, Cynthia Fuchs. "Positive Effects of The Multiple Negative: Explaining The Success of Black Professional Women." American Journal of Sociology. Vol. 78, January, 1973, pp. 912-935.

1060
Fadayomi, Theophilus Oyeyemi. "Black Women In The Labor Force: An Investigation Of Factors Affecting The Labor Force Participation of Black Women In The United States." Doctoral Dissertation, University of Pennsylvania, 1977, 199p.

1061
Fairclough, Alice B. "A Study Of Occupational Opportunities For Negro Women In New York City." Master's Thesis, New York University, 1929, 67p.

1062
"Federal Commission Orders Motion Picture Theatre In Michigan To Hire Negro Girl As Candy Counter Operator With Back Pay." Race Relations Law Review. Vol. 5, Fall, 1960, pp. 914-917.

1063
"Federal Women Concerned About Stereotype Positions." Washington Afro American. 14 July, 1973, pp. 9.

1064
"Female Negro Labor Efficient As White." New York Age. 11 March, 1922, pp. 1.

1065
Ferguson, Elaine. "The Relationship of Work Motivation To Selected Demographic Characteristics of Black Female Workers." Doctoral Dissertation, University of Houston, 1978, 143p.

1066
Fitcher, Joseph H. "Career Expectations of Negro Women Graduates." Monthly Labor Review. Vol. 90, November, 1967, pp. 36-42.

Fitcher, Joseph H. "Career Expectations Of Negro Women Graduates," in The Professional Woman, edited by Athena Theodore. Cambridge: Schenkman Publishing Company, 1971, 769p., pp. 427-440.

1067
"First Black Woman Heads Houston's Civil Service." Jet. Vol. 50, April 8, 1976, pp. 7.

1068
"First Black Woman Plate Printer For U. S. Bureau." Jet. Vol. 40, August 26, 1971, pp. 23.

1069
"For Black Girls, It's Worse," in The Job Crisis For Black Youth, by The Twentieth Century Fund Task Force On Employment Problems of Black Youth. New York: Praeger, 1971, 135p., pp. 77-96.

1070
Fox, Andrew. Black Teenage Girl Project. In School Neighborhood Youth Corps. Memphis, Tennessee: Social Service Delivery Systems, 1973, unpaged.

1071
Fulcher, Patsy G. "Aileen C. Hernandez and Eleanor R. Spikes: Sharing The Power And The Glory." Contact. Vol. 5, Fall, 1974, pp. 50-52, 63-64.

1072
Ginzberg, Eli and Dale L. Hiestand. "Employment Patterns of Negro Men And Women," in The American Negro Reference Book,

edited by John P. Davis. New Jersey: Prentice-Hall, 1966, 969p., pp. 205-250.

1073
"The Girl Who Wouldn't Give Up." Ebony. Vol. 23, December, 1967, pp. 113-114, 116, 118.

1074
Glover, Robert W., Alexis Herman and Allan King. "Minority Women, Professional Work." Manpower Magazine. Vol. 7, July, 1975, pp. 8-12.

1075
Gordon, Eugene and Cyril Briggs. The Position of Negro Women. New York: Workers Library Publishers, 1935.

1076
"Government Girl." Sepia. Vol. 13, July, 1964, pp. 47-51.

1077
Granston, Fannie. "First Lady Vows To Help Black Women." Jet. Vol. 47, October 3, 1974, pp. 16.

1078
Graves, Earl G. "Salute To The Working Woman." Black Enterprise. Vol. 8, August, 1977, pp. 3.

1079
Green, Barbara M. "Upgrading Black Women In The Supervisory Ranks." Personnel. Vol. 46, November/December, 1969, pp. 47-50.

1080
Gump, Janice P. and L. Wendell Rivers. "A Consideration Of Race In Efforts To End Sex Bias," in Issues Of Sex Bias And Sex Fairness In Career Interest Measurement, edited by Esther E. Diamond. Washington, D. C.: National Institute of Education, Department of HEW, 1975, 219p., pp. 123-139.

1081
Guthrie, Harold W. "The Prospect of Equality of Incomes Between White And Black Families Under Varying Rates of Unemployment." Journal of Human Resources. Vol. 5, Fall, 1970, pp. 431-446.

1082
Hamilton, Kelly. Goals And Plans Of Black Women. New York; Exposition Press, 1975, 79p.

1083
"A Harbor - The Colored Working Girls' Home In Toledo, Ohio." The Crisis. Vol. 21, April, 1921, pp. 262-263.

1084
Harley, Sharon. "Northern Black Female Workers: Jacksonian Era," in The Afro American Woman: Struggles And Images,

edited by Sharon Harley and Rosalyn Terborg-Penn. New York: Kennikat Press, 1978, 137p., pp. 5-16.

1085
Harrison, Algea O. and Joanne H. Minor. "Interrole Conflict, Coping Strategy, And Satisfaction Among Black Working Wives." Journal Of Marriage And The Family. Vol. 40, November, 1978, pp. 799-805.

1086
Haynes, Elizabeth Ross. "Two Million Negro Women At Work." The Southern Workman. Vol. 51, February, 1922, pp. 64-72.

1087
Heaston, Patricia Yvonne Wright. "An Analysis of Selected Role Perceptions Among Successful Black Women In The Professions." Doctoral Dissertation, Northwestern University, 1975, 142p.

1088
Herman, Alexis M. "Black Women In The Labor Force." The Black Collegian. Vol. 9, May/June, 1979, pp. 30, 32, 35.

1089
Hernandez, Aileen C. "Equal Employment Opportunities For Women: Problems, Facts and Answers." Contact. Vol. 3, Fall, 1973, pp. 9-12.

1090
________________. "Small Change For Black Women." Ms. Vol. 3, August, 1974, pp. 16-18.

1091
Hiestand, Dale L. Economic Growth And Employment Opportunities For Minorities. New York: Columbia University Press, 1964, 127p.

1092
Hobbs, Clark S. "The Old Conditions Are Changing." The Aframerican Woman's Journal. Vol. 2, Summer/Fall, 1941, pp. 30-31.

1093
________________. "The Whip Changes Hands." The Aframerican Woman's Journal. Vol. 2, Summer/Fall, 1941, pp. 29-30.

1094
Huck, James R. "Determinants of Assessment Center Ratings For White and Black Females And The Relationship Of These Dimensions To Subsequent Performance Effectiveness." Doctoral Dissertation, Wayne State University, 1974, 168p.

1095
Hunter, Clarence. "Negro Women Urged In High -Federal Posts." Evening Star. 14 March, 1964.

1096
Hutchins, Grace. Women Who Work. New York: International Publishers, 1952, 96p.

1097
"Improvement For Negro Women Workers." Service. Vol. 11, August, 1946, pp. 19.

1098
"In Factory And Field: Black Women And Slavery In America, 1808-1860," in We Were There: The Story of Working Women In America, by Barbara Mayer Wertheimer. New York: Pantheon Books, 1977, 427p., pp. 107-127.

1099
Iota Phi Lambda Sorority. Survey On White Collar Occupations For Negro Women, March-August, 1947. Iota Phi Lambda Sorority, 1948, 11p.

1100
Jackson, Raymond J. "Black Women In Administration (From The Point of View Of A Black Man)." The Crisis. Vol. 83, December, 1976, pp. 353, 362.

1101
Jason, Grace Atkins. "A Study Of The Occupations Followed By Hampton Institute's Women Graduates of The School of Education And Home Economics." Master's Thesis, Northwestern University, 1941, 74p.

1102
Jefferson, Margo. "Should Black Women Work?" Contact. Vol. 3, Fall, 1973, pp. 33-34.

1103
Jensen, Beverly, "Black And Female, Too." Black Enterprise. Vol. 6, July, 1976, pp. 26-29.

1104
"Jobs For Colored Women." Baltimore American. 9 August, 1918.

1105
Johnson, Toki Schalk. "Education And The Arts Make History." Chicago Courier. 7 April, 1963.

1106
Jones, Barbara Ann Posey. "The Contributions of Black Women To The Incomes of Black Families: An Analysis of The Labor Force Participation Rates of Black Women." Doctoral Dissertation. Georgia State University, 1973, 158p.

1107
Jones, Sylvia M. "Career Plans For Black Women." Afro American Magazine. November 25, 1972, pp. 11.

1108
Kellor, Frances A. "Opportunities For Southern Negro Women In Northern Cities." Voice Of The Negro. Vol. 2, July, 1905, pp. 470-473.

1109
Kilson, Marian. "Black Women In The Professions, 1890-1970." Monthly Labor Review. Vol. 100, May, 1977, pp. 38-41.

1110
King, Allan G. "Labor Market Racial Discrimination Against Black Women." Review of Black Political Economy. Vol. 8, Summer, 1978, pp. 325-335.

1111
Klugh, Eolyn C. "Colored Girls At Work In Boston." Opportunity. Vol. 6, October, 1928, pp. 295-299.

1112
LaBeau, Fay Bowman. "A Study Of The Incomes Of Two Hundred Women Graduated From The College At Hampton Institute, Virginia, 1926-1933." Master's Thesis, Cornell University, 1935, 64p.

1113
"Labor Department Publication Explains Black Women's Job Experience." Black News Digest. September 29, 1975, pp. 6.

1114
"Labor Force Activity of Married Women In Relation To Child Status And Family History - Multivariate Analysis," in Women In The Labor Force, by James A. Sweet. New York: Seminar Press, 1973, 211p., pp. 89-111.

1115
"Lady In The Tank." Norfolk Journal And Guide. 24 February, 1973, pp. 11.

1116
"Lady Selectman." Ebony. Vol. 14, September, 1959, pp. 35-36, 38.

1117
"Lady Weatherman." Ebony. Vol. 10, November, 1954, pp. 59-62.

1118
Landry, Bart and Margaret P. Jendrek. "Employment of Wives In Middle Class Black Families." Journal of Marriage And The Family. Vol. 40, November, 1978, pp. 787-797.

1119
Lanham, Florence B. "Income Supplementing Occupations; An Approach To Program Planning For Economically Disadvantaged Homemakers." Master's Thesis, Howard University, 1969, 69p.

1120
Latimer, Magnolia L. "The Problem of Unemployed Women."

Opportunity. Vol. 14, November, 1936, pp. 342-343.

1121
"Leather Craft." Ebony. Vol. 2, September, 1947, pp. 29-33.

1122
Lee, LaVerne Lillian. "The Negro Woman Worker." Master's Thesis, Atlanta University, 1945, 34p.

1123
Lemieux, Melba. "Black Women Assert Themselves." The Black Collegian. Vol. 6, May/June, 1976, pp. 4-6, 8, 10, 12, 14.

1124
__________. "Careers For Women In The '70s." The Black Collegian. Vol. 7, May/June, 1977, pp. 4.

1125
"Light Colored Girls." Columbus Journal. 4 August, 1918.

1126
Lissner, Will. "Negro Women Pay Up 53% in Decade In City Area." New York Times. 12 August, 1962.

1127
McKenney, Nampeo D. R. "Profile of Black America - The Woman." Black Enterprise. Vol. 2, August, 1971, pp. 17.

1128
McKenzie, Marjorie. "Against The Lean Years." The Aframerican Woman's Journal. Vol. 3, Summer, 1943, pp. 6-7.

1129
Mednick, Martha T. Shuck, and Gwendolyn Randall Puryear. "Motivational and Personality Factors Related To Career Goals of Black Women." Journal of Social And Behavioral Sciences. Vol. 21, Winter, 1975, pp. 1-30.

1130
Mellon, Steven Joseph, Jr. "Instrumentality-Expectancy Theory Of Work Motivation: A Modification And Empirical Test Of Its Implication For Disadvantaged Black Females In Job Training Programs." Doctoral Dissertation, University of Houston, 1975, 182p.

1131
Metcalf, Zaida. "Negro Applicants at The Vocational Adjustment Bureau." Opportunity. Vol. 18, December, 1940, pp. 365-368.

1132
Metropolitan Applied Research Center. Improving Employment Opportunities For Female Black Teenagers In New York City. Washington, D. C.: Department of Labor, Employment And Training Administration, 1977, 262p.

1133
Minorities And Women In State And Local Government, 1973, Vol. 1, U. S. Summary. Washington, D. C.: Equal Employment Opportunity Commission, 1974, 197p.

1134
"The Minority Woman: Doubly Protected," in Affirmative Action And The Woman Worker: Guidelines For Personnel Management, by Jennie Farley. New York: American Management Association, 1979, 225p., pp. 93-113.

1135
"Minority Women's Employment Programs," in...To Form A More Perfect Union...Justice For American Women. Report Of The National Commission of The Observance of International Women's Year. Washington, D. C.: G. P. O., 1976, 382p., pp. 296-297.

1136
Moss, Judith Gordon. "A Comparative Study of Types of Volunteer Activities of Higher Occupational Status Black And White Women." Master's Thesis, Atlanta University, 1973, 29p.

1137
"Mrs. Washington On Labor Question." Norfolk Journal And Guide. 25 November, 1916, pp. 1.

1138
"The Negro," in Woman's Work In Municipalities, by Mary Ritter Beard. New York: D. Appleton & Company, 1915, 344p., pp. 182-195.

1139
"Negro Woman Is Technician In Dep't of Agriculture." Oklahoma Eagle. 6 March, 1943.

1140
"Negro Women Contribute To Nation's Welfare." Service. Vol. 10, February, 1946, pp. 11.

1141
"Negro Women Employees Show 450,000 Increase." Black Dispatch. 5 March, 1949.

1142
"Negro Women In Gainful Occupations," in Women In Gainful Occupations, 1870-1920, by Joseph A. Hill. Washington, D. C.: G. P. O., 1929, 416p., pp. 109-121.

1143
"Negro Women Prove To Be Satisfactory Workers At Depot." Birmingham Age-Herald. 15 June, 1918.

1144
"Negro Women Workers." Opportunity. Vol. 5, July, 1927, pp. 191.

1145
"Negro Women Workers." Survey Midmonthly. Vol. 75, March, 1939, pp. 87.

1146
"Negro Women Workers Is Study Subject." Evening Star. 27 March, 1964.

1147
"Negro Women Workers Plea." Chicago Tribune. 19 July, 1918.

1148
Nelson, Charmeynne D. "Myths About Black Women Workers In Modern America." Black Scholar. Vol. 6, March, 1975, pp. 11-15.

1149
"New Careers For The New Woman." Ebony. Vol. 26, July, 1971, pp. 31-35.

1150
Nobel, Jeanne L. "Four Phases Mark Expansion of Job Opportunities For College-Bred Women." Amsterdam News. 19 June, 1954, pp. 7, 18.

1151
"Non-White Women In The Illinois Labor Force," "Employed Non-White Illinois Women," "Unemployed Non-White Women," "Income Of Non-White Illinois Women," "Weeks Worked By Non-White Illinois Women; "Non-White Women Workers In Eight Illinois Labor Market Areas," in Women Workers In Illinois, by The Bureau of Employment Security. Illinois: Department of Labor, 1964, 92p., pp. 42-66, 83-92.

1152
Norton, Eleanor Holmes. "Affirmative Action For Both Minorities and Women: The Road To Real Reform." Contact. Vol. 5, Fall, 1974, pp. 12, 14-15.

1153
Oaxana, Ronald. "Male-Female Wages Differentials In Urban Labor Markets." International Economic Review. Vol. 14, October, 1973, pp. 693-709.

1154
O'Leary, Virginia Elizabeth. "The Work Acculturation of 72 Black Women Into The Labor Force Trainee Orientation." Doctoral Dissertation, Wayne State University, 1969, 97p.

1155
Ostlund, Leonard A. "Occupational Choice Patterns of Negro Women." Journal of Negro Education. Vol. 26, Winter, 1957, pp. 86-91.

1156
"Our Women Wage-Earners." Norfolk Journal And Guide. 3 March, 1917, pp. 4.

1157
Ovington, Mary White. "On The Black Woman As Breadwinner," in Roots of Bitterness: Documents Of The Social History of American Women, edited by Nancy F. Cott. New York: Dutton & Company, 1972, 373p., pp. 343-347.

1158
"Pearl Makers." Ebony. Vol. 2, May, 1947, pp. 27-30.

1159
Perrella, Vera C. "Women And The Labor Force." Monthly Labor Review. Vol. 91, February, 1968, pp. 1-12.

1160
Pleck, Elizabeth H. "A Mother's Wages: Income Earnings Among Married Italian and Black Women, 1896-1911," in The American Family In Social-Historical Perspective, edited by Michael Gordon. New York: St. Martin's Press, 1978, 580p., pp. 490-510.

1161
Powell, W. H. R. The Negro And The Bread Line. The Danger Of His Remaining, Some Things He Should Do To Get Out, And Is Negro Womanhood Equal To Its Task Of Constructive Leadership In These Days of Distressing Unemployment. Philadelphia: James Printing Company, 1931, 22p.

1162
Pressman, Sonia. "Job Discrimination And The Black Woman." The Crisis. Vol. 77, March, 1970, pp. 103-108.

1163
"Problems of Black Girls Are Worse." Sacramento Observer. 1 June, 1972, pp. D-17.

1164
"Problems of Negro Women," in Four Consultations, by the U. S. President's Commission on The Status of Women. Washington, D. C.: G. P. O., 1963, 38p.

1165
"Professional Women." The Woman's National Magazine. Vol. 4, April, 1937, pp. 86-87, 94.

1166
"The Professions: More Skilled, Higher Paid, But..." in Working Women: A Study of Women In Paid Jobs, edited by Ann Seidman. Boulder, Colorado: Westview Press, 1978, 217p., pp. 113-114.

1167
"Protest Sent To Wilson." New York Post. 25 September, 1918.

1168
"Put Girls on Elevators of State House." Norfolk Journal And Guide. 6 March, 1943.

1169
"Race Woman Appointed In Dept. of Agri." Philadelphia Independent. 7 March, 1943.

1170
"Race Woman Gets Important U.S.D.A. Post." National Negro Health News. Vol. 12, April/June, 1944, pp. 23.

1171
Reden, W. F. and Reuben Taylor. "Lucille Went To College." The Crisis. Vol. 42, November, 1935, pp. 347.

1172
Reid, Ira De A. "Social Studies In Pictures III - Black And White Women Workers In The United States, 1890-1930." Opportunity. Vol. 11, May, 1933, pp. 136.

1173
"The Relationship Between Nonwhite Housing And Labor Force Participation of Nonwhite Wives," in Married Women In The Labor Force: An Economic Analysis, by Glen G. Cain. Chicago: University of Chicago Press, 1966, 159p., pp. 143-148.

1174
"Restored To Job." The Crisis. Vol. 62, March, 1955, pp. 171.

1175
Rice, Rhonda Ferrell. "Comparison Analysis of Labor Force Changes Among Black And White Females In The United States From 1960-1970." Master's Thesis, Atlanta University, 1977, 36p.

1176
Robinson, Anna Jones. "The Negro Woman In The Professions." The Messenger. Vol. 7, July, 1923, pp. 765-766.

1177
Robinson, Florence Ann. "A Study Of The Occupational Choices Of The Negro Women of The Senior Classes In Atlanta Colleges, 1940-1941, In Relation to Possible Employment." Master's Thesis, Atlanta University, 1941, 55p.

1178
Robinson, Sarah B. "The Occupational Aspirations of Young Black and White Females: Levels, Atypicality, And Work Commitment." Doctoral Dissertation, University of Texas at Austin, 1978, 163p.

1179
Ross, Ruth N. "The Negro Girl Goes Job Hunting." Urban West. Vol. 1, November/ December, 1967, pp. 13-14, 31.

1180
"Rug Weaver." Ebony. Vol. 1, May, 1946, pp. 31-34.

1181
Sarpy, Lynn. "Jobs Offering The Greatest Opportunities For Black Women." The Black Collegian. Vol. 6, May/June, 1976, pp. 15, 66.

1182
__________. "Problems of Black Women In The Labor Market." The Black Collegian. Vol. 7, May/June, 1977, pp. 6, 8, 10, 12.

1183
Sayre, Anne. "Negro Woman At Work." Service. Vol. 13, March, 1949, pp. 10.

1184
"Says Negro Women Are Holding Many Employment Gains." Call And Post. 6 July, 1946.

1185
"Seek Back Wages For Arkansas Women Workers." The Crisis. Vol. 42, April, 1935, pp. 119.

1186
"Seek To Raise Morale of Girl Federal Workers." Norfolk Journal And Guide. 17 October, 1942.

1187
Sexton, Patricia Cayo. "Minority Group Women." Paper presented at the Workshop On Research Needed To Improve The Employment and Employability of Women. Washington, D. C.: June, 1974, 21p.

1188
Sharpe, Lynn. "Are We Taking Jobs From Our Men?" Essence. Vol. 5, March, 1975, pp. 46, 95.

1189
Shea, John R. "Welfare Mothers: Barriers To Labor Force Entry." Journal of Human Rources. Vol. 8, Supplement, 1973, pp. 90-102.

1190
Sheppard, Harold. "Age And Migration Factors In The Socioeconomic Conditions of Urban Black And White Women," in New Perspectives On Older Workers. Kalamazoo, Michigan: The W. E. Upjohn Institute for Employment Research, 1971, 90p., pp. 37-70.

1191
"Should Wives Quit Work To Make New Jobs? Working Wives Chorus 'No' To Idea." Jet. Vol. 19, March 2, 1961, pp. 18.

1192
Smith, Marie. "Policy Posts Sought." Washington Post. 14 December, 1963, pp. F-12.

1193
"Some Specific Proposals. Workshop II: Blacks And Other Minority Women," in Working Women: A Study of Women In Paid Jobs, edited by Ann Seidman. Boulder, Colorado: Westview Press, 1978, 217p., pp. 148-149.

1194
Sorkin, Alan L. "Education, Occupation and Income of Nonwhite Women." Journal of Negro Education. Vol. 41, Fall, 1972, pp. 343-351.

1195
____________. "Occupational Status and Unemployment of Nonwhite Women." Social Forces. Vol. 49, March, 1971, pp. 393-398.

1196
Stone, Louise D. "On The Job And Over 40." Contact. Vol. 3, Fall, 1973, pp. 42-43.

1197
Struyk, Ramond J. "Explaining Variations In The Hourly Wage Rates of Urban Minority Group Females. Journal of Human Resources. Vol. 8, Summer, 1973, pp. 349-364.

1198
Swain, Johnnie dee. "Regional Comparison of Black And White Women Economic Activities In Segmented Labor Markets." Doctoral Dissertation, Syracuse University, 1977, 161p.

1199
"Swift Ordered To Hire 12 Negro Women." Jet. Vol. 1, December 13, 1951, pp. 19.

1200
"Television Makeup Lady." Ebony. Vol. 4, February, 1949, pp. 27-30.

1201
"Three Colored Girls Give Up Jobs But Hold To Race Pride." New York Age. 20 January, 1923, pp. 1.

1202
Tillman, Katherine D. "Paying Professions For Colored Girls." Voice Of The Negro. Vol. 4, January/February, 1907, pp. 54-56.

1203
Toote, Gloria E. A. "Women In The Work Force: A Rising Reality." Contact. Vol. 3, Fall, 1973, pp. 29-31.

1204
"Tradition And Employment." Opportunity. Vol. 2, March, 1924, pp. 1.

1205
"The Triple Jeopardy of Black And Other Minority Women." in Working Women: A Study of Women In Paid Jobs, edited by Ann Seidman. Boulder, Colorado: Westview Press, 1978, 217p., pp. 59-69.

1206
"Two Women Appointed to N. Y. State, City Posts." Jet. Vol. 25, January 16, 1964, pp. 4.

1207
U. S. Department of Labor, Women's Bureau. Facts On Women Workers of Minority Races. Washington, D. C.: G. P. O., 1974, 9p.

1208
____________________. The Legal Status Of Women In The United States of America. January 1, 1938: Final Report, Giving Summary of All States Combined. Bulletin # 157. Washington, D. C.: G. P. O., 1942, 88p.

1209
____________________. "Minority Race Women In The Work Force," "Occupations of Minority Race Women," in 1975 Handbook On Women Workers. Bulletin #297 Washington, D. C.: G. P. O., 1975, 435p., pp. 41-45; 102-106.

1210
____________________. The Negro Woman Worker. Washington, D. C.: G. P. O., 1938, 17p.

1211
____________________. The Negro Woman In The United States - New Roles - New Challenges. Washington, D. C.: G. P. O., 1967, 10p.

1212
____________________. "Negro Women - Major Occupational Groups," "Negro Women - Individual Occupations," in Changes In Women's Occupations, 1940-1950. Bulletin #253. Washington, D. C.: G. P. O., 1954, 104p., pp. 9-12; 31-35.

1213
____________________. Negro Women And Their Jobs. Washington, D. C.: G. P. O., 1954, 10p.

1214
____________________. "Negro Women In Chicago And Atlanta," in The Employment of Women In Offices. Bulletin #120. Washington, D. C.: G. P. O., 1934, 126p., pp. 92.

1215
U. S. Department of Labor, Women's Bureau. Negro Women In The Population And In The Labor Force. Washington, D. C.: G. P. O., 1966, 34p.

1216
____________________. Negro Women - In The Population And In The Labor Force. Washington, D. C.: G. P. O., 1967, 41p.

1217
____________________. "Negro Women Workers," in 1954 Handbook On Women Workers. Bulletin # 255. Washington, D. C.: G. P. O., 1954, 75p., pp. 18-20.

1218
____________________. Negro Women Workers In 1960. Bulletin #287. Washington, D.C.: G. P. O., 1964, 55p.

1219
____________________. "Nonwhite Women In The Labor Force in 1965," "Occupations of NonWhite Women," in 1965 Handbook On Women Workers. Bulletin # 290. Washington, D. C.: G. P. O., 1965, 319p., pp.7; 101-102.

1220
____________________. "Nonwhite Women In The Labor Force," in 1969 Handbook On Women Workers. Bulletin # 294. Washington, D. C.: G. P. O., 1969, 384p., pp. 10-11.

1221
____________________. "Nonwhite Women Workers," in 1952 Handbook of Facts on Women Workers. Bulletin #242. Washington, D. C.: G. P. O., 1952, pp. 24-26.

1222
____________________. "Unemployment Among Foreign-Born and Negro Women," in Employment Fluctuations And Unemployment of Women: Certain Indications From Various Sources, 1928-1931. Bulletin #113. Washington, D. C.: G. P. O., 1933, 236p., pp. 7.

1223
____________________. "Weekly Earnings Of Negro Women," in Wages of Women in 13 States. Bulletin #85. Washington, D. C.: G. P. O., 1931, 211p., pp. 117-134.

1224
____________________. White and Negro Women Workers," in Women's Occupations Through Seven Decades. Bulletin #218. Washington, D. C.: G. P. O., 1947, 257p, pp. 38-39.

1225
Voight, Daisy. "It's Crystal Ball Time. "Essence. Vol. 5,

March, 1975, pp. 48-49, 96-98, 100.

1226
Wallace, Phyllis A. Pathways To Work: Unemployment Among Black Teenage Females. Massachusetts: Lexington Press, 1974, 117p.

1227
"Washerwoman And Schoolteacher," in Sharecroppers All, by Arthur F. Raper. Chapel Hill: University of North Carolina Press, 1941, 281p., pp. 107-117.

1228
"We Would Never Have Made It Without Momma," The American Woman: Who Was She?" by Anne Firor Scott. New Jersey: Prentice-Hall, 1971, 182p., pp. 32-36.

1229
Willacy, Hazel and Harvey J. Hilaski. "Working Women In Urban Poverty Neighborhoods." Monthly Labor Review. Vol. 93, June, 1970, pp. 35-38.

1230
Williams, Eugene, Sr. "Job Satisfaction And Self-Concept As Perceived By Black Female Paraprofessional Trainees." Doctoral Dissertation, University of Miami, 1972, 125p.

1231
Williams, Fannie B. "Colored Women of Chicago." The Southern Workman. Vol. 43, October, 1914, pp. 564-566.

1232
________________. "An Extension of The Conference Spirit." Voice Of The Negro. Vol. 1, July, 1904, pp. 300-303.

1233
________________. "The Problem of Employment For Negro Women." The Southern Workman. Vol. 32, September, 1903, pp. 432-437.

1234
Williams, Louise M. "The Negro Working Woman." The Messenger. Vol. 5, July, 1923, pp. 763.

1235
"Woman Gets Manpower Post In Illinois." Jet. Vol. 39, February 11, 1971, pp. 31.

1236
"Woman Gets Top Labor Dept. Post In Philadelphia." Jet. Vol. 40, August 12, 1971, pp. 18.

1237
"Woman Labor Leader Urges Black Risk Firms Train More Women." Jet. Vol. 40, August 19, 1971, pp. 44.

1238
"Woman May Get High-Ranking State Dept. Post." Jet. Vol. 30, July 7, 1966, pp. 3.

1239
"Woman Passes N. Y. Stock Exchange Exam." Jet. Vol. 3, May 7, 1953, pp. 18.

1240
"The Woman's Conference." The Southern Workman. September, 1899, pp. 344-346.

1241
"Women," in Selected Documents Pertaining To Black Workers Among The Records of The Department of Labor And Its Component Bureaus, 1902-1969," compiled by Debra L. Newman. Washington, D. C.: National Archives and Records Service, 1977, 53p., pp. 48-53.

1242
"Women At Work." Service. Vol. 7, December, 1943, pp. 6.

1243
"Women Garbage Workers." Jet. Vol. 48, August 28, 1975, pp. 46.

1244
"Women Occupy New Jobs." Journal of The National Association of College Women. #19, 1941-1943, pp. 11-12.

1245
"Women On The Rise." Sepia. Vol. 13, April, 1964, pp. 8-13.

1246
"Women Prove Good Workers." Service. Vol. 11, September, 1946, pp. 8.

1247
"Women Who Act Like Men." Jet. Vol. 3, April 2, 1953, pp. 26-29.

1248
"Women Workers." Opportunity. Vol. 3, August, 1925, pp. 226.

1249
"Women Workers," in The Shadow Of The Plantation, by Charles S. Johnson. Chicago: University of Chicago Press, 1934, 215p., pp. 114-118.

1250
"Women Workers In Indianapolis." The Crisis. Vol. 37, June, 1930, pp. 189-191.

1251
"Women's Bureau Studies Problems of Negro Women Workers." Opportunity. Vol. 17, February, 1939, pp. 56.

1252
Woodson, Carter G. "The Negro Washerwoman: A Vanishing Figure." Journal of Negro History. Vol. 15, July, 1930, pp. 269-277.

1253
"Work For Negro Women In Norfolk." The Southern Workman. Vol. 28, November, 1899, pp. 413-415.

1254
"Work Or Fight For Negro Women Urged." New York Tribune. 22 September, 1918.

1255
"The Working Woman And The Men In Her Life." Black Enterprise. Vol. 8, August, 1977, pp. 14-17, 50.

Guidance And Career Counseling

1256
Buckner, Phiphine Kirven. "A Proposed Guidance Program For Negro Girls In Newport News, Virginia." Master's Thesis, Hampton Institute, 1951, 35p.

1257
Dubose, Kathryn Elizabeth. "The Guidance Implications Of A Study of The Work, The Work Interests, And The Attitudes of One Hundred Negro Women." Master's Thesis, The Ohio State University, 1942, 63p.

1258
Scott, Patricia Bell. "Preparing Black Women For Nontraditional Professions: Some Considerations For Career Counseling." Journal of The NAWDAC. Vol. 40, Summer, 1977, pp. 135-139.

1259
Stevenson, Gloria. "Counseling Black Teenage Girls." Occupational Outlook Quarterly. Vol. 19, Summer, 1975, pp. 2-13.

Hotel Industry

1260
"A Job For Hotel Women." Service. Vol. 7, September, 1943, pp. 29.

1261
"Negro Girls For Bellhops." New York World. 14 April, 1918.

1262
Nivens, Beatryce. "At Home In The Hotel Industry." Essence. Vol. 10, July, 1979, pp. 20, 22, 25.

1263
"Women Hotel Workers." Service. Vol. 7, October, 1942, pp. 7.

Industry And Organized Labor

1264
Anderson, Mary. "The Negro Woman Worker." American Federationist. Vol. 39, October, 1932, pp. 1114-1120.

1265
Bishop, Samuel H. "Industrial Conditions of Negro Women In New York." The Southern Workman. Vol. 39, September, 1910, pp. 525-528.

1266
"The Case Of The Women Strikers." Norfolk Journal And Guide. 29 September, 1917, pp. 4.

1267
Cheyney, Alice S. "Negro Woman In Industry." Survey. Vol. 46, April 23, 1921, pp. 119.

1268
"Colored Women In Industry." The Southern Workman. Vol. 48, April, 1919, pp. 167-168.

1269
Colson, Myra H. "Negro Home Workers In Chicago." Social Services Review. Vol. 2, September, 1928, pp. 385-413.

1270
"Complete Survey of Race Women In Local Industries." New York Age. 22 March, 1919.

1271
Consumer's League of Eastern Pennsylvania. Colored Women As Industrial Workers In Philadelphia; A Study Made By The Consumer's League Of Eastern Pennsylvania. Philadelphia: Consumer's League of Eastern Pennsylvania, 1920, 47p.

1272
Davis, John P. "Maid-Well Garmert Case." The Crisis. Vol. 41, December, 1934, pp. 356-357.

1273
"Employment of Negro Women," in The Negro In The Petroleum Industry, by Carl B. King. Philadelphia: University of Pennsylvania Press, 1969, 96p., pp. 65-67.

1274
"Factory Girls Resent Abuse." Norfolk Journal And Guide. 3 March, 1917, pp. 3.

1275
"Factory Girls Told of Their Opportunities." Norfolk Journal And Guide. 29 November, 1919.

1276
"Female Employment," in The Negro In The Department Store

Industry, by Charles R. Perry. Philadelphia: University of Pennsylvania Press, 1971, 155p., pp. 23.

1277
"Female Employment," in The Negro In The Drug And Manufacturing Industry, by F. Marion Fletcher. Philadelphia: University of Pennsylvania Press, 1970, 149p., pp. 2.

1278
"Female Employment," in The Negro In The Furniture Inudstry, by William E. Fulmer. Philadelphia: University of Pennsylvania Press, 1973, 207p., pp. 26-28.

1279
"Female Employment," in The Negro In The Lumber Industry, by John C. Howard. Philadelphia: University of Pennsylvania Press, 1970, 97p., pp. 43-44.

1280
"Female Employment," in The Negro In The Paper Industry, by Herbert R. Northrup. Philadelphia: University of Pennsylvania Press, 1969, 233p., pp. 70-72.

1281
"Female Employment," in The Negro In The Public Utilities Industries, by Bernard E. Anderson. Philadelphia: University of Pennsylvania Press, 1970, 261p., pp. 28.

1282
"Female Employment," in The Negro In The Rubber Tire Industry, by Herbert R. Northrup. Philadelphia: University of Pennsylvania Press, 1969, 134p., pp. 39.

1283
"Female Employment," in The Negro In The Supermarket Industry, by Gordon F. Bloom and F. Marion Fletcher. Philadelphia: University of Pennsylvania Press, 1972, 226p., pp. 22.

1284
"Female Employment," in The Negro In The Tobacco Industry, by Herbert R. Northrup. Philadelphia: University of Pennsylvania Press, 1970, 107p., pp. 15.

1285
"Garment Workers' Unions Welcome Colored Women In Women's Wear Industry." New York Age. 8 September, 1923, pp. 1.

1286
Goffredsen, Svend. "Young Chicago Girl A CIO Union Leader." Opportunity. Vol. 25, April/June, 1947, pp. 104-105.

1287
Grover, Anju. "The History And Development Of The Activities Of The National Women's Trade Union League of The United States, 1903-1929." Master's Thesis, Howard University, 1967, 106p.

1288
Hatcher, Lillian. "A Woman Laborite Gives Her Views On Labor Draft." The Aframerican Woman's Journal. Vol. 5, March, 1945, pp. 6, 20.

1289
Hochman, Julius. "Organizing The Dressmakers." American Federationist. Vol. 36, December, 1929, pp. 1462-1467.

1290
Huger, Phannye Brinson. "Study of The Techniques of Group Work Employed By The International Ladies' Garmern Workers' Union, Local No. 122, Among Negroes In Atlanta, Georgia." Master's Thesis, Atlanta University, 1944, 57p.

1291
"Industrial Condition of Negro Women In New York City." The Southern Workman. Vol. 39, October, 1910, pp. 525-528.

1292
"Industrial Slavery," in America's Working Women, by Rosalyn Baxandall, Linda Gordon and Susan Reverby. New York: Random House, 1976, 399p., pp. 34-35.

1293
Irwin, Helen B. "Conditions In Industry As They Affect Negro Women." Proceedings of The National Conference of Social Work. 46th Annual Session, 1919, pp. 521-524.

1294
Jackson, Mary E. "The Colored Woman In Industry." The Crisis. Vol. 17, November, 1918, pp. 12-17.

1295
Lepowsky, Martha. "Negro Women In Industry." Master's Thesis, New York University, 1940, 91p.

1296
Lewis, Mollie V. "Negro Women In Steel." The Crisis. Vol. 45, February, 1938, pp. 54.

1297
McDougald, Gertrude E. A New Day For The Colored Woman Worker. A Study of The Colored Women In Industry In New York City. New York: Charles P. Young, 1919, 39p.

1298
Martinez, Sabina. "Negro Woman In Organized Labor." The Aframerican Woman's Journal. Vol. 2, Summer/Fall, 1941, pp. 17.

1299
"Mills Open To Colored Labor." Norfolk Journal And Guide. 15 September, 1917, pp. 1.

1300
Morrow, Henry G. "A Comparison Of White And Negro Women In

Industry In New York City." Master's Thesis, New York University, 1940, 77p.

1301
"The Negro And The United Mine Workers of America," in Work, Culture, and Society In Industralizing America, by Herbert G. Gatman. New York: Knopf, 1976, 343p., pp. 199-201.

1302
"The Negro Woman Worker: A Study of Negro Women In The Industries of Indianapolis." The Southern Workman. Vol. 59, August, 1930, pp. 375-377.

1303
"Negro Women In Industry." Opportunity. Vol. 9, April, 1931, pp. 105.

1304
____________________. Opportunity. Vol. 13, September, 1935, pp. 286.

1305
"Negro Women In Industry: Preliminary Report for Bulletin #20, 1922," in Women Bureau File, RG86, #2, Correspondence Relating To Surveys. Washington, D. C.: National Archives and Records Service.

1306
"Negro Women In New York Industry." New York Post. 21 March, 1919.

1307
"Negro Women in Organized Labor." The Aframerican Woman's Journal. Vol. 2, Summer/Fall, 1941, pp. 11-13.

1308
"Negro Women in South Carolina Industries." Opportunity. Vol. 2, May, 1924, pp. 146-147.

1309
"The Negro's Life, 1901-1910: Negroes And The Ladies Waist Makers Union," in A Documentary History of The Negro People In The United States, Vol. 1., edited by Herbert Aptheker. New York: Citadel Press, 1951, 942p., pp. 844.

1310
Newsome, Nora. "The Negro Women In The Trade Union Movement." The Messenger. Vol. 5, July, 1923, pp. 60-61.

1311
Paul, Ruth Frances. "Negro Women In Industry." Master's Thesis, Temple University, 1940, 70p.

1312
Porter, Ruth R. "Negro Women In The Clothing, Cigar And Laundry Industries of Philadelphia, 1940." Journal of Negro Education. Vol. 12, Winter, 1943, pp. 21-23.

1313
Poston, Ted. "Making of Mamma Harris." New Republic. Vol. 103, November 4, 1940, pp. 624-626.

1314
Sayre, Helen B. "Negro Women In Industry." Opportunity. Vol. 2, August, 1924, pp. 242-244.

1315
Shields, Emma L. "A Half-Century In The Tobacco Industry." The Southern Workman. Vol. 51, September, 1922, pp. 419-425.

1316
__________. "Negro Women And The Tobacco Industry." Life And Labor. May, 1921, pp. 142-144.

1317
"A Study of Negro Women In Industry." The Southern Workman. Vol. 58, September, 1929, pp. 420-422.

1318
"A Trade Union Leader Speaks: An Interview With Doris Turner." Women's Rights Law Reporter. Vol. 1, Fall/Winter, 1972-1973, pp. 73-75.

1319
U. S. Department of Labor, Women's Bureau. "Daily Hours of Negro Women," "Weekly Hours of Negro Women," "Wages of Negro Women," in Women in Florida Industries. Bulletin #80. Washington, D. C.: G. P. O., 1930, 113p., pp. 25, 29, 49-54.

1320
__________. "Earnings and Hours of Negro Women," in Employment of Women In Tennessee Industries. Bulletin #149. Washington, D. C.: G. P. O., 1937, 63p., pp. 38-42.

1321
__________. "Earnings of Negro Women," in Women In Arkansas Industries. Bulletin #124. Washington, D. C.: G. P. O., 1935, 45p., pp. 12-13.

1322
__________. "Earnings of Negro Women," in Women In Arkansas Industries, A Study of Hours, Wages, and Working Conditions. Bulletin #26. Washington, D. C.: G. P. O., 1923, 85p., pp. 30-31.

1323
__________. "Earnings of Negro Women," in Women In Tennessee Industries: A Study of Hours, Wages and Working Conditions. Bulletin #56. Washington, D. C.: G. P. O., 1927, 120p., pp. 39-44.

1324
U. S. Department of Labor, Women's Bureau. "Earnings of Negro Women Workers," in Women In Alabama Industries: A Study of Hours, Wages and Working Conditions. Bulletin # 34. Washington, D. C.: G. P. O., 1924, 86p., pp. 52-56.

1325
________________. "Earnings of Negro Women," in Women in Mississippi Industries: A Study of Hours, Wages and Working Conditions. Bulletin #55. Washington, D. C.: G. P. O., 1926, 89p., pp. 18-19.

1326
________________. "Earnings of Negro Workers." in Women In Oklahoma Industries: A Study of Hours, Wages and Working Conditions. Bulletin #48 Washington, D. C.: G. P. O., 1926, 118p., pp. 31-32.

1327
________________. "The Employment of Negro Women," in Women in South Carolina Industries: A Study of Hours, Wages and Working Conditions. Bulletin #32. Washington, D. C.: G. P. O., 1923, 128p., pp. 81-85.

1328
________________. "Nativity And Race," in A Survey of Laundries And Their Women Workers In 23 Cities. Bulletin #78. Washington, D. C.: G. P. O., 1930, 164p., pp. 87-88.

1329
________________. "The Negro Woman Worker," in Women At Work: A century of Industrial Change. Bulletin #115. Washington, D. C.: G. P. O., 1934, 60p., pp. 33-37.

1330
________________. "The Negro Woman Worker," in Women At Work: A Century of Industrial Change. Bulletin #161. Washington, D. C.: G. P. O., 1939, 80p., pp. 58-64.

1331
________________. "Negro Women," in Women In Kentucky Industries, 1937. Bulletin #162. Washington, D. C.: G. P. O., 1938, 38p., pp. 15.

1332
________________. Negro Women In Industry. Bulletin #20. Washington, D. C.: G. P. O., 1922, 65p.

1333
________________. Negro Women In Industry In 15 States. Bulletin #70. Washington, D. C.: G. P. O., 1929, 74p.

1334
U. S. Department of Labor, Women's Bureau. "The Negro Worker," in Women In Georgia Industries: A Study of Hours, Wages and Working Conditions. Bulletin #22. Washington, D. C.: G. P. O., 1922, 89p., pp. 31-39.

1335
__________. "The Negro Worker," in Women In Missouri Industries: A Study of Hours and Wages. Bulletin #35. Washington, D. C.: G. P. O., 1924, 27p., pp. 39-44.

1336
__________. "Negro Workers In Cotton Mills," in Lost Time And Labor Turnovers In Cotton Mills: A Study of Cause And Extent. Bulletin #53. Washington, D. C.: G. P. O., 1926, 201p., pp. 133-134.

1337
__________. "Wages, Negro Women," in Women in Texas Industries: Hours, Wages, Working Conditions, and Home Work. Bulletin #126. Washington, D. C.: G. P. O., 1936, 81p., pp. 27-28.

1338
U. S. Equal Employment Opportunity Commission. Hearings On Utilization of Minority and Women Workers In Certain Major Industries. Washington, D. C.: G. P. O., 1969, 712p; 1971, 705p.

1339
Waldman, Elizabeth. "Changes In The Labor Activity of Women." Monthly Labor Review. Vol. 93, June, 1970, pp. 10-18.

1340
Wesley, Charles H. "On Agriculture and Industry - Industry," in A Documentary History of The Negro People In The United States, 1910-1932, edited by Herbert Aptheker. New Jersey: Citadel Press, 1973, 754p., pp. 607-609.

1341
"When Ladies Meet..." Headlines. Vol. 1, January, 1945, pp. 17-19.

1342
"Woman Union Leader Wins Back Job, $16,648 Wages." Jet. Vol. 41, October 7, 1971, pp. 22.

1343
"Women Are Finding Steady Employment." Norfolk Journal And Guide. 17 February, 1923, pp. 3.

1344
"Women and Child Care - Negro Women In Industry." Monthly Labor Review. Vol. 15, July, 1922, pp. 116-118.

1345
"Woman and Child Labor - Colored Workers. (Women In Missouri Industries)." Monthly Labor Review. Vol. 19, November, 1924, pp. 131-132, 1075-1076.

1346
"Women in Alabama Industries." Monthly Labor Review. Vol. 19, August, 1924, pp. 126-128.

1347
"Women In Industry." National Notes. Vol. 32, November, 1930, pp. 8.

1348
"Women In Industry - Negro Women in Industry In Fifteen States." Monthly Labor Review. Vol. 29, September, 1929, pp. 554-556.

1349
"Women In Industry and Child Labor - Colored Women In Industry In Philadelphia." Monthly Labor Review. Vol. 12, May, 1921, pp. 1046-1048,

1350
Woods, Sylvia. "You Have To Fight For Freedom," in Rank And File: Personal Histories by Working-Class Organizers, edited by Alice Lynd and Staughton Lynd. Boston: Beacon Press, 1973, 296p., pp. 111-129.

1351
"Working Women's Union." Norfolk Journal And Guide. 19 May, 1919, pp. 1.

Library Science

1352
"American Library Association Names First Black President-Elect." Black Scholar. Vol. 6, July/August, 1975, pp. 50-51.

1353
"Black Woman Is Appointed Montana State Librarian." Jet. Vol. 45, December 6, 1973, pp. 32.

1354
Bolden, Ethel Evangeline Martin. "Susan Dart Butler, Pioneer Librarian." Master's Thesis, Atlanta University, 1959, 31p.

1355
"Colored Assistants for N. Y. Library." New York Age. 19 June, 1920.

1356
"Detroit's Top Librarian." Ebony. Vol. 27, November, 1971, pp. 115-116.

1357
DeView, Lucille. "Emancipated Librarian." McCalls. Vol. 98, April, 1971, pp. 46.

1358
"Dr. Jean Blackwell Hutson And The Schomburg Center For Research in Black Culture." Black Monitor. Vol. 3, April, 1978, pp. 6, 12-14.

1359
"First Black Woman Heads Library System In Detorit." The Negro History Bulletin. Vol. 33, April, 1970, pp. 100.

1360
"First Negro Librarian Wins $500 Grolier Award." Jet. Vol. 8, July 14, 1955, pp. 17.

1361
"Librarian of Johnson Publishing Co. Paid Tributes at Final Rites." Jet. Vol. 43, January 18, 1973, pp. 14-15.

1362
Lubin, Maurice A. "An Important Figure In Black Studies: Dr. Dorothy B. Porter." CLA Journal. Vol. 16, June, 1973, pp. 514-518.

1363
"135th St. Librarian Visits Colored Libraries In South." New York Age. 19 November, 1921, pp. 1.

1364
Rhodes, Lelia Gaston. "A Critical Analysis of The Career Backgrounds of Selected Black Female Librarians." Doctoral Dissertation, The Florida State University, 1975, 251p.

1365
"Wins Award." Jet. Vol. 17, February 11, 1960, pp. 38.

Life Insurance

1366
"Cases - Evelyn Robinson," in Women In The Organization, edited by Harold H. Frank. Philadelphia: University of Pennsylvania Press, 1977, 31op., pp. 99-123.

1367
"Life Insurance." The Woman's National Magazine. Vol. 5, April, 1938, pp. 83.

1368
Livingston, Omeda F. "A Study of Women Executives In Life Insurance Companies Owned And Operated By Negroes With Implications for Business Education." Doctoral Dissertation, New York University, 1964, 162p.

Migrant Labor

1369
"Letters From Black Migrants," in America's Working Women, edited by Rosalyn Baxandall, Linda Gordon and Susan Reverby. New York: Random House, 1976, 399p., pp. 133.

1370
"Living On The Road," in Women of Crisis: Lives of Struggle and Hope, by Robert Coles and Jane Hallowell Coles. New York: Delacorte Press, 1978, 297p., pp. 11-70.

Miners

1371
"Chicago Woman Miner." Tuskegee Messenger. Vol. 12, July/September, 1936, pp. 24.

1372
"Lady Miner Digs Her Job: A Young Mother of Eight Strikes Coal." Ebony. Vol. 29, October, 1974, pp. 116-118, 120, 122.

Modeling

1373
"Artists Model." Ebony. Vol. 3, February, 1948, pp. 63-66.

1374
"Charm School Charges 'Racist Journalism' Against Time, Inc." Jet. Vol. 40, July 29, 1971, pp. 14.

1375
"Chicago's Most Photographed Model." Jet. Vol. 8, August 25, 1955, pp. 46-47.

1376
"Darm Glamour, Negro Models." Newsweek. Vol. 60, September 3, 1962, pp. 69.

1377
"A Day With A Model." Pulse. Vol. 4, December, 1946, pp. 14-15.

1378
Grange, Hamlin. "Model On Her Way To The Top." Sacramento Observer - National Scene. May, 1979, pp. 6.

1379
"Have Black Models Really Made It?" Ebony. Vol. 25, May, 1970, pp. 152-154, 156, 158, 160.

1380
"How To Become A Paris Model." Jet. Vol. 2, August 28, 1952, pp. 32-38.

1381
Jenkins, Walter. "Gay Thomas: Making It Big In Swift World of Glamor." Black Stars. Vol. 28, April, 1979, pp. 52-56.

1382
Johnson, Eunice W. "Successful Black Models in Europe." Ebony. Vol. 32, August, 1977, pp. 157-159.

1383
"Lynn is Model of Many Moods." Jet. Vol. 25, January 23, 1964, pp. 42-43.

1384
"Meet The Top Models." Negro Achievement. Vol. 9, September, 1952, pp. 10-12, 44.

1385
Morgan, Ted. "I'm The Biggest Model, Period." New York Times Magazine. August 17, 1975, pp. 12-14, 16, 18, 20, 22.

1386
"Most Photographed Models." Ebony. Vol. 14, October, 1959, pp. 102-104, 106.

1387
Murphy, Frederick D. "Black Models Have Their Say." Encore. Vol. 4, April 7, 1975, pp. 30-33.

1388
"Negro Models; A Band of Beautiful Pioneers." Life. Vol. 52, June 29, 1962, pp. 87-88.

1389
"New Model Agency Makes History." Headines And Pictures. Vol. 3, September, 1946, pp. 43.

1390
"New York's Hottest Model." Jet. Vol. 2, August 14, 1952, pp. 34-35.

1391
"No. 1 Black Model Keeps Her Mind In 'Right' Places." Jet. Vol. 48, May 8, 1975, pp. 48.

1392
Sims, Naomi. "It Takes More Than Beauty To Make A Model." Essence. Vol. 1, August, 1970, pp. 14.

1393
"Swirl of Bright Hues." Life. Vol. 52, June 29, 1962, pp. 83-86.

1394
"Those Sleek Black Beauties." Newsweek. Vol. 85, May 5, 1975, pp. 68.

1395
"Top Model." Jet. Vol. 48, May 8, 1975, pp. 48.

1396
"Top Negro Model Makes Debut In Paris." Ebony. Vol. 15, September, 1960, pp. 61-62, 64, 66.

1397
"What Happened To The Bradford Models?" Our World. Vol. 9, February, 1954, pp. 30-37.

1398
"Why Some Pretty Women Don't Make Good Models." Jet. Vol. 7, December 2, 1954, pp. 26-30.

1399
"Young Woman In A White World." Ebony. Vol. 21, August, 1966, pp. 69-70, 72-74.

Postal Workers

1400
"Charleston, S. C. Gets First Negro Postmistress." Jet. Vol. 6, September 9, 1954, pp. 8.

1401
"Former School Teacher Is First Negro Woman to Be Employed As Post Office Money Order Clerk." Philadelphia Tribune. 19 December, 1942.

1402
Hall, Henry. "The Adjustment of Negro Female Clerks To Working Conditions In The Atlanta Branch of The United States Post Office." Master's Thesis, Atlanta University, 1970, 79p.

1403
"Heads Executive Committee of the Postal Auxiliary." Norfolk Journal And Guide. 18 July, 1925, pp. 1.

1404
"Nation vs. Indiana." Nation. Vol. 76, January 29, 1903, pp. 86.

1405
"Postal Security Aide." Jet. Vol. 40, September 2, 1971, pp. 25.

1406
"She Kept The Mail Coming." Headlines And Pictures. Vol. 2, December, 1945, pp. 24.

1407
"This Week In Black History." Jet. Vol. 47, October 10, 1974, pp. 53.

Sales Ladies

1408
"Colored Saleswomen Sucess In St. Louis." New York Sun. 1 July, 1918.

1409
"Colored Woman Holds An Unusual Position." Opportunity. Vol. 19, January, 1941, pp. 22-23.

1410
"Department Store Taking Salesgirls." Norfolk Journal And Guide. 14 November, 1942.

1411
"Girl Clerks Employed in Birmingham." Philadelphia Independent. 11 April, 1943.

1412
"Indianapolis Store Gets First Negro Salesgirls." Jet. Vol. 2, October 9, 1952, pp. 6.

Sea Industries

1413
"Longshore - Women." Jet. Vol. 41, October 7, 1971, pp. 22.

1414
"Negro Woman Sea Captain Retires; Georgia Smith Was In Command Twenty-Two Years." Black Dispatch. 15 August, 1936.

1415
"A Pair of Lubbers Take To The Sea." Ebony. Vol. 21, April, 1966, pp. 112-114.

1416
"Queen of The Shrimpers." Ebony. Vol. 21, November, 1965, pp. 131-134, 136-137.

1417
"Woman, 62 Years Old, Returns To Ship Duty." Jet. Vol. 40, May 6, 1971, pp. 18.

Secretaries

1418
"Automation And The Black Secretary." New Lady. Vol. 2, October, 1969, pp. 12-17.

1419
"Colored Woman Now Private Secretary To Harlem Banker." New York Age. 26 January 1924, pp. 1.

1420
Mason, Helen S. "Now We Are Three: Capitol Hill Secretaries." Pulse. Vol. 6, July, 1948, pp. 2-5.

1421
"Stricken 1st Black Secretary To U. S. President Feted." Jet. Vol. 40, May 27, 1971, pp. 13.

Social Services

1422
Ashton, Harroldean. "Married Social Workers in Social Agencies; A Study of Private Social Agency Policies And Practices, Experiences and Attitudes Toward The Hiring And Employment of Married Social Workers With Minor Children." Master's Thesis, Howard University, 1962, 182p.

1423
Booker, Grace C. "Cynthia Henderson: A Negro Pioneer In Social Welfare In Kansas, 1879-1923." Master's Thesis, Howard University, 1953, 50p.

1424
Bryson, Seymore, Harold Bardo and Constance Johnson. "Black Female Counselor And The Black Male Client," in Perspectives On Afro American Women, edited by Willa D. Johnson and Thomas L. Green. Washington, D. C.: Educational Community Counselors Associates, 1975, 197p., pp. 66-72.

1425
"Cases - Vanessa Green," in Women In The Organization, edited by Harold H. Frank. Philadelphia: University of Pennsylvania Press, 1977, 310p., pp. 92-98.

1426
"14 Get Social Work Diploma." Norfolk Journal And Guide. 4 June, 1927, pp. 8.

1427
Hall, Winona R. "Janie Porter Barrett, Her Life And Contributions To Social Welfare In Virginia." Master's Thesis, Howard University, 1954, 31p.

1428
Jackson, Jacquelyne J. "Black Female Sociologists," in Black Sociologists: Historical And Contemporary Perspectives, edited by James E. Blackwell and Morris Jonowitz. Chicago: University of Chicago Press, 1975, 415p., pp. 267-295.

1429
Kernan, Michael. "She Can't Stop Helping People." Washington Post. 9 October, 1970, pp. B-1.

1430
U. S. Department of Labor, Women's Bureau. "Negro Women," in The Outlook For Women In Social Work: General Summary. Bulletin #235-8. Washington, D. C.: G. P. O., 1952, 93p., pp. 59-61.

<u>Sports Car Racer</u>

1431
"Nitro Nellie." <u>Ebony</u>. Vol. 27, November, 1971, pp. 63-64.

1432
"Woman Sports Car Racer." <u>Ebony</u>. Vol. 13, December, 1957, pp. 107-110.

<u>Telephone Service And Repair</u>

1433
"Climbing To Top In A Man's World." <u>Ebony</u>. Vol. 28, September, 1973, pp. 79-80, 84, 86.

1434
"The Girl Behind The Voice; Telephone Operators.." <u>Ebony</u>. Vol. 12, August, 1957, pp. 94, 96-98.

<u>Transportation</u>

1435
"Black Nurse Drives Truck." <u>Jet</u>. Vol. 44, September 6, 1973, pp. 32-33.

1436
"Black Woman Gets First Interstate Truck Permit." <u>Jet</u>. Vol. 46, May 9, 1974, pp. 46.

1437
"Black Women Enter H'way Construction Industry." <u>Jet</u>. Vol. 50, April 8, 1976, pp. 52.

1438
"Boss of California's Freeways." <u>Ebony</u>. Vol. 32, June, 1978, pp. 147-148, 150, 152.

1439
"Carriers In Court." <u>Headlines And Pictures</u>. Vol. 1, April, 1945, pp. 6.

1440
"Carter Nabs Black Woman For National RR Board." <u>Jet</u>. Vol. 56, April 19, 1979, pp. 12.

1441
"Chicago Hires First Female Bus Driver: Black Woman." <u>Jet</u>. Vol. 46, July 11, 1974, pp. 53.

1442
"Colored Women Porters." <u>Brooklyn Eagle</u>. 12 May, 1918.

1443
"First Subway Motorwoman Begins Job Training." <u>Norfolk Journal And Guide</u>. 24 February, 1973, pp. 8.

1444
"First Woman Highway Engineer." Afro American Magazine. November 25, 1972, pp. 10.

1445
"Hands Across The Table." The Brown American. Vol. 5, Summer, 1943, pp. 6.

1446
Johnson, Bill. "Women Enter The Highway Construction Crafts." Dawn Magazine. January/February, 1976, pp. 16-17, 19.

1447
"Ladies of The Steel Road." The Brown American. Vol. 5, Summer, 1944, pp. 10.

1448
"Miss. Has 1st Negro Woman Train Caller." Philadelphia Independent. 9 May, 1943.

1449
"Negro Women Advance As Pennsylvania Railroad Men Go To War." The Brown American. Vol. 5, Winter/Spring, 1944, pp. 10.

1450
"Negro Women Advance In Pennsylvania Railroad." Service. Vol. 9, September, 1944, pp. 15.

1451
"Negro Women In Transportation." The Negro Traveler. Vol. 1, January/February, 1945, pp. 16, 39; December, 1945, pp. 23.

1452
Queen, Bill. "Leave The Driving To Sister." Dawn Magazine. December 13, 1975, pp. 6, 19.

1453
"Railway Line Advertises For Employees." Norfolk Journal And Guide. 17 October, 1942.

1454
"Replace Men With Women on D. C. Railroad." Philadelphia Independent. 11 April, 1943.

1455
"Train Women For Ohio Street Cars." Norfolk Journal And Guide. 1 March, 1943.

1456
"Women At Work: A Railroad At War." Pulse. Vol. 2, March, 1944, pp. 20-21.

Welders

1457
"Welder Is A Lady." Ebony. Vol. 18, August, 1963, pp. 58, 60, 62, 64.

FAMILY LIFE

Birth Control And Family Planning

1458
"Abortion Law Seen Difference In Illinois, North Carolina By Courts." Jet. Vol. 39, February 18, 1971, pp. 18.

1459
"Alabama Halts Sterilization of Retarded Youngsters." Jet. Vol. 44, August 16, 1973, pp. 23.

1460
Beasley, Joseph D., Carl L. Hunter, and Ann Fischer. "Attitudes and Knowledge Relevant to Family Planning Among New Orleans Negro Women." American Journal of Public Health. Vol. 56, November, 1966, pp. 1847-1857.

1461
Berry, William E. "Furor Mounts Over Sterilization of Blacks." Jet. Vol. 44, August 2, 1973, pp. 20-21.

1462
"Birth Control Ideals Changing." Sacramento Observer. 1 June, 1972, pp. D-10.

1463
"Black Churchmen Oppose Abortion As Genocide." Jet. Vol. 44, July 26, 1973, pp. 44.

1464
"Black Family Planning." Sacramento Observer. 1 June, 1972, pp. D-10.

1465
"A Black Girl's Abortion Saga." Jet. Vol. 43, March 22, 1973, pp. 21.

1466
Black Women's Liberation Group, Mount Vernon, New York. "State-

ment on Birth Control," in Sisterhood Powerful, by Robin Morgan. New York: Vintage Books, 1970, 577p., pp. 360-361.

1467
"Blacks View Limitations on Number In Family As Genocide Effort By U. S." Jet. Vol. 40, August 5, 1971, pp. 20-21.

1468
Bogue, Donald J. "Family Planning In The Negro Ghettos of Chicago." The Milbank Memorial Fund Quarterly. Vol. 48, April, 1970, pp. 283-307.

1469
"Bonus For Sterilization Offered In Illinois Bill." Jet. Vol. 44, May 10, 1973, pp. 22.

1470
Bremner, Judy Bradley. "Abortion; Black Women And Selected Personal Characteristics, Knowledge Items And Attitudes." Master's Thesis, Atlanta University, 1973, 75p.

1471
Cade, Toni. "The Pill: Genocide or Liberation," in The Black Woman: An Anthology, edited by Toni Cade. New York: Signet Books, 1970, 256p., pp. 162-169.

1472
"Calif. Woman Seeks $50,000 For Sterilization." Jet. Vol. 6 September 23, 1954, pp. 51.

1473
Campbell, Arthur. "Fertility and Family Planning Among Non-White Married Couples in The United States." Eugenics Quarterly. Vol. 12, September, 1965, pp. 124-131.

1474
"Cash-Or-Sterilization Plan Comes Under Fire." Jet. Vol. 44, August 23, 1973, pp. 14.

1475
Cherniak, Donna and Allen Feingold. "The Pill Controversy - Letter to the Editor." Ramparts. Vol. 10, June, 1972, pp. 64-65.

1476
Cochrane, Carl M., Clark E. Vincent, C. Allen Haney and Robert Michielutte. "Motivational Determinants of Family Planning Clinic Attendance." Journal of Psychology. Vol. 84, May, 1973, pp. 33-43.

1477
Coleman, Marsha. "Are Abortions For Black Women Racist?" The Militant. Vol. 21, January, 1972, pp. 19.

1478
"Despite Dangers, Women Still Preper The Pill." Jet. Vol. 48, December 4, 1975, pp. 27.

1479
"Edelin: Women Should Have Right To Have Abortion." Jet. Vol. 49, January 1, 1976, pp. 47.

1480
Engerman, Stanley L. "Changes In Black Fertility, 1880-1940," in Family And Population in Nineteenth Century America, edited by Tamara K. Hareven and Maris A. Vinovskis. New Jersey: Princeton University Press, 1978, 250p., pp. 126-153.

1481
"Federal Judge Sets Rules for Ala. Sterlizations." Jet. Vol. 45, January 24, 1974, pp. 5.

1482
"First Black Woman Heads Center For Family Planning." Jet. Vol. 43, January 18, 1973, pp. 20.

1483
Fisch, Maria Alba. "Internal Versus External Ego Orientation And Family Planning Effectiveness Among Poor Black Women." Doctoral Dissertation, Columbia University, 1973, 145p.

1484
Frazier, E. Franklin. "Birth Control For More Negro Babies." The Negro Digest. Vol. 3, July, 1945, pp. 41-44.

1485
__________. "The Negro and Birth Control." Birth Control Review. March, 1933, pp. 68-70.

1486
Furstenburg, Frank F. "Attitudes Toward Abortion Among Young Blacks (Based On a Study of 300 Young Negro Women in Baltimore, Maryland)." Studies In Family Planning. Vol. 3, April, 1972, pp. 66-69.

1487
Harris, Theresa E. "Family Planning Practices Of A Selected Group of Black Married Women Of Child-Rearing Age From The Western Division of San Francisco." Master's Thesis, California State University, 1971, 84p.

1488
Haney, C. Allen, Robert Michielutte, Clark E. Vincent and Carl M. Cochrane. "Legitimacy, Illegitimacy and Live Birth Ratios In A Black Population." Journal of Health And Social Behavior. Vol. 13, September, 1972, pp. 303-310.

1489
Hill, Adelaide Cromwell and Frederick S. Jaffe. "Negro Fertility And Family Size Preferences: Implications for Programming of Health and Social Services," in The Negro American, edited by Talcott Parsons and Kenneth B. Clark. Boston: Beacon Press, 1967, 781p., pp. 205-224.

1490
Hudgins, John. "Is Birth Control Genocide?" Black Scholar. Vol. 4, November/December, 1972, pp. 34-37.

1491
Hughes, Blanche R. "Abortion: Perception and Contemporary Genocide Myth: A Comparative Study Among Low-Income Pregnant Black and Puerto Rican Women." Doctoral Dissertation, New York University, 1973, 178p.

1492
"Is Birth Control A Menace To Negroes?" Jet. Vol. 6, August 19, 1954, pp. 52-55.

1493
Johnson, Robert E. "Legal Abortion: Is It Genocide or Blessing in Disguise?" Jet. Vol. 43, March 22, 1973, pp. 12-19.

1494
Jones, Carolyn. "Abortion and Black Women." Black America. #5, September, 1970, pp. 48-49.

1495
Jordan, Vernon, Jr. "To Be Equal - Scandal Shows Experimenters Still Busy." Afro American. 28 July, 1973, pp. 4.

1496
"Jury Upholds Woman's Sterilization Suit." Jet. Vol. 48, August 21, 1975, pp. 14.

1497
Kanter, John F. and Melvin Zelnik. "Sexual Experience of Young Unmarried Women In The United States." Family Planning Perspectives. Vol. 4, October, 1972, pp. 9-18.

1498
Kashif, Lonnie. "Black Women Spearheads Anti-Abortion Campaign." Muhammad Speaks. 21 March, 1975, pp. 18.

1499
Kennard, Gail. "Sterilization Abuse." Essence. Vol. 5, October, 1974, pp. 66-67, 85-86.

1500
Lang. F. "Sickle Cell and The Pill; Birth Control Pills Dangerous to Black Women." Ramparts. Vol. 10, February, 1972, pp. 14, 16, 18.

1501
Lindsey, Kay. "Birth Control and The Black Woman." Essence. Vol. 1, October, 1970, pp. 56-57, 70-71.

1502
Mayhew, Bruce H., Jr. "Behavioral Observability and Compliance With Religious Proscriptions On Birth Control," Social Forces. Vol. 47, 1968, pp. 60-70.

1503
McFall, Joseph A., Jr. "Impact of VD on The Fertility of The U. S. Black Population, 1880-1950." Social Biology. Vol. 20, March, 1973, pp. 2-19.

1504
McNeil, Merriel Rose. "Fertility Among Blacks In The Southern Black Belt, 1950 to 1970." Master's Thesis, Atlanta University, 1977, 65p.

1505
Michielutte, Robert, Allen C. Haney, Clark E. Vincent and Carl M. Cochrane. "Early Sexual Experiences and Pregnancy Wastage In Two Cultures." Journal of Comparative Family Studies. Vol. 4, Fall, 1973, pp. 225-238.

1506
"More Black Women Are Getting Legal Abortions." Jet. Vol. 42, June 29, 1972, pp. 15.

1507
"Negro Women Avoiding Children." Norfolk Journal And Guide. 5 March, 1925, pp. 3.

1508
"New Miracles in Birth Control." Jet. Vol. 1, March 6, 1952, pp. 24-27.

1509
"Poor Should Have Option for Sterilization." Jet. Vol. 45, November 1, 1973, pp. 15.

1510
Presser, Harriet B. "The Timing of The First Birth, Female Roles and Black Fertility." Milbank Memorial Fund Quarterly. Vol. 49, July, 1971, pp. 329-361.

1511
Reed, Julia. "Marriage and Fertility in Black Female Teachers." Black Scholar. Vol. 1, January/February, 1970, pp. 22-28.

1512
Robbins, Lillie M. "Attitudes Toward Birth Control Among Female Students Enrolled In Atlanta University Summer Session, 1967. Master's Thesis, Atlanta University, 1971, 60p.

1513
"Rules Will Not Stop Sterilization: HEW." Jet. Vol. 44, August 30, 1973, pp. 5.

1514
Sanger, Margaret. "The Case For Birth Control." The Crisis. Vol. 41, June, 1934, pp. 176-177.

1515
Sanger, Margaret. "Love Or Babies: Must Negro Mothers Choose?" The Negro Digest. Vol. 4, August, 1946, pp. 3-8.

1516
Slater, Jack. "Sterilization: Newest Threat To The Poor." Ebony. Vol. 28, October, 1973, pp. 150-152, 154, 156.

1517
Smith, Mary. "Birth Control And The Negro Woman." Ebony. Vol. 23, March, 1968, pp. 29-32, 34, 36-37.

1518
"Sterilization of Females to Resume in Alabama." Jet. Vol. 46, September 12, 1974, pp. 5.

1519
"Sterilization of Welfare Mothers in S. C. Draws Fire." Jet. Vol. 44, August 9, 1973, pp. 24-25.

1520
"Strick Sterilization Rules Proposed by HEW Officials." Jet. Vol. 45, October 11, 1973, pp. 68.

1521
Thompson, M. Cordell. "Black Youngsters Are Sterilized by Alabama Agency." Jet. Vol. 44, July 19, 1973, pp. 12-15.

1522
Tietze, Christopher and Sarah Lewit. "Patterns of Family Limitation in A Rural Negro Community." American Sociological Review. Vol. 18, October, 1953, pp. 563-564.

1523
Treadwell, Mary. "Is Abortion Black Genocide?" Family Planning Perspectives. Vol. 4, January, 1972, pp. 4-5.

1524
Turner, Castellano B. and William A. Darity. "Fears of Genocide Among Black Americans As Related To Age, Sex, and Region." American Journal of Public Health. Vol. 63, December, 1973, pp. 1029-1034.

1525
Valien, Preston and Ruth E. Vaughn. "Birth Control Attitudes and Practices Of Negro Mothers." Sociology and Social Research. Vol. 35, July/August, 1951, pp. 415-421.

1526
Valien, Preston and Alberta Price Fitzgerald. "Attitudes of the Negro Mother Toward Birth Control." American Journal of Sociology. Vol. 55, November, 1959, pp. 279-283.

1527
Vaughn, Ruth Ercell. "Attitudes of 100 Negro Mothers of Nashville, Tennessee Toward Birth Control." Master's Thesis, Fisk University, 1950, 51p.

1528
Walker, Lynn. "On Supreme Court's Abortion Decision." Essence. Vol. 4, June, 1973, pp. 19.

1529
Weathers, Maryanne. "Black Women And Abortion." The Second Wave. Vol. 1, Summer, 1971, pp. 5.

1530
Wiggins, Lillian. "What of Women And Their Safe Abortions?" Washington Afro American. 12 April, 1975, pp. 9.

1531
Williams, Barbara A. "Family Planning and The Black Perspective." Essence. Vol. 4, September, 1973, pp. 18.

Childrearing and Motherhood

1532
Abbott, Grace. "A Message to Colored Mothers." The Crisis. Vol. 39, October, 1932, pp. 311.

1533
"Aid For The Working Mother." Service. Vol. 11, May, 1947, pp. 8.

1534
Anderson, Mable B. "Child-Rearing Practices of Negro Migrant Mothers In Three Pennsylvania Counties." Doctoral Dissertation, Pennsylvania State University, 1965, 215p.

1535
"An Appeal For Working Mothers." Norfolk Journal And Guide. 7 October, 1916, pp. 1.

1536
Bartz, Karen W. and Elain S. Levine. "Childrearing By Black Parents: A Description and Comparison to Anglo and Chicano Parents." Journal of Marriage and The Family. Vol. 40, November, 1978, pp. 709-719.

1537
Bell, Robert R. "Lower-Class Negro Mothers And Their Children." Integrated Education. Vol. 2, December, 1964, pp. 23-27.

1538
____________. "The Lower Class Negro Mother's Aspiration For Her Children." Social Forces. Vol. 43, May, 1965, pp. 493-500.

1539
Berry, Pike. Birthed Into Glory. Boston: Christopher: 1966, 201p.

1540
"The Black Mammy Monument." New York Age. 6 January, 1923, pp. 4.

1541
"The Black Mother." The Crisis. Vol. 5, December, 1912, pp. 78.

1542
Brookins, Geraldine Kearse. "Maternal Employment: Its Impact On The Sex Roles and Occupational Choices of Middle and Working Class Black Children." Doctoral Dissertation, Harvard University, 1977, 130p.

1543
Bullock, Dorothy Josephine. "An Analysis of Cases of Negro Working Mothers Known To The Family Welfare Society, Atlanta, Georgia, 1940-1942. Master's Thesis, Atlanta University, 1943, 48p.

1544
Burns, Jacqueline. "Effects on Parents' Child Rearing Practices Of Their Children's Participation In The UPO Pre-School Program In Washington, D. C." Master's Thesis, Howard University, 1966, 186p.

1545
Busby, Everett Charles. "Pre-School Problems and Resources to Meet Such Problems As Seen By Twenty-eight Austin Negro Mothers." Master's Thesis, University of Texas at Austin, 1953, 44p.

1546
Carter, Ross. "The Negro Woman And Foster Care: Motivating And Deterring Factors." Master's Thesis, Howard University, 1964.

1547
Cunnigen, Donald. "Power Of A Black Mother's Touch." The Crisis. Vol. 84, December, 1977, pp. 477-478.

1548
Dougherty, Molly Crocker. Becoming A Woman In Rural Black Culture. New York: Holt, Rinehart & Winston, 1978, 111p.

1549
________________________. "Maturation and Motherhood: Becoming A Woman In Rural Black Culture." Doctoral Dissertation, The University of Florida, 1973, 241p.

1550
DuBois, W. E. B. "The Black Mother." The Crisis. Vol. 79, December, 1972, pp. 328.

1551
Eggleston, Cecilia. "What A Negro Mother Faces." Forum. Vol. 100, August, 1938, pp. 59-62.

1552
Epps, Edgar G. Irwin Katz and Leland Axelson. "Relation of Mother's Employment to Intellectual Performance of Negro College Students." Social Problems. Vol. 11, Spring, 1964, pp. 414-419.

1553
Fourtune, Hilda O. "A Study of The Power Position Of Mothers In Contemporary Negro Family Life in New York City." Doctoral Dissertation, New York University, 1963, 159p.

1554
Gregory, Patty. "Child Rearing Practices of Negro Mothers Of The Professional Class." Master's Thesis, Howard University, 1951, 69p.

1555
Guthrie, Alchibia Robinson. "A Proposed Plan Establishing Day Nursery Centers For Children of Working Negro Mothers In Washington, D. C.: Master's Thesis, Howard University, 1942, 73p.

1556
Harris, Joan Ricks. "Black/White and Socioeconomic Status As Factors In Maternal Attitudes Toward Child-Rearing Practices And The Use Of Health Care In Families With And Without An Educable Mentally Retarded Child." Doctoral Dissertation, The Florence Heller Graduate School for Advanced Studies In Social Welfare, 1976, 251p.

1557
__________________. "Ethnicity And Socio-Economic Status As Factors In Patterns of Child-Rearing Among Working Mothers." Master's Thesis, California State University, 1965, 151p.

1558
Hendricks, Leo Edward, Jr. "The Effect of Family Size, Child Spacing and Family Density on Stress In Low Income Black Mothers And Their Preadolescent Children." Doctoral Dissertation, University of North Carolina at Chapel Hill, 1977, 167p.

1559
Holman, Zephyr L. "Maternal Care of Negro Women In Chicago." Master's Thesis, University of Chicago, 1932.

1560
"It's Up To The Women." Service. Vol. 6, June, 1942, pp. 3.

1561
Jenkins, Jennie M. "The Role of The Mother In Helping Children To Adjust to Foster Care." Master's Thesis, Howard University, 1955, 60p.

1562
Jones, Mary Ann Dixon. "A Study of The Need For A Day Care Center For Negroes In Saint Louis: An Analysis of The Need For Day Care Centers of Sixty Families In One Negro Neighborhood In St. Louis, Missouri." Master's Thesis, St. Louis University, 1948, 48p.

1563
Kammi, Constance K. "Socio-Economic Class Differences in The Preschool Socialization Practices of Negro Mothers." Doctoral Dissertation, University of Michigan, 1965, 159p.

1564
Kammi, Constance K. and Norma L. Radin. "Class Differences In The Socialization Practices of Negro Mothers." Journal Of Marriage and The Family. Vol. 29, May, 1967, pp. 302-310.

1565
Keough, M. Adrienne. "Dimensionalities and Discrepancies In Maternal Perception Of The Vocational Interests of Caucasian and Negro Mothers." Doctoral Dissertation, The Catholic University of America, 1970, 76p.

1566
Lee, Irene K. and Marjorie Smith. "Opinions About Sex Education Held By Low Income Negro Mothers." Journal of Home Economics. Vol. 61, May, 1969, pp. 359-362.

1567
"Medic Finds Black Mothers Downgraded." Jet. Vol. 45, October 25, 1973, pp. 44.

1568
Morrow, Betty Hearn. "A Comparison of Eight-Year Old Children Born To Young Black Adolescents and Those Born to Comparable Mothers In Their Early Twenties." Doctoral Dissertation, University of Miami, 1978, 138p.

1569
"A Mother Appeals To Mothers." Headlines And Pictures. Vol. 2, June, 1946, pp. 15.

1570
Myers, Lena Wright. "Mothers From Families of Orientation As Role Models For Black Women." Northwest Journal of African And Black American Studies. Vol. 2, Winter, 1974, pp. 7-9.

1571
"To Negro Motherhood on Mother's Day." The Aframerican Woman's Journal. Vol. 1, Spring, 1940, pp. 28.

1572
"Negro Mothers Aided By Lunch Program" Service. Vol. 7, March, 1943, pp. 10.

1573
North, George E. and O. Lee Buchanan. "Maternal Attitudes In A Poverty Area." Journal of Negro Education. Vol. 37, Fall, 1968, pp. 418-425.

1574
Osborne, Gwendolyn E. "Motherhood In The Black Community." The Crisis. Vol. 84, December, 1977, pp. 479, 482-484.

1575
Parkhurst, Jessie W. "The Role of The Black Mammy In The Plantation Household." Journal of Negro Education. Vol. 23, July, 1938, pp. 349-369.

1576
Peters, Marie Ferguson. "Nine Black Families: A Study of Household Management and Childrearing In Black Families With Working Mothers." Doctoral Dissertation, Harvard University, 1976, 339p.

1577
Radin, Norma and Constance Kamii. "The Child-Rearing Attitudes of Disadvantaged Negro Mothers and Some Educational Implications." Journal of Negro Education. Vol. 34, Spring, 1965, pp. 138-146.

1578
Ross, Joel A. "The Effect of Recommendations Made By An Expert to Negro Mothers of Low Socioeconomic Status When Recommendations Are Supported Or Negated By A Peer." Doctoral Dissertation, Hofstra University, 1971, 75p.

1579
Rothenburger, Leila A. "America's Most Courageous Woman." Christian Century. Vol. 47, December 24, 1930, pp. 587-588.

1580
Rutland, Eva. The Trouble With Being A Mama. Nashville: Abingdon Press, 1964, 143p.

1581
Slater, Jack. "Three Profiles In Courage: Mothers Overcome Grief At Deaths Of Their Children." Ebony. Vol. 28, March, 1973, pp. 94-96, 98, 100-102, 104, 106.

1582
Smith, Audrey and William J. Reid. "Child Care Arrangements Of AFDC Mothers In The Work Incentive Program." Child Welfare. Vol. 52, December, 1973, pp. 651-681.

1583
Smith, Dennis Elliott. "Independent Training Of Their Male Offspring By Lower Class Black Mothers With High And Low Achievement Motivation." Doctoral Dissertation, Wayne State University, 1974, 85p.

1584
Snow, Jacqueline E. "A Hueristic Study of Black Female Heads of Households and Black Females Who Are Not Heads of Households And Their Involvement With Their Children's Educational Development, Camden, New Jersey." Doctoral Dissertation, Rutgers University, 1976, 139p.

1585
Tatje, Terrence Andresen. "Mother-Daughter Dyadic Dominance In Black American Kinship." Doctoral Dissertation, Northwestern University, 1974, 460p.

1586
Theiner, Patricia Ann. "Expectations Of A Day Care Facility By Low Income Negro Mothers." Master's Thesis, The Catholic University of America, 1968, 116p.

1587
Thomas, Naomi Jean. "The Employment Experience of Forty Negro Mothers Receiving Aid To Dependent Children In Marin County And Its Effect On Their Families During The War and Post-War Period." Master's Thesis, Indiana University, 1948, 66p.

1588
Trufant, Carol Ann. "The Effects of Familial Support Systems On Black Mothers' Childrearing Attitudes And Behavior And on Their Childrens' Competence." Doctoral Dissertation, Michigan State University, 1977, 161p.

1589
Waldman, Elizabeth. "Children of Working Mothers, March, 1974." Monthly Labor Review. Vol. 97, January, 1975, pp. 64-67.

1590
Webster, Staten W. "Some Correlates of Reported Academically Supportive Behaviors of Negro Mothers Toward Their Children." Journal of Negro Education. Vol. 34, Spring, 1965, pp. 114-120.

1591
West, Frankie L. "A Mother-Dauthter Study of Thirty Families As Bases For A Vocational Guidance Program." Master's Thesis, Hampton Institute, 1964, 81p.

1592
West, Stan. "Mothers In Show Biz!! How Easy Is It?" Right On. Vol. 8, June, 1979, pp. 61-64.

1593
White, Joyce. "Lessons on Motherhood." Essence. Vol. 10, May, 1979, pp. 88-90.

1594
Winters, Wilda Glasgow. "Black Mothers In Urban Schools: A Study of Participation And Alienation." Doctoral Dissertation. Yale University, 1975, 167p.

1595
"Working Mothers." Opportunity. Vol. 9, September, 1931, pp. 267.

1596
"Working Mothers," in Negro Problems In Cities, by T. J. Woofter, Jr. College Park, Maryland: McGrath Publishing Company, 1969, 284p., pp. 192-193.

1597
Wyatt, Gail Elizabeth. "The Relationship of Life and Locus Of Control Attributions To Cognitive Aspects of The Black Mother/Child Interaction." Doctoral Dissertation, University of California at Los Angeles, 1973, 187p.

Family

1598
Abzug, Robert H. "The Black Family During Reconstruction," in Key Issues In The Afro American Experience, Vol. 2, by Nathan Huggins, Martin Kilson and Daniel Fox. New York: Harcourt, Brace, Javonovich, 1971, 272p., pp. 26-41.

1599
Agresti, Barbara Finlay. "The First Decades of Freedom: Black Families in A Southern County, 1870-1885." Journal of Marriage and The Family. Vol. 40, November, 1978, pp. 697-706.

1600
"The Anatomy of Exploitation - The Family," in Time On The Cross: The Economics of American Negro Slavery, by Robert William Fogel and Stanley L. Engerman. Boston: Little, Brown, 1974, 286p., pp. 126-144.

1601
Bernard, Jesse S. Marriage And Family Among Negroes. New Jersey: Prentice Hall, 1966, 160p.

1602
Billingsley, Andrew. Black Families In White America. New Jersey: Prentice Hall, 1968, 218p.

1603
Billingsley, Andrew and Marilyn Cynthia Greene. "Family Life Among The Free Black Population in the 18th Century." Journal of Social and Behavioral Sciences. Vol. 20, Spring, 1974, pp. 1-18.

1604
Blackburn, Cleo Walter. "Five Hundred Negro Families of Chester, Pennsylvania." Master's Thesis, Fisk University, 1936, 132p.

1605
Carry, Saidie Edwina. "The Origin and Family Patterns of Thirty-six Negro Common-Law Families of Nashville, Tennes-

see." Master's Thesis, Fisk University, 1942, 97p.

1606
"Color Him Father," in Beautiful, Also, Are The Souls Of My Black Sisters: A History of The Black Woman In America, by Jeanne Noble. New Jersey: Prentice-Hall, 1978, 353p., pp. 90-108.

1607
DuBois, W. E. B. The Negro American Family. Cambridge, Massachusetts: M. I. T. Press, 1909, 156p.

1608
"Economic Status of Black Family," in The State Of Black America, 1979. New York: National Urban League, 1979, 250p., pp. 25-20.

1609
Edwards. G. Franklin. "Marriage and Family Life Among Negroes." Journal of Negro Education. Vol. 32, Fall, 1963, pp. 451-465.

1610
Farrakhan, L. "The Black Woman." Essence. Vol. 2, January, 1972, pp. 30-31,

1611
"The Family," in The Shadow of The Plantation, by Charles S. Johnson. Chicago: The University of Chicago Press, 1934, 215p., pp. 47-102.

1612
"Family Life," in Black New Orleans, 1860-1880," by John W. Blassingame. Chicago: University of Chicago Press, 1973, 301p., pp. 79-105.

1613
Frazier, E. Franklin, The Negro Family In The United States. Chicago: University of Chicago Press, 1966, 372p.

1614
Furstenburg, Frank, Theodore Hershberg and John Modell. "Family Structure, Ethnicity, and Social Mobility: An Historical and Comparative Analysis of The Black Family In Philadelphia. American Sociological Association, 68th Annual Meeting, 1973.

1615
Gossett, Ruth Ross. "So Few Men: A Study of Black Widowhood." Doctoral Dissertation, Syracuse University, 1976, 148p.

1616
Gutman, Herbert G. The Black Family In Slavery And Freedom, 1750-1925. New York: Pantheon Books, 1976, 664p.

1617
Gutman, Herbert G. "Persistent Myths About The Afro-American Family." The Journal of Interdisciplinary History. Vol. 6, Autumn, 1975, pp. 181-210.

Gutman, Herbert G. "Persistent Myths About The Afro-American Family," in The Afro-American Family In Social-Historical Perspective, edited by Michael Gordon. New York: St. Martin's Press, 1978, 580p., pp. 467-489.

1618
Haney, C. Allen, Clark E. Vincent, Robert Michielutte and Carl M. Cochrane. "Characteristics of Black Women in Male and Female Households." Journal of Black Studies. Vol. 6, December, 1975, pp. 136-157.

1619
Henry, Curtis Charles. "The Spatial Interaction of Black Families In Suburban Cities In The Bay Area: A Study Of Black Subsystem Linkage." Doctoral Dissertation, University of California, Berkely, 1978, 378p.

1620
Jackson, Jacquelyn J. "Comparative Lifestyles and Family And Friend Relationships Among Older Black Women." The Family Coordinator. Vol. 21, 1972, pp. 477-485.

1621
Jones, Bobby F. "A Cultural Middle Passage: Slave Marriage and Family In The Ante-Bellum South." Doctoral Dissertation, University of North Carolina at Chapel Hill, 1965, 273p.

1622
Jones, Curtis Joseph. "Differences and Similarities Between Two Parent and Mother-Child Black Families Residing In A Lower Socio-Economic Census Tract." Doctoral Dissertation, Michigan State University, 1974, 203p.

1623
King, Charles E. "The Maternal Negro Family of Barrow County, Georgia." Master's Thesis, University of Michigan, 1940, 60p.

1624
Kulikoff, Allan. "The Beginnings of The Afro American Family In Maryland," in The American Family In Social-Historical Perspective, edited by Michael Gordon. New York: St. Martin's Press, 1978, 580p., pp. 444-466.

1625
Lammermeier, Paul J. "The Urban Black Family of The Nineteenth Century: A Study of Black Family Structure in The Ohio Valley, 1850-1880." Journal of Marriage and The Family. Vol. 35, August, 1973, pp. 440-456.

1626
Lowe, Edwina Electa. "Attitudes Of Negro Women Toward Family Disorganization in Two Contrasting Communities. Master's Thesis, Fisk University, 1940, 60p.

1627
Martin, Elmer P. The Black Extended Family. Chicago: University of Chicago Press, 1978.

1628
"The Negro Family," in The Negro In America: The Condensed Version of Gunnar Myrdal's An American Dilemma, by Arnold Rose. New York: Harper & ROw, 1948, 324p., pp. 294-296.

1629
Pleck, Elizabeth H. "The Two-Parent Household: Black Family Structure In Late Nineteenth Century Boston." Journal of Social History. Vol. 6, Fall, 1972, pp. 3-31.

Pleck, Elizabeth H. "The Two-Parent Household: Black Family Structure In Late Nineteenth Century Boston," in The American Family in Social-Historical Perspective, edited by Michael Gordon. New York: St. Martin's Press, 1973, 428p., pp. 152-177.

1630
"Psychiatrist Sees Racism Eroding Black Family Life." Jet. Vol. 48, May 29, 1975, pp. 23.

1631
Rainwater, Lee and William L. Yancey. The Moynihan Report And The Politics of Controversy. Cambridge: M. I. T. Press, 1967, 493p.

1632
Randolph, Mary Elizabeth. "A Case Study of Thirty Family Desertions Among Fifteen Negro and Fifteen White Clients of The Atlanta Family Welfare Society." Master's Thesis, Atlanta University, 1943, 42p.

1633
Robinson, Patricia Ann. "The Moynihan Report And The Negro Family: A Critical Analysis." Master's Thesis, Atlanta University, 1972, 142p.

1634
Robinson, Seanie Mary. "The Negro Professional Family In A Southern Town." Master's Thesis, Fisk University, 1947, 283p.

1635
Scanzoni, John H. The Black Family In Modern Society. Boston: Allyn & Bacon, 1971, 353p.

1636
Schency, Mary-Lou. "A Southern Negro Girl in A White Northern Family: A Case Study." Social Work. Vol. 14, July, 1969,

pp, 77-83.

1637
Schweninger, Loren. "A Slave Family In The Ante-Bellum South." Journal of Negro History. Vol. 60, January, 1975, pp. 29-44.

1638
Scott, Patricia Bell. "An Analysis of Research Studies of Black Family Life Reported In The Journal of Marriage and The Family. 1973." Master's Thesis, University of Tennessee, 1973, 76p.

1639
Shifflett, Crandall A. "The Household Compositon of Rural Black Families: Louisa County, Virginia, 1880." The Journal of Interdisciplinary History. Vol. 6, Autumn, 1975, pp. 235-260.

1640
"The Slave Family," in The Negro In Colonial New England, 1620-1776, by Lorenzo J. Greene. New York: Columbia University Press, 1942, 404p., pp. 191-217.

1641
"The Slave Family," in The Slave Community: Plantation Life In The Ante-Bellum South, by John W. Blassingame. New York: Oxford University Press, 1972, 262p., pp. 77-103.

1642
"The Slave Family, Slave Sexual Behavior, and Slave Sales," in Slavery and The Numbers Game: A Critique of Time On The Cross, by Herbert G. Gutman. Chicago: University of Illinois Press, 1975, 183p., pp. 88-164.

1643
Stack, Carol B. All Our Kin: Strategies For Survival In A Black Community. New York: Harper & Row, 1974, 175p.

1644
____________. "The Kindred of Viola Jackson: Residence And Family Organization Of An Urban Black American Family," in Afro-American Anthropology: Contemporary Prespectives, edited by Norman E. Whitten, Jr. and John F. Szwed. New York: The Free Press, 1970, 468p., pp. 303-311.

1645
Staples, Robert. The Black Family: Essays And Studies. Belmont, California: Wadsworth Publishing Company, 1971, 393p.

1646
Staples, Robert. "The Status of Black Women: Sex, Marriage and The Family," in Perspectives On Afro American Women, edited by Willa D. Johnson and Thomas L. Green. Washington, D. C.: Educational Community Counselors Associates, Inc., 1975, 197p., pp. 45-47.

1647
Steinman, Anne and David Fox. "Attitudes Toward Women's Family Role Among Black and White Undergraduates." The Family Coordinator. Vol. 19, October, 1970, pp. 363-367.

1648
"Study Put Lie To Old Myths About Black Family." Jet. Vol. 40, August 12, 1971, pp. 54.

1649
Sudarkasa, Niara. "An Exposition on The Value Premises Underlying Black Family Studies." Journal of The National Medical Association. Vol. 67, May, 1975, pp. 235-239.

1650
TenHouten, Warren. "The Black Family: Myth and Reality." Psychiatry. Vol. 33, May, 1970, pp. 145-173.

1651
"To Knit Together The Broken Ties of Family Kinship," in Black Women In Nineteenth Century American Life: Their Words, Their Thoughts, Their Feelings, by Bert James Loewenberg and Ruth Bogin. University Park: The Pennsylvania State University Press, 1976, 355p., pp. 37-123.

1652
Turner, Clarence Rollo. "Some Theoretical and Conceptual Consideration for Black Family Studies." Black Lines: A Journal of Black Studies. Vol. 11, Summer, 1972, pp. 13-27.

1653
Ware, Cellestine. "The Black Family and Feminism," in The First Ms. Reader, edited by Francine Klagsbrun. New York: Warner, 1973, 282p., pp. 36-41.

1654
White, Priscilla and Patricia Scott. "The Role of Black Women in Black Families: Teaching About Black Families on A Predominantly White Campus," in Perspectives on Afro-American Women, edited by Willa D. Johnson and Thomas L. Green. Washington, D. C.: Educational Community Counselors Associates, Inc., 1975, 197p., pp. 187-195.

1655
Whittington, James. "Some Approaches to Afro American Family Structure: A Brief Review and Cirtique." Journal of Social and Behavioral Sciences. Vol. 19, Summer/Fall, 1972, pp. 18.

1656
Williams, J. Allen, Jr., and Robert Stockton. "Black Family Sturcture and Function: An Empirical Examination of Some Suggestions Made By (Andrew) Billingsley." Journal of Marriage and The Family. Vol. 35, February, 1973, pp. 39-49.

Marriage and Divorce

1657
"Are Child Brides Fit For Marriage?" Jet. Vol. 5, Feburary 11, 1954, pp. 18-20.

1658
"Are Doctors' Wives Jealous?" Jet. Vol. 6, June 24, 1954, pp. 30.

1659
"Baseball Wives." Jet. Vol. 2, June 12, 1952, pp. 52-57.

1660
"Battered Wives Strike Back." Bronze Thrills. Vol. 27, March, 1978, pp. 34.

1661
Berry, Bill. "Husbands of Well Known Women: Behind Every Successful Woman There Is..." Ebony. Vol. 33, April, 1978, pp. 154-158.

1662
__________. "Interracial Marriages In The South." Ebony. Vol. 32, June, 1978, pp. 64-66, 68, 70, 72.

1663
"Black Women To Be Hurt More By 'Reverse Alimony'." Jet. Vol. 56, June 14, 1979, pp. 50.

1664
Bontemps, Alex. "Startling New Attitudes On Interracial Marriage." Ebony. Vol. 30, September, 1975, pp. 144-146, 148, 150-151.

1665
Breiter, Toni. "Battered Women: When Violence Is Linked To Love." Essence. Vol. 10, June, 1979, pp. 74-75, 121, 123-124, 126, 128-129.

1666
Britton, John H. "Women Study in Shadows, But Give Men Strength To Fight." Jet. Vol. 25, February 13, 1964, pp. 22-28.

1667
Chavis, William M. and Gladys J. Lyles. "Divorce Among Educated Black Women." Journal of the National Medical Association. Vol. 67, March, 1975, pp. 128-134.

1668
"Common Law Marriage." Jet. Vol. 2, May 1, 1952, pp. 44-48.

1669
"Divorce And Raising A Fatherless Child." Essence. Vol. 6, October, 1975, pp. 26.

1670
"Do Career Women Make Good Wives?" Jet. Vol. 1, April 17, 1952, pp. 40-46.

1671
"Do Pretty Women Make Good Wives?" Jet. Vol. 3, May 28, 1953, pp. 24-27.

1672
"Do Working Women Make Better Wives?" Jet. Vol. 6, May 27, 1954, pp. 56-57.

1673
"Does Mixed Marriage Hurt Race Relations?" Jet. Vol. 2, July 3, 1952, pp. 20-25.

1674
"Educated Black Women Lead Fewer Men to Altar." Jet. Vol. 46, September 19, 1974, pp. 8.

1675
Fichter, Joseph H. "Marriage and Motherhood of Black Women Graduates," in Woman In A Man-Made World: A Socioeconomic Handbood, edited by Nona Glazer-Malbin and Helen Youngelson Waehrer. Chicago: Rand McNally, 1972, 443p., pp. 203-207.

1676
Gorham, Thelma T. "Negro Army Wives." The Crisis. Vol. 50, January, 1943, pp. 21-22.

1677
Haggerty, Sandra. "A Black Sister Looks At Polygamy." Sacramento Observer. 1 June, 1972, pp. D-10.

1678
Hopkins, Ann A. "The 'New' Black Woman." Essence. Vol. 2, January, 1972, pp. 42-43, 54, 60.

1679
"How Often Do Men Marry The Other Woman?" Jet. Vol. 6, July 15, 1954, pp. 28-29.

1680
"Inter-marriage." The Crisis. Vol. 20, April, 1925, pp. 251.

1681
Jones, Vickie. "Divorce: Two Women Who Experienced It." Essence. Vol. 4, April, 1974, pp. 52-53, 95.

1682
Kisner, Ronald E. "The Problems of Baseball Wives." Jet. Vol. 50, April 22, 1976, pp. 21-23, 50.

1683
________________. "The Problems of Black Wives and Famous Athletes." Jet. Vol. 45, February 21, 1974, pp. 20-24.

1684
Lefcowitz, Myron J. Differences Between Negro And White Women in Marital Stability and Family Structure: A Multiple Regression Analysis. Winconsin: Institute for REsearch on Poverty, 1968.

1685
Lewis, Shawn D. "Black Women/White Men: The 'Other' Mixed Marriage." Ebony. Vol. 33, January, 1978, pp. 37-39, 41-42.

1686
______________. "Why I'm Not Married." Ebony. Vol. 32, September, 1977, pp. 120, 122, 124, 126, 128, 130.

1687
"The Marriage Ceremony," in First Days Amongst The Contrabands, by Elizabeth Hyde Botume. Boston: Lee & Shepard Publishers, 1893, 286p., pp. 157-167.

1688
"Negro Women With White Husbands." Jet. Vol. 1, February 21, 1952, pp. 24-29.

1689
Pierce, Ponchita. "Divorce and Negro Women." Ebony. Vol. 22, July, 1967, pp. 84-86, 90-92.

1690
________________. "Marriage and The Educated Black Woman." Ebony. Vol. 28, August, 1973, pp. 160-163.

1691
"POW Wife." Ebony. Vol. 26, January, 1971, pp. 111.

1692
"Problems of Second Wives." Ebony. Vol. 15, July, 1960, pp. 55-58, 60.

1693
Robinson, Louie. "Why Wives Become Unfaithful." Jet. Vol. 5, January 7, 1954, pp. 16-18.

1694
Rutledge, Essie Manual. "Marital and Family Relations of Black Women." Doctoral Dissertation, University of Michigan, 1974, 176p.

1695
Shaw, Louis B. Economic Consequences of Marital Disruption For Women In Their Middle Years. Washington, D. C.: Department of Labor, Employment and Training Administration, 1978, 30p.

1696
"Should Husbands Be Told About Cheating Wives?" Jet. Vol. 7, December 16, 1954, pp. 18-20.

1697
"The Truth About Army Wives." Jet. Vol. 6, September 2, 1954, pp. 28-30.

1698
"Waiting Wives." Ebony. Vol. 23, February, 1968, pp. 44-46, 48-50, 52.

1699
West, Hollie I. "...But A Scarcity of Black Men." Washington Post. 23 July, 1972, pp. E-1.

1700
White, Joyce. "Women Speak!" Essence. Vol. 10, June, 1979, pp. 75, 129, 131.

1701
"Why More White Men Are Marrying Negro Women." Jet. Vol. 4, December 3, 1953, pp. 18-21.

1702
"Wives of Negro Millionaires." Jet. Vol. 1, January 17, 1952, pp. 56-61.

1703
"Wives of POWs Want Privacy When Husbands Return." Jet. Vol. 43, Feburary 15, 1973, pp. 8-9.

Matriarchy

1704
"Bias, Poverty, Urban Living Increase Black Fatherless Homes." Jet. Vol. 39, March 25, 1971, pp. 28.

1705
"Black Adoption: Black Women as Household Heads." Sacramento Observer. 1 June, 1972, pp. D-20.

1706
"Characteristics of Families Headed by Women, March, 1968." Welfare In Review. January/February, 1970, pp. 16-20.

1707
Davis, Angela. "The Myth of The Black Matriarch," in The First Ms. Reader, edited by Francine Klagsbrun. New York: Warner, 1973, 282p., pp. 241-249.

1708
DeRamus, Betty. "Taking Another Look At The Matriarchy: Did Those Strong Women Ever Cry?" New Lady. Vol. 3, April/May, 1970, pp. 3-4.

1709
Dietrich, Kathryn Thomas. "The Myth of The Black Matriarchy," in Woman In A Man-Made World: A Socioeconomic Handbook, edited by Nona Glazer-Malbin and Helen Y. Waehrer. Chicago:

Rand McNally, 1972, 443p., pp. 279-286.

1710
Dietrich, Kathryn Thomas. "A Re-Examination of The Myth of Black Matriarchy." Journal of Marriage and The Family. Vol. 37, May, 1975, pp. 367-374.

1711
Frazier, E. Franklin. "The Black Matriarchate," in The Black Sociologists: The First Half Century, edited by John Bracey, August Meier and Elliot Rudwick. California: Wadsworth, 1971, 186p., pp. 124-135.

1712
Furstenberg, Frank, Theodore Hershberg and John Modell. "The Origins of The Female Headed Black Family: The Impact of The Urban Experience." Journal of Interdisciplinary History. Vol. 6, Autumn, 1975, pp. 211-233.

1713
Genovese, Eugene. "The Slave Family, Women - A Reassessment of Matriarchy, Emasculation, Weakness." Southern Voices. Vol. 2, August/September, 1974, pp. 9-16.

1714
Gonzalez, Nancie L. "Toward A Definition of Matrifocality," in Afro-American Anthropology: Contemporary Perspectives, edited by Norman E. Whitten, Jr. and John F. Szwed. New York: The Free Press, 1970, 468p., pp. 231-243.

1715
Honig, Marjorie Hanson. The Impact of The Welfare System on Labor Supply and Family Stability: A Study of Female Heads of Families." Doctoral Dissertation, Columbia University, 1971.

1716
Hyman, Herbert H. and John S. Reed. "Black Matriarchy Reconsidered: Evidence From Secondary Analysis of Sample Surveys," Public Opinion Quarterly. Vol. 33, Summer, 1969, pp. 346-354.

1717
Jackson, Jacquelyne J. "Black Women In A Racist Society," in Racism and Mental Health, edited by Charles V. Willie, Barnard Kramer and Bertram Brown. Pittsburgh: University of Pittsburgh Press, 1973, 604p., pp. 185-268.

1718
Kaiser, Evelyn L. "The Unattached Negro Woman On Relief: A Study of Fifty Unattached Negro Women On Relief In The Compton District Office of The State Relief Administration of California In Los Angeles." Master's Thesis, University of Southern California, 1939, 166p.

1719
Kriesberg, Louis. Mothers In Poverty: A Study of Fatherless Families. Chicago: Aldine Publishing Company, 1970, 356p.

1720
La Point, Velma DeVonne. "A Descriptive Survey of Some Perceptions and Concerns of Black Female Single Parent Families In Lansing, Michigan." Doctoral Dissertation, 1977, 140p.

1721
Lincoln. C. Eric. "A Look Beyond The Matriarchy." Ebony. Vol. 21, August, 1966, pp. 111-114, 116.

1722
Mack, Delores. "Where The Black Matriarchy Theorists Went Wrong." Psychology Today. Vol. 4, January, 1971, pp. 24.

1723
McBroom, Patricia. "The Black Matriarchy: Healthy or Pathological?" Science News. Vol. 94, October 19, 1968, pp. 394

1724
"More Black Families Headed by Women," in Characteristics Of Black Suburbanites, by Eunice S. Grier. Washington, D. C.: Center for Metropolitan Studies, 1973, 53p., pp. 16, 18.

1725
Parker, Seymore. "Characteristics of Negro Mothers in Single Headed Households." Journal of Marriage and The Family. Vol. 28, November, 1966, pp. 507-513.

1726
Rubin, Roger H. "Matriarchal Themes in Black Family Literature: Implications for Family Life Education." The Family Coordinator. Vol. 27, January, 1978, pp. 33-41.

1727
__________. Matricentric Family Structure And The Self-Attitudes of Negro Children. Palo Alto, California: R & E Research Associates, 1976, 75p.

1728
Sawhill, Isabel V. Black Women Who Head Families: Economic Needs and Economic Resources. Washington, D. C.: Department of Health, Education and Welfare, 1978, 13p.

1729
Schwartz, Michael. "Northern United States Negro Matriarchy: Status Versus Authority." Phylon. Vol. 26, Spring, 1965, pp. 18-24.

1730
Shelton, Isabelle. "Professor Dispels Myth of Black Matriarchy." Evening Star. 7 April, 1972.

1731
"Some Special Needs: Negro Women and Women Heads of Families," in Sex and The Marketplace: American Women At Work, by Juanita Kreps. Baltimore: The Johns Hopkins University Press, 1971, 117p., pp. 7.

1732
Staples, Robert. "The Matricentric Family System: A Cross-Cultural Examination." Journal of Marriage and The Family. Vol. 34, February, 1972, pp. 156-165.

1733
__________. The Myth of the Black Matriarchy." Black Scholar. Vol. 1, January/February, 1970, pp. 8-16.

1734
Strodtbeck, Fred L. "The Poverty-Dependency Syndrome of the ADC Female-Based Negro Family." American Journal of Orthopsychiatry. Vol. 34, March, 1964, pp. 216-217.

1735
"Study Shows Women Head Third of Black Families." Jet. Vol. 46, August 29, 1974, pp. 7.

1736
Veasey, Jess F. "Black Youth's Reading Skills and Achievements From Single Parent Homes With Mother As Head of the Household Compared With Those Where Both Parents Were Present," in Perspectives on Afro American Women, edited by Willa D. Johnson and Thomas L. Green. Washington, D. C.: Educational Community Counselors Associates, Inc., 1975, 197p., pp. 173-186.

1737
Walker, Lewis. "Composition And Role Structure of The Female Based Negro Family." Master's Thesis, The Ohio State University, 1961.

1738
Weisman, Carol Sachs. "An Analysis of Female Dominance In Urban Black Families." Doctoral Dissertation, The Johns Hopkins University, 1973, 219p.

1739
Zimmerman, Judith Joan. "The Concept of Maternal Responsibility In A Selected Sample of Large, Low Income, Negro Families." Master's Thesis, The Catholic University of America, 1961, 83p.

Unwed Mothers

1740
Arline, Catherine et al. "Romantic Love - Its Conception And Role Among Low-Income Unwed Mothers." Master's Thesis, Howard University, 1967, 83p.

1741
Baldwin, Maxine. "A Study of Services Rendered Twenty-six Unmarried Mothers In The House of Hope, Washington, D. C., 1946-1947." Master's Thesis, Atlanta University, 1947, 44p.

1742
Bernell, James W. "Newer Approaches in The Management of The Pregnant Unmarried Adolescent." National Medical Association Journal. Vol. 64, November, 1972, pp. 483-487, 507.

1743
Bieber, Toby B. "A Comparison of Negro Wed and Unwed Mothers." Doctoral Dissertation, Columbia University, 1963, 138p.

1744
Billingsley, Andrew and Amy T. Billingsley. "Illegitimacy And Patterns of Negro Family Life," in The Unwed Mother, edited by Robert W. Roberts. New York: Harper & Row, 1966, 270p., pp. 131-157.

1745
Borlick, Martha M. "The Effects of A Parent Group Discussion Program on Parental Learning of Unwed, Expectant Negro Adolescent Girls From Low-Income Families." Doctoral Dissertation, University of Maryland, 1966, 235p.

1746
Burnham, Frusilla. "Black-White Differences In Illegitimacy: An Examination of The Effects of Socio-Economic Differences, Marital Stability and Educational Attainment." Doctoral Dissertation, Florida State University, 1977, 153p.

1747
Clay, Fannie Candis. "The Adjustment Problems of Unwed Mothers in The High School." Master's Thesis, Fisk University, 1957, 61p.

1748
"Concern For Whipper Home." Bulletin of The Medico-Chirurgical Society of The District of Columbia. Vol. 6, May/September, 1949, pp. 2.

1749
Condon, Ruth Helen. "A Study of Colored Unmarried Minor Mothers In The District of Columbia From July 1, 1937 to June 30, 1938." Master's Thesis, The Catholic University of America, 1939, 75p.

1750
Dixon, Richard Davis. "Out-Of-Wedlock Conceptions: Illegitimate Births and Alternative Resolutions Among Young, Poor, Urban, Black Females." Doctoral Dissertation, Emory University, 1976, 314p.

1751
Eisenberg, Florence H. "Reference Group Behavior and The Negro Adolescent Unwed Mother." Master's Thesis, The Catholic University of America, 1963, 72p.

1752
Eisenmeier, Anne Marie. "A Study of Sixty Unmarried Negro Mothers Receiving Services From The St. Vincent de Paul Society, Milwaukee, Wisconsin, June, 1936 to June, 1943." Master's Thesis, St. Louis University, 1944, 112p.

1753
Ewer, Phyllis and James O. Gibbs. "Relationship With Putative Father and Use of Contraceptives In A Population of Black Ghetto Adolescent Mothers." Public Health Reports. September/October, 1975, pp. 417-423.

1754
"Finds Stigma Lessened For Unwed Mothers." Jet. Vol. 39, March 25, 1971, pp. 28.

1755
Flesch, Katharina. "Two Hundred Forty-eight Negro Unmarried Mothers, A Study of Two Hundred Forty-eight Negro Unmarried Mothers and Of Certain Services Provided for Them by Social and Health Agencies in Metropolitan Detroit. Master's Thesis, Wayne State University, 1945, 92p.

1756
Frigg, Martelle Daisy. "An Analysis of Illegitimacy By Natural Areas in Memphis, Tennessee." Master's Thesis, Fisk University, 1954, 51p.

1757
Furstenberg, Frank F. "Premarital Pregnancy Among Black Teenagers." Transaction. Vol. 7, May, 1970, pp. 52-55.

1758
Gorman, Mary Estelle. "A Study of Colored Minor Unmarried Mothers In The District of Columbia, July 1, 1937 to June 30, 1938." Master's Thesis, The Catholic University of America, 1939, 74p.

1759
Grape, Helen Hayes. "Factors Influencing The Decision of Afro American Unmarried Mothers Who Retain Custody of Their Children." Master's Thesis, Atlanta University, 1968, 57p.

1760
Haney, C. Allen, Robert Michielutte, Carl M. Cochrane and Clark E. Vincent. "Some Consequences of Illegitimacy In A Sample of Black Women." Journal of Marriage and The Family. Vol. 37, May, 1975, pp. 359-366.

1761
Harper, Helena H. "A Study of Colored Unmarried Mothers In Los Angeles." Master's Thesis, University of Southern California, 1932.

1762
Hertz, Hilda. "Negro Illegitimacy In Durham, North Carolina." Master's Thesis, Duke University, 1944, 110p.

1763
Hertz, Hilda and Sue W. Little. "Unmarried Negro Mothers In A Southern Urban Community." Social Forces. Vol. 23, October, 1944, pp. 73-79.

1764
Himes, Joseph. "Some Reactions To A Hypothetical Premarital Pregnancy by 100 Negro College Women." Marriage and Family Living. Vol. 26, August, 1964, pp. 344-349.

1765
Hunter, Sarah Margureite. "A Study of Twenty-five Unmarried Negro Mothers Served By The Family Welfare Society." Master's Thesis. Atlanta University, 1945, 48p.

1766
Insley-Casper, R. "The Negro Unmarried Mother of New York." Opportunity. Vol. 12, June, 1934, pp. 172-173.

1767
James, W. F. Bernall, Pauline M. James, and Edgar Walker. "Some Problems of Sexual Growth in Adolescent Underprivileged Unwed Black Girls." Journal of the National Medical Association. Vol. 69, September, 1977, pp. 631-633.

1768
Karr, Rosemary Josephine. "Assistance to Unmarried Mothers, Social Security Commission, St. Louis, July 1, 1940 to December 31, 1940." Master's Thesis, St. Louis University, 1942, 83p.

1769
Mann, Andrea Sands. "A Study of Selected Factors Influencing The Birth Control Practices of The Teenage Negro Unmarried Mother." Master's Thesis, The Catholic University of America, 1969, 68p.

1770
McGarigle, Marjorie. "A Study of Colored Unmarried Minor Mothers In The District of Columbia, July 1, 1932 to June 30, 1938. Master's Thesis, The Catholic University of America, 1939, 66p.

1771
McIntyre, Jennie J. "Illegitimacy: A Case of Stretched Values?" Doctoral Dissertation, Florida State University, 1966, 102p.

1772
Medonis, Gwen C. "The Negro Adolescent Unmarried Mother and Her Relationship With Significant Persons Before and After Pregnancy." Master's Thesis, The Catholic University of America, 1921, 35p.

1773
Monaster, Rebecca. "The Effect of A Continuing Eduction-for-Girls Program On The Self-Concept and Locus of Control Of

A Selected Group of Negro Adolescent Unmarried Mothers." Doctoral Dissertation, Wayne State University, 1967, 244p.

1774
Munchrath, Donald P. "The Unmarried Negro Father As He Is Viewed By A Selected Group of Unmarried Negro Mothers In Washington, D. C." Master's Thesis, The Catholic University of America, 1962, 92p.

1775
"Out of Wedlock Births Drop For Blacks, Rate Increases For Whites." Jet. Vol. 40, May 6, 1971, pp. 10.

1776
Peace, Marva et al. "Attitudes of Lower Class Negroes Towards Illegitimacy." Master's Thesis, Atlanta University, 1966, 188p.

1777
Poinsett, Alex. "A Despised Minority." Ebony. Vol. 21, August, 1966, pp. 48-50, 52-54.

1778
Pope, Hallowell. "Unwed Mothers and Their Sex Partners," in The Black Family: Essays and Studies, edited by Robert Staples. Belmont, California: Wadsworth Publishing Company, 1971, 393p., pp. 349-365.

1779
Reilly, Andelaide Stephanie. "The Relationship of 55 Negro Adolescent Unmarried Mothers Toward Their Own Mothers." Master's Thesis, The Catholic University of America, 1962, 88p.

1780
Reiner, Beatrice. "The Real World of The Teenage Negro Mother." Child Welfare. Vol. 47, 1968, pp. 391-386.

1781
Reynolds, Josephine Katherine. "Problems of Forty-four Negro Unmarried Mothers In St. Louis, Missouri, March, 1940 - March, 1941." Master's Thesis, St. Louis University, 1941, 88p.

1782
Rippy, Creighton L. "The Young Black Unwed Mother: Some Findings Concerning The Perception of Deviance." Master's Thesis, Wayne State University, 1977, 57p.

1783
Robinson, Louie. "Are More Coeds Becoming Unwed Mothers?" Jet. Vol. 5, January 14, 1954, pp. 18-20.

1784
Smith, Ernestine Latson. " 'To Have And To Hold' Project: A Study of Twenty-five Negro Teenage Unwed Mothers In Volusia

County, Florida." Master's Thesis, Atlanta University, 1968, 49p.

1785
Smith, Ollivette. "A Study of Unmarried Negro Motherhood As Encountered In The Census Tracts, District 17, 18, 19, 28, 29, 33, and 34, in Atlanta, Georgia, in 1947." Master's Thesis, Atlanta University, 1948, 34p.

1786
Talbot, Sylvia Evadney Ross. "An Inquiry Into The Knowledge Of Selected Aspects of Conception and Contraception of A Group of Unmarried, Pregnant Negro Girls Sixteen Years Of Age and Under." Doctoral Dissertation, Columbia University, 1969, 152p.

1787
Terrell, Caryl. "Financial Troubles Vanishing Homes For Unwed Mothers." Jet. Vol. 43, January 11, 1973, pp. 12-14.

1788
"Unwed, Teen Mothers Double; New School Codes For Them." Jet. Vol. 39, February 11, 1971, pp. 24.

1789
Vaughn, Priscilla Nevette. "A Study of A Selected Group of Illegitimately Pregnant Residents Served By The Florence Crittenton Home, Washington, D. C. in 1960." Master's Thesis, The Catholic University of America, 1963, 53p.

1790
Westney, Guida Elaine. "The Comparative Effects of A Group Discussion Program And A Lecture Program On The Self-Concept, Attitudes Toward Pregnancy and Manifest Anxiety of Unwed Primigravid, Negro Adolescent Girls." Doctoral Dissertation, University of Maryland, 1972, 121p.

1791
White, Joyce. "Single Motherhood." Essence. Vol. 4, November, 1973, pp. 54-55.

1792
Whitted, Christine. "Supports In The Black Community: Black Unmarried Mothers Who Kept Their Babies And Achieved Their Educational And/Or Professional Goals." Doctoral Dissertation, Columbia University Teachers College, 1978, 346p.

1793
Wilkinson, Grace W. "An Analysis of Case Work Treatment of Twenty-five Unmarried Mothers Carried By A Fmaily Agency During The Year, 1946." Master's Thesis, Howard University, 1947, 49p.

1794
Wright, Elizabeth C. "Trends In Planning With Unmarried Mother Mothers; A Comparative Study of Prospective Mothers Admitt-

ed To The Florence Crittenton Home In Washington, D. C., From January 1 Through June 30, In 1940 And 1945, With Whom The Social Service Department of The Home Had Responsibility In Planning For The Disposition of The Child." Master's Thesis, The Catholic University of America, 1947, 54p.

1795
Young, Ellen Lanius. "A Study of Requests for Service and Its Availability to Unmarried Mothers in Nashville and Davidson County, Tennessee." Master's Thesis, Vanderbilt University, 1949, 67p.

GENERAL WORKS

1796
Bambara, Toni Cade. The Black Woman; An Anthology. New York: New American Library, 1970, 256p.

1797
"Beautiful Black Women Pay Tribute To Her 200-Year Sojourn." Ebony. Vol. 30, August, 1975, pp. 159-160.

1798
"The Black Woman," in Reference Library Of Black America, edited by Harry A. Ploski. New York: Bellwether Publishing Company, 1971, 245p., pp. 196-221.

1799
"The Black Woman In The 1980s: The View From Now." Black Male/Female Relationships. Vol. 1, June/July, 1979, pp. 6-9.

1800
"The Burden of Black Women," in The Selected Writings of W. E. B. DuBois, by Walter Wilson. New York: Mentor Books, 1970, 384p., pp. 277-279.

1801
Carson, Josephine. Silent Voices; The Southern Negro Woman Today. New York: Delacorte Press, 1969, 273p.

1802
Crummell, Alexander. "The Black Woman of The South." American Missionary Magazine. Vol. 42, April, 1888, pp. 105-107.

1803
Daniels, Henri A. "The Concerned Black Woman." Afro American Magazine. November 25, 1972, pp. 6-7.

1804
"First Ladies of Colored America." The Crisis. Vol. 49, September, 1942, pp. 287-291; October, 1942, pp. 319-322; November, 1942, pp. 351-354.

1805
"First Ladies of Colored America." The Crisis. Vol. 50, January, 1943, pp. 15-18; February, 1943, pp. 47-50; March, 1943, pp. 79-82; April, 1943, pp. 111-114; May, 1943, pp. 143-146; June, 1943, pp. 175-178; July, 1943, pp. 207-210; September, 1943, pp. 271-274; October, 1943, pp. 303-306; November, 1943, pp. 335-338.

1806
Garland, Phyl. "Builders of A New South." Ebony. Vol. 21, August, 1966, pp. 27-30, 34, 36-37.

1807
Hackley, Emma Azalia. The Colored Girl Beautiful. Kansas City, Missouri: Burton Publishing Company, 1916, 206p.

1808
Hare, Nathan and Julia Hare. "Black Women, 1970." Transaction. Vol. 8, November, 1970, pp. 65-68.

1809
Harper, Francis Ellen Watkins."Colored Women of America." Englishwoman's Review. January 15, 1878, pp. 10-15.

1810
Higgins, Chester. Black Woman. New York: McCall Publishing Company, 1970, lv.

1811
Hill, Adelaide Cromwell. "The Afro-American Woman's Contribution to Society." Women's Education. Vol. 7, December, 1968, pp. 1, 7.

1812
Hobson, Elizabeth. A Report Concerning The Colored Women of The South. Baltimore: J. Murphy & Company, 1896, 15p.

1813
Hudson, Alva B. "Reading Achievements, Interests, And Habits of Negro Women." Master's Thesis, University of Chicago, 1931, 71p.

1814
Jackson, Jacquelyne J. Black Women: Their Problems And Power. New York: Barron's Educational Series, 1974.

1815
Jefferson, Olive Ruth. "The Southern Negro Woman." Woman's Council Table. 1893, pp. 91-94.

1816
Johnson, Willa D. and Thomas L. Green. Perspectives On Afro American Women. Washington, D. C.: Educational Community Counselors Associates, Inc., 1975, 197p.

1817
Ladner, Joyce A. "The Black Woman Today." Ebony. Vol. 32,

August, 1977, pp. 33-36, 38, 40, 42.

1818
Ladner, Joyce A. Tomorrow's Tomorrow: The Black Woman. New York: Doubleday, 1971, 304p.

Ladner, Joyce A. "Tomorrow's Tomorrow: The Black Woman," in The Death of White Sociology, edited by Joyce A. Ladner. New York: Random House, 1973, 476., pp. 414-428.

1819
________________. "The Women: Conditions of Slavery Laid The Foundation For Their Liberation." Ebony. Vol. 30, August, 1975, pp. 76-78, 80-81.

1820
Lerner, Gerda. Black Women In White America; A Documentary History. New York: Pantheon Books, 1972, 630p.

1821
Lifton, Robert Jay. The Woman In America. Boston: Houghton Mifflin, 1965, 293p.

1822
"More Black Women Than Men In The Suburbs," in Characteristics of Black Suburbanites, by Eunice S. Grier. Washington, D. C.: Washington Center for Metropolitan Studies, 1973, 53p., pp. 11, 13.

1823
Mossell, N. F. The Work of The Afro-American Woman. Philadelphia: G. S. Ferguson, 1894, 178p.

1824
Negro Women. Newspaper Clippings, 1900-1920. 5 vol. Clippings #231. Hampton, Virginia: Hampton Institute, Peabody Collection

1825
"Negro Women In National Affairs.: Norfolk Journal And Guide. 26 September, 1925, pp. 7; 10 October, 1925, pp. 13; 31 October, 1925, pp. 13.

1826
"The New Negro Woman." The Messenger. Vol. 7, July, 1923, pp. 757.

1827
Noble, Jeanne L. "The American Negro Woman," in The American Negro Reference Book, edited by John P. Davis. New Jersey: Prentice-Hall, 1966, 969p.

1828
Norment, Lynn. "Tomorrow's Black Woman: Independent, Smart, Feminine." Ebony. Vol. 32, August, 1977, pp. 44-46, 48.

1829
Picott, J. Rupert. "To The Women, We Look." *The Negro History Bulletin*. Vol. 39, May, 1976, pp. 583.

1830
"The Position of the Negro Woman." *Public Opinion*. Vol. 36, February 4, 1904, pp. 142.

1831
Reed, Ruth. "The Negro Woman of Gainesville, Georgia." Master's Thesis, University of Georgia, 1921, 61p.

1832
Reid, Inez. *Together Black Women*. New York: Emerson Hall Publishers, 1972, 383p.

1833
Render, Sylvia Lyons. "Afro-American Women: The Outstanding and The Obscure." *The Quarterly Journal of The Library Of Congress.* Vol. 32, October, 1975, pp. 306-321.

1834
Robinson, Dorothy. "Black Women...Expectations and Demands," in *Woman In The Year 2000,* by Maggie Tripp. New York: Arbor House Publishing Company, 1974, 302p., pp. 40-43.

1835
Slaughter, Diana T. "Becoming An Afro-American Woman." *School Review*. Vol. 80, February, 1972, pp. 299-318.

1836
Smith, Madeline R. "Negro Women of Today." *Norfolk Journal And Guide*. 5 May, 1923, pp. 4.

1837
Staples, Robert. *The Black Woman In America*. Chicago: Nelson-Hall, 1973, 269p.

1838
Steward, Susan M. "Colored American Women." *The Crisis*. Vol. 3, November, 1911, pp. 33-34.

1839
Tcholakian, Arthur. *Majesty of The Black Woman*. New York: Van Nostrand Reinhold, 1971, 169p.

1840
Terrell, Mary Church."Progress And Problem of Colored Women." *Home Mission College Review*. Vol. 2, March, 1929, pp. 41-48.

1841
Valien, Preston and Caroll Horton. "Some Demographic Characteristics of Outstanding Negro Women." *Journal of Negro Education*. Vol. 23, Fall, 1954, pp. 406-420.

1842
Washington, Booker T. "The New Negro Woman." Lend A Hand. Vol. 15, October, 1895, pp. 254.

1843
Washington, Booker T. (Mrs.). "Are We Making Good?" in A Documentary History of The Negro People In The United States, 1910-1932, edited by Herbert Aptheker. New Jersey: Citadel Press, 1973, 754p., pp. 120-123.

1844
Watkins, Mel. To Be A Black Woman: Portraits In Fact And Fiction. New York: Morror, 1970, 285p.

1845
"What the Negro Woman is Doing For Herself." Colored Alabamian. Vol. 7, March 15, 1913, pp. 2-3.

1846
"Women - Black Women," in Sourcebook of Equal Opportunity. Chicago: Marquis Academic Media, 1977, 686p., pp. 603-607.

1847
"Women Leaders." Ebony. Vol. 4, July, 1949, pp. 19-22.

1848
"Women On The Rise." Sepia. Vol. 13, April, 1964, pp. 8-12.

1849
Wright, Odessa M. "Achievements of Negro Women Since 1865." Master's Thesis, The State University of Iowa, 1931, 93p.

1850
Young, Gwendolyn. "Black Women On The Move - But Where?" The Crisis. Vol. 84, April, 1977, pp. 153-154.

HEALTH AND BEAUTY

Beauty

1851
Accent African: Traditional and Contemporary Hair Styles For The Black Woman. New York: Col-Bob Associates, 1973, 30p.

1852
"Are Negro Girls Getting Prettier?" Ebony. Vol. 21, February, 1966, pp. 25-28, 30-31.

1853
"Are The Prettiest Girls From Washington?" Jet. Vol. 5, January 21, 1954, pp. 20-23.

1854
"The Barbara Walden Story: From Actress to Beauty Consultant." Sepia. Vol. 19, August, 1970, pp. 72-75.

1855
"The Beautiful Black Woman: Beauty Questions You Want To Know - But Never Asked." Dawn Magazine. Vol. 7, May, 1979. pp. 12.

1856
"The Beautiful Black Woman: The Secret of Beautiful Hair." Dawn Magazine. Vol. 7, May, 1979, pp. 10.

1857
"Beauty is Blooming and Business Booming." Encore. Vol. 5, January 19, 1976, pp. 45.

1858
"Beverly Johnson's Brightest Color Secrets; Choices of Negro Models." Harper's Bazaar. Vol. 108, April, 1975, pp. 84-85.

1859
"A Black Woman's Guide to Skin Care." McCalls. Vol. 104, February, 1977, pp. 140, 202.

1860
"Black Women Are Three of Ten Best-Coiffed." Jet. Vol. 56, January 16, 1975, pp. 56.

1861
"Black Women Prefer Own Look." Dawn Magazine. Vol. 3, October, 1975, pp. 4.

1862
"Blackwomen's Beauty Guide." Mademoiselle. Vol. 77, May, 1973, pp. 225-226.

1863
Bouleware, Lemuel Ross. "Color and Cosmetics To Make American Negro Women Charming." Master's Thesis, Hampton Institute, 1946, 54p.

1864
Campbell, E. Simms. "Are Black Women Beautiful?" The Negro Digest. Vol. 9, June, 1951, pp. 16-20.

1865
"Does Detroit Have The Prettiest Society Girls?" Jet. Vol. 6, July 29, 1954, pp. 46-48.

1866
"For New Glamour Today: Beauty...From Head To Toe." Pulse. Vol. 4, April, 1946, pp. 16-17.

1867
"For Today's Active Black Woman, Wigs Are A Fashion Convenience." Black Monitor. Vol. 3, November, 1978, pp. 9.

1868
Fornay, Alfred. "The Beautiful Black Woman." Ebony. Vol. 32, February, 1977, pp. 138-142.

1869
Garland, Phyl. "The Natural Look." Ebony. Vol. 21, June, 1966, pp. 142-144, 146, 148.

1870
"Glorifying Negro Womanhood." Service. Vol. 5, June, 1941, pp. 7.

1871
"Harlem Versus Hollywood: Which Has The Most Beautiful Negro Girls?" Jet. Vol. 2, June 5, 1952, pp. 32-38.

1872
"How Beauty Sells Beauty - Avon's Field Support Program." The Gibson Report. Vol. 18, May, 1978, pp. 1-4.

1873
"How Long Do Glamor Girls Last." Jet. Vol. 6, June 10, 1954, pp. 60-62.

1874
"How Negro Beauties Charm Europe's Men." Jet. Vol. 1, November 8, 1951, pp. 61-65.

1875
"Ideal Type of Negro Beauty." New York Age. 6 August, 1914.

1876
"Lena Horne Beauty Products." Jet. Vol. 20, October 19, 1961, pp. 62.

1877
"Lena Horne Cosmetics Company Opens 7th Branch Office in Atlanta, Georgia." Jet. Vol. 19, August 7, 1960, pp. 21.

1878
"Making Black Hair More Beautiful." McCalls. Vol. 105, November, 1977, pp. 92, 94, 96, 98, 256.

1879
Mathis, Cynthia H. "The Concept of Feminine Beauty in Novels By Negroes." Master's Thesis, Fisk University, 1937.

1880
McNair, Barbara. The Complete Book of Beauty For The Black Woman. New Jersey: Prentice-Hall, 1972.

1881
Miller, Melba. The Black is Beautiful Beauty Book. New Jersey: Prentice-Hall, 1974, 113p.

1882
"Most Beautiful Women in Negro Society." Jet. Vol. 4, December 17, 1953, pp. 44-48.

1883
"New Hair Care!" Dawn Magazine. Vol. 6, August, 1978, pp. 24.

1884
"The Perfect Negro Beauty." Jet. Vol. 1, March 13, 1952, pp. 32-38.

1885
Peterson, P. "Color is True; Cosmetics for Black Women." New York Times Magazine. July 10, 1973, pp. 76-77.

1886
"Question of Style." Newsweek. Vol. 74, October 6, 1969, pp. 104.

1887
Riddle, Beve. "Beauty Power." New Lady. Vol. 3, March, 1970, pp. 13-15, 46.

1888
Rodgers, Evelyn. "Is Ebony Killing Black Women?" Liberator. Vol. 6, May, 1966, pp. 12-13.

1889
Rosenthal, Richard. "Cosmetics For The Black Woman." Urban West. Vol. 3, July/August, 1970, pp. 20-21, 28-29, 36-37.

1890
Sims, Naomi. "Skin Care." The Black Collegian. Vol. 7, May/June, 1977, pp. 20, 22, 24, 64.

1891
"Solving Cosmetic Problems for Black Women - Perfectly." Vogue. Vol. 164, August, 1974, pp. 57.

1892
Uggams, Leslie and M. Fenton. The Leslie Uggams Beauty Book. New Jersey: Prentice-Hall, 1966.

1893
"What Is The Age For Beauty?" Ebony. Vol. 14, November, 1958, pp. 43-44, 46, 48.

1894
"What Is The Perfect Figure?" Jet. Vol. 2, June 26, 1952, pp. 32-38.

1895
"Why Hollywood Won't Glamorize Negro Girls." Jet. Vol. 4, September 17, 1953, pp. 56-61.

1896
Young, A. S. "Beauty In Negro Women." Sepia. Vol. 12, September, 1963, pp. 42-48.

Beauty Pageants and Queens

1897
"America's Miss Golden Brown." Norfolk Journal And Guide. 3 October, 1925, pp. 8.

1898
Baraka, Imamu A. "The Coronation of The Black Queen." Black Scholar. Vol. 1, June, 1970, pp. 46-48.

1899
"Black Co-ed Named Queen of Drake U. Relays." Jet. Vol. 40, May 13, 1971, pp. 52.

1900
"Black College Queens for 1977-1978." Ebony. Vol. 33, April, 1978, pp. 64-66, 68, 70, 72, 74, 76.

1901
"Beauty Queen Hits Bias in 'Miss America' Contest." Jet. Vol. 2, May 22, 1952, pp. 5.

1902
"Beauty Queens of 1959." Ebony. Vol. 14, September, 1959, pp. 114-116, 118-120.

1903
"Black Beauty in Other Pageants." Encore. Vol. 7, September, 1978, pp. 36.

1904
"Black Campus Queens Featured in April Ebony." Jet. Vol. 50. April 1, 1976, pp. 14.

1905
Brown, Clarence. "New Boom In Black Beauty Pageant Queens." Jet. Vol. 42, August 17, 1972, pp. 20-24.

1906
"Brown Beauty With Courage." Ebony. Vol. 21, October, 1966, pp. 102, 104-5.

1907
"Campus Queens." Ebony. Vol. 30, April, 1975, pp. 78-80, 82, 84-86.

1908
"Date Foul-up Leaves Contest Without Winner in Atlanta." Jet. Vol. 49, February 19, 1976, pp. 24.

1909
"Daughter of Preacher Says God Helped Her Win Teen-age Pageant." Jet. Vol. 40, August 19, 1971, pp. 12.

1910
Davis, Dorothy. "Positively Black Is The Word For Miss Black America." Encore. Vol. 7, September 18, 1978, pp. 34-36.

1911
"A Dream Becomes A Rose." Sepia. Vol. 13, May, 1964, pp. 13-16.

1912
"1st Black Beauty Chosen 'Miss Henry Ford College'." Jet. Vol. 39, February 11, 1971, pp. 31.

1913
"First Black Cherry Blossom Princess." Ebony. Vol. 25, July, 1970, pp. 104-107.

1914
"First Black Finalist In Alabama Beauty Pageant." Jet. Vol. 40, June 3, 1971, pp. 26.

1915
"First Negro Beauty Queen to See Paris." Jet. Vol. 6, October 28, 1954, pp. 26-27.

1916
"Fraternity Queens." Jet. Vol. 5, February 4, 1954, pp. 26-29.

1917
"Glamor At Fisk." Headlines. Vol. 1, December, 1944, pp. 27.

1918
"Hal Jackson Productions Sues 'Other' Miss Black Teenage America Group." Jet. Vol. 41, October 7, 1971, pp. 57.

1919
"Kentucky Beauty Queen Wins On Her Second Try." Jet. Vol. 44, August 9, 1973, pp. 17.

1920
Kisner, Ronald E. "Miss Indiana Makes Bid for Miss America." Jet. Vol. 40, September 9, 1971, pp. 58-61.

1921
"Miss Black America Title Goes To Florida." Jet. Vol. 40, September 16, 1971, pp. 52.

1922
"Miss Black Chicago." Jet. Vol. 40, August 26, 1971, pp. 61.

1923
"Miss Festival: Tan Toast of France." Ebony. Vol. 15, August, 1960, pp. 93-95.

1924
"Miss Fine Brown Frame." Ebony. Vol. 2, May, 1947, pp. 47-50.

1925
"Miss Indiana." Jet. Vol. 40, July 15, 1971, pp. 33.

1926
"Miss Soul Princess Wins Scholarship, Cash, Prizes." Jet. Vol. 40, July 15, 1971, pp. 28.

1927
"Miss St. Augustine." Norfolk Journal And Guide. 9 April, 1927, pp. 11.

1928
"Miss Universe Contestant." Ebony. Vol. 15, September, 1960, pp. 118-122.

1929
"Miss Victory." Headlines. Vol. 1, August, 1944, pp. 15.

1930
"Miss Wyoming: Proud Black Beauty Queen." Jet. Vol. 46, June 6, 1974, pp. 46-47.

1931
"Negro Coed Queen at Norte Dame U." Jet. Vol. 4, November 5, 1953, pp. 15.

1932
"New Teen-Age Queen Plans for Career In Psychology." Jet. Vol. 44, August 16, 1973, pp. 64.

1933
"1954: Banner Year for Beauty Queens." Jet. Vol. 7, December 23, 1954, pp. 10-14.

1934
"1977 Black College Queens: Beauty, Brains, Versatility." Ebony. Vol. 32, April, 1977, pp. 146-148, 150, 152-153.

1935
"Replaces White Queen." Jet. Vol. 44, April 5, 1973, pp. 25.

1936
"Talented Queen." Jet. Vol. 42, July 20, 1972, pp. 40.

1937
"Teen Beauty Queen." Jet. Vol. 46, August 29, 1974, pp. 44.

1938
Thompson, Cordell S. "Miss Black America Hits Jackpot." Jet. Vol. 38, September 17, 1970, pp. 48-51.

1939
"The Truth About Beauty Contests." Jet. Vol. 3, February 26, 1953, pp. 26-31.

1940
"What Happens to Beauty Queens?" Jet. Vol. 1, March 20, 1952, pp. 32-39.

1941
Williams, Saundra. "Face To Face With Miss Black America." Seventeen. Vol. 28, March, 1969, pp. 151.

1942
"Winsome Miss Wilberforce." Headlines. Vol. 1, December, 1944, pp. 26.

Fashions

1943
Bonaparte, Anna M. Wilkie. "A Guide to Good Grooming And Clothing For Negro High School Girls." Master's Thesis, Hampton Institute, 1951, 85p.

1944
Bruton, Mozelle Cornelia. "A Study of Clothing Expenditures of Eighth and Ninth Grade Girls, A. L. Lewis Junior High School, Jacksonville, Florida." Master's Thesis, Hampton Institute, 1948, 69p.

1945
Coleman, Jettie Laura. "Selected Factors Which Influence The Purchasing of Clothes By Groups of Housewives and Profess-

ional Women." Master's Thesis, Prairie View A & M College, 1950, 54p.

1946
Dawkins, Irma Handy. "Educational Needs Having Implications For The Home Economics Program. X. In The Area of Clothing of Eight and Ninth Grade Negro Girls, Lincoln Parish, Louisiana." Master's Thesis, Iowa State College, 1944, 119p.

1947
"Do Negro Women Overdress?" Jet. Vol. 6, June 24, 1954, pp. 40-42.

1948
"Ebony Fashion Fair Answers What's Going On?" Jet. Vol. 40, September 16, 1971, pp. 40-41.

1949
"Ebony Fashion Fair Breaks Attendance Records In Cross-Country Swing." Jet. Vol. 41, October 21, 1971, pp. 40-42.

1950
"Ebony Fashion Fair Draws Record Throng To New York Dates." Jet. Vol. 47, October 24, 1974, pp. 16-18.

1951
"Ebony Fashion Fair Honored In Hour-Long NBC Telecase In Chicago." Jet. Vol. 47, September 26, 1974, pp. 56-58.

1952
"Ebony Fashion Fair Launches 78-City Tour For "Big Whirl'." Jet. Vol. 47, October 3, 1974, pp. 12-14.

1953
"Ebony Fashion Fair Lures Record 9,700 To Chicago Shows." Jet. Vol. 47, November 28, 1974, pp. 12-15.

1954
"Ebony Fashion Fair Makes Debut Before A Capacity Crowd." Jet. Vol. 41, September 30, 1971, pp. 51-54.

1955
"Ebony Fashion Fair Scores As Peek-A-Boo Delight In Los Angeles." Jet. Vol. 56, April 26, 1979, pp. 13-16.

1956
"Fashions By L'Tanya." Ebony. Vol. 2, August, 1947, pp. 24-27.

1957
"Fashion's Flower Child." Ebony. Vol. 23, March, 1968, pp. 56-58.

1958
"Girl Is Prize Winner, As Costume Designer." New York Age. 1 April, 1922, pp. 1, 5.

1959
Kelly, June. "Moriah Graham: Fashion Illustrator." *Encore*. Vol. 4, April 7, 1975, pp. 26.

1960
Lazard, Lydia Beecher. "Becomingness of Textile Colors For Seven Typical Pigmentations Found In Selected Groups of Negro Women." Master's Thesis, Tuskegee Institute, 1949, 37p.

1961.
"Mike Douglas Television Show To Present Fashion Fair." *Jet*. Vol. 47, November 14, 1974, pp. 44-46.

1962
"Paris Model Has Dazzling Wardrobe." *Jet*. Vol. 1, December 6, 1951, pp. 40-41.

1963
Peanort, Erline Keene. "A Study of The Clothing Needs and Interests of 275 Sixth and Seventh Grade Girls In Portsmouth, Virginia." Master's Thesis, Hampton Institute, 1952, 56p.

1964
Rodgers, Evelyn. "New Fashions for Afro-American Women." *Liberator*. Vol. 6, August, 1966, pp. 12-13.

1965
Sims, Naomi. "A Gift Truly Liberating." *Encore*. Vol. 4, June 23/July 4, 1975, pp. 56-58.

1966
Watson, Eunice Neal. "A Study of The Clothing Program of High School Girls in Greene County, Georgia." Master's Thesis, Hampton Institute, 1950, 68p.

1967
Weaver, Charlotte Ann. "A Study of Motivations in Clothing Selection And Expenditure In A Selected Group of Negro Women." Master's Thesis, Howard University, 1970, 20p.

Health

1968
Aging Black Women: Selected Readings For The National Caucus on The Black Aged. Washington: College and University Press, 1975, 449p.

1969
Allen, Chaney. *I'm Black And I'm Sober*. Minneapolis: CompCare Publications, 1978, 279p.

1970
Barnes, Kiser D. "Women Continue Health Tradition." *Afro American Magazine*. November 25, 1972, pp. 7-8, 11.

1971
Barr, Lillie Mae. "A Study of Seventy Venerally Infected Women Patients Served by The Rapid Treatment Center, Gallinger Hospital, Washington, D. C.: Master's Thesis, Atlanta University, 1948, 48p.

1972
Bartholomew, R. A. "Syphilis As A Complication of Pregnancy In The Negro." American Medical Association Journal. Vol. 83, July, 1924, pp. 172-174.

1973
Benton, Lucille Katherine. "A Study of The Dietary Habits of Eighth Grade Home Economics Girls at Lincoln Park Academy, Fort Pierce, Florida. "Master's Thesis, Hampton Institute, 1952, 66p.

1974
"Black Named President of Health Organization" Jet. Vol. 44, September 6, 1973, pp. 57.

1975
Bouleware, T. M. "A Negro Demonstration Center for Maternal and Newborn Care in Alabama." National Negro Health News. Vol. 12, April/June, 1944, pp. 1.

1976
Bradley, Fanette Susan. "A Study of Fifteen Gynecological Patients at Grady Hospital, Atlanta, Georgia, During 1946-1947. "Master's Thesis, Atlanta University, 1947, 33p.

1977
"Cancer High Among Black Women; Linked To Alcohol." Jet. Vol. 55, November 9, 1978, pp. 54.

1978
"The Care of Women and Children," in The Health of Slaves On Southern Plantations, by William Dosite Postell. Gloucester, Massachusetts: Peter Smith, 1970, 231p., pp. 111-128.

1979
Clarke, Lillian Brosier. "The Breakfast-Eating Habits of 87 Eighth Grade Girls Enrolled in Homemaking in the George P. Phenix School." Master's Thesis, Hampton Institute, 1950, 64p.

1980
Clarke, Mildred I. "Cancer and The Black Woman." Essence. Vol. 3, October, 1972, pp. 12.

1981
Coleman, Josephine Gordie. "The Emotional and Interpersonal Relationship Problems of Women Diagnosed With Toxemia of Pregnancy During Hospitalization." Master's Thesis, Atlanta University, 1960, 44p.

1982
Dickens, Helen O. "New Hope For Women In The Fight Against Cancer." *New Lady*. Vol. 4, May, 1971, pp. 29, 33-34.

1983
"Diet Craze Among Black Women May Be Slow Death." *Jet*. Vol. 49, February 19, 1976, pp. 45.

1984
Drayton, Mary Hunter. "A Study of The Cumulative Records and Food Habits of Seventh Grade Girls." Master's Thesis, Virginia State College, 1951, 44p.

1985
Dunston, Beverly N. "Pica, Hemoglobin, and Pre-Maturity And Perinatal Mortality: An Experimental Investigation of The Relationships Between Pica, Hemoglobin Levels, and Pre-Maturity And Perinatal Mortality Among A Clinic Population of Married Negro Pregnant Women." Doctoral Dissertation, New York University, 1961, 196p.

1986
Evans, Virgie A. "Problems Presented By Syphilitic Expectant Mothers Known to Provident Hospital In 1946." Master's Thesis, Howard University, 1947, 50p.

1987
Frankel, Barbara. *Childbirth In The Ghetto: Folk Beliefs of Negro Women In A North Philadelphia Hospital Ward*. Palo Alto, California: R & E Research Associates, 1977, 124p.

1988
Gayles, J. N., Jr. "Health Brutality and The Black Life Cycle." *Black Scholar*. Vol. 5, May, 1974, pp. 2-9.

1989
Greene, E. H. "Observations of 500 Laparotomies in Negro Women." *Southern Medical Journal*. Vol. 28, December, 1935, pp. 1147-1150.

1990
Greenlee, Claudia. "Why Women Behave As They Do." *The Negro*. Vol. 3, September, 1945, pp. 4-5.

1991
Grier, Marian E. "Hair Care For The Black Patient." *American Journal of Nursing*. Vol. 76, November, 1976, pp. 1781.

1992
Harper, Laura Jane. "Dietary Practices of Three Samples of Women: A Longitudinal and Cross-Sectional Study." Doctoral Dissertation, Michigan State University, 1956, 144p.

1993
Henderson, Callie Margaret James. "A Study of The Relationship

Between Self Esteem and the Month Prenatal Care Was Initiated In a Group of Low Socio-Economic Pregnant Mothers." Master's Thesis, California State University, 1972, 78p.

1994
Henton, Comradge L. "The Effect of Socio-Economic and Emotional Factors on the Onset of Menarche Among Negro and White Girls." Journal of Genetic Psychology. Vol. 98, June, 1961, pp. 255-264.

1995
Hess, Alfred F. and Lester J. Unger. "Diet of the Negro Mother in New York City." Journal of the American Medical Association. Vol. 70, March 30, 1918, pp. 900-902.

1996
Hough, Clara. "Case Studies of Thirteen Negro Girls Infected With The Puerile Type of Tuberculosis." Master's Thesis, University of Cincinnati, 1939, 115p.

1997
Hudson, Sara Thompson. "Dietary Habits of 100 Pregnant Negro Women, Macon County, Alabama, 1946-1947." Master's Thesis, Tuskegee Institute, 1947, 85p.

1998
Huenman, Ruth. "Nutrition of Mother and Young Child." Service. Vol. 10, May, 1946, pp. 13-14.

1999
Johnson, Georgia A. "The Black Female: Her Image and Choice of Medical Care," in Perspectives on Afro American Women, edited by Willa D. Johnson and Thomas L. Green. Washington, D. C.: Educational Community Counselors Associates, Inc., 1975, 197p., pp. 54-60.

2000
Johnson, Joseph T. On Some of The Apparent Peculiarities Of Parturition in The Negro Race, With Remarks On Race Pelves In General. New York: W. Wood, 1875, 36p.

2001
Kaul, Lalita, Donna B. Standard, Mamidanna S. Rao and Diosdado E. Ulep. "Management of Obesity in Black Females In A Community Model Clinic: A Preliminary Study." Journal of The National Medical Association. Vol. 71, #1, 1979, pp. 81-83.

2002
Lewis, Beulah Ables. "A Case Study of Tuberculosis Mortality Among Negro Women, 1933-1935." Master's Thesis, Atlanta University, 1937, 60p.

2003
Linder, Charlotte Bernice. "A Study of Thirty-five Negro Girls Under Treatment For Veneral Disease Infection in Grady Hospital and The Atlanta Health Center, #1, Atlanta, Georgia,

From December, 1945 Through January, 1946." Master's Thesis, Atlanta University, 1946, 32p.

2004
Lobel, Suzanne. "Another Black Disease: 'Sle' - A Type of Arthritis Whose Victims Are Mostly Black Women." Essence. Vol. 4, September, 1973, pp. 50-51.

2005
Major, Benjamin. "A Woman Has A Choice." New Lady. Vol. 2, November, 1969, pp. 41, 57.

2006
"Maternity Hospital Plans Forming." Norfolk Journal And Guide. 29 September, 1923, pp. 1.

2007
McCray, Ernestine H. "An Evaluation of Outcomes of Pregnancy of Women With Low Income Who Received Nutrition Counseling." Master's Thesis, Howard University, 1974, 194p.

2008
Meyers, Linda Dee. "Definition, Prevalence, and Correlates of Iron Deficiency Anemia in Black and White American Women - An Epidemiologic Analysis." Doctoral Dissertation, Cornell University, 1978, 243p.

2010
Milholland, John E. (Mrs.). "Talks About Women." The Crisis. Vol. 1, March, 1911, pp. 29.

2011
Miller, Ruth Patsy. "A Study of Thirty-six Non-Follow Up Negro Mothers in Postpartum Clinic, Grady Hospital, Atlanta, Georgia." Master's Thesis, Atlanta University, 1947, 29p

2012
Minor, Carrye Mae Hall. "A Dietary Survey of the Home Economics Girls of Douglas High School As A Basis for Establishing A Functional and Educative Lunch Program." Master's Thesis, Hampton Institute, 1951, 122p.

2013
Mitchell, Gwendoline Stephenson. "A Cross-Cultural Assessment of the Food Habits and Life Styles of Urban Black Female Adolescent." Doctoral Dissertation, Howard University, 1979.

2014
Moraghan, Loretta C. "A Study of the Household Contracts of Fifty Negro Mothers With Active Pulmonary Tuberculosis." Master's Thesis, The Catholic University of America, 1939.

2015
"Negro Mothers' and Babies' Mortality Rates." Social Service Review. Vol. 15, June, 1941, pp. 343-346.

2016
New York Association for Improving the Condition of The Poor. Health Work For Mothers and Children In A Colored Community; Including A Study of Veneral Disease As A Prenatal Problem. New York: New York Association for Improving the Condition of the Poor, 1924, 15p.

2017
"The Physique of Negro Women." Opportunity. Vol. 1, May, 1923, pp. 22.

2018
"Pill Hypertension Risk Less For Black Women." Jet. Vol. 56, June 14, 1979, pp. 27.

2019
Powell, Ellen Grett. "A Study of The Dietary Habits of One Hundred Girls of the Sam Houston High School, Huntsville, Texas." Master's Thesis, Hampton Institute, 1951, 64p.

2020
Rochat, R. W. "Pap Smear Screening: Has It Lowered Cervical Cancer Mortality Among Black Americans?" Phylon. Vol. 38, December, 1977, pp. 429-447.

2021
Rollins, Carl G. "Danger Zone: Fallopian Tubes." Essence. Vol. 1, August, 1970, pp. 58.

2022
Roman, Charles V. "The Negro Woman and The Health Problem." Journal of The National Medical Association. Vol. 7, July/September, 1915, pp. 182.

2023
Saunders, Vincent E., Jr. "A Memo to Negro Women: Uterine Cancer Can Be Reduced." The Negro Digest. Vol. 10, August, 1961, pp. 25-30.

2024
"A Simple Test For Breast Cancer." Ebony. Vol. 30, April, 1975, pp. 64-65.

2025
Simpson, Clay Eddie, Jr. "Comparison of Pregnancy Outcome Related to Prenatal Care Between Private and Service Negro Patients in Oklahoma County." Doctoral Dissertation, The University of Oklahoma, 1968, 59p.

2026
Sims, Naomi. All About Health And Beauty For The Black Woman. New York: Doubleday, 1976, 296p.

2027
Slesinger, Doris Peyser. "The Utilization of Preventive Medical Services By Urban Black Mothers: A Sociocultural

Approach." Doctoral Dissertation. University of Wisconsin, 1973, 218p.

2028
Smith, Odette K. "A Study of The Food Habits of A Selected Group of Black Women Students at Howard University." Master's Thesis, Howard University, 1973, 149p.

2029
"Southern Black Women's Milk Has High DDT Level." Jet. Vol. 50, May 6, 1976, pp. 9.

2030
Spires, Ruth Andrews. "A Study of The Dietary Practices of Twenty-one Adolescent Girls in The Jackson County Training School." Master's Thesis, Hampton Institute, 1952, 66p.

2031
Stone, I. S. "Ovarine Tumor In A Mulatto." Washington Medical Annals. Vol. 17, July, 1918, pp. 253.

2032
Tandy, Elizabeth C. "Infant and Maternal Mortality Among Negroes." National Negro Health News. Vol. 7, April/June, 1939, pp. 19-21.

2033
Tisdale, James E. "Black Women and Drugs." A Losing Combination." Essence. Vol. 1, September, 1970, pp. 54-57.

2034
"Warning To Black Women." Encore. Vol. 8, April 2, 1979, pp. 5-6.

2035
Watkins, Elizabeth L. "The Decision of Negro Mothers To Seek Prenatal Care." Doctoral Dissertation, Harvard University, 1966.

2036
__________. "Low Income Negro Mothers - Their Decision to Seek Prenatal Care." American Journal of Public Health. Vol. 58, April, 1968, pp. 655-776.

2037
Wright, Bettie Ann. "A Study of Selected Factors Related to Prenatal Nutrition Counseling of Black Women." Master's Thesis, Howard University, 1971, 91p.

HISTORY

2038
Abrams, Josephine Scott. "The Treatment of Negro Women During Slavery." Master's Thesis, Y. M. C. A. Graduate School, 1936.

2039
"Antislavery Labors - Sojourner Truth," in Black Protest: Issues and Tactics, by Robert D. Dirk. Connecticut: Greenwood Press, 1974, 338p., pp. 223-227.

2040
Aptheker, Herbert. "The Negro Woman." Masses and Mainstream. Vol. 2, February, 1949, pp. 10-17.

2041
Astrachan, Anthony. "The Black Woman As A Slave." Encore. Vol. 4, June 23/July 4, 1975, pp. 34-35.

2042
Beal, Frances M. "Slave of a Slave No More: Black Women In Struggle." Black Scholar. Vol. 6, March, 1975, pp. 2-10.

2043
Bennett, Lerone. "The Negro Woman." Ebony. Vol. 15, August, 1963, pp. 38-46.

2044
__________. "No Crystal Stair: The Black Woman In History." Ebony. Vol. 32, August, 1977, pp. 164-165, 167-168, 170.

2045
"Black Bondage - White Pedestal," in A History of Women In America, by Carol Hymowitz and Michaele Weissman. New York: Bantam Books, 1978, 400p., pp. 40-63.

2046
"Black Heroine Fredom Fighters In The Civil War," in Black Women Makers of History: A Portrait, by George F. Jackson. Sacramento: Fong & Fong, 1977, 289p., pp. 65-76.

2047
"Black Heroine Freedom Fighters of Bygone Years, in Black Women Makers of History: A Portrait, by George F. Jackson. Sacramento: Fong & Fong, 1977, 289p., pp. 7-64.

2048
"Black Heroine Freedom Fighters Of The Twentieth Century," in Black Women Makers of History: A Portrait, by George F. Jackson. Sacramento: Fong & Fong, 1977, 289p., pp. 105-152.

2049
"The Black Revolution," in A Pictorial History of Women In America, by Ruth Warren. New York: Crown Publishers, 1975, 228p., pp. 196-202.

2050
"Black Women," in Founding Mothers: Women of America In The Revolutionary Era, by Linda Grant De Pauw. Boston: Houghton Mifflin, 1975, 228p., pp. 70-98.

2051
"Black Women In Colonial America," in We Were There: The Story of Working Women in America, by Barbara Mayer Wertheimer. New York: Pantheon Books, 1977, 427p., pp. 26-37.

2052
"Black Women Pioneers in California and Nebraska," in Black Women Makers of History: A Portrait, by Geroge F. Jackson. Sacramento: Fong & Fong, 1977, 289p., pp. 77-104.

2053
Bovoso, Carole. "Discovering My Foremothers." Ms. Vol. 6, September, 1977, pp. 56-59.

2054
A Century of Progress Of Negro Women. An Address Delivered Before the Chicago Women's Federation, June 30, 1933. New Orleans, Dillard University, Amistad Research Center.

2055
Clarke, John Henrik. "The Black Woman: A Figure In World History." Essence. Vol. 2, May, 1971, pp. 26-29; June, 1971, pp. 36-39; July, 1971, pp. 42-44.

2056
"The Colored Woman of To-Day," in Progress Of A Race Or The Remarkable Advancement of The Afro-American, by H. F. Kletzing and W. H. Crogman. New York: Negro University Press, 1897, 664p., pp. 191-228.

2057
Coombs, Orde. "The Black Woman Finds Her Roots." Redbook. Vol. 149, October, 1977, pp. 56, 60, 62, 67.

2058
Crawford, Margo. "Diamond in Dirt Theory of Slavery, Seasoning

The Female Slave," in Perspectives On Afro American Women, edited by Willa D. Johnson and Thomas L. Green. Washington, D. C.: Educational Community Counselors, Inc., 1975, 197p., pp. 22-33.

2059
Crowder, Ralph L. "Black Women: A Neglected Dimension in History." The Black Collegian. Vol. 9, May/June, 1979, pp. 103-109.

2060
Dannett, Sylvia G. L. Profiles of Negro Womanhood. Vol. 1, 1619-1900. New York: Educational Heritage, Inc., 1966, 352p.

Dannett, Sylvia G. L. Profiles of Negro Womanhood. Vol. 2, 20th Century. New York: Educational Heritage, Inc., 1966, 352p.

2061
Davis, Angela. "Reflections On The Black Woman's Role In The Community of Slaves." Black Scholar. Vol. 3, December, 1971, pp. 2-15.

Davis, Angela. "Reflections On The Black Woman's Role In The Community of Slaves." The Massachusetts Review. Vol. 13, Winter/Spring, 1972, pp. 80-100.

2062
Dean, Deola Edith. "The Ante-Bellum Slave Woman, 1830-1865: A General Survey. Master's Thesis, Atlanta University, 1975, 45p.

2063
Diggs, Irene. "DuBois and Women: A Short Story of Black Women 1910-1932." A Current Bibliography On African Affairs. Vol. 7, Summer, 1974, pp. 260-303.

2064
Distaff To History. Philadelphia: Joseph V. Baker Associates, n.d., 26p.

2065
Douglas, Emily. Remember The Ladies; The Story of Great Women Who Helped Shape America. New York: Putnam, 1966, 254p.

2066
Fleming, John E. "Slavery, Civil War and Reconstruction: A Study of Black Women in Microcosm." The Negro History Bulletin. Vol. 38, August/September, 1975, pp. 430-433.

2067
"Free At Last," in Beautiful, Also, Are The Souls of My Black Sisters: A History of The Black Woman In America, by Jeanne Noble. New Jersey: Prentice-Hall, 1978, 353p., pp. 50-71.

2068
Furr, Arthur. Democracy's Negroes. Boston: House of Edenboro, 1947, 315p.

2069
Gardner, Mary Elizabeth. The Role of Women In American History, 1789-1860." Master's Thesis, Howard University, 1942, 146p.

2070
Garrett, Romeo B. "Women," in Famous First Facts About Negroes. New York: Arno Press, 1972, 212p., pp. 194-200

2071
"Great Women in Negro History." Sepia. Vol. 7, February, 1959, pp. 70.

2072
Harley, Sharon and Rosalyn Terborg-Penn. The Afro American Woman: Struggles and Images. New York: Kennikat Press, 1978, 137p.

2073
Hines, Miriam Jacqueline. "The Black Woman As Reflected In Selected Afro-American Newspapers and Related Sources, 1875-1895." Master's Thesis, Atlanta University, 1975, 70p.

2074
Hudson, Gossie H. "Women, Too, In American History." The Crisis. Vol. 81, August/September, 1974, pp. 229-231.

2075
Jackson, George F. Black Women Makers of History: A Portrait. Sacramento: Fong & Fong, 1977, 289p.

2076
Jones, Anna H. "A Century's Progress For The American Colored Woman." Voice of The Negro. Vol. 2, September, 1905, pp. 631-633.

2077
Katz, Maude W. "The Negro Woman and The Law." Freedomways. Vol. 2, Summer, 1962, pp. 278-286.

2078
"Letters From Negro Women, 1827-1950." Masses And Mainstream. Vol. 4, February, 1951, pp. 24-33.

2079
Loewenberg, Bert James and Ruth Bogin. "American Negro Women: Four Nineteenth Century Selections." The Sarah Lawrence Journal. Spring, 1969, pp. 27-52.

2080
____________________. Black Women In 19th Century American Life: Their Words, Their Thoughts, Their

Feelings. Pennsylvania: Pennsylvania State University Press, 1976, 520p.

2081
Lutz, Alma. Crusade For Freedom: Women In The Anti-Slavery Movement. Boston: Beacon Press, 1968, 338p.

2082
McDonald, Elsie J. "The Task of Negro Womanhood, 1925." Encore. Vol. 4, June 23/July 4, 1975, pp. 38, 40.

2083
McKenzie, Marjorie. Fifty Years of Progress For Negro Women. Pittsburgh: Courier Publishing Company, 1950.

2084
Moore, Frank. Women of The War: Their Heroism and Self Sacrafice. Hartford, Connecticut: S. S. Scranton & Company, 1866, 596p.

2085
Murphy, Ella Louise. "Women In The Abolition Movement: 1830-1860." Master's Thesis, Howard University, 1935, 83p.

2086
"The Negro Woman in American Life," in Negro Builders and Heroes, by Benjamin Brawley. Chapel Hill: University of North Carolina Press, 1937, 315p.

2087
"Negro Women in Freedom's Battles." Freedomways. Vol. 7, Fall, 1967, pp. 302-315.

2088
"Negro Women's Contribution Enrich American Culture." Los Angeles Sentinel. 31 January, 1963.

2089
"The Negro Response to Brown Martyrdom, 1859 - From The Colored Women of Brooklyn," in A Documentary History of The Negro People In The United States, Vol. 1. edited by Herbert Aptheker. New York: Citadel Press, 1951, 942p., pp. 441-442.

2090
Neverdon-Morton, Cynthia. "The Black Woman's Struggle For Equality In The South, 1895-1925," in The Afro American Woman: Struggles and Images, edited by Sharon Harley and Rosalyn Terborg-Penn. New York: Kennikat Press, 1978, 137p., pp. 43-57.

2091
Newman, Debra L. "Black Women In The Era of The American Revolution In Pennsylvania." Journal of Negro History. Vol. 61, July, 1976, pp. 276-289.

2092
Noble, Jeanne. Beautiful, Also, Are The Souls Of My Black Sisters: A History of The Black Woman In America. New York: Prentice-Hall, 1978, 353p.

2093
__________. "Status of The Black American Woman," in World Encyclopedia of Black Peoples, Vol. 1. Michigan: Scholarly Press, 1975, 317p., pp. 143-158.

2094
Painter, Diann Holland. "The Black Woman In American History," in Women's Lives: Perspectives on Progress and Change, edited by Virginia Lee Lassier and Joyce Jennings Walstedt. Newark: University of Delaware, 1977, 245p., pp. 85-92.

2095
"The Peculiar Institution," in Black Women Makers of History: A Portrait, by George F. Jackson. Sacramento: Fong & Fong, 1977, 289p., pp. 1-6.

2096
"Public Addresses of Negro Women," in The Oratory of Negro Leaders: 1900-1968, by Marcus H. Bouleware. Connecticut: Negro Universities Press, 1969, 312p., pp. 98-113.

2097
Salter, Kwame S. "Black Women: From The Background to The Fore-front." Essence. Vol. 5, March, 1975, pp. 8.

2098
Savage, Rosalind. "Some Aspects of The Life of The Free Afro-American Woman, 1830-1860." Master's Thesis, Atlanta University, 1976, 59p.

2099
"She Who Would Be Free. Resistance. (The Negro Woman In Slavery, in The Civil War and Reconstruction)." Freedomways. Vol. 2, Winter, 1962, pp. 60-70.

2100
Shockley, Ann Allen. "The Negro Woman In Retrospect: Blueprint for The Future." The Negro History Bulletin. Vol. 29, December, 1965, pp. 55-56, 62.

2101
Sillen, Samuel. Women Against Slavery. New York: Masses And Mainstream, 1955, 102p.

2102
Sinclair, Anne. "Studies in Rebellion: Creating The Legend." Essence. Vol. 6, November, 1975, pp. 28, 78.

2103
Sisters of B. C. D. Black Woman's Role In The Revolution. New York: Jihad Productions, 1969, 18p.

2104
"Slave Women," in Women In The American Economy: A Documentary History, 1675-1929," by W. Elliot Brownlee and Mary M. Brownlee. Connecticut: Yale University Press, 1976, 350p., pp. 92-98.

2105
Slavery Illustrated In Its Effects Upon Women And Domestic Society. Boston: Issac Knapp, 1837, 127p.

2106
Smart-Grosnenor, Vertamae. "Why 'Where You From' Has Replaced 'What's Your Sign'; It's About Roots." Mademoiselle. Vol. 83, July, 1977, pp. 96-97, 154.

2107
Spruill, Julia C. Women's Life and Work In The Southern Colonies. Chapel Hill: University of North Carolina Press, 1938, 426p.

2108
Strong, Augusta. "Black Women In Freedom's Battles," in A Freedomways Reader: Afro-Americans In The Seventies, edited by Ernest Kaiser. New York: International Publishers, 1977, 432p., pp. 307-324.

2109
Terborg-Penn, Rosalyn. "Black Male Perspectives On The Nineteenth Century Woman," in The Afro American Woman: Struggles And Images, edited by Sharon Harley and Rosalyn Terborg-Penn. New York: Kennikat Press, 1978, 137p., pp. 28-42.

2110
Terrell, Mary Church. "The Progress of Colored Women." Voice Of The Negro. Vol. 1, July, 1904, pp. 291-294.

2111
"To Be A Slave," in Beautiful, Also, Are The Souls Of My Black Sisters: A History of The Black Woman In America, by Jeanne Noble. New Jersey: Prentice-Hall, 1978, 353p., 31-49.

2112
"The Unbelievable World of Women in Retrospective." Washington Afro American. 29 December, 1973, pp. 8.

2113
Ware, Gilbert. "Sitting In The Driver's Seat." Encore. Vol. 4, June 23/July 4, 1975, pp. 14-15.

2114
Washington, Booker T. (Mrs.). "The Gain In The Life of The Negro Woman." Outlook. January 30, 1904.

2115
Williams, Fannie Barrier. Present Status and Intellectual Progress of Colored Women. Address Before the Congress of Representative Women. Chicago, 1898, 15p.

2116
"Women Activists and The Anti-Slavery Movement," in A Pictorial History of Women In America, by Ruth Warren. New York: Crown Publishers, 1975, 228p., pp. 85-88.

2117
Woodson, Carter G. "Negro Women Eligible To Be Daughters of The American Revolution." The Negro History Bulletin. Vol. 7, November, 1943, pp. 36, 39.

JOURNALISM

The Press

2118
"Afro-American Women in Journalism," in The Afro-American Press And Its Editors, by I. Garland Penn. New York: Arno Press, 1969, 565p., pp. 367-427.

2119
"Black Ventures." Time. Vol. 95, May 4, 1970, pp. 79-80.

2120
"Blames On Playboy Rep. Big Essence Mag. Shakeup." Jet. Vol. 40, May 20, 1971, pp. 52.

2121
"The Brown Lady." The Brown American. Vol. 4, June, 1941, pp. 13-15; July, 1941, pp. 8-10.

2122
"Chicago Paper Names First Woman Managing Editor." Jet. Vol. 47, November 14, 1974, pp. 19.

2123
"Co-ed Editor Seeks To Set Example For White Daily Newspapers." Jet. Vol. 40, August 12, 1971, pp. 41.

2124
Davis, Marguerite Ross. "A Survey and Analysis of The Opportunities for Negro Women In Journalism." Master's Thesis, Kansas State College of Agriculture and Applied Science, 1942, 66p.

2125
"Early History of Negro Women in Journalism. Short Biographies of About 20 Early Negro Women Journalists." The Negro History Bulletin. Vol. 28, Summer, 1965, pp. 178-179, 193.

2126
"1st Black Religious Editor of Kansas City Newspaper." Jet. Vol. 40, July 1, 1971, pp. 19.

2127
"Foreign Correspondent." Headlines. Vol. 1, December, 1944, pp. 24.

2128
"Girls To Have Column In The New York Age." New York Age. 2 April, 1921, pp. 1.

2129
"Ladies of The Press," in Blacks In Communications: Journalism, Public Relations and Advertising, by Meyer L. Stein. New York: Julian Messner, 1972, 191p., pp. 79-96.

2130
"Magazine Called Essence, Aimed at Helping Black Women." National Now Times. Vol. 11, July, 1978, pp. 2.

2131
"Making Waves," in Up From The Footnote: A History of Women Journalists, by Marion Marzolf. New York: Hastings House, 1977, 310p., pp. 90-92.

2132
Minor, Valena S. "Crashing The Fourth Estate." Pulse. Vol. 2, August, 1944, pp. 32-33.

2133
"Nations First Black Woman Press Secretary Appointed." Jet. Vol. 45, November 15, 1973, pp. 28.

2134
"New Magazines for Women," in The Black Press, U. S. A., by Roland E. Wolseley. Ames: Iowa State University Press, 1971, 274p., pp. 129-132.

2135
"Society Editors." Ebony. Vol. 15, March, 1950, pp. 52-56.

2136
Thurman, Sue Bailey. "The Negro Woman In The Magazine Press." The Aframerican Woman's Journal. Vol. 1, Spring, 1940, pp. 7, 26.

2137
"The Press." Encore. Vol. 4, June 23/July 4, 1975, pp. 74.

2138
"Today's Women Journalists," in The Black Press, U. S. A., by Roland E. Wolseley. Ames: Iowa State University Press, 1971, 274p., pp. 204-209.

2139
Washington, Jacqueline. "She Wants To Be A Journalist." Quill.

Vol. 56, November, 1968, pp. 47.

2140
"White House Reporter - Alice Dunnigan." Opportunity. Vol. 26, Spring, 1948, pp. 52, 66-67.

Radio and Television

2141
"American Negro Woman Russian Radio Announcer." Los Angeles Sentinel. 19 April, 1945.

2142
"Blacks vs. the News Media." Encore. Vol. 4, May 19, 1975, pp. 48.

2143
Brandt, Pat. "Edith Huggins: WCAU - TV's First Lady of The News...This Is Her Inside Story." New Lady. Vol. 2, September, 1969, pp. 12-18, 42-45.

2144
"Colored Woman Is First Radio 'Trouble Shooter'." Louisville Defender. 3 April, 1943.

2145
Douglas, Pamela. "An Inside Perspective on The Black Woman TV Executive." Contact. Vol. 5, Spring, 1974, pp. 46.

2146
"Facing Up To Black Women." Essence. Vol. 10, July, 1979, pp. 18.

2147
"Few Black Women Have Managerial Jobs in TV." Jet. Vol. 50, April 22, 1976, pp. 29.

2148
"Frisco Woman Honored For Broadcast Work." Jet. Vol. 49, January 22, 1976, pp. 29.

2149
Hall, Chatwood. "American Negro Woman Now Russian Radio Announcer." Chicago Defender. 14 April, 1945.

2150
Jewell, Karen Sue Warren. "An Analysis of The Visual Development Of A Stereotype: The Media's Portrayal of Mammy and Aunt Jemima As Symbols of Black Womanhood." Doctoral Dissertation, The Ohio State University, 1976, 170p.

2151
"Mrs. Mastermind of TV's Black Tech School." Ebony. Vol. 27, May, 1972, pp. 102-104, 106-107.

2152
"Pretty Face On The Move." Encore. Vol. 8, April 2, 1979, pp. 48.

2153
Ramsey, Alvin. "Through A Glass Whitely: The Television Rape of Miss Jane Pittman." Black World. Vol. 23, August, 1974, pp. 31-36.

2154
Tait, Eric V., Jr. "Women Behind Television." Essence. Vol. 10, June, 1979, pp. 37-38.

2155
"Theresa Merrit Denies 'Black Mama' Image On TV." Jet. Vol. 46, September 19, 1974, pp. 61.

2156
"TV News Hens." Ebony. Vol. 21, October, 1966, pp. 44-46, 50.

2157
"Upsurge In TV News Girls." Ebony. Vol. 26, June, 1971, pp. 168-170, 172, 174-176.

2158
"Woman News Director May Be South's First." Jet. Vol. 43, January 25, 1973, pp. 16.

2159
Wood, Bill. "Black Women in Television News." Essence. Vol. 3, July, 1972, pp. 30-31, 58.

2160
Wright, C. M. "Carol Jenkins Beating The System." Contact. Vol. 5, Fall, 1974, pp. 9-11.

LAW AND LAW ENFORCEMENT

Crime and Delinquency

2161
Aery, William Anthony. "Helping Wayward Girls." The Southern Workman. Vol. 44, November, 1915, pp. 598.

2162
"Black Girl Named in London Sex Scandal." Jet. Vol. 44, June 14, 1973, pp. 33.

2163
"Black Woman Bandit Nabs $2,600 From Chicago Bank." Jet. Vol. 47, December 5, 1974, pp. 13.

2164
Brown, Martha Ivory. "Social Types Among Delinquent Girls In Atlanta." Master's Thesis, Atlanta University, 1949, 47p.

2165
Brown, W. K. "Black Female Gangs In Philadelphia." International Journal of Offender Therapy and Comparative Criminology. Vol. 21, #3, 1977, pp. 221-228.

2166
Clayton, Edward T. "Famous Negro Madames." The Negro Digest. Vol. 9, August, 1951, pp. 27-31.

2167
Diggs, Ellen Irene. "A Study of Fifty Delinquent Negro Girls In The City of Atlanta." Master's Thesis, Atlanta University, 1933.

2168
Duncan, Emily. "Runaway Girls." The Negro. Vol. 4, March, 1946, pp. 57.

2169
Kallstrom, Dale W. "A Study of the Perceptual Organization of Black and White Delinquent and Non-Delinquent Juvenile

Females." Doctoral Dissertattion, University of Florida, 1970, 87p.

2170
"Lady Racketters: New Crime Menance." Ebony. Vol. 6, June, 1952, pp. 46-50.

2171
"Lynched: A Woman." The Crisis. Vol. 4, August, 1912, pp. 196-197.

2172
Morrow, Oneita Burton. "Family Factors In Sex Delinquency of The Negro Girl." Master's Thesis. Northwestern University, 1935, 67p.

2173
Murchison, Carl. "Mental Tests and Other Concomitants of Some Negro Women Criminals." Pedagogical Seminary and Journal of Genetic Psychology. Vol. 33, September, 1926, pp. 527-530.

2174
Thompson, M. Cordell. "Blacks Charge Bias In Police Investigation of Five Murder Cases of Black Women." Jet. Vol. 41, October 28, 1971, pp. 12-14.

2175
Thompson, Era Bell. "Girl Gangs of Harlem." The Negro Digest. Vol. 9, March, 1951, pp. 38-42.

2176
Von Hentig, Hans. "The Criminality of The Colored Woman." Doctoral Dissertation, University of Colorado, 1942.

Von Hentig, Hans. "The Criminality of The Colored Woman." University of Colorado Studies. Vol. 1, May, 1942, pp. 231-260.

Judges and Lawyers

2177
Ainsworth, Marilyn. "Woman in Law." Essence. Vol. 6, August, 1975, pp. 51, 76, 78.

2178
Alpha Kappa Alpha Sorority. Negro Women In The Judiciary. Chicago: AKA Sorority, 1968, 24p.

2179
American Law and The Black Community, Viewed by Black Women Lawyers. Boston: Boston University, Afro American Studies Program, n. d., 70p.

2180
"At The University of Minnesota Law School: A Together Prof." Ebony. Vol. 27, May, 1972, pp. 39-43.

2181
"A Black Woman Civil Rights Lawyer," in The American Woman: Who Was She?" by Anne Firor Scott. New Jersey: Prentice-Hall, 1971, 182p., pp. 32-36.

2182
"Black Woman Is Judge." Miami Herald. 6 January, 1974, pp. 2-A.

2183
"Black Woman Is Named Narcotics Judge in N. Y." Jet. Vol. 46, May 30, 1974, pp. 6.

2184
"Black Woman Judge in Ga. to Continue Juvenile Work." Jet. Vol. 43, February 15, 1973, pp. 14.

2185
"Black Woman Nominated for Appeals Court Judgeship." Jet. Vol. 48, July 24, 1975, pp. 12.

2186
"Carter Takes Black Woman For N. Y. Federal Branch." Jet. Vol. 54, June 1, 1978, pp. 17.

2187
"Clark Grad Is State's First Female Asst. Atty. Gen." Jet. Vol. 47, November 7, 1974, pp. 5.

2188
"Cleveland Woman Becomes Marines' First Woman Judge." Jet. Vol. 44, May 24, 1973, pp. 32.

2189
"Colored Girl Enters Fordham Law School." New York Age. 1 October, 1921, pp. 1.

2190
"Counselor At Large." Our World. Vol. 5, February, 1950, pp. 56-57.

2191
"A Day In The Life of A Media Executive." Black Enterprise. Vol. 5, August, 1974, pp. 29-31.

2192
"Dean Named for Howard Law School." Washington Post. 30 January, 1969.

2193
Feinberg, Lawrence. "D. C. Black Lawyer Named to Judgeship." Washington Post. 5 July, 1975, pp. C-1.

2194
"First Black Woman Gets Louisiana Judge Post." Jet. Vol. 45, February 21, 1974, pp. 9.

2195
"First Colored Girls To Receive Degrees In Law." New York Age. 17 June, 1922, pp. 1.

2196
"First Negro Woman Judge in U. S. A." The Crisis. Vol. 46, September, 1939, pp. 257, 262.

2197
"1st Woman, Black, Named Pres. Student Bar Assn." Jet. Vol. 50, May 27, 1976, pp. 29.

2198
"Howard Grad Becomes First Black Female Navy Lawyer." Jet. Vol. 48, April 10, 1975, pp. 29.

2199
"Howard Law Dean Quits, Raps Nabrit." Washington Post. 28 February, 1969.

2200
Hughes, Joyce A. "The Black Portia." The Crisis, Vol. 82, May, 1975, pp. 167-172.

2201
Jensen, Beverly. "Alexander, Harris, Kennedy, Motley and Murray: Attorneys-at-Law." Black Enterprise. Vol. 8, August, 1977, pp. 19-24.

2202
"Judge Bolin." Opportunity. Vol. 17, August, 1939, pp. 226.

2203
Kulzer, Barbara A. "Invisible Woman" Role Perception in Welfare Litigation." Black Law Journal. Vol. 2, Winter, 1972, pp. 257-281.

2204
"Lady Lawyers." Ebony. Vol. 2, August, 1947, pp. 18-21.

2205
"Lady Lawyers." Jet. Vol. 3, January 22, 1953, pp. 14-18.

2206
"Lawyer Is Truly A Lady: J. Lafontant, U. S. Deputy Solicitor General." Ebony. Vol. 28, April, 1973, pp. 146-149.

2207
Morrison, A. "Top Woman Civil Rights Lawyer." Ebony. Vol. 18, January, 1963, pp. 50-52.

2208
"Negro Woman Named to Philadelphia Law Dept." Jet. Vol. 4, July 30, 1953, pp. 8.

2209
Odom, Karen. "Black And Female In Law." Chicago Defender. 22 March, 1975, pp. 13.

2210
"Only Woman Law Dean Is Howard Graduate." New York Age. 19 August, 1922, pp. 1.

2211
"Philadelphia's Tough Lady Judge." Sepia. Vol. 14, October, 1965, pp. 8-10, 12, 14-15.

2212
Pierce, Ponchita. "The Mission of Marion Wright." Ebony. Vol. 21, June, 1966, pp. 94-97, 102-104, 106-108.

2213
Ramsey, Sephyr M. "Negro Women Lawyers of State of California." California Eagle. 14 September, 1944.

2214
Sampson, Edith. "Legal Profession Followed by Nation's Best Known Socialites." Chicago Defender. 4 May, 1935.

2215
Terrell, Mary C. "Needed Women Lawyers." The Negro Digest. Vol. 1, September, 1943, pp. 57-59.

2216
Voight, Daisy. "To Be A Lawyer." Essence. Vol. 6, December, 1975, pp. 44, 74.

2217
Washington, Michelle. "Constance Baker Motley: Black Woman, Black Judge." Black Law Journal. Vol. 1, Summer, 1971, pp. 172-179.

2218
Whaley, Ruth W. "Women Lawyers, Lot Not Easy." New York Age. 29 October, 1949, pp. 27.

2219
"Widow is First N. Y. Woman Marshall." Norfolk Journal And Guide. 26 December, 1942.

2220
Wiggins, Lillian. "Justics In America and Women Lawyers." Washington Afro American. 12 April, 1975, pp. 7-8.

2221
Williams, Barbara J. "Black Women In Law." Black Law Journal. Vol. 1, Summer, 1971, pp. 171.

2222
"Woman Judge Nominated For County Prosecutor Post." Jet. Vol. 48, September 4, 1975, pp. 25.

2223
"Woman Lawyer Provides Advice to Diggs on Africa." Jet. Vol. 41, January 6, 1972, pp. 22.

2224
"Woman Lawyer to Head U. S. Compensation Board." Jet. Vol. 46, May 2, 1974, pp. 12.

2225
"Women Lawyers to Discuss Current Cases." Washington Afro American. 15 March, 1975, pp. 9.

2226
"Young Negro Attorney May Be First Woman Police Prosecutor In Nation: Appointed to Replace Ted Williams." Cleveland Call & Post. 12 December, 1946.

Law Enforcement

2227
"Black Woman To Head Male Bronx, N. Y. Prison." Jet. Vol. 55, November 23, 1978, pp. 5.

2228
"Black Women Appointed to Legal Posts in Major Cities." Jet. Vol. 47, Feburary 20, 1975, pp. 28.

2229
Brown, Julia Clarice. I Testify: My Years As An Undercover Agent For The F. B. I. Belmont, California: Western Islands Publishing Company, 1966, 296p.

2230
"Chicago's Lady Gangbuster." Our World. Vol. 7, June, 1952, pp. 63-65.

2231
"FBI Recruits First Black Female Special Agent Ever." Jet. Vol. 49, February 26, 1976, pp. 8.

2232
"First Female Guards Work At Ohio State Reformatory." Jet. Vol. 50, July 22, 1976, pp. 54.

2233
"Joan A. Burt First Woman in D. C. Parole Board." Washington Afro American. 6 January, 1976, pp. 1.

2234
"L. A. Woman Named Police Commissioner; First." Jet. Vol. 39, March 11, 1971, pp. 44.

2235
"Lady Bailiff." Ebony. Vol. 2, August, 1947, pp. 48.

2236
"Lady Detective." Ebony. Vol. 4, February, 1949, pp. 46-47.

2237
Mason, B. J. "Warden With A Conscience." Ebony. Vol. 29, September, 1973, pp. 70-72, 74, 76.

2238
"Merritt, Anna, First Negro Woman Federal Probation Officer." Sepia. Vol. 11, April, 1962, pp. 23.

2239
"New York Names Black Woman to Head Female Prison." Jet. Vol. 42, September 21, 1972, pp. 6.

2240
"Routine Job." Jet. Vol. 47, February 27, 1975, pp. 48.

2241
"Two Negro Women First To Serve on Texas Juries." Jet. Vol. 7, December 30, 1954, pp. 9.

2242
"Woman Guard Protests Firing at N. J. Prison." Jet. Vol. 45, March 14, 1974, pp. 29.

Legislation

2243
"Assemblywoman Proposes Bill For Women's Rights." Jet. Vol. 40, April 8, 1971, pp. 8.

2244
Katz, William Loren. "Black/White Fight Against Slavery And For Women's Rights In America." Freedomways. Vol. 16, 4th quarter, 1976, pp. 230-236.

2245
Legislative Review of Concerns of Women Based On The Black Women's Action Plan. Houston, Texas: National Women's Conference, November 18-21, 1977.

2246
Sedwick, Cathy and Reba Williams. "Black Women And The Equal Rights Amendment." Black Scholar. Vol. 7, July/August, 1976, pp. 24-29.

2247
Timberlake, Constance H. "Black Women and The ERA." Encore. Vol. 5, December 20, 1976, pp. 10-11.

2248
Washington, Patricia Lee. "The Black Women's Agenda: An Investigation Into Strategies For Change." Doctoral Dissertation, Arizona State University, 1978, 198p.

Police Women

2249
"Ambassador of Goodwill For Police Department." Ebony. Vol. 19, March, 1964, pp. 40.

2250
"America's Most Glamorous Negro Cop." Jet. Vol. 6, September 2, 1954, pp. 54-55.

2251
"Atlantic City to Have Colored Policewomen." New York Age. 11 March, 1922, pp. 1.

2252
"Birmingham Accepts It's First Black Policewoman." Jet. Vol. 44, September 20, 1973, pp. 21.

2253
"Black D. C. Policewoman First of Her Sex to Be Killed." Jet. Vol. 46, October 10, 1974, pp. 54.

2254
"Black Policewoman, White Officer in Flint Shootout." Jet. Vol. 49, January 15, 1976, pp. 8.

2255
"Chicago Policewoman Retired at 63; Served For 25 Years." Norfolk Journal And Guide. 10 April, 1943.

2256
"Colored Policewomen." Philadelphia Ledger. 12 June, 1922.

2257
"Colored Woman Named to Police Force in Baltimore, Md." Opportunity. Vol. 16, March, 1938, pp. 91.

2258
"First Negro Woman Police Sgt. on Narcotics Council." Jet. Vol. 25, February 20, 1964, pp. 26.

2259
Horton, Joseph. "Black Women in Blue." Sepia. Vol. 21, November, 1972, pp. 56-62.

2260
"Houston (Tex.) Police Force Gets 1st Woman Officer." Jet. Vol. 4, July 30, 1953, pp. 8.

2261
"L. A. Woman Named Police Commissioner; First." Jet. Vol. 39, March 11, 1971, pp. 44.

2262
"Lady Cops; Policewomen Are Gentler, Prettier Arm of Law." Ebony. Vol. 9, September, 1954, pp. 26-28.

2263
"Madeline Fletcher Trial Begins in Flint, Mich." Jet. Vol. 50, June 3, 1976, pp. 53.

2264
"Mrs. Grace Murphy Made Policewoman In Detroit." Chicago

Defender. 7 May, 1921, pp. 1.

2265
"Needs of Policewomen." New York Age. 14 January, 1922, pp. 4.

2266
"Pennsylvania Gets First Black Woman Trooper." Jet. Vol. 44, August 16, 1973, pp. 24.

2267
Perry, Harmon. "Black Is First Woman on Atlanta SWAT Team." Jet. Vol. 50, April 15, 1976, pp. 28-29.

2268
"Sergeant Strange: West Coast's Veteran Negro Policewoman Lives Dangerously and Likes It." Our World. Vol. 8, January, 1953, pp. 29-30.

2269
"Seven or Eight Policewomen in Chicago Gain Equal Status With Men as 65 Policewomen are Integrated With Men Police." Jet. Vol. 20, August 17, 1961, pp. 46-47.

2270
Smith, Alice Ward. "Colored Police Women of Washington." The Southern Workman. Vol. 51, March, 1922, pp. 135-136.

2271
"TV's Tough Lady Cop." Jet. Vol. 47, November 14, 1974, pp. 58-60.

2272
Voight, Daisy. "Ms Policeperson." Essence. Vol. 5, April, 1975, pp. 11.

2273
"Woman Top Grad of New Orleans Police Academy." Jet. Vol. 47, October 9, 1975, pp. 18.

Rehabilitation

2274
Bailey, Lottie Louise. "Negro Women Prisoners In Atlanta, Georgia: A Study of Arrest and Detention In The Municipal Prison, 1937." Master's Thesis, Atlanta University, 1938, 62p.

2275
Blount, George W. "Delaware Industrial School for Negro Girls." The Southern Workman. Vol. 63, January, 1934, pp. 17-20.

2276
Clark, William E. "The Katy Ferguson Home." The Southern Workman. Vol. 52, May, 1923, pp. 228-230.

2277
Clecker, Patricia. "Jive Dope Fiend Whoes: In The Street And In Rehabilitation," in Women in Ritual and Symbolic Roles, edited by Judith Hochsmith and Anita Spring. New York: Plenum Press, 1978, 289p., pp. 269-285.

2278
Davis, J. E. "A Virginia Asset: The Virginia Industrial School for Colored Girls." The Southern Workman. Vol. 49, August, 1920, pp. 357-364.

2279
Ellis, Willielee. "A Study of The Factors Influencing The Recidivism of Twenty Girls at the Barrett School for Girls, Glen Burnie, Maryland, January, 1948 - February, 1951." Master's Thesis, Atlanta University, 1951, 54p.

2280
"For Delinquent Girls." New York Age. 27 May, 1922, pp. 4.

2281
French, Laurence. "The Incarcerated Black Female: The Case of Social Double Jeopardy." Journal of Black Studies. Vol. 8, March, 1978, pp. 321-335.

2282
Haith, M. Edwina. "An Analysis of The Classification Program Utilized In An Institution for Delinquent Girls." Master's Thesis, Howard University, 1952, 64p.

2283
Howard, Gwendolyn. "The Perceptions of Incarcerated Black Mothers And Their Concerns For Their Children: An Exploratory Study With Implications For Schools." Doctoral Dissertation, Atlanta University, 1976, 91p.

2284
"Judge Jean Norris Tells of Experiences With Delinquent Girls In Women's Court." New York Age. 2 May, 1925, pp. 3.

2285
"The Katy Ferguson Home And Its Work For Erring Girls." New York Age. 14 October, 1922, pp. 1.

2286
Kelley, Ruby Mitchell. "An Analysis of the Factors Associated With The Delinquency of Twenty-five Girls Committed to The Georgia Training School for Negro Girls for 1943-1947." Master's Thesis, Atlanta University, 1948, 79p.

2287
Mann, Geraldine H. "The Development and Growth of the Service for Delinquent Girls In The Protective Services Division, Department of Public Welfare, Baltimore, Maryland." Master's Thesis, Howard University, 1950, 66p.

2288
McCleave, Wilma Loree. "A Study of the History and Development of the State Training School for Negro Girls, Kinston, North Carolina." Master's Thesis, Atlanta University, 1948, 19p.

2289
Mondesire, Dorothy Camille. "A Study of the Factors Associated With the Delinquency of 25 Girls Committed to The Kruse School, Marshallton, Delaware, 1943-1947." Master's Thesis, Atlanta University, 1948, 50p.

2290
Moulden, Maxine Charlotte. "A Sociometric Study of The Brooklyn Training School for Girls, Summer of 1948." Master's Thesis, Atlanta University, 1949, 41p.

2291
Norris, Catherine White. "A Consideration of Factors Attributing To Recividism In A Girl's Training School." Master's Thesis, Atlanta University, 1966, 48p.

2292
Perry, Emma Louise. "A Study of The Background of The First Twenty-six Girls Admitted to The State Training School For Negro Girls In North Carolina." Master's Thesis, Atlanta University, 1945, 41p.

2293
"School of Welfare For Colored Girls Is Ready to Open." Norfolk Journal And Guide. 12 September, 1925, pp. 8.

2294
Small, Juanita Josephine. "A Study of The Social Histories Of 32 Negro Women Committed to A State Reformatory for Women for The First Time, September, 1941 - August, 1942." Master's Thesis, Atlanta University, 1943, 36p.

2295
Smith, Stella Mae. "Intense Experiences of Black and White Female Prisoners." Doctoral Dissertation, University of Florida, 1973, 170p.

2296
"The Virginia Industrial School for Wayward Colored Girls." The Southern Workman. Vol. 52, August, 1923, pp. 398-400.

2297
"Virginia's Care of Delinquent Girls." The Southern Workman. Vol. 45, August, 1916, pp. 444.

2298
Watson, Edythe Roberts. "The Concept of Institutional Care In Relation to Personnel Selections At the Maryland Training School for Colored Girls For the Period, 1937-1947." Master's Thesis, Atlanta University, 1948, 38p

LITERATURE

2299
Bannon, B. A. "Authors and Editors; Alice Walker's Books And Beliefs on The Black Woman." Publishers Weekly. Vol. 198, August 31, 1970, pp. 195-197.

2300
Bell, Marilynn Powe. "Using The Black Female Autobiography To Teach Freshman College English." Doctoral Dissertation, University of Michigan, 1977, 100p.

2301
Bell, Rosann Pope. "For Colored Girls Who Have Considered Suicide When The Rainbow Is Enuf." The Black Collegian. Vol. 7, May/June, 1977, pp. 48-49.

2302
Bell, Rosann Pope, Bettye J. Parker and Beverly Sheftall. Sturdy Black Bridges: Visions of Black Women In Literature. New York: Anchor Press, 1979.

2303
Billingslea, Alma Jean. "Feminism In The Works of Gwendolyn Brooks." Master's Thesis, Atlanta University, 1971, 51p.

2304
"Black Women Write." American Libraries. Vol. 5, December, 1974, pp. 607.

2305
Bond, Jean Carey. "For Colored Girls Who Have Considered Suicide..." Freedomways. Vol. 16, 3rd quarter, 1976, pp. 187-191.

2306
Brewton, Butler Emanuel. "Richard Wright's Thematic Treatment of Women In Uncle Tom's Children, Black Boy and Native Son." Doctoral Dissertation, Rutgers University, 1978, 251p.

2307
Brown, Frank L. "Chicago's Great Lady of Poetry." Black World. Vol. 11, December, 1961, pp. 53-57.

2308
Brown, Martha Hursey. "Images of Black Women: Family Roles In Harlem Renaissance Literature." Doctoral Dissertation, Carnegie-Mellon University, 1976, 279p.

2309
Bullock, Penelope Laconia. "The Treatment of The Mulatto In American Fiction From 1826-1902." Master's Thesis, Atlanta University, 1944, 162p.

2310
" 'Caged Bird' May Win National Book Award." Jet. Vol. 39, February 11, 1971, pp. 40.

2311
Campbell, Jo. "American Griot: Actress Brings Afro American Writers To Her Audiences." African Woman. #13, January/ February, 1978, pp. 23.

2312
Chambers, Kenneth L. "Black Men In The Poetry of Gwendolyn Brooks." Master's Thesis, Atlanta University, 1975, 71p.

2313
Childress, Alice. "A Woman Playwright Speaks Her Mind," in Anthology of The American Negro In The Theatre: A Critical Approach, edited by Lindsay Patterson. New York: Publishers Company, 306p., pp. 75-79.

2314
Dance, Daryl. "Black Eve or Madonna? A Study of The Antithetical Views of the Mother in Black American Literature," in Perspectives On Afro American Women, edited by Willa D. Johnson and Thomas L. Green. Washington, D. C.: Educational Community Counselors Associates, Inc., 1975, 197p., pp. 103-111.

2315
Dandridge, Rita B. "The Black Woman As A Freedom Fighter In Langston Hughes' Simple's Uncle Sam." CLA Journal. Vol. 18, December, 1974, pp. 273-283.

2316
Doyle, Mary Ellen (Sister). "The Heroine of Black Novels," in Perspectives On Afro American Women, edited by Willa D. Johnson and Thomas L. Green. Washington, D. C.: Educational Community Counselors Associates, Inc., 1975, 197p., pp. 112-125.

2317
Durden, Frances Collier. "Negro Women In Poetry From Phillis Wheatley to Margaret Walker." Master's Thesis, Atlanta University, 1947, 123p.

2318
Evans, Dorothy C. "The World of The Black Woman: The Poetry Of Gwendolyn Brooks." Master's Thesis, Howard University, 1972, 81p.

2319
Exum, Pat Crutchfield. Keeping The Faith: Writings By Contemporary Black American Women: Connecticut: Fawcett, 1974, 228p.

2320
Fisher, Jerilyn Beth. "The Minority Woman's Voice: A Cultural Study of Black and Chicano Fiction." Doctoral Dissertation, The American University, 1978, 38p.

2321
Fleissner, Robert F. "That Cheek of Night: Toward The Dark Lady." CLA Journal. Vol. 16, March, 1973, pp. 312-323.

2322
Giddings, Paula. "A Special Vision, A Common Goal." Encore. Vol. 4, June 23/July 4, 1975, pp. 44, 46, 48.

2323
Giovanni, Nikki. Night Comes Softly: Anthology of Black Female Voices. Newark: Medic Press, 1970, 97p.

2324
Graham, Beryl Caroline. "Treatment of Black American Women In Children's Encyclopedias." The Negro History Bulletin. Vol. 39, May, 1976, pp. 596-598.

2325
Haki, Justice. "Colored Girls: A New Game For An Old Profession." Blacknews. Vol. 3, March, 1978, pp. 22-23.

2326
Harriott, Frank. "Life Of A Pulitzer Poet." The Negro Digest. Vol. 8, August, 1950, pp. 14-16.

2327
Harris, Carol Ann. "Black Women In Langston Hughes' Poetry And Short Fiction." Master's Thesis, Atlanta University, 1972, 74p.

2328
Hopkins, Pauline E. "Famous Women of The Negro Race: V. Literary Workers." The Colored American Magazine. Vol. 4, April, 1902, pp. 370-371.

2329
Howard, Lillie Pearl. "Zora Neale Hurston: A Non-Revolutionary Black Artist." Doctoral Dissertation, University of Mexico, 1975, 242p.

2330
Ivy, Nadine Marie. "The Invisible Woman: An Examination of

Richard Wright's Treatment of Female Characters In Uncle Tom's Children and Native Son." Master's Thesis, The Ohio State University, 1974, 68p.

2331
Jackson, Jacquelyne. "A Critique of Lerner's Work on Black Women and Further Thoughts." Journal of Social and Behavioral Sciences. Vol. 21, Winter, 1975, pp. 63-89.

2332
James, Annie Deloris. "Images of The Black Woman In Selected Fiction By Black Males." Master's Thesis, The Ohio State University, 1974, 103p.

2333
Johnson,Beulah V. "The Treatment of The Negro Woman As A Major Character In American Novels, 1900-1950." Doctoral Dissertation, New York University, 1955, 556p.

2334
Johnson, Gloria J. "Hurston's Folk: The Critical Significance of Afro American Folk Tradition in Three Novels And The Autobiography." Doctoral Dissertation, University of California at Irvine, 1978.

2335
Kalamyu ya Salaam. "The Sound of Sisters Singing: A Mini-Anthology of Black Women Poets." The Black Collegian. Vol. 9, May/June, 1979, pp. 90-93.

2336
Kane, Patricia and Doris Y. Wilkinson. "Survival Strategies: Black Women in Ollie Miss and Cotton Comes to Harlem." Critique. Vol. 16, #1, 1974, pp. 101-109.

2337
Kent, George E. "The Black Woman In Faulkner's Works, With The Exclusion of Disey." Phylon. Vol. 35, December, 1974, pp. 430-441.

2338
Kidd, Davis. "Black Women In The Poetry of Nikki Giovanni." Master's Thesis, Atlanta University, 1977, 46p.

2339
Mathis, Cynthia Hamilton. "The Concept of Feminine Beauty In Novels By Negroes." Master's Thesis, Fisk University, 1937, 99p.

2340
Miller, Jeanne-Marie A. "Images of Black Women In Plays By Black Playwrights." CLA Journal. Vol. 20, June, 1977, pp. 494-507.

2341
Miller, Katherine Lois. "Lorraine Hansberry and The Drama of Human Affirmation." Master's Thesis, Atlanta University,

1973, 56p.

2342
Molette, Barbara. "They Speak, Who Listens? Black Women Playwrights." Black World. Vol. 25, April, 1976, pp. 28-34.

2343
"The Negro Woman in American Literature. Speeches by Sarah E. Wright, Abbey Lincoln, Alice Childress and Paule Marshall at The Harlem Writers' Guild Writers' Conference At the New School for Social Research, New York City, Spring, 1965." Freedomways. Vol. 6, Winter, 1966, pp. 8-25.

2344
"Poetess Gwendolyn Brooks to Get Schools' First Honorary Doctorate Degree." Jet. Vol. 45, April 29, 1971, pp. 31.

2345
Porter, Dorothy B. "Selected Writings By Negro Women." Women's Education. Vol. 7, December, 1968, pp. 4-5.

2346
Potter, Velma R. "New Politics, New Mothers." CLA Journal. Vol. 16, December, 1972, pp. 247-255.

2347
Powell, Bertie Jefferess. "An Analysis of The Dominant Themes In The Selected Literature By Afro-American Women With Recommendations For Inclusion In The High School Curriculum." Doctoral Dissertation, University of Pittsburgh, 1974, 268p.

2348
"Public Opinion and The Negro Woman As Expressed In Fiction." Tuskegee Messenger. Vol. 9, February, 1933, pp. 3.

2349
Pyne-Timothy, Helen. "Perceptions of the Black Woman in The Works of Claude McKay." CLA Journal. Vol. 19, December, 1975, pp. 152-164.

2350
Royster, Beatrice Horn. "The Ironic Vision of Four Black Women Novelists: A Study of The Novels of Jessie Fauset, Nella Larsen, Zora Neale Hurston, and Ann Petry." Doctoral Dissertation, Emory University, 1975, 219p.

2351
Rushing, Andrea Benton. "Images of Black Women in Afro-American Poetry." Black World. Vol. 24, September, 1975, pp. 18-30.

Rushing, Andrea Benton. "Images of Black Women in Afro-American Poetry," in Afro American Women: Struggles And Images, edited by Sharon Harley and Rosalyn Terborg-Penn. New York: Kennikat Press, 1978, 137p., pp. 74-86.

2352
Sample, Maxine J. Cornish. "The Portrayal of The Black Woman In The Works of Paule Marshall." Master's Thesis, Atlanta University, 1977, 62p.

2353
Shange, Ntozake. For Colored Girls Who Have Considered Suicide, When The Rainbow Is Enuf: A Choreopoem. New York: MacMillan, 1977, 64p.

2354
"She Takes Her Poetry To The People." African Woman. #15, May/June, 1978, pp. 24-25.

2355
Shinn, T. J. "Women In The Novels of Ann Petry." Critique. Vol. 16, #1, 1974, pp. 110-120.

2356
Skeeter, Sharyn J. "Black Women Writers: Levels of Identity." Essence. Vol. 4, May, 1973, pp. 58-59.

2357
Somers, Linda. "The Visual Imagery Predominant In Gwendolyn Brooks As Exemplified In Annie Allen, The Bean Eaters, A Street In Bronzeville, In The Mecca, Family Pictures." Master's Thesis, Atlanta University, 1970, 70p.

2358
"Speak The Truth To The People," in Beautiful, Also, Are The Souls of My Black Sisters: A History of The Black Woman In America, by Jeanne Noble. New Jersey: Prentice-Hall, 1978, 353p., pp. 146-208.

2359
Stone, Carol Anne. "A Study Of The Major Black Women Novelists of The Late 1940's." Master's Thesis, Atlanta University. 1971, 43p.

2360
Sylvander, Carolyn Wedin. "Jessie Redmon Fauset, Black American Writer: Her Relationships, Biographical and Literary, With Black and White Writers, 1910-1935." Doctoral Dissertation, University of Wisconsin, 1976, 374p.

2361
"Teacher Writes Book, Assails White People." Jet. Vol. 38, September 3, 1970, pp. 31.

2362
Thompson, Enola. "Jessie Fauset As Interpreter of Negro Life." Master's Thesis, Drake University, 1939, 75p.

2363
"U. S. Seeks to Burn Black Mistress." Jet. Vol. 2, September 18, 1952, pp. 51.

2364
Walker, Alice. In Love and Trouble: Stories of Black Women. New York: Harcourt, Brace, Javanovich, 1973, 138p.

2365
______. In Search of Our Mother's Gardens: The Creativity of Black Women In The South." Ms. Vol. 2, May, 1974, pp. 64-70.

2366
Ward, Hazel Mae. "The Black Woman As Character: Images In The American Novel, 1852-1953." Doctoral Dissertation, University of Texas at Austin, 1977, 301p.

2367
Washington, Mary Helen. Black Eyed Susans: Classic Stories By And About Black Women. New York: Anchor Books, 1975, 163p.

2368
______. "Black Women Image Makers." Black World. Vol. 23, August, 1974, pp. 10-18.

2369
Wood, Darlene Iva. "The Fictional Writings of Jessie Fauset." Master's Thesis, Atlanta University, 1975, 97p.

2370
"Woman Poet Gets $5,800 Ford Foundation Award." Jet. Vol. 3, April 23, 1953, pp. 37.

2371
"Women on Women." Essence. Vol. 7, May, 1976, pp. 20, 22, 78.

2372
"Writing Schoolmarm." Ebony. Vol. 7, July, 1952, pp. 23-26.

2373
"Yale Poetry Prize Won By Negro Girl." Opportunity. Vol. 20, December, 1942, pp. 372.

MAGAZINES

2374
Aframerican Woman's Journal
Washington, D. C.: National Council of Negro Women
1940-1950

2375
Afro-American Woman Magazine
New York: Afro-American Woman Publishing Company
1969-

2376
Bessie Coleman Aero News
Phoenix, Arizona: Bessie Coleman Aero Clubs
1930-

2377
Black Male/Female Relationships
San Francisco: Black Think Tank, Inc.
1979-

2378
Essence
New York: Hollingsworth Group, Inc.
1971-

2379
Journal of The College Alumnae Club of Washington, D. C.
Washington, D. C.: College Alumnae Club
1925-1950

2380
Journal of The National Association of College Women
Washington, D. C.: National Association of College Women
1924-1948

2381
Mystique
Chicago:
1974-

2382
National News Bulletin
National Association of Colored Graduate Nurses
1928-

2383
National Notes
Chicago: National Association of Colored Women
1927-1966

2384
The Negro Woman's World
Washington, D. C.:
1934-1936

2385
New Lady
Hayward, California: Mecco Enterprises, Inc.
1966-

2386
The Woman's National Magazine
Chicago:
1936-1941

2387
The X-Ray
Washington, D. C.: Zeta Phi Beta Sorority
1928-

2388
Southern Woman's Magazine
Nashville, Tennessee:
1916-

2389
Women United
Washington, D. C.: National Council of Negro Women

2390
The Women's Voice (Newspaper)
Washington, D. C.:
1939-

2391
The Worker
Washington, D. C.: National Training School for Women and Girls
1915-

MEDICINE, NURSING, AND RELATED AREAS

Dentistry

2392
Alpha Kappa Alpha Sorority. Women In Dentistry. Chicago: AKA Sorority, 1972, 27p.

2393
"Army's First Female Dental Intern Completes Studies." Jet. Vol. 47, October 3, 1974, pp. 18.

2394
"Black Women In Dentistry." Bulletin of The Lincoln Dental Society. Vol. 28, #4, 1972, pp. 32.

2395
"Dental Dean." Ebony. Vol. 28, March, 1973, pp. 84-86, 88.

2396
"Howard's First Lady of Dentistry." Ebony. Vol. 23, April, 1968, pp. 103-104, 106-108.

2397
"New Howard Dean Stresses Comprehensive Dental Plan." Jet. Vol. 49, November 20, 1975, pp. 24.

2398
U. S. Department of Labor, Women's Bureau. "Negro Women," in The Outlook for Women In Occupations In Medical and Other Health Services: Women Dentists. Bulletin #203, #9. Washington, D. C.: G. P. O., 1945, 21p., pp. 9.

2399
West, Charles H. "Negroes In Dentistry - An Outline: Negro Women In Dentistry." The Meharry-Dent. Vol. 15, January, 1957, pp. 13-15.

Hospital Workers

2400
"Black Woman To Head N. Y. Hospital." Jet. Vol. 39, March 11, 1971, pp. 46.

2401
"Career Women Gets High N. Y. Hospital Post." Jet. Vol. 2, August 14, 1952, pp. 24.

2402
"First Black Woman Heads Major Teaching Hospital." Jet. Vol. 42, August 24, 1972, pp. 17.

2403
Sheridan, Wanda. "Women On The Move." The Auricle. Vol. 26, #1, 1977, pp. 4-6.

Medicine

2404
Alexander, Leslie L. "Susan Smith McKinney, M. D., 1847-1918: First Afro-American Woman Physician In New York State." Journal of The National Medical Association. Vol. 67, March, 1975, pp. 173.

2405
Alpha Kappa Alpha Sorority. Women In Medicine. Chicago: AKA Sorority, 1971, 32p.

2406
Anderson, Monroe. "Doctor to Teen-Agers." Ebony. Vol. 28, December, 1972, pp. 47-48, 50, 54, 56, 58.

2407
"Arkansas School Graduates First Negro Doctor." Jet. Vol. 2, June 5, 1952,pp. 61.

2408
"Black Female Medics - Dr. Jacqueline Coates Howell." Black Excellence. Vol. 2, December, 1978/January-February, 1979, pp. 16.

2409
Bolden, Hilda M. "The Negro Woman In Medicine." The Woman's National Magazine. Vol. 8, February, 1941, pp. 8, 14, 16.

2410
Brown, Sara W. "Colored Women Physicians." The Southern Workman. Vol. 52, December, 1923, pp. 580-593.

2411
"Can A Colored Woman Be A Physician?" The Crisis. Vol. 40, February, 1933, pp. 33-34.

2412
Davis, George. "A Healing Hand In Harlem." New York Times Magazine. April 22, 1979, pp. 40-42, 44, 50, 54, 56.

2413
"Discovery In Medical Science By A Negro Girl." American Missionary Magazine. Vol. 76, June, 1922, pp. 76.

2414
"Dorothy Boulding Ferebee, M. D., 1898-." Journal of The National Medical Association. Vol. 62, March, 1970, pp. 177.

2415
"Dr. Rebecca Lee, First Negro Woman Medical Graduate." Bulletin of The Medico-Chirurgical Society of The District of Columbia. Vol. 6, January, 1949, pp. 3.

2416
DuBois, W. E. B. "The Woman's Medical College." The Crisis. Vol. 26, August, 1923, pp. 154.

2417
"E. Mae McCarroll, A. B., M. D., M. S. P. H., 1898-: First Lady of The NMA." Journal of the National Medical Association. Vol. 65, November, 1973, pp. 544-545.

2418
Edwards, Lena Frances and Sister Anthony Scally. "Dr. Lena Edwards: People Lover." The Negro History Bulletin. Vol. 39, May, 1976, pp. 592-595.

2419
"First 2 Negro Girls Enter Texas U. Med School." Jet. Vol. 6, September 9, 1954, pp. 13.

2420
Foye, A. Frances. "Medical Training of Women." The Howard Alumnus. Vol. 5, January, 1927, pp. 83-84, 99.

2421
"Glamour Chases Germs." Headlines And Pictures. Vol. 2, May, 1946, pp. 36-37.

2422
"Ky. Medical School Admits 1st Negro Woman." Jet. Vol. 4, September 24, 1953, pp. 21.

2423
"Lady Doctor to Migrant Workers." Ebony. Vol. 17, February, 1962, pp. 59-60, 62, 64, 66, 68.

2424
"Lady Heart Specialist." Sepia. Vol. 13, July, 1964, pp. 14-18.

2425
"Med School Mom." Ebony. Vol. 27, September, 1972, pp. 40-42, 44, 46, 48.

2426
"Medical," in Black Women Makers of History: A Portrait, by George F. Jackson. Sacramento: Fong & Fong, 1977, 289p., pp. 269-271.

2427
"Medico-Chi Vice Presicent - 1948." Bulletin of The Medico-Chirurgical Society of The District of Columbia. Vol. 5, February, 1948, pp. 4.

2428
"Meharry Faculty Member First Woman To Win The Coveted Strecker Award." Jet. Vol. 40, May 27, 1971, pp. 49.

2429
Mitchell, Doris. "The Challenge Goes On." Encore. Vol. 4, June 23?July 4, 1975, pp. 70-71, 73.

2430
"The Negro Woman In Medicine." Bulletin of The Medico-Chirurgical Society of The District of Columbia. Vol. 5, February, 1948, pp. 4.

2431
"Negro Woman Medic To Teach at White Ky. College." Jet. Vol. 4, December 10, 1953, pp. 21.

2432
"New Day, New Doctor." Ebony. Vol. 19, April, 1964, pp. 27-30, 33-35.

2433
"Our Lady Asclepiads." Journal of The National Medical Association. Vol. 60, March, 1968, pp. 136-137, 163.

2434
"Outstanding Women Doctors." Ebony. Vol. 19, May, 1964, pp. 68-70, 72-74, 76.

2435
"Petticoat Medics." Ebony. Vol. 3, February, 1948, pp. 19-20.

2436
Robinson, Carolyn J. "Black Woman, Can Medicine Be For You?" Essence. Vol. 6, August, 1975, pp. 66.

2437
"She Chose Medicine For A Career." Negro Achievement. Vol. 6, June, 1952, pp. 16, 56.

2438
Steward, S. Maria. Women In Medicine; A Paper Read Before The National Association of Colored Women's Clubs, Wilberforce,

Ohio, August 6, 1914. Wilberforce: Maria S. Steward, 1914, 24p.

2439
U. S. Department of Labor, Women's Bureau. "Negro Women," in The Outlook for Women In Occupations In The Medical Services: Women Physicians. Bulletin #203 #7. Washington, D. C.: G. P. O., 1945, 28p., pp. 13-14.

2440
"West Virginia's Director of Mental Health." Ebony. Vol. 19, January, 1964, pp. 63-68.

2441
"Woman In White." Headlines And Pictures. Vol. 2, August, 1945, pp. 40.

2442
"Woman Medic Gets Humanity Award." Jet. Vol. 39, February 4, 1971, pp. 30.

2443
"Woman Medic Gets Job." Headlines. Vol. 1, November, 1944, pp. 42.

2444
"Women In White." Our World. Vol. 6, February, 1951, pp. 15-19.

2445
"Women Physicians Graduated From Howard University, 1872-1967." Journal of The National Medical Association. Vol. 60, March, 1968, pp. 152-154.

2446
"Women Physicians Graduated From Meharry Medical College, 1891-1967." Journal of The National Medical Association. Vol. 60, March, 1968, pp. 154-155.

2447
"Women's Auxiliary of The National Medical Association, 1973 Convention Highlights." Journal of The National Medical Association. Vol. 65, November, 1973, pp. 562.

2448
Young, Stark. "Virgilian Ladies; Negro Medicine." New Republic. Vol. 82, March 27, 1935, pp. 187-188.

Nursing

2449
Adams, Eleanor. "Red Cross Widens Opportunities For Nursing Aid And Instruction." National Negro Health News. Vol. 16, October/December, 1948, pp. 1-4.

2450
"AKA Sorority Protests Jim Crowing of Nurses." The Crisis. Vol. 42, September, 1935, pp. 284.

2451
"American Nurses Association Admits Negro Nurses." National Negro Health News. Vol. 14, July/September, 1946, pp. 23.

2452
"American Nurses' Association Widens Use of Negro Nurses In War Effort." National Negro Health News. Vol. 12, October/December, 1944, pp. 21.

2453
"The American Red Cross and Home Nursing." National Negro Health News. Vol. 13, January/March, 1945, pp. 2-4.

2454
"Angels In White." The Brown American. Vol. 1, December, 1936, pp. 4-5.

2455
"The Angels of Saigon." Ebony. Vol. 21, August, 1966, pp. 44-46.

2456
"Another Public Health Nursing School Proposed For South." National Negro Health News. Vol. 6, October/December, 1938, pp. 23-24.

2457
"Appoint Nurse To Red Cross Board." National Negro Health News. Vol. 12, April/June, 1944, pp. 22.

2458
"Arkansas State Nurses Association to Admit Negro Nurses." National Negro Health News. Vol. 18, January/March, 1950, pp. 27.

2459
"Army Nurses." National Negro Health News. Vol. 12, January. March, 1944, pp. 7.

2460
"Army Nurses." Pulse. Vol. 2, March, 1944, pp. 18.

2461
"Army Nursing and Negro Nurses." The American Journal of Nursing. Vol. 42, December, 1942, pp. 1386-1387.

2462
"Assistant To Consultant In Negro Nursing NNCSW Appointed." National Negro Health News. Vol. 12, October/December, 1944, pp. 21.

2463
"At Yale Nursing School." Headlines. Vol. 1, September, 1944, pp. 32.

2464
Austin, B. F. "The Need of Nurses Aids." Service. Vol. 9, February, 1945, pp. 14.

2465
"Ban on Colored Army Nurses Continues To Go Unexplained." Pittsburgh Courier. 4 March, 1944.

2466
Bell, Wilhelmina. "Practical Nurses In Durham." National Negro Health News. Vol. 16, October/December, 1948, pp. 5-6.

2467
"Bellvue Hospital To Open Doors To Colored Nurses." New York Age. 28 May, 1921, pp. 1.

2468
"Bigger Program Started At St. Philip School of Nursing." National Negro Health News. Vol. 9, October/December, 1941, pp. 30.

2469
"Black Health Expert Named Univ. of Colo. Nursing Dean." Jet. Vol. 56, June 21, 1979, pp. 16.

2470
Bolden, Adeline. "Angels of Mercy With Brown Faces." Service. Vol. 6, July, 1942, pp. 21-24.

2471
Bousfield, M. O. "The Adventure of Public Health Nursing." The Southern Workman. Vol. 61, January, 1932, pp. 33-37.

2472
Branch, Marie F. "Ethnic Minorities In Nursing." Urban Health. Vol. 6, August, 1977, pp. 49-52.

2473
Brewman, Martha P. "Negro Nurse." Nation. Vol. 175, August 23, 1952, pp. 160.

2474
Brockenborough, Harriet Doty. "The Relationship Between Performance On The Scholastic Aptitude Test and The NLN State Board Examination Scores For Nursing Students." Master's Thesis, Howard University, 1970, 56p.

2475
Brown, Rosa L. "A Negro Nurse In The Glades." Opportunity. Vol. 15, November, 1937, pp. 336-338.

2476
Burgess, Audrey. 1985...Baccalaureate Degree For Nursing Practice: Impact on Black Health Care Providers And Health Care of Blacks. Nashville: Meharry Medical College, 1979, 24p.

2477
"Cadet Nurse Corps." Pulse. Vol. 1, November, 1943, pp. 6-7.

2478
"Cadet Nurses In Training." Service. Vol. 9, February, 1945, pp. 31.

2479
"Cadet Nurses Ready For Service." Service. Vol. 9, September, 1944, pp. 11.

2480
Carnegie, Mary Elizabeth. "Are Negro Schools of Nursing Needed Today?" Nursing Outbook. Vol. 12, February, 1964, pp. 53-56.

2481
________________. "The Impact of Integration on The Nursing Profession." The Negro History Bulletin. Vol. 28, April, 1965, pp. 154-155, 168.

2482
________________. "Nurse Training Becomes Nursing Education at Florida A & M College." Journal of Negro Education. Vol. 17, Spring, 19-8, pp. 200-204.

2483
Carnegie, Mary Elizabeth and E. M. Osborne. "Integration In Professional Nursing." The Crisis. Vol. 69, January, 1962, pp. 5-9.

2484
Chayer, Mary Ella. "Mary Eliza Mahoney." American Journal of Nursing. Vol. 54, April, 1954, pp. 429-431.

2485
Cobb, William M. "The Negro Nurse and The Nation's Health." Journal of Negro Education. Vol. 20, Winter, 1951, pp. 126-130.

2486
Cofer, Audre. "Autobiography of A Nurse." American Journal Of Nursing. Vol. 74, October, 1974, pp. 1836-1838.

2487
Coles, Anna B. "The Howard University School of Nursing In Historical Perspective." Journal of The National Medical Association. Vol. 61, March, 1969, pp. 105-118.

2488
"Collegiate Nursing Course at Dillard University." National Negro Health News. Vol. 11, October/December, 1943, pp. 18.

2489
"Colored Nurses Are Now In The Majority On The Harlem Hospital Staff." New York Age. 16 June, 1923, pp. 1.

2490
"Colored Registered Nurses Will Be Called To Colors." Norfolk Journal And Guide. 6 October, 1917, pp. 1.

2491
"Completed Red Cross Home Nursing Course." National Negro Health News. Vol. 13, October/December, 1945, pp. 8.

2492
Cornely, Paul B. "A Study of Negro Nursing." Public Health Nursing. Vol. 34, August, 1942, pp. 449-451.

2493
"A Course In Public Health Nursing." National Negro Health News. Vol. 2, January/March, 1934, pp. 6.

2494
Cox, Pearl Belden. "The Gray Ladies." Pulse. Vol. 4, February, 1946, pp. 24-25.

2495
Deming, Dorothy. "The Negro Nurse In Public Health." Opportunity. Vol. 15, November, 1937, pp. 333-335.

2496
Dodd, R. A. " Training Negro Nurses." Survey. Vol. 45, March 26, 1921, pp. 926-927.

2497
Doyle, A. "Rural Nursing Among Negroes." Public Health Nurse. Vol. 12, December, 1920, pp. 981-985.

2498
"The Education of The Negro Nurse." National Negro Health News. Vol. 4, January/March, 1936, pp. 9-10.

2499
"Educational Facilities For Colored Nurses and Their Employment." Public Health Nurse. Vol. 17, April, 1925, pp. 203-204.

2500
Elmore, Joyce Ann. "A History of Freedman's Hospital Training School for Nurses in Washington, D. C., 1894-1901." Master's Thesis, The Catholic University of America, 1965, 109p.

2501
"Enrollment of Negroes in Nursing Schools Rises." National Negro Health News. Vol. 13, January/March, 1945, pp. 2.

2502
Eshleman, Fannie and Marian L. Dannenberg. "Tuberculosis Training For Colored Student Nurses." Public Health Nurse. Vol. 15, June, 1923, pp. 301-303.

2503
"The Establishment of Negro Hospitals And The Progress of Negro Nurses," in The History of Nursing In North Carolina, by Mary Lewis Wyche. Chapel Hill: University of North Carolina Press, 1938, 151p., pp. 126-131.

2504
Ferguson, Elizabeth R. "Nurse-Midwives Serve A Rural County." National Negro Health News. Vol. 11, April/June, 1943, pp. 11-13.

2505
Ferris, Louanne. I'm Done Crying. New York: M. Evans, 1969, 275p.

2506
"First Colored Nurse Goes To Glenn Dale." Washington Tribune. 30 September, 1939.

2507
"The First Graduating Class of The Tuskegee School of Mid-Wifery." Journal of The National Medical Association. Vol. 34, May, 1942, pp. 107-109.

2508
"First Negro Nurse Named Chicago TV Supervisor." Jet. Vol. 4, September 17, 1953, pp. 18.

2509
"First Nurses Arrive in European Theatre of Operations." Opportunity. Vol. 22, Fall, 1944, pp. 178.

2510
"5 Nurses, Discharged After Walkout From Upshur, Plan Appeal." Washington Evening Star. 3 March, 1945.

2511
"5,728 Colored Nurses In United States." Tuskegee Messenger. Vol. 9, June, 1933, pp. 8.

2512
"Flint-Goodridge Again Will Train Nurses; Also Mid-Wives." National Negro Health News. Vol. 10, July/September, 1942, pp. 39.

2513
"Flint-Goodridge School of Nurse Midwifery." National Negro Health News. Vol. 11, January/March, 1943, pp. 25.

2514
"Freedman's Hospital School of Nursing." Opportunity. Vol. 20, June, 1942, pp. 182-183.

2515
The Freedman's Hospital School of Nursing, 1894-1973. Washington, D. C.: Howard University, 1973, 44p.

2516
Gage, Nina D. and Alma C. Hampt. "Some Observations on Negro Nursing in The South." Public Health Nursing. Vol. 24. December, 1932, pp. 674-680/

2517
Goldstein, Rhoda L. "Negro Nurses in Hospitals." American Journal of Nursing. Vol. 60, February, 1960, pp. 215-217.

2518
"Good Home Nursing Means Better Health." Service. Vol. 10, October, 1945, pp. 18-19.

2519
"A Good Samaritan - IVNS Bedside Care On Call." Pulse. Vol. 5, June, 1947, pp. 3-4.

2520
"Graduates of Red Cross Nursing Class." Chicago Defender. 30 April, 1921, pp. 9.

2521
"Group Votes A Welcome to Race Members." Chicago Defender. 1 June, 1940.

2522
Gunter, Laurie Martin. "A Comparative Study of The Interest Patterns of Nurses At Selected Levels." Master's Thesis, Fisk University, 1953, 45p.

2523
"Handful of U. S. Nurses Guards Health of All Negroes." Chicago Defender. 24 January, 1948.

2524
Hawkins, Charles C. "The Health Service Program and The School Nurse in Negro Colleges and Universities." The National News Bulletin. Vol. 13, September, 1939, pp. 1.

2525
"The Health of Nurses." National Negro Health News. Vol. 18. April/June, 1950, pp. 11.

2526
Hecht, Amy Blatchford. "Men and Black Students Entering Nursing: A Comparative Study of Factors In Vocational Choice." Doctoral Dissertation, University of Virginia, 1977, 171p.

2527
Heisler, Anna. "Negro Public Health Nurses Employed In The United States From 1938-1942." National Negro Health News. Vol. 10, October/December, 1942, pp. 19-23.

2528
Henry, Esther P. "Public Health Nursing Is Expanding." National Negro Health News. Vol. 17, January/March/April/June, 1949, pp. 14-15.

2529
"Here are 20 Nurses the Army Says It Won't Use." PM. 21 January, 1945, pp. 12.

2530
"Highlights of Wartime Nursing: Nursing Council." National Negro Health News. Vol. 11, January/March, 1943, pp. 26.

2531
Holt, Rackham. "Brown Women in White." The Negro Digest. Vol. 3, December, 1944, pp. 9-13.

2532
"Home Nursing Class Graduates." National Negro Health News. Vol. 11, July/September, 1943, pp. 6.

2533
"Home Nursing Program of The American Red Cross." National Negro Health News. Vol. 12, January/March, 1944, pp. 3-4.

2534
"Hospital Turns Down Negro Nurses Who Responded To Polio Emergency." PM. 15 December, 1944, pp. 11.

2535
"A Hospital's Prejudice." The Crisis. Vol. 35, December, 1928, pp. 405-406, 422.

2536
"Institute For Colored Nurses." National Negro Health News. Vol. 9, April/June, 1941, pp. 54.

2537
Jones, Charlie Mae. "How Black American Nursing Students View Their Educational Experiences In Baccalaureate Nursing Programs In Ohio." Master's Thesis, The Ohio State University, 1969, 69p.

2538
Jones, Elizabeth. "The Negro Woman In The Nursing Profession." The Messenger. Vol. 7, July, 1923, pp. 764-765.

2539
King, H. B. "The Colored Nurse Helps Solve The Health Problem In Memphis." National Negro Health News. Vol. 8, January/March, 1940, pp. 35.

2540
Landis, H. R. M. "Negro Nurse In Public Health Work." Child Health Bulletin. Vol. 3, January, 1927, pp. 18-20.

2541
Lemat, Harry. "Provident Hospital and Training School." Voice Of The Negro. Vol. 3, December, 1906, pp. 559-561.

2542
Lincoln School For Nurses: 100th Anniversary. New York: Lincoln School for Nurses, 11p.

2543
Lynch, C. Maude H. "The Negro College and Nursing." Opportunity. Vol. 13, Summer, 1945, pp. 124-125.

2544
"Mable Keaton Staupers, R. N., 1890-." Journal of the National Medical Association. Vol. 61, March, 1969, pp. 198-199.

2545
McMurdy, Robert. "Negro Women as Trained Nurses." The Southern Workman. Vol. 43, January, 1914, pp. 31-35.

2546
Maddux, Willa M. "Nursing Professions Traced From Origin To Present Day." Chicago Defender. 4 May, 1935.

2547
Margaret Murray Washington Vocational High School, Practical Nursing Department. Tenth Anniversary Album. Washington, D. C.: Public Schools of The District of Columbia, 1957, 44p.

2548
Marriner, Jessie L. "Public Health Nurse of The Negro Race In Alabama, Their Place In The Public Health Program of The State." Public Health Nurse. Vol. 15, June, 1923, pp. 304-307.

2549
Mathis, Annie Maie. "Negro Public Health Nursing In Texas." The Southern Workman. Vol. 56, July, 1927, pp. 302-303.

2550
Mercy Hospital and School For Nurses. Annual Report, 1923-1926. Philadelphia: Mercy Hospital, 1926.

2551
Meyers, Sarah B. "The Negro Problem As It Appears To A Public Health Nurse." American Journal of Nursing. Vol. 19, January, 1918, pp. 278-281

2552
Miller, Lucile V. "A Bird's Eye View of the Experimental Forward Trend in The Field of Public Health Nursing." The Aframerican Woman's Journal. Vol. 3, Summer, 1943, pp. 18-19.

2553
Minor, N. J. "Status of The Colored Public Health Nurse In Virginia." Public Health Nurse. Vol. 16, May, 1924, pp. 243-244.

2554
"Missing An Opportunity - An Appeal To Negro Nurses." National Negro Health News. Vol. 9, October/December, 1941, pp. 27.

2555
"Mississippi Nurse Heads Mixed Staff." Jet. Vol. 5, January 28, 1954, pp. 29.

2556
Moran, Ella Payne. She Wasn't Even A Nurse. New York: Vantage Press, 1974, 223p.

2557
"National Nurse Group Votes to Drop Color Bar." National Negro Health News. Vol. 8, April/June, 1940, pp. 48.

2558
"Navy, Red Cross Pass Buck on Taking Negro Nurses." PM. 28 January, 1945, pp. 14.

2559
"Navy Refuses to Lift Its Ban on Negro Nurses." Chicago Defender. 6 Janaury, 1945.

2560
"Negro Cadets At Army Hospitals." National Negro Health News. Vol. 13, April/June, 1945, pp. 22.

2561
"The Negro Nurse." Opportunity. Vol. 15, November, 1937, pp. 325.

2562
"Negro Nurse Commissioned in Navy." National Negro Health News. Vol. 13, April/June, 1945, pp. 22.

2563
"Negro Nurse Elected to Board Membership, Florida State Nurses Association." National Negro Health News. Vol. 16, January/March, 1948, pp. 24.

2564
A Negro Nurse In Republican Spain. New York: The Negro Committee to Aid Spain, n. d., 14p.

2565
"The Negro Nurse In Seventeen Agencies." National Negro Health News. Vol. 9, October/December, 1941, pp. 28-29.

2566
"Negro Nurse Joins Navy." PM. 8 March, 1945, pp. 15.

2567
"Negro Nurse on N. Y. U. Faculty." National Negro Health News. Vol. 13, April/June, 1945, pp. 22.

2568
"Negro Nurse Receives Honorable Mention." National Negro Health News. Vol. 14, October/December, 1945, pp. 13-14.

2569
"Negro Nurse Situation." Headlines. Vol. 1. February, 1945, pp. 5.

2570
"Negro Nurses Admitted To Oklahoma State Association." National Negro Health News. Vol. 15, October/December, 1947, pp. 23.

2571
"Negro Nurses and Teachers Receive Scholarships." National Negro Health News. Vol. 8, April/June, 1940, pp. 48.

2572
"Negro Nurses And The War Effort." National Negro Health News. Vol. 11, July/September, 1943, pp. 5-6.

2573
"Negro Nurses And The War Effort." National Negro Health News. Vol. 12, January/March, 1944, pp. 14.

2574
"Negro Nurses at the Nurses' Biennial Convention." National Negro Health News. Vol. 14, October/December, 1946, pp. 13.

2575
"Negro Nurses Attend Graduate Training Course in West Virginia." National Negro Health News. Vol. 7, April/June, 1939, pp. 12.

2576
"Negro Nurses Do Their Share To Keep Them Flying." Service. Vol. 9, October, 1944, pp. 12.

2577
"Negro Nurses Enrolled For Graduate Study." National Negro Health News. Vol. 7, October/December, 1939, pp. 24.

2578
"Negro Nurses In Britain." Headlines And Pictures. Vol. 1, April, 1945, pp. 14.

2579
"Negro Nurses In North Carolina Dissolve Their Organization." National Negro Health News. Vol. 17, October/December, 1949, pp. 27.

2580
"Negro Nurses In Public Health." National Negro Health News. Vol. 17, January/March/April/June, 1949, pp. 14.

2581
"Negro Nursing Personnel." National Negro Health News. Vol. 11, October/December, 1943, pp. 16.

2582
"Negro Nurses Serving With The U. S. Army Nursing Corps." National Negro Health News. Vol. 10, April/June, 1942, pp. 4.

2583
"Negro Professional Nurses (Graduates and Students) By State." National Negro Health News. Vol. 16, October/December, 1948, pp. 7.

2584
"Negro Public Health Nurse." Public Health Nursing. Vol. 34, August, 1942, pp. 452-454.

2585
"Negro Public Health Nurses." National Negro Health News. Vol. 8, October/December, 1940, pp. 24-25.

2586
"Negro Public Health Nurses In The United States In 1931 And 1938." National Negro Health News. Vol. 6, July/September, 1938, pp. 24-25.

2587
"Negro Public Health Nurses Increase In Number and Quality." National Negro Health News. Vol. 13, July/September, 1945, pp. 17.

2588
"Negro Women As Trained Nurses In Chicago." Survey. Vol. 31, November 8, 1913, pp. 159-180.

2589
"Negroes Enter Nursing Class, Boston City College." Morehouse Journal of Science. Vol. 3, October, 1929, pp. 159.

2590
"Negroes Nurse Nazis." Headlines. Vol. 1, December, 1944, pp. 21.

2591
Nichols, Franklin O. "Opportunities and Problems of Public Health Nursing Among Negroes." Public Health Nurse. Vol. 15, March, 1924, pp. 121-123.

2592
"The 1946 Census of Public Health Nurses." National Negro Health News. Vol. 14, October/December, 1946, pp. 16-18.

2593
"The 1947 Census of Public Health Nurses." National Negro Health News. Vol. 15, July/September, 1947, pp. 15-17.

2594
"Nurse Ban Lifted." Headlines. Vol. 1, September, 1944, pp. 9,

2595
"Nurses Aids: Women At Work." Pulse. Vol. 1, July, 1943, pp. 28.

2596
"Nurses Aides Answer The Call." Service. Vol. 16, March, 1952, pp. 6.

2597
"Nurses In Scotland." Headlines. Vol. 1, October, 1944, pp. 10.

2598
"Nurses Render Valuable Service." Service. Vol. 9, May, 1945, pp. 30.

2599
"$168,000 Grant Made For Education of Negro Nurses." National Negro Health News. Vol. 9, April/June, 1941, pp. 56.

2600
Osborne, Estelle M. "Status and Contribution of The Negro Nurse." Journal of Negro Education. Vol. 18, Summer, 1949, pp. 364-369.

2601
"Our Negro Nurses." American Journal of Nursing. Vol. 46, August, 1946, pp. 512.

2602
"Our Nurses." National Negro Health News. Vol. 4, July/September, 1936, pp. 16.

2603
"Our Nurses in Australia." The Crisis. Vol. 51, April, 1944, pp. 107-108.

2604
Pitrone, Jean Maddern. Trailblazer: The Negro Nurse In The American Red Cross. New York: Harcourt, Brace, 1969, 191p.

2605
"A Plea For Negro Nurses Aides." National Negro Health News. Vol. 11, January/March, 1943, pp. 5.

2606
"A Plea For Negro Nurse Aides." Service. Vol. 7, February, 1943, pp. 31.

2607
"Professional Training For Nurses." Service. Vol. 10, September, 1945, pp. 14.

2608
"Psychiatric Nursing." National Negro Health News. Vol. 12, October/December, 1944, pp. 22.

2609
"Public Health Nursing." National Negro Health News. Vol. 1, January/March, 1933, pp. 13.

2610
"Public Health Services of WPA To Be Surveyed." National Negro Health News. Vol. 7, January/March, 1939, pp. 30.

2611
"Refresher Course For Negro Nurses." National Negro Health News. Vol. 11, July/Septmeber, 1943, pp. 6.

2612
Riddle, Estelle M. "Negro Nurses: The Supply And Demand." Opportunity. Vol. 15, November, 1937, pp. 327-329.

2613
________________. "The Negro Nurse and The War." Opportunity. Vol. 21, April, 1943, pp. 44-45, 92.

2614
________________. "The Nurse Shortage." Opportunity. Vol. 25, Winter, 1947, pp. 22-23.

2615
________________. "The Training and Placement of Negro Nurses." Journal of Negro Education. Vol. 4, January, 1935, pp. 42.

2616
Rivington, Ann. "We're On The March, Say Negro Nurses." The Worker. 31 January, 1943, pp. 15.

2617
Roberts, Abbie. "Nursing Education and Opportunities For The Colored Nurse." Proceedings of the National Conference of Social Work. 55th Annual Session, 1928, pp. 183-185.

2618
Rodgers, William. "The Public Health Nurse In The Modern Treatment of Tuberculosis Among The Negroes." National Negro Health News. Vol. 5, January/March, 1937, pp. 28-29.

2619
Ruffin, Osolee M. "Jim-Crowing Nurses." The Crisis. Vol. 37, April, 1930, pp. 123, 139-140.

2620
"Scholarships for Negro Nurses." National Negro Health News. Vol. 13, January/March, 1945, pp. 15.

2621
Smith, Charlotte P. "The Public Health Nurse and Veneral Disease Education." National Negro Health News. Vol. 13, January/March, 1945, pp. 14-15.

2622
Speaks, Rheva A. "The U. S. Cadet Nurse Corps at Freedman's Hospital, Washington, D. C." National Negro Health News. Vol. 11, July/September, 1943, pp. 9-10.

2623
"Special Courses For Nurses." National Negro Health News. Vol. 12, October/December, 1944, pp. 21.

2624
Staupers, Mabel K. "The Black Nurse and Nursing Goals." Journal of The National Medical Association. Vol. 62, July, 1970, pp. 304-305

2625
________________. "The Negro Nurse." Opportunity. Vol. 20, November, 1942, pp. 332-333.

2626
________________. "The Negro Nurse Advances." National Negro Health News. Vol. 10, April/June, 1942, pp. 5-8.

2627
________________. "The Negro Nurse In America." Opportunity. Vol. 15, November, 1937, pp. 339-341.

2628
________________. No Time For Prejudice; A Story Of The Integration Of Negroes In Nursing In The United States. New York: MacMillan, 1961, 206p.

2629
________________. "Present Status of The Negro Nurse In The Army Nursing Corps." The Aframerican Woman's Journal. Vol. 1, #4, 1941, pp. 34-35, 37.

2630
Stocker, Joseph. "Brown Nurse to Redskins." The Negro Digest. Vol. 8, October, 1950, pp. 70-73.

2631
"Student Nurses Assn. Get Funds To Recruit Blacks." Jet. Vol. 46, September 12, 1974, pp. 24.

2632
Tatum, Jane Anne. "Some Factors Associated With The Selection of Nursing As A Career." Master's Thesis, Howard University, 1959, 122p.

2633
Taylor, Eola Lyons. "The Training of Negro Nurses in The South." Opportunity. Vol. 15, November, 1937, pp. 330-331.

2634
Taylor, Lois. "Nurse Education at Hampton Institute." *Opportunity*. Vol. 22, April/June, 1944, pp. 83, 100.

2635
"Tennessee Nursing Association Admits Negro Nurses." *National Negro Health News*. Vol. 14, October/December, 1946, pp. 14.

2636
"Top Nurse in Uniform; Highest Ranking Negro Woman In The U. S. Army Nurse Corps." *Ebony*. Vol. 21, September, 1966, pp. 50, 52, 54.

2637
"Tuskegee To Train Nurses." *Service*. Vol. 7, September, 1943, pp. 6-7.

2638
"University of Illinois To Train Black Women As Nurses' Assistants." *Jet*. Vol. 40, July 29, 1971, pp. 44.

2639
U. S. Department of Labor, Women's Bureau. "Negro Women," in *The Outlook for Women in Occupations In The Medical and Other Health Services: Professional Nurses*. Bulletin #203 #3. Washington, D. C.: G. P. O., 1945, 66p., pp. 21-23.

2640
Vessells, Alma. "Negro Nurses." *National Negro Health News*. Vol. 16, October/December, 1948, pp. 9-10.

2641
Voight, Daisy. "Nurse - Widwives - One Answer To The Doctor Shortage." *Essence*. Vol. 5, December, 1974, pp. 92.

2642
"Volunteer Nurses Aid War Program." *Service*. Vol. 7, May, 1943, pp. 47.

2643
Wallace, Ernestine Marie. "A Study of Negro Nursing Services In Atlanta, Georgia." Master's Thesis, Atlanta University, 1945, 55p.

2644
Wells, Marjorie. "Only Negro Nurse in Kenny Institute." *Our World*. Vol. 3, March, 1948, pp. 31-32.

2645
Westney, Guida. "The Black Nurse In The 20th Century." *The Message*. Vol. 41, October, 1975, pp. 20-22.

2646
Wilkins, Roy. "Black Women in White." *The Negro Digest*. Vol. 1, April, 1943, pp. 61-63.

2647
Wilkins, Roy. "No Negro Nurses Wanted." The Crisis. Vol. 52, February, 1945, pp. 40.

2648
__________. "Nurses Go To War." The Crisis. Vol. 50, February, 1943, pp. 42-44.

2649
"Woman In White." Jet. Vol. 3, April 30, 1953, pp. 26-28.

2650
"The Woman In White." Pulse. Vol. 3, October, 1945, pp. 19.

2651
Worthy, William. The Story of The Two First Colored Nurses To Train In The Boston City Hospital. Boston, n.p., 1942, 15p.

2652
Zierden, Connie. "Student Nurse at St. Joseph's." Interracial Review. Vol. 22, February, 1949, pp. 26-28.

Pharmacy

2653
"Black Woman Elected President of Pharmacists." Jet. Vol. 56, August 30, 1979, pp. 6.

2654
"Manufacturing Chemists Award Race Woman Medal." Norfolk Journal And Guide. 12 September, 1925, pp. 1, 6.

2655
"Woman Pharmacist Opens Drug Store." New York Age. 4 June, 1921, pp. 1.

MORAL AND SOCIAL CONDITIONS

2656
Adams, John H., Jr. "Rough Sketches." Voice of The Negro. Vol. 1, August, 1904, pp. 323-326.

2657
"Are Bachelor Girls Less Moral?" Jet. Vol. 6, June 10, 1952, pp. 24-26.

2658
Baker, Thomas N. The Negro Woman. Philadelphia: A. M. E. Book Concern, n.d., 16p.

Baker, Thomas N. "The Negro Woman." Alexander's Magazine. Vol. 3, December 15, 1906, pp. 71-85.

2659
"Better Treatment For Our Women." Norfolk Journal And Guide. 11 August, 1923, pp. 8.

2660
Bowser, Rosa D. "What Role Is the Educated Negro Woman To Play In The Uplifting of Her Race?' in Twentieth Century Negro Literature Or A Cyclopedia Of Thought on The Vital Topics Relating To The American Negro, by Daniel W. Culp. Toronto: J. L. Nichols, 1902, 472p., pp. 177-182.

2661
Burroughs, Nannie Helen. "Not Color But Character." Voice of The Negro. Vol. 1, July, 1904, pp. 277-279.

2662
Cantor, M., K. Rosenthal and L. Wilker. "Social And Family Relations of Black Aged Women in New York City." Gerontologist. Vol. 15, October, 1975, pp. 64.

2663
"City of Single Women." Ebony. Vol. 14, February, 1959, pp. 19-22, 24-25.

2664
"Colored Girls In Harlem Subject of Discussion At Urban League Conference." New York Age. 24 January, 1920.

2665
"Do Pretty Girls Go Wrong in Harlem?" Jet. Vol. 1, January 3, 1952, pp. 36-40.

2666
Fowler, Anne Clarke. "The Contemporary Negro Subculture: An Exploratory Study of Lower Class Negro Women In New Orleans." Doctoral Dissertation, Tulane University, 1970, 296p.

2667
Fulton, David B. A Plea For Social Justics For The Negro Woman. New York: Lincoln Press Association, 1912, 11p.

2668
Guzman, Jessie P. "The Social Contributions of The Negro Woman Since 1940." The Negro History Bulletin. Vol. 11, January, 1948, pp. 86-94.

2669
"Harlem Girls Are Warned of Pitfalls That Infest the Paths of Gay Living." New York Age. 14 April, 1924, pp. 1.

2670
Harvey, Marion."A Study of The Social and Educational Adjustment of A Group of Colored Girls Who Migrated From The Deep South To Washington, D. C." Master's Thesis, The Catholic University of America, 1941.

2671
Hayes, Rosalind. "Confessions of a Pin-Up Girl." Jet. Vol. 1, March 27, 1952, pp. 22-25.

2672
Hunton, Addie. "Negro Womanhood Defended." Voice of The Negro. Vol. 1, July, 1904, pp. 280-282.

2673
Lantz, Ragni. "The Pleasures and Problems of The Bachelor Girl." Ebony. Vol. 21, August, 1966, pp. 102-104, 106-108.

2674
Lasker, Bruno. All Colors, A Study Outline of Women's Part In Race Relations. New York: The Woman's Press, 1926, 153p.

2675
"Let Us Make A Mighty Effort and Arise," in Black Women In Nineteenth Century American Life: Their Words, Their Thoughts, Their Feelings, by Bert James Loewenberg and Ruth Bogin. University Park: Pennsylvania State University, Press, 1976, 255p., pp. 181-279.

2676
Lopata, Helena Znaniecki. "Social Relations of Black And White Widowed Women In A Northern Metropolis." American Journal of Sociology. Vol. 78, January, 1973, pp. 1003-1010.

2677
Malden, Martin Barnaby. For The Protection of Negro Womanhood. Washington, D. C.: G. P. O., 1915, 4p.

2678
Major, Gerri. "The New Image of The Socialite." Ebony. Vol. 21, August, 1966, pp. 63-64, 66-68.

2679
"Our Women and The Soldiers." Norfolk Journal And Guide. 15 September, 1917, pp. 4.

2680
Stewart, Dorothy Granberry. "The Social Adjustment of Black Females At A Predominantly White University." Doctoral Dissertation, University of Connecticut, 1971, 112p.

2681
Tayleur, Eleanor. "Negro Women." Outlook. Vol. 76, January 30, 1904, pp. 266-271.

2682
Washington, Booker T. (Mrs.). "Social Improvement of The Plantation Woman." Voice of The Negro. Vol. 1, July, 1904, pp. 288-290.

2683
Williams, Fannie B. "The Colored Girl." Voice of The Negro. Vol. 2, June, 1905, pp. 400-403.

2684
Williams, Sylvania F. "The Social Status of The Negro Woman." Voice of The Negro. Vol. 1, July, 1904, pp. 298-300.

ORGANIZATIONS AND INSTITUTIONS

2685
"Associationism and Reform: 1890-1920; Black Women's Organizations," in Women Together, by Judith Papachristou. New York: Knopf, 1976, 273p., pp. 120-124.

2686
Barrett, Harris (Mrs.). "Negro Women's Clubs and The Community." The Southern Workman. Vol. 39, January, 1910, pp. 33-34.

2687
Bowen, Margaret Davis. "Educational Work Of A National Professional Sorority of Negro College Women." Master's Thesis. University of Cincinnati, 1935, 165p.

2688
Brown, Annie O. W. "A Study of The Organizations of Negro Women In Maryland With Implications For The Education of Negro Girls." Master's Thesis, Hampton Institute, 1944, 55p.

2689
Brown, Charlotte Hawkins. "Cooperation Between White and Colored Women." Missionary Review of The World. Vol. 45, June, 1922, pp. 484-487.

2690
Bynes, Sallie Connell. "Activities of Fifty Chapters of The New Homemakers of America of The Schools of Tennessee." Master's Thesis, Hampton Institute, 1949, 71p.

2691
"Class," in Before The Ghetto: Black Detroit In The Nineteenth Century. Chicago: University of Illinois Press, 1973, 254p., pp. 156-157.

2692
"Clubs And Organizations," in Black Women Makers of History:

A Portrait, by George F. Jackson. Sacramento: Fong & Fong, 1977, 289p., pp. 153-166.

2693
Cromwell, J. W. "War Work Council." The Crisis. Vol. 17, January, 1919, pp. 116-117.

2694
Current, Gloster B. "Women in The N.A.A.C.P." The Crisis. Vol. 66, April, 1959, pp. 205-210.

2695
Curtis, Julia Childs. "A Girls' Clubhouse." The Crisis. Vol. 6, October, 1913, pp. 294-296.

2696
Dillon, J. M. "Black Women: United For A Cause." The Black Collegian. Vol. 9, May/June, 1979, pp. 47-48, 50, 113.

2697
A Directory of Black Women's Organizations of Metropolitan Washington. Washington, D. C.: Howard University, Institute for Urban Affairs and Research, 1978, 101p.

2698
"Do Sororities Have A Future?" Headlines And Pictures. Vol. 1, June, 1945, pp. 22-24.

2699
DuBois, W. E. B. "The Battle of Washington." The Crisis. Vol. 30, July, 1925, pp. 114-115.

2700
__________. "A Christian Basis." The Crisis. Vol. 29, March, 1925, pp. 201-202.

2701
Fernandis, Sarah C. "Inter-racial Activities of Baltimore Women." The Southern Workman. Vol. 51, October, 1922, pp. 482-484.

2702
Fields, Emma L. "The Women's Club Movement In The United States, 1877-1900." Master's Thesis, Howard University, 1948, 117p.

2703
"First National Conference of Colored Women, July 29-31, 1895, Boston, Massachusetts." The Woman's Era. Vol. 2, September, 1895, 14p.

2704
Gardner, Mary E. B. "The Negro Woman: Her Role As Participant In Volunteer Community Activities In Westchester Communities." Doctoral Dissertation, New York University, 1961, 196p.

2705
Gilliard, Robert. "Alpha To Omega: A History of Black Fraternities and Sororities." The Black Collegian. Vol. 5, November/December, 1974, pp. 42, 46j 48.

2706
"Home For Friendless Girls." The Crisis. Vol. 3, April, 1912, pp. 254.

2707
Home For Aged Colored Women. Annual Report, 1863-1914. Boston: Home For Aged Colored Women, 1914.

2708
Hunton, Addie W. "Caring for Young Women." The Crisis. Vol. 2. July, 1911, pp. 121-122.

2709
______________. "The Club Movement in California." The Crisis. Vol. 5, December, 1912, pp. 90-92.

2710
______________. "A Social Center at Hampton, Va." The Crisis. Vol. 4, July, 1912, pp. 145-146.

2711
______________. "State Conventions." The Crisis. Vol. 2, September, 1911, pp. 210-212.

2712
______________. "Women's Clubs: Caring For The Children." The Crisis. Vol. 2, June, 1911, pp. 78-79.

2713
"Inter-racial Activities in The South." The Crisis. Vol. 21, April, 1921, pp. 249-250.

2714
"Inter-racial Co-operation: Constructive Measures Recommended by Southern White Women." The Southern Workman. Vol. 50, January, 1921, pp. 35-37.

2715
Lerner, Gerda. "Early Community Work of Black Club Women." Journal of Negro History. Vol. 59, April, 1974, pp. 158-167.

2716
Long, Nira Hardon. "International Women's Year." The Crisis. Vol. 82, May, 1975, pp. 159-161.

2717
Milholland, John E. (Mrs.). "Talks About Women." The Crisis. Vol. 1, February, 1911, pp. 28.

2718
Moore, Rosa A. "The Co-operative Women's Civic League." The Southern Workman. Vol. 53, April, 1924, pp. 186-187.

2719
Neely, Sara E. "Women of Philadelphia and Their Activities." The Crisis. Vol. 51, May, 1944, pp. 150-152.

2720
"Negro Women's Clubs." Public Opinion. Vol. 30, April 18, 1901, pp. 492.

2721
"New Black Women's Group Demands Equal Rights." Jet. Vol. 50, June 3, 1976, pp. 8.

2722
"The Ninth Crusade." The Crisis. Vol. 25, March, 1923, pp. 213-217.

2723
Post, H. Christian. "Black Women's Organizations: More Fun And Games." Tuesday Magazine. January, 1977, pp. 8-9.

2724
Proctor, Jennie. "Women's Responsibility in Building Up The N.A.A.C.P." The Crisis. Vol. 12, July, 1916, pp. 140-141.

2725
"Professional Woman's Club." New York Age. 1 December, 1923, pp. 8.

2726
Sibley, James L. "Homemakers' Clubs For Negro Girls." The Southern Workman. Vol. 44, February, 1915, pp. 81-86.

2727
Spaulding, Asa T. The Impact of The Changing World In Women's Organizations - Economically; An Overall Picture of The Economic Situation As It Relates To The Negro People. Washington, D. C.: National Council of Negro Women, 1956, 15p.

2728
Steward, Susan M. "Women's Clubs: Colored American Women." The Crisis. Vol. 3, November, 1911, pp. 33-34.

2729
Taylor, Alice. "The Institute at Bay Breeze." Journal of The National Association of College Women. #14, 1937, pp. 19-21.

2730
Terborg-Penn, Rosalyn. "Discrimination Against Afro-American Women In The Woman's Movement, 1830-1920," in The Afro American Woman: Struggles And Images, edited by Sharon Harley and Rosalyn Terborg-Penn. New York: Kennikat Press, 1978, 137p., pp. 17-27.

2731
Terrell, Mary Church. "The Club Work of Colored Women." The Southern Workman. Vol. 30, 1901, pp. 435-438.

2732
______________. "The History of The Club Women's Movement." The Aframerican Woman's Journal. Vol. 1, Summer/Fall, 1940, pp. 34-38.

2733
"Their Sisters' Keepers." Ebony. Vol. 23, March, 1968, pp. 81-82, 84, 86.

2734
"Thirty-six Black Women's Organizations." The Black Collegian. Vol. 9, May/June, 1979, pp. 48-49.

2735
"To Protect Negro Girls." Public Opinion. Vol. 32, February 13, 1902, pp. 206.

2736
U. S. Department of Labor, Women's Bureau. Preliminary Report Of The Women's Bureau 50th Anniversary Conference, Held June 11-13, 1970. Washington, D. C.: G. P. O., 1970, 6 vol.

2737
"The Utopia Neighborhood Club." The Crisis. Vol. 25, March, 1923, pp. 208-210.

2738
"Varied Views Emerge From Black Women's Conference." Muhammad Speaks. Vol. 14, 2 May, 1975, pp. 18.

2739
"Virginia Women's Inter-racial Program." The Southern Workman. Vol. 51, January, 1922, -p. 3.

2740
Washington, Margaret Murray. "Club Work Among Negro Women," in The New Progress Of A Race, by J. L. Nichols and William H. Crogman. Naperville, Illinois: J. L. Nichols & Company, 1929, 480p., pp. 177-209.

2741
Williams, Fannie B. "The Club Movement Among Colored Women of America," in A New Negro For A New Century, by Booker T. Washington, Chicago: American Publishing House, 1900, 428p., pp. 378-405.

2742
______________. "Club Movement Among Negro Women," in Progress Of A Race, by J. L. Nichols and William H. Crogman. Naperville, Illinois: J. L. Nichols & Company, 1929, 280p., pp. 197-231.

2743
Williams, Fannie B. "The Club Movement Among The Colored Women." Voice of The Negro. Vol. 1, March, 1904, pp. 99-102.

2744
Wilson, Inez R. "New York's Committee of One Hundred." The Crisis. Vol. 36, July, 1929, pp. 229, 245-246.

2745
"Woman Power At The N.A.A.C.P." Ebony. Vol. 30, April, 1975, pp. 88-90, 92.

2746
"Women Leaders Discuss Mobilization for Freedom." Jet. Vol. 1, April 10, 1952, pp. 10.

2747
"Women's Clubs." The Crisis. Vol. 4, May, 1912, pp. 38-39.

2748
"Women's Clubs." Ebony. Vol. 32, July, 1977, pp. 70-73, 76, 78, 80.

2749
"Women's Council of Portsmouth In Interesting Meet." Norfolk Journal And Guide. 9 April, 1927, pp. 8.

2750
"Women's Welfare Club Bring Joy to Many Needy." Norfolk Journal And Guide. 24 January, 1925, pp. 10.

Alpha Kappa Alpha Sorority

2751
"AKA." The Brown American. Vol. 2, January, 1937, pp. 16.

2752
"AKA Dedicates Founders Tribute At Howard University." Jet. Vol. 54, February 16, 1978, pp. 24.

2753
"AKA's, Deltas, Fete Anniversary." Ebony. Vol. 14, November, 1958, pp. 141-142, 144, 146.

2754
"AKA's Provides $16,500 Total For National Projects." National Negro Health News. Vol. 14, October/December, 1946, pp. 24.

2755
"AKA's 69th Year." Jet. Vol. 51, February 24, 1977, pp. 13.

2756
"Alpha Kappa Alpha." The Brown American. Vol. 5, November/December, 1941, pp. 17.

2757
"Alpha Kappa Alpha." Headlines. Vol. 1, February, 1945, pp. 45.

2758
"The Alpha Kappa Alpha." Howard University Journal. Vol. 11, October 24, 1913, pp. 6.

2759
"Alpha Kappa Alpha At Institute." New York Age. 20 January, 1923, pp. 7.

2760
"Alpha Kappa Alpha Boule In Philadelphia Was Notable Occasion." New York Age. 10 January, 1925, pp. 9.

2761
"Alpha Kappa Alpha Health Program." Bulletin of The Medico-Chirurgical Society of The District of Columbia. Vol. 6, October, 1949, pp. 4.

2762
"The Alpha Kappa Alpha Sorority." Howard University Journal. Vol. 11, February 7, 1913, pp. 3.

2763
"Alpha Kappa Alpha Sorority Boule." Opportunity. Vol. 2, February, 1924, pp. 63.

2764
"The Alpha Kappa Alpha Sorority Continues Health Project And Established National Non-Partisan Council." The Aframerican Woman's Journal. Vol. 1, #4, 1941, pp. 38.

2765
"Alpha Kappa Alpha Sorority Holds First Meeting Of The Year." New York Age. 13 October, 1923, pp. 8.

2766
"Alpha Kappa Alpha Sorority Observes Founder's Day." Norfolk Journal And Guide. 7 February, 1925, pp. 10.

2767
"Alpha Kappa Alpha Soros Celebrate Its Founders' Day." New York Age. 31 January, 1925, pp. 10.

2768
"Barbara Phillips Heads AKA Sorority." Black Excellence. Vol. 2, December, 1978/January-February, 1979, pp. 36.

2769
Boyer, Sallie C. "Visit With Ethel Hedgeman Lyle: Founder of The Alpha Kappa Alpha Sorority." The Brown American. Vol. 5, November/December, 1941, pp. 18-19.

2770
Chisholm, Flora B. "Full-Time Health Education Program of The Alpha Kappa Alpha Sorority." *National Negro Health News*. Vol. 15, October/December, 1947, pp. 11-13.

2771
Cobbs, Bessie E. "Health On Wheels In Mississippi; The Rural Health Project of The Alpha Kappa Alpha Sorority." *American Journal of Nursing*. Vol. 41, May, 1941, pp. 551-554.

2772
Jackson, Ida Louise. "National Non-Partisan Council on Public Affairs." *Opportunity*. Vol. 20, November, 1942, pp. 327-329.

2773
"Margaret Flagg Holmes, AKA Founder, Dies at 87." *Jet*. Vol. 49, February 26, 1976, pp. 14.

2774
McRae, Michele L. "National Club Notes - Alpha Kappa Alpha." *Philadelphia Afro American*. 21 December, 1976.

2775
"Outgoing National President of Sorority Honored." *Headlines And Pictures*. Vol. 3, September, 1946, pp. 40.

2776
Parker, Marjorie H. *Alpha Kappa Alpha: In The Eye Of The Beholder*. Washington, D. C.: AKA Sorority, 1979, 205p.

2777
________________. *Alpha Kappa Alpha Sorority: 1908-1958*. Washington, D. C.: AKA Sorority, 1958, 140p.

2778
Poole, Charlotte. "The Alpha Kappa Alpha Sorority National Projects: Non-Partisan Council on Public Affairs." *Pulse*. Vol. 1, September, 1943, pp. 4-5; October, 1943, pp. 20-21, 31.

2779
"Social Progress - AKA." *Opportunity*. Vol. 3, July, 1925, pp. 221; December, 1925, pp. 387.

2780
"Sorority Makes Final Payment On UNCF Pledge." *Black Excellence*. Vol. 2, December, 1978/January-February, 1979, pp. 36.

2781
"Sorority Play Well Recieved." *Norfolk Journal And Guide*. 7 May, 1927, pp. 4.

2782
"Sorors Observe Vocational Week, May 31-June 6th." *Norfolk Journal And Guide*. 6 June, 1925, pp. 2.

2783
Turner, Zatella R. "Alpha Kappa Alpha Sorority's Wartime Program." The Aframerican Woman's Journal. Vol. 3, Summer, 1943, pp. 22-23.

Association of Deans of Women and Advisors To Girls In Negro Schools

2784
Bolton, Ina A. "The Organization of The Office of The Dean of Women." Quarterly Review of Higher Education Among Negroes. Vol. 8, October, 1940, pp. 254-255.

2785
Cuthbert, Marion. "The Dean of Women At Work." Journal of The National Association of College Women. April 13-14, 1928, pp. 39-44.

2786
Davis, Hilda. "The Fifth Deans' Conference Meets." Journal of The National Association of College Women. #11, 1933-1934, pp. 58-59.

2787
National Association of Deans of Women. Findings of A Conference on Current Problems and Programs In Higher Education of Negro Women, June 5-12, 1944. Atlanta: Spelman College, 1944, 15p.

2788
"Proceedings of The Eleventh Annual Meeting of The Association of Women and Advisors of Girls." Quarterly Review of Higher Education Among Negroes. Vol. 8, October, 1940, pp. 228.

2789
"Proceedings of The Twelfth Annual Meeting of The Association of Deans of Women and Advisors to Girls in Negro Schools. Quarterly Review of Higher Education Among Negroes. Vol. 9, October, 1941, pp. 178-183.

2790
Rambo, Thelma Mitchell. "A Dean's Program." Journal of The National Association of College Women. #13, 1936, pp. 58-60.

2791
"Remarks of The President at the Public Session, Eleventh Annual Conference, Association of Deans of Women and Advisors to Girls In Negro Schools." Quarterly Review of Higher Education Among Negroes. Vol. 8, October, 1940, pp. 249.

2792
Slowe, Lucy D. "The Dean's Conference At Fisk." Journal of The National Association of College Women. April 5-6, 1929, pp. 14-15.

2793
Slowe, Lucy D. "Some Impressions From Two Conferences of Deans of Women." Journal of The National Association of College Women. #12, 1935, pp. 38-39.

2794
____________. "What Is A Dean of Women?" Journal of The National Association of College Women. April 8-10, 1926, pp. 53-56.

2795
"Summary of Seventh Deans' Conference." Journal of The National Association of College Women. #13, 1936, pp. 54-57.

2796
"Summary of The Conference of Deans and Advisors To Women In Colored Schools." Journal of the National Association of College Women. April 13-14, 1928, pp. 37-39.

2797
Tancil, Elaine. "The Deans of Women Hold Their Second Conference." Journal of The National Association of College Women. 1930-1931, pp. 8-9.

Association of Southern Women For The Prevention of Lynching

2798
Barber, Henry E. "The Association of Southern Women For the Prevention of Lynching, 1930-1942." Phylon. Vol. 34, December, 1973, pp. 378-389.

2799
Butler, Franklin W. "Southern Women Against Lynching: A Study of An Anti-Lynching Organization, 1930-1942." Master's Thesis, Atlanta University, 1974, 62p.

Bennett College

2800
"Bennett College For Women." The Southern Workman. Vol. 63, May, 1934, pp. 131.

2801
"Bennett College Extends Health Service." National Negro Health News. Vol. 12, July/September, 1944, pp. 23.

2802
"Bennett College Girls Perform Unique Stunts." Norfolk Journal And Guide. 26 November, 1927, pp. 10.

2803
"Bennett College Homemaking Institute Popular." Norfolk Journal And Guide. 30 April, 1927, pp. 11.

2804
"A Brief Historical Account of the Founding and Development of Bennett College," in Two Centuries of Methodist Concern: Bondage, Freedom and Education of Black People, by James P. Brawley. New York: Vantage Press, 1974, 606p., pp. 155-175.

2805
"Dr. D. D. Jones Inaugurated President of Bennett College." Norfolk Journal And Guide. 4 June, 1927, pp. 5.

2806
"Girls Tell Why They Selected Bennett College." Norfolk Journal And Guide. 8 October, 1927, pp. 10.

2807
Gleed, Carrie. "The Tuskegee Party At Bennett College." Tuskegee Messenger. Vol. 7, December, 1931, pp. 2, 15

2808
Hamilton, Velma B. "An Adventure in Women's Education." Journal of The National Association of College Women. #12, 1935, pp. 32-33.

2809
Heningburg, Alphonse. "Founders Day At Bennett College For Women." Tuskegee Messenger. Vol. 7, December, 1931, pp. 2, 15.

2810
Hughes, Walter J. "The Health Program of Bennett College." National Negro Health News. Vol. 18, January/March, 1950, pp. 1-3.

2811
"Inauguration of Dr. David D. Jones As President of Bennett College For Women." Norfolk Journal And Guide. 4 June, 1927, pp. 1.

2812
Marteena, Constance H. "A College For Girls - Bennett College." Opportunity. Vol. 16, October, 1938, pp. 036-307.

2813
Pinkard, Nancy L. "Mademoiselle's College Board Collegues From Bennett College." Pulse. Vol. 5, September, 1947, pp. 20-21, 30.

2814
Player, Willa. "Improving College Education For Women At Bennett College." Doctoral Dissertation, Columbia University, 1948.

2815
"Survey of The Month - Achievement of Bennett College." Opportunity. Vol. 13, February, 1935, pp. 60.

2816
Tate, Merze. "The Justification of A Women's College." Journal of The National Association of College Women. #14, 1937, pp. 22-26.

2817
Taylor, Lois. "Social Action At Bennett College." Opportunity. Vol. 20, January, 1942, pp. 8-10.

2818
Turner, John G. "Radio At Bennett College." Opportunity. Vol. 21, January, 1943, pp. 8-10.

2819
"Young Women Who Direct Student Government At Bennett College." Norfolk Journal And Guide. 9 April, 1927, pp. 5.

Big Sisters

2820
"Brooklyn Big Sisters Open Their House." New York Age. 4 March, 1922, pp. 8.

2821
"Brooklyn Colored Women Resent Prejudice By The Roosevelt Hotel." New York Age. 19 May, 1923, pp. 1.

Black Women Organized For Action

2822
Gant, Liz. "Black Women Organized For Action - They Collect Political IOU's." Essence. Vol. 7, October, 1976, pp. 46, 128, 131.

Black Women's Community Development Foundation

2823
Black Women's Community Development Foundation. Annual Report, 1972. Washington, D. C.: Black Women's Community Development Foundation, 1972, 15p.

2824
Terrell, Angela. "Priority: Liberating Black Communities." Washington Post. 1 April, 1973.

2825
Trescott, Jacqueline. "Juvenile 'Habilitation'." Washington Star. 29 March, 1973, pp. D-4.

2826
White, Joyce. "Black Women's Community Development Foundation." Essence. Vol. 6, February, 1976, pp. 44-45.

Campfire Girls

2827
Carrington, Catherine E. "An Evaluative Study of Recruiting

and Training Twenty-five Volunteers for Camp Fire Girls In Atlanta, Georgia, From August, 1984 to January, 1949." Master's Thesis, Atlanta University, 1951, 49p.

Chi Eta Phi Sorority

2828
"The History of Chi Eta Phi," in The Freedman's Hospital School of Nursing, 1894-1973. Washington, D. C.: Howard University, 1973, 44p., pp. 41-42.

2829
Miller, Helen Sullivan. The History of The Chi Eta Phi Sorority, Inc., 1932-1967. Washington, D. C.: Association For the Study of Negro Life and History, 1968, 244p.

Colored Women's Civic League

2830
"Colored Women's League Holds Mass Meeting." New York Age. 30 June, 1923, pp. 8.

2831
"Colored Women's League To Hold A Mass Meeting, Friday, June 22." New York Age. 23 June, 1923, pp. 6.

2832
"Women's Civic League And Work Accomplished." New York Age. 28 July, 1923, pp. 8.

2833
"Women's Civic League Thanked By Mrs. Hylan." New York Age. 29 September, 1923, pp. 8.

Daughter Elks

2834
"Daughter Elks Issue Final Call, Roanoke Meet." Norfolk Journal And Guide. 14 May, 1927, pp. 10.

2835
"Demands High Standards of Womanhood." Norfolk Journal And Guide. 13 June, 1925, pp. 7.

2836
"Elk Daughters Celebrate Fifteenth Anniversary." Norfolk Journal And Guide. 16 June, 1917, pp. 1.

2837
"Elk Daughters Fun Revue." Norfolk Journal And Guide. 16 April, 1927, pp. 4.

2838
"Pays Stirring Tribute To Mrs. Emma V. Kelley." Norfolk Journal And Guide. 4 June, 1927.

2839
"State Daughter Elks Conclude Banner Session." Norfolk Jour-and Guide. 28 May, 1927, pp. 7.

2840
"State Meeting of Daughter Elks A Marked Success." Norfolk Journal And Guide. 6 June, 1925. pp. 7.

2841
"Women Elks Wage Hot Contest Over Election of Rules." Norfolk Journal And Guide. 5 September, 1925, pp. 1.

Delta Sigma Theta Sorority

2842
"Alpha Chapter of Dleta Sigma Theta Initiates." Howard University Journal. Vol. 11, April 18, 1913.

2843
"AKA's, Deltas, Fete Anniversity." Ebony. Vol. 14, November, 1958, pp. 141-142, 144, 146.

2844
"Bio Notes on Delta's Founders." Delta. Vol. 66, January/February, 1979, pp. 4-5.

2845
Celebration of The Fiftieth Anniversary of The Founding of Delta Sigma Theta Sorority, January 12-13, 1963. Washington, D. C.: Delta Sigma Theta Sorority, 1963.

2846
"Changing Hands." Jet. Vol. 40, September 16, 1971, pp. 16.

2847
"College Women Open Frat Home At Howard." New York Age. 18 November, 1922, pp. 2.

2848
Comer, Brenda. "Delta's Oldest Member, Eloise LeQuey." Delta. Vol. 66, January/February, 1979, pp. 8.

2849
"Delta Sigma Theta - 66 Years of Forceful Heritage." Delta. Vol. 66, January/February, 1979, pp. 6-7, 10.

2850
"Delta Sigma Theta Annual Meeting." Norfolk Journal And Guide. 17 December, 1927, pp. 5.

2851
"Delta Sigma Theta Helps Others From Africa to Alaska." Los Angeles Sentinel. 23 April, 1964.

2852
"Delta Sigma Theta Sends Delegate to Convention Of Intercolle-

giate Socialist Society." *Howard University Journal*. Vol. 11, January 16, 1914, pp. 1, 5.

2853
"Deltas Culminate Golden Anniversary." *St. Louis American*. 9. January, 1964, pp. 6.

2854
"Delta's Program Reflects Public Service Commitment." *Jet*. Vol. 50, April 22, 1976, pp. 32.

2855
"Deltas Set Pace." *Headlines*. Vol. 1, October, 1944, pp. 11.

2856
Gilliam, Dorothy. " 'Kulsini' Countdown." *Washington Post*. 31 March, 1976, pp. F-1.

2857
"Monument Dedication." *The Delta*. Vol. 66, April, 1979, pp. 5.

2858
"Paragraphs of News - Delta Sigma Theta." *Howard University Journal*. Vol. 11, January 9, 1914, pp. 6.

2859
Peterson, Maurice. "Deltas Go Hollywood." *Essence*. Vol. 6, May, 1976, pp. 30, 32, 77.

2860
"Regional Conference Delta Sigma Theta Sorority." *Tuskegee Messenger*. Vol. 4, January 12, 1929, pp. 7.

2861
"Sororities." *The Woman's National Magazine*. Vol. 8, February, 1944, pp. 5.

2862
"A Sorority Organized." *Howard University Journal*. Vol. 11, February 11, 1913, pp. 6.

2863
Vroman, Mary Elizabeth. *Shaped To Its Purpose: Delta Sigma Theta - The First Fifty Years*. New York: Random House, 1965, 213p.

Federation of Colored Women's Clubs

2864
"Aftermath of The Women's Federation." *New York Age*. 5 August, 1922, pp. 5.

2865
"Alabama Club Women." *New York Sun*. 20 September, 1900.

2866
"Annual Convention of The South Carolina Federation of Colored Women's Clubs." *New Era*. 8 July, 1922.

2867
"Annual Session of Alabama Club Women Largely Attended at Decatur." *Tuskegee Messenger*. Vol. 9, July/August, 1933, pp. 1, 7.

2868
"Appeal To Clubwomen." *Norfolk Journal And Guide*. 13 January, 1916, pp. 7.

2869
"Appreciation of Colored Women, Resolution Agreed to By The House and Senate, February 6, 1918." *The Southern Workman*. Vol. 47, June, 1918, pp. 315.

2870
Blauvelt, Mary Taylor. "The Race Problem As Discussed By Negro Women." *American Journal of Sociology*. Vol. 6, March, 1901, pp. 662-672.

2871
"Chicago Women To Attend Northwestern Federation." *Chicago Defender*. 16 July, 1921, pp. 5.

2872
"Colored Women Clubs Federate." *Wilmington Journal*. 3 August, 1916.

2873
"Colored Women's Clubs Help In Denver Health Week Program." *National Negro Health News*. Vol. 15, January/March, 1947, pp. 5.

2874
"Colored Women's Federation." *The Southern Workman*. Vol. 52, December, 1923, pp. 572-573.

2875
"Colored Women's Federation Meeting." *The Southern Workman*. Vol. 41, July, 1912, pp. 398-399.

2876
Davis, Elizabeth L. *The Story of The Illinois Federation of Colored Women's Clubs, 1900-1922*. Chicago, n.p., 1922, 137p.

2877
"Delaware State Federation of Colored Women's Clubs Hold Annual Session." *Wilmington Advocate*. 28 October, 1922.

2878
Federation of Colored Women." *The Southern Workman*. Vol. 40, August, 1911, pp. 453.

2879
"A Group of State Federation Workers." Norfolk Journal And Guide. 11 July, 1925, pp. 1.

2880
Hunton, Addie W. "The Southern Federation of Colored Women." Voice of The Negro. Vol. 2, December, 1905, pp. 850-854.

2881
__________. "Women's Clubs - State Convention." The Crisis. Vol. 2, September, 1911, pp. 210-211.

2882
Jones, Laurence C., (Mrs.). What The Mississippi Women Are Doing. Braxton, Mississippi: Mississippi State Federation of Colored Women's Clubs, n.d., 27p.

2883
"Mississippi Women In 13th Annual Session." New York Age. 12 November, 1921, pp. 2.

2884
Moton, Jennie B. "Findings of Thirty-fifth Annual Session of Colored Club Women in Alabama." Tuskegee Messenger. Vol. 11, August/September, 1935, pp. 7.

2885
Mundy, Alberta V. "Women's Club Activities: State And Local." Tuskegee Messenger. Vol. 12, July/September, 1936, pp. 4-5.

2886
"The 19th Annual Session of Woman's Federation of Clubs." Philadelphia Tribune. 10 July, 1915.

2887
"State Federation of Colored Women's Clubs." The Southern Workman. Vol. 37, December, 1908, pp. 674-648.

2888
"Virginia Federation of Colored Women." The Southern Workman. Vol. 44, September, 1915, pp. 467-468.

2889
"Woman's View of The New Deal: Thirty-third Annual Convention of Alabama Federation of Colored Women's Clubs." Tuskegee Messenger. Vol. 10, July, 1934, pp. 1, 8.

Girl Scouts

2890
Bolton, Edna Couch. "A Study of A Selected Number of Girls Participating In The Negro Girl Scout Camping Program of Atlanta, Georgia, In The Summer of 1948." Master's Thesis, Atlanta University, 1949, 39p.

2891
Burnley, Alfreda Elizabeth. "An Analysis of The Services Rendered By Volunteer Leaders Working With The Girl Scouts of District Seven In Louisville, Kentucky." Master's Thesis, Atlanta University, 1947, 36p.

2892
Campbell, S. S. (Mrs.). "Negro Girl Scouting, Duval County, Florida." National Negro Health News. Vol. 9, July/September, 1941, pp. 19.

2893
Dews, Phyllis Wheatley. "An Analysis of Girl Scouting And The Activities Engaged In By Ten Negro Troops In Atlanta, Georgia." Master's Thesis. Atlanta University, 1946, 55p.

2894
Dumetz, Bettye Jane. "A Study of The Relationship Between Registration, Participation And The Quality of Group Work Found In Negro Girl Scout Troops In Atlanta, Georgia." Master's Thesis, Atlanta University, 1948, 43p.

2895
Gentry, Annamelia. "A Study of The Community Implications of Girl Scout Work In Portsmouth, Ohio." Master's Thesis, Atlanta University, 1945, pp. 45.

2896
"Girl Scouts In Richmond." Journal of The National Association of College Women. #14, 1937, pp. 70.

2897
Higginbotham, Velena. "A College Woman's Plea For High School Girls." Journal of The National Association of College Women. #12, 1935, pp. 42-43.

2898
Hill, Alyce M. "Girl Scouts and Preparedness." National Negro Health News. Vol. 9, April/June, 1941, pp. 3.

2899
__________. "Scouting For Colored Girls In Washington." National Negro Health News. Vol. 8, October/December, 1940, pp. 9.

2900
Lewis, Margaret C. "Negro Girl Scouts in The Health Field." National Negro Health News. Vol. 13, January/March, 1945, pp. 9-11.

2901
Myles, Jacqueline. "Girl Scouts: Informal Education Of Our Youth." Pulse. Vol. 1, June, 1943, pp. 18.

2902
Payne, Mary J. "The Origin and Development of Scouting For

Negro Girls In Jefferson County, Alabama." Master's Thesis, Tuskegee Institute, 1948, 77p.

2903
Ridley, Bernice Blount. "The Girl Scout Program In Bibb County, 1945-1962." Master's Thesis, Atlanta University, 1963, 128p.

2904
Sturrup, Verneka A. "The History and Development of Negro Girl Scouting In Miami, Florida." Master's Thesis, Atlanta University, 1946, 29p.

2905
Tillman, Carmen. "A Study of The Development and Program of Camp Seguin, Bexar County Council of Girl Scouts, San Antonio, Texas, 1947." Master's Thesis, Atlanta University, 1948, 42p.

International Council of Women

2906
"Colored Women Hold 3-Day Session In Washington of World International Council." New York Age. 18 Augsut, 1923, pp. 5.

2907
"Colored Women's International Council." The Southern Workman. Vol. 52, January, 1923, pp. 7-10.

2908
"The International Council of Women." The Crisis. Vol. 21, November, 1920, pp. 57.

2909
"International Council of Women Meets." Tuskegee Messenger. Vol. 6, August 30, 1930, pp. 7.

2910
"The International Council of Women of The Darker Races," in A Documentary History of The Negro People In The United States, 1910-1932, edited by Herbert Aptheker. New Jersey: Citadel Press, 1973, 574p., pp. 616-618.

2911
"International Organization of Colored Women Is Formed." New York Age. 26 August, 1922, pp. 5.

League For Community Service

2912
Farley, Ena L."Caring And Sharing Since World War I: The League For Community Service - A Black Volunteer Organization in Boston." Umoja. Vol. 1. Summer, 1977, pp. 1-12.

Links

2913
"4,000 Attend Annual Links Convention In Washington." Jet. Vol. 46, July 25, 1974, pp. 18.

2914
"Links Award." Jet. Vol. 39, February 11, 1971, pp. 40.

2915
"Links Open Unique Exhibit At Cleveland Art Museum." Jet. Vol. 54, February 23, 1978, pp. 46-47.

2916
"Links Present Memorial Awards." Sacramenta Observer Magazine. Vol. 16, June 14-20, 1979, pp. C-1.

2917
"Links Seek Bright Youth; Women's Organization Backs National Program." Ebony. Vol. 16, June, 1961, pp. 124-129.

2918
"Lynchburg Links." Jet. Vol. 46, May 9, 1974, pp. 40.

2919
Parrish, Mildred. "Julia Purnell: Links National President." Black Excellence. Vol. 2, December, 1978/January-February, 1979, pp. 9.

2920
Ratcliffe, Robert M. "Links Have Warmth and Friendship." The Crisis. Vol. 61, April, 1954, pp. 209-213.

2921
Trigg, Eula S. "Washington, D. C. Chapter of Links, Inc.; Friendship And Service." The Negro History Bulletin. Vol. 39, May, 1976, pp. 584-589.

National Association For The Relief of Destitute Colored Women And Children

2922
Montgomery, Winfield S. Fifty Years of Good Works of The National Association For The Relief of Destitute Colored Women And Children. Washington, D. C.: National Association for The Relief of Destitute Colored Women And Children, 1913, 34p.

2923
National Association For The Relief of Destitute Colored Women And Children. Annual Report. Washington, D. C.: Smith Brothers, 1913, 17p.

National Association Of Beauty Culture School Owners And Teachers

2924
Joyner, Marjorie S. "National Association of Beauty Culture School Owners and Teachers." The Aframerican Woman's Journal. Winter/Spring, 1947-1948, pp. 5.

National Association of Black Professional Women In Higher Education

2925
"Black Women's Group Urges Changes In Education." Jet. Vol. 48, April 29, 1976, pp. 58.

National Association of Black Women Attorneys

2926
"The Politics of Alertness: A Tribute to Attorney Wilhelmina Jackson Rolark and The National Association of Black Women Attorneys." Black Monitor. Vol. 3, January, 1978, pp. 4, 7, 12-13.

National Association of College Women

2927
Atwood, Charlotte. "Washington Honors The Founders." Journal of The National Association of College Women. #12, 1935, pp. 24-27.

2928
Brodnax, Anna F. "Branch Organization." Journal of The National Association of College Women. April 8-10, 1926, pp. 36-42.

2929
Carter, Mary M. "The Educational Activities of The National Association of College Women, 1923-1960." Master's Thesis, Howard University, 1962, 129p.

2930
"College Women Form Association." Norfolk Journal And Guide. 3 January, 1925, pp. 3.

2931
Cook, Vivian J. "The N.A.C.W. Faces A Changing World." Journal of The National Association of College Women. #11, 1933-1934, pp. 5-13.

2932
"Delaware Women Organize First." Journal of The National Association of College Women. #18, 1941, pp. 24-25.

2933
"Eleventh Annual Convention." Journal of The National Association of College Women. #11, 1933-1934, pp. 63-64.

2934
Howard, Juanita P. "What May We Expect Of The National Asso-

ciation of College Women?" Journal of The National Association of College Women. April 5-6, 1929, pp. 7-10.

2935
Hudley, Mary S. "The National Association of College Women." Opportunity. Vol. 3, June, 1925, pp. 185.

2936
"An Interpretation of Objectives and Accomplishments of The National Association of College Women." Journal of The National Association of College Women. #24, 1947, pp. 34-29.

2937
"Membership of Active Branches." Journal of The National Association of College Women. #18, 1941, pp. 64-67.

2938
"Minutes - Sixth Annual Convention, April 5-6, 1929, Washington, D. C.." Journal of The National Association of College Women. April 5-6, 1929, pp. 12-14

2939
"The National Holds Its Silver Anniversary." Journal of The National Association of College Women. #21, 1948, pp. 21-26.

2940
"The National's First Fellowship Award." Journal of The National Association of College Women. #20, 1947, pp. 42-43.

2941
Nicholson, Nellie. "How Can We Interest All College Women In The Formation and Support of City and State College Women's Clubs?" Journal of The National Association of College Women. April 25-26, 1924, pp. 30-32.

2942
"Nineteenth Annual Convention." Journal of The National Association of College Women. #19, 1941-1943, pp. 45-51.

2943
"Officers and Chairman of Committees of The National Association of College Women During The Years From 1924-1941," Journal of The National Association of College Women. #18, 1941, pp. 72-74.

2944
"Proceedings - Fifth Annual Convention, April 13-14, 1928, Atlantic City, New Jersey." Journal of the National Association of College Women. April 13-14, 1928, pp. 10-19.

2945
"Proceedings - Fourth Annual Convention, April 21-23, 1927, Washington, D. C." Journal of The National Association of College Women. April 21-23, 1927, pp. 9-23.

2946
"Proceedings - Sixth Annual Convention, April 5-6, 1929, Washington, D. C." Journal of The National Association of College Women. April 5-6, 1929, pp. 12-14.

2947
"Proceedings - Third Annual Convention, April 8-10, 1926, New York City." Journal of The National Association of College Women. April 8-10, 1926, pp. 6-19.

2948
"Program - Twelfth Annual Convention." Journal of The National Association of College Women. #12, 1935, pp. 67-68.

2949
"Report of The Activities and Findings of The Committee on Standards, National Association of College Women, 1923-1933." Journal of The National Association of College Women. #18, 1941, pp. 74-77.

2950
"Report of The First Annual Convention of The Permanent Organization." Journal of The National Association of College Women. April 25-26, 1924, pp. 43.

2951
"Report of The President To The Silver Anniversary Convention." Journal of The National Association of College Women. #21, 1948, pp. 31-35.

2952
Shaw, Esther Popel. "Our Thirteenth - In Ohio, 1936." Journal of The National Association of College Women. #13, 1936, pp. 61-63.

2953
________________. "The Tenth Milestone." Journal of The National Association of College Women. #11, 1933-1934, pp. 29.

2954
"The Story of The National Unfolds." Journal of The National Association of College Women. #18, 1941, pp. 6-23.

2955
Taylor, Nellie. "An Interpretation of Objectives and Accomplishments of The National Association of College Women: An Interview With The President, Miss Alice G. Taylor." Journal of The National Association of College Women. #20, 1947, pp. 34-39.

2956
"Twenty-fifth Anniversary Suggestion To The College Alumnae Club." Journal of The National Association of College Women. #12, 1935, pp. 28.

2957
"Twenty-first Annual Convention." Journal of The National Association of College Women. #20, 1947, pp. 77-78.

2958
"Twenty-second Annual Convention." Journal of The National Association of College Women. #20, 1947, pp. 75-76.

2959
"Twenty-third Annual Convention." Journal of The National Association of College Women. #20, 1947, pp.73-74.

2960
Washington, Alethea H. "The National - What Now?" Journal of The National Association of College Women. #14, 1937, pp. 63-64.

2961
"Who's Who In National Association of College Women." Journal of The National Association of College Women. April 16-18, 1925, pp. 55-59.

2962
"Widening Circles of The N.A.C.A." Journal of The National Association of College Women." #10, 1932-1933, pp. 43-45.

2963
"Wilmington Branches Out." Journal of The National Association of College Women. #18, 1941, pp. 31-32.

National Association Of Colored Graduate Nurses

2964
"Annual Meeting of The Colored Graduate Nurses, Atlanta, Georgia." National Negro Health News. Vol. 15, April/June, 1947, pp. 22.

2965
"The Annual Report of The Executive Secretary." The National News Bulletin. Vol. 13, September, 1939, pp. 5, 8.

2966
Bobo, Ferrol G. "A Report From California." The National News Bulletin. Vol. 13, September, 1939, pp. 6-7.

2967
Lee, B. M. Kelley. "The National Association of Graduage Nurses Close Epoch Making Session In Jacksonville." Norfolk Journal And Guide. 5 September, 1925, pp. 7, 9.

2968
NACGN - Four Decades of Service. New York: National Association of Colored Graduate Nurses, n.d., 8p.

2969
National Association of Colored Graduate Nurses. The National

Health Act of 1939 - A Special News Bulletin. June, 1939, 6p.

2970
"National Association of Colored Graduate Nurses Reports Progress." National Negro Health News. Vol. 7, October/December, 1939, pp. 23.

2971
"National Association of Colored Nurses." National Negro Health News. Vol. 4, July/September, 1936, pp. 18.

2972
"Negro Nurses." National Negro Health News. Vol. 12, April/June, 1944, pp. 7-8.

2973
"Officers and Chairmen of Committees of The N.A.C.G.N." The National News Bulletin. Vol. 13, September, 1939, pp. 7.

2974
Smith, Gloria. "From Invisibility To Blackness: The Story of The National Black Nurses' Association." Nursing Outlook. Vol. 23, April, 1975, pp. 225-229.

2975
Staupers, Mabel K. "History of The National Association of Colored Graduate Nurses." National Negro Health News. Vol. 6, April/June, 1938, pp. 11-15.

2976
Thoms, Adah B. Pathfinders: A History of The Progress of Colored Graduate Nurses. New York: Kay Printing House, 1929, 240p.

2977
Winder, Eleanor Hill. "A Brief History of The Contributions of The National Association of Colored Graduate Nurses." Master's Thesis, Fisk University, 1953, 37p.

National Association of Colored Women

2978
Aery, William A. "National Association of Colored Women." The Southern Workman. Vol. 41, September, 1912, pp. 533-539.

2979
Bogle, Bonnie. "A Club Woman's Reverie." National Notes. Vol. 31, February, 1929, pp. 6.

2980
Bruce, Josephine B. "Afterglow of The Women's Convention." Voice of The Negro. Vol. 1, November, 1904, pp. 541-543.

2981
"Club List. Names of The Clubs of The National Association of

Colored Women," in A New Negro For A New Century, by Booker T. Washington. Chicago: American Publishing House, 1900, 428p., pp. 406-428.

2982
"Conference of Negro Women." Survey. Vol. 40, August 3, 1918, pp. 513.

2983
Dunnigan, Alice A. "Republican Women Plot to Put National Association of Colored Women in Spotlight." Black Dispatch. 29 August, 1953.

2984
Fauset, Jessie. "The 13th Biennial of The N.A.C.A." The Crisis. Vol. 24, October, 1922, pp. 257-260.

2985
Hamilton, Tullia Kay Brown. "The National Association of Colored Women, 1896-1920." Doctoral Dissertation, Emory University, 1978, 173p.

2986
Hunter, Jane. "The Phillis Wheatley Department of The National Association of Colored Women." National Notes. Vol. 31, January, 1929, pp. 10.

2987
Hunton, Addie W. "The Detroit Convention of The National Association of Colored Women." Voice of The Negro. Vol. 3, July, 1906, pp. 589-593.

2988
____________. "The National Association Of Colored Women." The Crisis. Vol. 2, May, 1911, pp. 17-18.

2989
____________. "The National Association of Colored Women," in A Documentary History of The Negro In The United States, 1910-1932, edited by Herbert Aptheker. New Jersey: Citadel Press, 1973, 754p., pp. 32-36.

2990
Jackson, M. M. Hubert (Mrs.). "Club Women's View of National Negro Health Week." National Negro Health News. Vol. 3, April/June, 1935, pp. 35; Vol. 5, January/March, 1937, pp. 10-13.

2991
Kendrick, Ruby Moyse. "The National Association of Colored Women's Clubs Meets for Fiftieth Anniversary." The Aframerican Woman's Journal. Fall, 1946, pp. 31.

2992
"Mothers In Council." The Crisis. Vol. 8, October, 1914, pp. 285-288.

2993
"The National Association of Colored Women, 1904," in A Documentary History of The Negro People In The United States, Vol. 1, edited by Herbert Aptheker. New York: Citadel Press, 1969, 942p., pp. 889-890.

2994
"National Association of Colored Women." The Southern Workman. Vol. 49, September, 1920, pp. 391-392; Vol. 53, October, 1924, pp. 439-440; Vol. 55, October, 1926, pp. 436-437.

2995
National Association of Colored Women, 1896-1952. Washington, D. C.: NACW, 1953, 147p.

2996
National Association of Colored Women. Biennial Financial Report To The Nineteenth Bieneial Convention Of the National Association of Colored Women, July 19-26, 1935. Cleveland, Ohio: NACA, 1935, 26p.

2997
__________. Directory, 1936. n.p., n.p., 1936, 68p.

2998
__________. Directory, 10th Annual Convention, July 10-13, 1906. Detroit: Wilson Printing Company, 1906, 8p.

2999
__________. Eighth Biennial Convention of The National Association of Colored Women, July 23-27, 1912. Hampton, Virginia: Hampton Institute, 1912, 6p.

3000
__________. Fifth Convention of The National Association of Colored Women, Bethel A.M.E. Church, July 9-14, 1906. Detroit: N.A.C.A., 1906, 6p.

3001
__________. Minutes of The Eleventh Biennial Convention of The National Association of Colored Women, Shorter Chapel A.M.E. Church, July 8-13, 1918. Denver: N.A.C.W., 1918, 110p.

3002
__________. Minutes of The Fifteenth Biennial Session of The National Association of Colored Women Held At Oakland, California, August 1-5, 1926. Oakland: N.A.C.W., 1926, 112p.

3003
__________. Minutes of The Tenth Biennial Convention of The National Association of Colored

Women, Bethel A.M.E. Church, August 7-10, 1916. Baltimore: N.A.C.W., 1916, 69p.

3004
National Association of Colored Women. Minutes of The Thirteenth Biennial Convention of the National Association of Colored Women, August 6-12, 1922, Held In Richmond, Virginia. Richmond: N.A.C.W., 1922, 86p.

3005
____________________. Minutes of The Twelfth Biennial Convention of The National Association of Colored Women, July 12-16, 1920, Held At Tuskegee Institute. Alabama: N.A.C.W., 1920, 71p.

3006
____________________. Nineteenth Biennial Convention of The National Association of Colored Women And Second Biennial Session National Association of Colored Girls, Cleveland, Ohio, Mt. Zion Congressional Church, July 22-26, 1935. Cleveland: N.A.C.W., 1935, 20p.

3007
____________________. Official Directory of The National Association of Colored Women. n.p., n.p., 1928.

3008
____________________. What You Should Know About It...How It Works...And What It Does. Washington, D. C.: N.A.C.W., 1959.

3009
"National Association of Colored Women's Clubs." Opportunity. Vol. 2, November, 1924, pp. 250-251.

3010
"Nation's Women To Talk Civil Rights At Seattle Convention." Chicago Defender. 31 July, 1948, pp. 5.

3011
"Negro Women Greet The Niagara Movement, 1907," in A Documentary History of The Negro People In The United States, Vol. 1, edited by Herbert Aptheker. New York: Citadel Press, 1969, 942p., pp. 913.

3012
"Negro Women To Meet In Richmond, Aug. 6-11." New York Age. 5 August, 1922, pp. 1.

3013
Parrish, Mary V. Fourth Statistical Report of The National Association of Colored Women, August 7-8, 1914. Louisville, Kentucky: American Baptist Press, 1914, 62p.

3014
"Past Presidents, N.A.C.W." National Notes. Vol. 32, July, 1930, pp. 11-14.

3015
Silone-Yates, Josephine. "The National Association of Colored Women." Voice of The Negro. Vol. 1, July, 1904, pp. 283-287.

3016
Stewart, Sallie W. "Call To The Biennial Meeting of The National Association of Colored Women, Inc." National Notes. Vol. 32, July, 1930, pp. 6.

3017
Terrell, Mary Church. "National Association of Colored Women." Howard's American Magazine. Vol. 4, November, 1899, pp. 26-31.

3018
Williams, Emily H. "The National Association of Colored Women." The Southern Workman. Vol. 43, August, 1914, pp. 481-483; Vol. 45, September, 1916, pp. 492-493; Vol. 51, December, 1922, pp. 543-544.

3019
"Work, Children, Home, Theme of National Association of Colored Women." Tuskegee Messenger. Vol. 9, October, 1953, pp. 6.

National Association of Negro Business and Professional Women

3020
Keene, Josephine B. National Directory of Negro Business and Professional Women. Philadelphia: Josephine Keene, 1942, 19p.

3021
National Association of Negro Business and Professional Women's Clubs. East Bay Area Club Directory. Oakland, fornia, 1967, 44p.

National Black Sisters Conference

3022
"Awakening of Black Nun Power: First National Black Sisters' Conference." Ebony. Vol. 23, October, 1968, pp. 44-46, 48-50.

3023
Haughey, John C. "Black Sisters Become Soul Sisters." America. Vol. 121, August 2, 1969, pp. 67.

3024
Kiely, Pat. "Cry For Black Nun Power: First National Black

Sisters Conference." Commonweal. Vol. 88, September 27, 1968, pp. 650.

3025
Park, J. Philip. "Black Nuns Relate To Black Power: National Black Sisters Conference." Christian Century. Vol. 85, October 16, 1968, pp. 1320-1322.

National Council of Negro Women

3026
Beal, Frances. "NCNW: To Sustain Our Growth..." Contact. Vol. 5, Fall, 1974, pp. 24, 26.

3027
Bethune, Mary McLeod. "Annual Report to The National Workshop Convention of the National Council of Negro Women." The Aframerican Woman's Journal. Vol. 3, #3, 1943, pp. 2-4.

3028
__________. "Council of Negro Women Makes History In 13 Years of Life." Chicago Defender. 18 December, 1948, pp. 6.

3029
"Beyond Bargaining." Pulse. Vol. 5, March, 1947, pp. 11, 33.

3030
"Brilliant Homage Paid The Ladies of Washington By The Governor." The Aframerican Woman's Journal. Vol. 1, Summer/Fall, 1949, pp 6.

3031
Brown, Jeanetta Welch. "The National Council of Negro Women." Pulse. Vol. 1, January, 1943, pp. 20-21, 35.

3032
"The Chicago Metropolitan Council Comes of Age." The Aframerican Woman's Journal. Vol. 3, Summer, 1943, pp. 25.

3033
"Conferences Attended and Participated in by the National Council of Negro Women." The Aframerican Woman's Journal. Fall, 1944, pp. 12-13.

3034
"Council of Negro Women Presents Bethune Awards." Jet. Vol. 44, August 2, 1973, pp. 51.

3035
"Defense Cooperation Program of the National Council of Negro Women, Inc." The Aframerican Woman's Journal. Vol. 1, #4, 1941, pp. 29-31.

3036
"Detroit Association of Women's Clubs Lauches $5,000 Drive

For Club House." The Woman's National Magazine. Vol. 8, February, 1941, pp. 7.

3037
"Excerpts From The Report Presented by The Executive Secretary." The Aframerican Woman's Journal. #3, 1943, pp. 6-10.

3038
"Dr. Dorothy Boulding Ferebee Receives From Mrs. Mary McLeod Bethune The Royal Mantle of The Presidency of The National Council of Negro Women." Bulletin of The Medico-Chirurgical Society of The District of Columbia. Vol. 6, November, 1948, pp. 12.

3039
Fosdick, Franklin. "War Among The Women." The Negro Digest. Vol. 8, February, 1950, pp. 21-25.

3040
Grant, Edmonia W. "Metropolitan Councils of Negro Women and Adult Education." The Aframerican Woman's Journal. Vol. 7, Winter, 1947, pp. 28, 32.

3041
"Hold Your Job." Service. Vol. 7, November, 1943, pp. 6-7.

3042
"International Deb Ball." Ebony. Vol. 16, December, 1960, pp. 45-46, 48, 50.

3043
Lewis, Carolyn. "Her Job: Leading Negro Women." Washington Post. 8 January, 1969.

3044
"Metropolitan Council Reports for 1943." The Aframerican Woman's Journal. Vol. 3, #3, 1943, pp. 18-19.

3045
Moore, Audrey. "Conference of Impressions." The Aframerican Woman's Journal. Vol. 2, Summer/Fall, 1941, pp. 16.

3046
National Council of Negro Women. Annual Conference. Washington, D. C.: NCNW, 1949.

3047
______________________________. Extracts Concerning The Color Question, From The Report of The Fourteenth Annual Executive Session of The National Council of Negro Women....March 26-29, 1903. Indianapolis: NCNW, 1903, 7p.

3048
______________________________. 14th Annual Conference. November 15-18, 1949. Washington, D. C.: NCNW, 1949.

3049
National Council of Negro Women. The Historical Cookbook of The American Negro. Washington, D. C.: Corporate Press, 1958, 144p.

3050
__________. The Impact of The Changing World on Women's Organizations - Economically. Washington, D. C.: NCNW, 1956, 14p.

3051
__________. Nineteenth Annual Convention, National Council of Negro Women, November 8-13, 1954. Washington, D. C.: NCNW, 1954, 17p.

3052
__________. Report, 1953-1957. Washington, D. C.: NCNW, 1957, 77p.

3053
__________. United We Build A Free World. Dedication Ceremony of The National Headquarters, October 15, 1944. Washington, D. C.: NCNW, 1944, 6p.

3054
__________. Women United; Souvenier Yearbook, Sixteenth Anniversary. Washington, D. C.: NCNW, n.d., 128p.

3055
"National Council of Negro Women Adopt Stevens House At UCLA As Project for The Ensuing Year." California Eagle. 23 June, 1949.

3056
"The National Council of Negro Women of The United States of America, Inc.: A Resume." The Aframerican Woman's Journal. Vol. 1, Spring, 1940, pp. 3.

3057
"National Council of Negro Women's Conference Findings." Opportunity. Vol. 19, November, 1941, pp. 343.

3058
"NCNW: Zeta Phi Betas Support Memorial Project." Sepia. Vol. 12, January, 1963, pp. 8-9.

3059
"NCNW Maps Plans to Extend Civil Rights at Conference." Chicago Defender. 3 July, 1948, pp. 16.

3060
"NCNW Workshop." Headlines. Vol. 1, November, 1944, pp. 11.

3061
"The NCNW's Bethune Memorial Project." Sepia. Vol. 11, December, 1962, pp. 26-27.

3062
"Negro Council Confers Awards on Group of Outstanding Women." Washington Evening Star. 20 June, 1949.

3063
"Negro Council Honors Mrs. Roosevelt As 'Woman of Year'." Washington Sunday Star. 11 February, 1945, pp. A-16.

3064
"Negro Women Hear President Pledge No Civil Rights Retreat." Washington Evening Star. 16 November, 1949.

3065
"Negro Women Plan Brotherhood Week Observance Here." Washington Star. 10 February, 1954.

3066
"Negro Women's Archives." The Aframerican Woman's Journal. Vol. 1, Summer/Fall, 1940, pp. 29-32.

3067
"Never Underestimate The Power of A Woman." Pulse. Vol. 5, December, 1947, pp. 16.

3068
"Permanent Headquarters Is Step in Right Direction, President Claims." Pittsburgh Courier. 1 January, 1944.

3069
"Program Emphasis of The New York Workshop." The Aframerican Woman's Journal. #3, 1943, pp. 5, 10.

3070
"Report of The Commission on Findings of The National Council of Negro Women." The Aframerican Woman's Journal. Vol. 2, Winter, 1941-1942, pp. 6-8.

3071
"The Report of The Committee on Findings, The Council Workshop Convention, New York City." The Aframerican Woman's Journal. #3, 1943, pp. 11-12.

3072
"Resolution To Mrs. Mary McLeod Bethune." Women United. Vol. 9, January, 1950, pp. 7, 10-12.

3073
Rockefeller, Nelson A. "Address Before The International Night Meeting of The Biennial Convention of The National Council of Negro Women." Washington, D. C.: NCNW, 1953.

3074
Sheppard, Kate I. "In Defense of NCNW." The Negro Digest. Vol. 8, July, 1950, pp. 98.

3075
"This Week in Black History." Jet. Vol. 47, December 12, 1974, pp. 39.

3076
Trescott, Jacqueline. "Dorothy Height, Feminist." Washington Post. 14 November, 1975, pp. C-3.

3077
"Washington NCNW Hears Norwegian." Chicago Defender. 25 December, 1948, pp. 8.

3078
Williams, Lorraine A. "The International Conference of The National Council of Negro Women." Journal of Negro Education. Vol. 26, Spring, 1957, pp. 204-206.

3079
Winston, E. Beulah. "The Significance of The NCNW Tenth Annual Workshop." The Aframerican Woman's Journal. December, 1945, pp. 4-5.

3080
"Women Organize Rights Movement." Lousiville Reader. 5 February, 1949.

3081
"Women's Group to Unveil Bethune Memorial In D. C." Jet. Vol. 46, July 11, 1974, pp. 6.

3082
Wright, Marion T. "The Challenge of Juvenile Delinquency to the National Council of Negro Women." The Aframerican Woman's Journal. Vol. 3, Spring, 1944, pp. 15-17.

National Federation of Afro American Women

3083
"Black Bourgeois Feminism Versus Peasant Values: Origins and Purposes of The National Federation of Afro-American Women," in The Golden Age of Black Nationalism, 1850-1925, by Wilson Jeremiah Moses. Hamden, Connecticut: Archon Books, 1978, 345p., pp. 103-131.

Order of The Eastern Star

3084
"Eastern Star Chapter Hears Annual Sermon." Tuskegee Messenger. Vol. 4, July 14-28, 1928, pp. 8.

3085
"Eastern Star Grand Chapter." New York Age. 24 June, 1922, pp. 5.

3086
"Eastern Star Women of N. Y. Hear Annual Sermon Preached." New York Age. 31 December, 1921, pp. 3.

3087
"Eastern Stars Hold Annual Session in N. Y." New York Age. 11 June, 1921, pp. 2.

3088
"Order of Eastern Star In Annual Meeting At Bethel A.M.E. Church." New York Age. 9 June, 1923, pp. 8.

3089
"Rosetta Chapter of Eastern Star Is Organized." Norfolk Journal And Guide. 14 May, 1927, pp. 3.

3090
"State Eastern Star Grand Lodge Session." Norfolk Journal And Guide. 15 September, 1923, pp. 5.

Phi Delta Kappa Sorority

3091
"Phi Delta Kappa Sorority." Philadelphia Tribune. 9 January, 1943.

Phillis Wheatley Association

3092
"Colored Girls Have Home In Cleveland." Detroit News. 29 March, 1918.

3093
"Colored Girls In Cleveland." The Crisis. Vol. 36, December, 1929, pp. 411-412.

3094
Doyle, Wilhelmina. "A Study of The History and Organization of The Phillis Wheatley Center, Greenville, South Carolina." Master's Thesis, Atlanta University, 1948, 25p.

3095
Hunter, Jane Edna Harris. A Nickle And A Prayer. Nashville: Parthenon Press, 1940, 198p.

3096
________________. "Twenty-fifth Anniversary Celebration of The Phillis Wheatley Association." The Southern Workman. Vol. 66, February, 1937, pp. 37-38.

3097
Parker, Thomas F. "The Phillis Wheatley Center." The Southern Workman. Vol. 54, November, 1925, pp. 497-504.

3098
"The Phillis Wheatley Campaign." The Southern Workman. Vol. 54, March, 1925, pp. 109.

3099
Smith, Naola Mae. "An Account of The Phillis Wheatley Home." National Notes. Vol. 32, July, 1930, pp. 15-16.

3100
Tyler, Ralph W. "The Phillis Wheatley Association: A Negro Woman's Achievement." The Southern Workman. Vol. 49, March, 1920, pp. 121-126.

Spelman College

3102
Adair, Margaret Smith. "An Index To The Spelman Messenger For The Period March, 1885 Through June, 1891." Master's Thesis. Atlanta University, 1963, 43p.

3103
Cash, Rubye Singleton. "A Followup Study of The Graudates of Spelman College, Atlanta, Georgia, for The Years 1947-1958." Master's Thesis, Atlanta University, 1960, 71p.

3104
"Commencement Features: Spelman Seminary." Voice of The Negro. Vol. 2, July, 1905, pp. 446.

3105
Dailey, Mozelle E. "A Study of The Success of Booker T. Washington High School Students Who Entered Spelman College During The Years 1936-1941." Master's Thesis, Atlanta University, 1946, 33p.

3106
Day, Marie Dansby. "An Index to The Spelman Messenger, November, 1891 Through June, 1898." Master's Thesis, Atlanta University, 1963, 32p.

3107
"Greetings Sent By Dr. Bowen To Spelman Seminary Upon The Celebration of Her Twenty-fifth Anniversary." Voice of The Negro. Vol. 3, May, 1906, pp. 456-357.

3108
"History of The Transfers of Land and Buildings In Connection With Development of The Plan of Affiliation of Atlanta University, Morehouse College and Spelman College," in A Candle In The Dark: A History of Morehouse College, by Edward A. Jones. Valley Forge, Pennsylvania: Judson Press, 1967, 380p., pp. 328-364.

3109
McDonnell, Henrietta Isabella. "The Reading Interests And Habits of The Spelman College Alumnae Classes From 1930 Through 1954." Master's Thesis. Atlanta University, 1957, 65p.

3110
Parks, John T. "A Comparative Study of The Measured Vocational Interests and Perferences of The Spelman Sophomores of 1947-1948, With Their Stated Vocational Interests and With Their Actual Work In 1952." Master's Thesis, Atlanta University, 1954, 57p.

3111
Read, Florence Matilda. The Story of Spelman College. Atlanta: Florence M. Read, 1961, 399p.

3112
Saine, Matilda Lynette. "A Comparison of The Effectiveness of Drills and Guided Free Reading As Mehtods For Improving The Reading Abilities of Twenty-eight Spelman College Freshmen." Master's Thesis, Atlanta University, 1942, 62p.

3113
"Spelman President Honored." Morehouse Journal of Science. Vol. 3, October, 1929, pp. 156.

3114
"Spelman Seminary Is Founded," in A Candle In The Dark: A History of Morehouse College, by Edward A. Jones. Valley Forge, Pennsylvania: Judson Press, 1967, 380p., pp. 44-47.

3115
"Spelman's Twenty-fifth Anniversary." Voice of The Negro. Vol. 3, May, 1906, pp. 322-323.

3116
Tapley, Lucy Hale. "Spelman College." Atlanta Historical Bulletin. Vol. 1, May, 1930, pp. 38-56.

3117
Washington, Josephine Henrietta. "An Analysis and Evaluation of The Experimental Data of The Will-Temperament Test Results of Sixty-seven Spelman Freshmen (Girls). Master's Thesis, Atlanta University, 1940, 46p.

3118
Wilson, Hulda A. "An Evaluation of The Materials Collection Of The Spelman College Library." Master's Thesis, Atlanta University, 1962, 31p.

Tuskegee Woman's Club

3119
"Members of Woman's Club Portray Historic Loves." Tuskegee Messenger. Vol. 5, March 9, 1929, pp. 7.

3120
"Tuskegee Woman's Club Holds First Meeting." Tuskegee Messenger. Vol. 1, October, 25, 1924, pp. 1.

3121
"Tuskegee Woman's Club Notes." Tuskegee Messenger. Vol. 5, February 9, 1929, pp. 8.

3122
Washington, Booker T. (Mrs.). "The Tuskegee Woman's Club." The Southern Workman. Vol. 49, August, 1920, pp. 365-369.

3123
"Women of Alabama Meet Here In Annual Session." Tuskegee Messenger. Vol. 4, June 30, 1928, pp. 1, 8.

Young Women's Christian Association

3124
Batterham, E. Rose. "Negro Girls And The Y.W.C.A." The Southern Workman. Vol. 48, September, 1919, pp. 437-441.

3125
Bell, Ruth Hamlin. "A History of The Phillis Wheatley Branch Of The Indianapolis Young Women's Christian Association, 1923-1944." Master's Thesis, Indiana University, 1948, 85p.

3126
Bond, J. Max. "The Rosenwald Y.W.C.A. Development For Negroes." Master's Thesis. University of Pittsburgh, 1931, 103p.

3127
"Busy Center of Activity In Harlem Is The Colored Women's Branch Y.W.C.A." New York Age. 10 November, 1923, pp. 7.

3128
"Chicago YWCA Hails Senior Women For Living History." Jet. Vol. 46, July 25, 1974, pp. 55.

3129
Cohron, Ruby Myra. "A Study of Fifty Volenteer Workers In The Phillis Wheatley Young Women's Christian Association, Atlanta, Georgia." Master's Thesis, Atlanta University, 1942, 63p.

3130
"Colored "Y" Workers In Attendance At Eastern Y.W.C.A. Conference." New York Age. 4 August, 1923, pp. 5.

3131
Colored Young Women's Christian Association, Third and Fourth Year's Report, May 1907-May, 1901. Washington, D. C.: Miner Institute, 1909, 15p.

3132
"Colored Y.W.C.A. Serves Thousands As A Bureau of Information and Direction." New York Age. 15 December, 1932, pp. 8.

3133
"Council of Colored Work For The National Board Y.W.C.A." New York Age. 17 June, 1922, pp. 7.

3134
"Discuss Extension of "Y" Work In South Among Negro Women." New York Age. 12 March, 1921, pp. 1.

3135
Drayton, Julia Camille. "A Study of The Inter-Club Council of

The Business and Professional Department, Phillis Wheatley Branch Y.W.C.A., Atlanta, Georgia, February 1947 to February, 1949." Master's Thesis, Atlanta University, 1949, 33p.

3136
Fauset, Jessie. "The "Y" Conference at Talladega." The Crisis. Vol. 26, September, 1923, pp. 213-215.

3137
Hunton, Addie W. "The Work of The National Board of The Young Women's Christian Association," in The New Voice In Race Adjustment, edited by A. M. Trawick. New York: Student Volunteer Movement, 1914, 230p., pp. 215-219.

3138
Mack, Ursulla Gertrude. "A Study of The Membership of The Industrial Department of The Phillis Wheatley Branch Young Women's Christian Association As A Basis For Program Planning." Master's Thesis, Atlanta University, 1946, 51p.

3139
McNeil, Delores Evelyn. "A History of The Blue Triangle Y.W.C.A. In Columbus, Ohio, 1918-1952." Master's Thesis, The Ohio State University, 1972, 90p.

3140
"Miss Bowles, Y Secretary Made Survey of Association Work On The Pacific Coast." New York Age. 4 August, 1923, pp. 2.

3141
"Much Progress Is Noted At Annual Meeting of Y.W.C.A." Norfolk Journal And Guide. 7 February, 1925, pp. 2.

3142
"National Board Y.W.C.A. Tells of Work With Colored Girls." New York Age. 14 May, 1921, pp. 2.

3143
"Nat'l Y.W.C.A. Board Holds 2nd Conference." New York Age. 25 August, 1923, pp. 2.

3144
"Negro Women Get 11 National YW Posts." New York Amsterdam News. 17 May, 1952.

3145
"New Home For Negro Women." Omaha Bee. 12 August, 1914.

3146
Olcott, Jane. The Work of Colored Women. New York: Y.W.C.A., 1919, 136p.

3147
Peebles, Alice Delores. "A Study of Selected Campers Known To The Phillis Wheatley Y.W.C.A., Atlanta, 1948." Master's Thesis, Atlanta University, 1949, 34p.

3148
"Phillis Wheatley Y.W.C.A. Is Now A Strong Institution." New York Age. 17 March, 1923, pp. 1, 2.

3149
Sloan, Vivian Louise. "A Compilation and Interpretation of The Social and Recreational Needs of The Negro Women and Girls of Atlanta, Georgia, With An Analysis of These Needs In Relationship To The Y.W.C.A. Program." Master's Thesis, Atlanta University, 1945, 46p.

3150
"Thirty-Eighth Anniversary Celebration of The Phillis Wheatley Y.W.C.A." Pulse. Vol. 1, July, 1943, pp. 25.

3151
Thomas, Ruth Adelle. "A Description of The Harlem Branch Young Women's Christian Association Extension Program." Master's Thesis, Atlanta University, 1951, 44p.

3152
Titus, Laura E. "A Negro Young Woman's Christian Association." The Southern Workman. Vol. 43, December, 1914, pp. 700-702.

3153
"Two Negro Women Get High Posts in YWCA." Jet. Vol. 2, May 22, 1952, pp. 8.

3154
Washington, Ella Jane. "A Study of The Co-ed Program of The Y-Teen Department of the Harlem Branch Young Women's Christian Association, October, 1947 - January, 1948." Master's Thesis, Atlanta University, 1948, 30p.

3155
"White "Y" Girls Want Colored Girls Out." New York Age. 19 November, 1921, pp. 1.

3156
Williams, Augustine J. "A Comparison of The Policies and Procedures of The National Y.W.C.A. and The Phillis Wheatley Y.W.C.A. of Washington, D. C.: Master's Thesis, Atlanta University, 1949, 39p.

3157
"Y Holds First Regional Confer'ce." Norfolk Journal And Guide. 12 February, 1927, pp. 8.

3158
"Y Work Among Women." New York Age. 3 December, 1921, pp. 4.

3159
"Y.W.C.A. Conference." The Southern Workman. Vol. 50, April, 1921, pp. 151-152; August, 1921, pp. 342-343; Vol. 54, September, 1925, pp. 392.

3160
"Y.W.C.A. Conference At Wilberforce." Tuskegee Messenger. Vol. 11, April/May, 1935, pp. 11.

3161
"Y.W.C.A. (Harlem)." The Brown American. Vol. 2, January, 1937, pp. 15, 17.

3162
"Y.W.C.A. Residence House Is Valuable Aid To Work." New York Age. 10 February, 1923, pp. 1.

3163
Young, Thomas W. "Phillis Wheatley Branch Y.W.C.A. Years Has Been Great Factor in Moral and Physical Development of Girls and Young Women of The Race." Norfolk Journal And Guide. 19 September, 1925, pp. 7.

3164
"Young Women's Christian Association." Norfolk Journal And Guide. 2 September, 1925, pp. 1.

3165
"The Young Women's Christian Association," in Recreation And Amusement Among Negroes In Washington, D. C.: A Sociological Analysis of The Negro In An Urban Environment, by William H. Jones. Washington, D, C.: Howard University Press, 1927, 216p., pp. 55-62.

Zeta Phi Beta Sorority

3166
Anderson, Anita. "Zeta Phi Beta Sorority Holds Annual Meeting in Washington, D. C." The Negro Woman's World. January, 1936, pp. 201.

3167
Bowman, LaBarbara. "Sorors and Soul Sisters." Washington Post. 6 August, 1970.

3168
"New Chapter Zeta Phi Beta Sorority Is Organized Here." Norfolk Journal And Guide. 24 December, 1927, pp. 7.

3169
"Zeta Phi Beta Sorority, Inc." Washington Afro American. 29 June/3 July, 1974, pp. 16.

3170
"Zeta Phi Beta Sorority Holds Its 5th Convention." New York Age. 10 January, 1925, pp. 9.

3171
"Zeta Phi Beta To Meet In Atlanta." New York Age. 22 December, 1923, pp. 5.

ORGANIZATIONS—ADDRESSES

3172
African American Women's Association
6222 A Street, N. E.
Washington, D. C. 20002

3173
Alpha Kappa Alpha Sorority
5211 S. Greenwood
Chicago, Illinois 60615

3174
Black Mothers United For Action
2406 26th Avenue
Oakland, California 94601

3175
Black Women Employment Program
Southern Regional Council
52 Fairlie Avenue, N. W.
Atlanta, Georgia 30303

3176
Black Women Organized For Action
5340 E. Olympic Boulevard
Los Angeles, California 90022

3177
Black Women's Agenda
1817 H Street, N. W.
Washington, D. C.

3178
Black Women's Association of Pittsburgh
P. O. Box 193
Pittsburgh, Pennsylvania 19103

3179
Black Women's Community Development Foundation
1028 Connecticut Avenue, N. W.
Washington, D. C. 20036

3180
Black Women's Employment Project
NAACP Legal Defense and Educational Fund, Inc.
10 Columbus Circle
New York, New York 10019

3181
Black Women's Institute
National Council of Negro Women
1817 H Street, N. W.
Washington, D. C.

3182
Black Women's Liberation Committee
346 West 20th Street
New York, New York 10010

3183
Black Women's Network
1522 K Street, N. W.
Washington, D. C. 20005

3184
Delta Sigma Theta Sorority
1717 New Hampshire Avenue, N. W.
Washington, D. C. 20009

3185
Links, Inc.
c/o Ms. Audrey Thorne
505 Laguardia Place
Apt. 21D
New York, New York 10012

3186
National Association of Black Women Attorneys
715 G Street, N. W.
Washington, D. C. 20001

3187
National Association of College Women
4620 Kossuth Avenue
St. Louis, Missouri 63115

3188
National Association of Minority Women In Buxiness
906 Grand
Suite 500
Kansas City, Missouri 64106

3189
National Black Feminist Organization
370 Lexington Avenue
Room 601
New York, New York 10017

3190
National Black Sisters Conference
3333 5th Avenue
Philadelphia, Pennsylvania 15213

3191
National Council of Negro Women
1817 H Street, N. W.
Washington, D. C.

3192
National Grand Chapter
Order of Eastern Star
5040 Joy Road
Detroit, Michigan 48204

3193
Organization of Black Women
New York University
21 Washington Place
New York, New York 10003

3194
Women's History Research Center, Inc.
2325 Oak Street
Berkeley, California 94708

3195
Zeta Phi Beta Sorority
1734 New Hampshire Avenue, N. W.
Washington, D. C. 20009

POLITICS AND GOVERNMENT

3196
Aba-Mecha, Barbara Woods. "Black Woman Activist In Twentieth Century South Carolina: Modjeska Monteith Simkins." Doctoral Dissertation, Emory University, 1978, 434p.

3197
Ainsworth, Marilyn. "Black Political Activists." Black Law Journal. Vol. 2, Summer, 1972, pp. 149-153.

3198
Alpha Kappa Alpha Sorority. Women In Politics. Chicago: AKA Sorority, 1969, 35p.

3199
Bailey, Peter. "The Lady To See In Pennsylvania." Ebony. Vol. 27, July, 1972, pp. 60.

3200
"Birmingham's Lady Mayor." Our World. Vol. 5, October, 1950, pp. 42.

3201
"Black and Female Power Rises in Public Life." Washington Evening Star. 24 August, 1974, pp. D-7.

3202
"Black Co-ed Wins Seat On Nevada Board of Regents." Jet. Vol. 47, December 26, 1974, pp. 28.

3203
"Black Female Mayor, 87, Didn't Want The Job." Jet. Vol. 48, September 4, 1975, pp. 24.

3204
"Black Mayor." Jet. Vol. 46, September 12, 1974, pp. 23.

3205
"Black Woman Appointed To White House Council." Jet. Vol. 40, June 3, 1971, pp. 27.

3206
"Black Woman Dr. Makes History, Gets Va. Post." Jet. Vol. 54, January 19, 1978, pp. 16.

3207
"Black Woman Enters Race For Lt. Gov. In Florida." Jet. Vol. 54, August 17, 1978, pp. 16.

3208
"Black Woman Gains Louisiana House Seat." Jet. Vol. 49, January 22, 1976, pp. 7.

3209
"Black Woman Holds Key to Democratic Harmony." Jet. Vol. 42, July 13, 1972, pp. 24-27.

3210
"Black Woman To Head Brown U. Student Body." Jet. Vol. 54, February 16, 1978, pp. 25.

3211
"Black Woman Wins La. Assembly Seat." Jet. Vol. 39, March 4, 1971, pp. 7.

3212
"Black Women In Electoral Politics. Focus (Joint Center for Political Studies. Vol. 1, August, 1973, 4p.

3213
"Black Women on Capitol Hill: Females In Government." Ebony. Vol. 29, June, 1974, pp. 122-124, 126-127.

3214
"Black Women Politicos Eased Out." Encore. Vol. 4, July 7-14, 1975, pp. 10.

3215
Britton, J. "Black Women in Politics: Do We Have A Future?" Essence. Vol. 5, March, 1975, pp. 80-81, 90.

3216
Brown, Geoffrey F. "Montant's First Black Legislator Scores Big During First Quarter." Jet. Vol. 48, July 10, 1975, pp. 22-23.

3217
Brown, Warren. "U. S. Congress Gets Three New Black Lawmakers." Jet. Vol. 43, November 30, 1972, pp. 20-26.

3218
__________. "Women Challenge System in Bids for Congress Seats." Jet. Vol. 43, September 28, 1972, pp. 12-16.

3219
Bryce, Herrington J. and Alan E. Warrick. "Black Women In Elective Office." Black Scholar. Vol. 6, October, 1974, pp. 17-20.

3220
Burke, Yvonne B. "Black Women in Politics.Today." Contact. Vol. 5, Fall, 1974, pp. 20, 24, 64.

3221
______________. "True Power - An Illusory Concept." Encore. Vol. 4, June 23/July 4, 1975, pp. 80.

3222
"California Legislature Gets Only Black Female Member." Jet. Vol. 48, August 7, 1975, pp. 23.

3223
Chamberlin, Hope. A Minority of Members: Women In The U. S. Congress. New York: Praeger, 1973, 374p.

3224
"Chicago Woman Gets High State Appointment." Jet. Vol. 44, August 9, 1973, pp. 18.

3225
Chisholm, Shirley. "Race, Revolution and Women." Black Scholar. Vol. 3, December, 1971, pp. 17-21.

3226
"City Near Los Angeles Elects Woman As Mayor." Jet. Vol. 44, June 21, 1973, pp. 17.

3227
"Colored G.O.P. Women Prepare To Organize." Columbus Journal. 14 March, 1918.

3228
"Colored Women Plan Inaugural Reception." Norfolk Journal And Guide. 24 January, 1925, pp. 11.

3229
"Colored Women Republicans Of Connecticut In State Convention At New Haven." New York Age. 10 May, 1924, pp. 7.

3230
"Colored Women Study Politics." Philadelphia Press. 22 August, 1919.

3231
"Cool-Headed Lady of The Crisis Bureau." Ebony. Vol. 23, June, 1968, pp. 56-58, 60, 62.

3232
"Councilwoman Named in Election Violation." Jet. Vol. 1, March 6, 1952, pp. 7.

3233
"Crusading Mom Seeks Seat In U. S. Congress." Jet. Vol. 39, March 4, 1971, pp. 5.

3234
Cummings, Judith. "Black Women in Public Life." Black Enterprise. Vol. 5, August, 1974, pp. 33-35.

3235
Dietsch, Robert. "Carter's HUD Secretary Is Sharp-Minded, Sharp-Tongued Woman Lawyer." Cincinnati Post And Times Star. 22 December, 1976.

3236
"Dr. Allen's Newest Patient: The City of Philadelphia." Ebony. Vol. 28, May, 1973, pp. 124-126, 128, 130-131.

3237
"First Black Assemblywoman." Sacramento Observer. 1 June, 1972, pp. D-21.

3238
"First Black Woman." Jet. Vol. 40, May 27, 1971, pp. 9.

3239
"First Black Woman Elected To Chicago City Council." Jet. Vol. 39, March 11, 1971, pp. 8.

3240
"First Black Woman in The U. S. House of Representatives: Congresswoman Shirley Chisholm." The Negro History History Bulletin. Vol. 33, May, 1970, pp. 128.

3241
"First Black Woman in Pennsylvania Governor's Cabinet." The Negro History Bulletin. Vol. 34, March, 1971, pp. 61.

3242
"First Black Woman is Named to Illinois Cabinet." Jet. Vol. 42, April 6, 1972, pp. 5.

3243
"First Black Woman Named by Carter As HUD Secretary." Arkansas Gazette. 22 December, 1976.

3244
"First Black Woman on Capitol Hill." Ebony. Vol. 24, February, 1969, pp. 58-59.

3245
"First Negro Woman Elected to Ill. Democrat Post." Jet. Vol. 6, May 20, 1954, pp. 8.

3246
"Fla's Only Black Female Rep. May Not Run Again." Jet. Vol. 50, July 22, 1976, pp. 21.

3247
"Former Congresswoman Burke Appointed Supervisor." Sacramento Observer Magazine. Vol. 16, June 14-20, 1979, pp. A-2.

3248
"Four In One; First Negro Woman to Head American Embassy." Time. Vol 85, May 28, 1965, pp. 23.

3249
"Getting Elected," In ...To Form A More Perfect Union... Justice For American Women. Report of The National Commission of The Observance of International Women's Year. Washington D. C.: G. P. O., 1976, 382p., pp. 41-44.

3250
Gill, Gerald R." 'Win or Lose - We Win': The 1952 Vice-Presidential Campaign of Charlotta A. Bass,: in The Afro American: Struggles and Images, edited by Sharon Harley and Rosalyn Terborg-Penn. New York: Kernikat Press, 1978, 137p., pp. 109-118.

3251
"Governor's Press Aide: In Louisiana Capitol, A Black Woman Helps To Break Old Barriers of Deep South Racism." Ebony. Vol. 29, September, 1974, pp. 72-74, 76, 78, 80.

3252
Harper, Marieta L. "Black Women and The Development of Black Politics." Journal of Afro-American Issues. Vol. 5, Summer, 1977, pp. 276-284.

3253
Horton, Luci. "The Distaff of Politics." Ebony. Vol. 29, December, 1973, pp. 48-54.

3254
____________. "Doris Davis: Her Honor The Mayor."Ebony. Vol. 28, September, 1973, pp. 105-108, 110, 112.

3255
"Illinois Legislature's 1st Black Woman Member Dies." Jet. Vol. 45, October 18, 1973, pp. 24.

3256
"In The Political Field:" The Woman's National Magazine. Vol. 7, April, 1940, pp. 53, 57.

3257
Jones, John E. "First Black Woman in Columbus Mayor's Council." Dawn Magazine. May 8, 1975, pp. 6, 17.

3258
Jones, Susie W. "Women's Responsibility for Government." The Aframerican Woman's Journal. Spring, 1944, pp. 8-9.

3259
"Jordan No. 1 Woman Choice for President, Polls Show. " Jet. Vol. 48, November 6, 1975, pp. 8.

3260
King, Mae C. "Oppression and Power: The Unique Status of The Black Woman in The American Political System." Social Science Quarterly. Vol. 56, June, 1975, pp. 116-128.

3261
Kramer, Dale. "America's Newest Diplomat." New Republic. Vol. 124, January 22, 1951, pp. 15-16.

3262
"Lady Mayor Mayersville." Ebony. Vol. 32, December, 1977, pp. 53-56.

3263
Lansing, Marjorie. "The Voting Pattern of American Black Wo-Women." Annual Meeting of the American Political Science Association. New Orleans, 1973.

3264
Lesher, S. "Short, Unhappy Life of Black Presidential Politics, 1972." New York Times Magazine. June 25, 1972, pp. 12-13.

3265
"Link Negro Councilwoman in Cleveland Vote Probe." Jet. Vol. 2, August 21, 1952, pp. 4.

3266
"Madame Secretary of State: The Honorable Vel Phillips." Black Excellence. Vol. 2, December, 1978/January-February, 1979, pp. 3-4.

3267
"Many Black Woman Qualify For Posts in Administration." Jet. Vol. 43, November 23, 1972, pp. 14.

3268
McCormack, Patricia. "Black Women in Politics...More Now Than Ever." Washington Post. 18 August, 1974, pp. F-8.

3269
"Michigan Swears in First Negro Woman Senator." Jet. Vol. 3, January 29, 1953, pp. 9.

3270
Miller, Judy Ann. "California's Black Lady Legislator." Black Politician. Vol. 2, Fall, 1970, pp. 14.

3271
_______________. "The Representative Is A Lady." Black Politician. Vol. 1, Fall, 1969, pp. 17-18.

3272
"More Black Women Hold Elected Political Offices." Jet. Vol. 45, September 27, 1973, pp. 31.

3273
"Mrs. Collins Crushed Foes To Win U. S. House Seat." _Jet_. Vol. 44, June 21, 1973, pp. 17.

3274
"Mrs. Collins Set To Enter Congress After Big Victory." _Jet_. Vol. 44, May 3, 1973, pp. 14.

3275
"Mrs. Lawson: Next U. S. Envoy to Denmark?" _Jet_. Vol. 19, January 26, 1961, pp. 3.

3276
"National Black Women's Political Group." _Sacramento Observer_. 1 June, 1972, pp. D-22.

3277
"The Negro Woman in Politics." _Ebony_. Vol. 21, August, 1966, pp. 96-100.

3278
"Negro Woman is First Named As Ambassador." _Washington Evening Star_. 19 May, 1965.

3279
"Negro Woman May Go as Envoy To Luxembourg." _Washington Evening Star_. 17 May, 1965.

3280
"Negro Women of Houston Register In Large Numbers." _Houston Chronicle_. 8 July, 1918.

3281
"New Envoy: Negro Woman; LBJ Picks Her For Luxembourg." _U. S. News and World Report_. Vol. 58, May 31, 1965, pp. 16.

3282
"New Kind of Candidate, She's Black." _Newsweek_. Vol. 79, February 24, 1972, pp. 24-26.

3283
"New York's New Lady Senator." _Sepia_. Vol. 13, May, 1964, pp. 35-39.

3284
"Once On Welfare, Black Woman Now Mayor Of Her Hometown in Taft, Okla." _Jet_. Vol. 44, June 21, 1973, pp. 18.

3285
"Our Lady in Luxembourg." _Sepia_. Vol. 14, December, 1965, pp. 18-22.

3286
"Our Lone Committeewoman." _Norfolk Journal And Guide_. 26 September, 1925, pp. 12.

3287
"Patricia Harris Picked For Top Post at HEW." Jet. Vol. 56, August 9, 1979, pp. 5.

3288
Poinsett, Alex. "Patricia Harris: HUD's Velvet-Gloved Iron Hand." Ebony. Vol. 34, July, 1979, pp. 33-34, 36.

3289
"Political Dynamite." Headlines. Vol. 1, November, 1944, pp. 15.

3290
"Political Leadership Group for Black Women is Formed by Detroit Representative." Jet. Vol. 41, February 3, 1972, pp. 7.

3291
Preece, Harold and Shirley Biondi. "Two New Black 'First' Ladies In Congress." Sepia. Vol. 21, October, 1972, pp. 46-48, 50, 52, 54, 56, 58, 60, 62.

3292
Prestage, Jewel. "Black Women Officeholders: The Case of State Legislators," in Women In The Professions, edited by Laurily Keir Epstein. Massachusetts: Lexington Books, 1975, 142p., pp. 81-96.

3293
"Profile: C. Delores Tucker, Top Black Woman in State Government." African Woman. September/October, 1976, pp. 41-42.

3294
"Republican Women Rally." Pulse. Vol. 5, December, 1947, pp. 7.

3295
"Republican Women To Give New Voters A Suffrage Course." New York Age. 1 March, 1924, pp. 1.

3296
"Republican Women Want Recognition In The Government." Norfolk Journal And Guide. 20 June, 1925, pp. 8.

3297
Robinson, Louie. "Women Lawmakers on The Move." Ebony. Vol. 27, October, 1972, pp. 48-56.

3298
Sanders, Charles. "Ambassador Is A Lady: Patricia Roberts Harris." Ebony. Vol. 21, January, 1966, pp. 23-26, 28, 30, 32.

3299
"Seek Black GOP Woman As A Booster For Reagan." Jet. Vol. 54, January 12, 1978, pp. 9.

3300
"Sexism, Racism Hamper Black Women Seeking Political Offices." Afro American. 28 August, 1973, pp. 18.

3301
"A Slim Past, But A Strong Future." Ebony. Vol. 32, August, 1977, pp. 89-92, 94, 96, 98.

3302
"Texas Senator May Become 14th Black in U. S. House." Jet. Vol. 40, July 1, 1971, pp. 8.

3303
"Top Black Woman Official Leaves To Do 'Own Thing'." Jet. Vol. 41, March 16, 1972, pp. 22.

3304
"21 Year-Old Woman In Washington Mayoral Race." Jet. Vol. 46, September 12, 1974, pp. 22.

3305
White, Joyce. "Women In Politics." Essence. Vol. 7, October, 1976, pp. 56-57, 96, 98.

3306
Williams, Frances Harriet. "A Woman Looks At Her Government." Opportunity. Vol. 21, April, 1943, pp. 73, 94.

3307
"Woman Named Deputy Mayor in Philly And Post Pays $34,000." Jet. Vol. 45, March 7, 1974, pp. 15.

3308
"Women Bring Hope To Politics Says Delegate." Washington Afro American. 24 November, 1973, pp. 7.

3309
"Women Hold Political Caucus in Washington." Jet. Vol. 44, June 21, 1973, pp. 7.

3310
"Women Hold 3 Day Parley In Washington." Norfolk Journal And Guide. 28 May, 1927, pp. 9.

3311
"Women Register Another Gain In Political Prestige." Norfolk Journal And Guide. 11 July, 1925, pp. 9.

3312
"Women Took Active Part In Atlantic City Conference of Colored Republicans." New York Age. 11 August, 1923, pp. 2.

3313
"Women Who Make State Laws." Ebony. Vol. 22, September, 1967, pp. 27-30, 32, 34.

PSYCHOLOGY AND MENTAL HEALTH

3314
Abrahams, Roger D. "Negotiating Respect: Patterns of Presentation Among Black Women." Journal of American Folklore. Vol. 88, January/March, 1975, pp. 58-80.

3315
Anthony-Welch, Lillian Doloris. "A Comparative Analysis of The Black Woman As Transmitter of Black Values, Based On Case Studies of Families in Ghana, And Among Jamaicans And Afro Americans in Hartford, Connecticut." Doctoral Dissertation, University of Massachusetts, 1976, 413p.

3316
Bagozzi, Richard P. "The Construct Validity of The Affective, Behavioral, and Cognitive Components of Attitude by Analysis of Convariance Structures." Multivariate Behavioral Research. Vol. 13, January, 1978, pp. 9-31.

3317
Battle, Kathryn W. "Attitudes of Relatives Toward Female Patients of Wassaic State School Who Are Ready For Convalescence." Master's Thesis, Howard University, 1953, 65p.

3318
Bingham, Rossie Rhillips. "The Concurrent Validity of Two Measures Operationalizing Holland's Theory Using A Sample of College Degree Black Women." Doctoral Dissertation, The Ohio State University, 1977, 102p.

3319
"Black Women Cooler Than White Feemes." Jet. Vol. 40, May 20, 1971, pp. 51.

3320
"Black Women Have Lowest Suicide Rate." Jet. Vol. 49, November 13, 1975, pp. 6.

3321
Blakley, Dorothy Tucker. "Internal and External Locus-of-Control and The Perception of Responsibility For Interpersonal Conflict Among Black Males and Females." Doctoral Dissertation, California School of Professional Psychology, 1976, 146p.

3322
Bonner, Marita O. "On Being Young - A Woman - And Colored." The Crisis. Vol. 31, December, 1925, pp. 63-65.

3323
Brandyburg, Mayme S. "A Study of The Expected and Actual Behavior of Negro Adolescent Girls In A Southern Rural Community." Master's Thesis, Hampton Institute, 1952, 40p.

3324
Brenman, Margaret. "Relationship Between Minority Group Membership and Group Identification In A Group of Urban Middle Class Negro Girls." Journal of Social Psychology. Vol. 11, February, 1940, pp. 171-197.

3325
Brown, Delindus R. and Wanda F. Anderson. "A Survey of The Black Woman and The Persuasion Process: The Study of Strategies of Identification and Resistance." Journal of Black Studies. Vol. 9, December, 1978, pp. 233-248.

3326
Burwell, Sherri Lynn. "The Soul of Black Women: The Hermeneutical Method of Analysis As Applied To The Novel Corredidora." Doctoral Dissertation, California School of Professional Psychology, 1979, 109p.

3327
Caliman, Alvis W. "Personality Adjustment of Aging Women." Doctoral Dissertation, Michigan State University, 1952, 115p.

3328
Campbell, Barbara L. "Systematic Desensitization: An Approach To The Treatment of Black Female Delinquent Adolescents." Doctoral Dissertation, California School of Professional Psychology, 1978, 82p.

3329
Chassin, Laurie. "Sex Role Identification, Sex-Role Preference and Psychopathology In Lower Class Black Adolescent Girls." Doctoral Dissertation, Columbia University, 1977, 141p.

3330
Chisholm, Helen E. "A Preliminary Study of Interpersonal Relations In A Girl's Reformatory." Master's Thesis, Howard University, 1939, 29p.

3331
Clark, Ellen Flanagan. "Selected Personality Characteristics of Primapara and Multipara Unmarried and Married Lower Class Negro Women." Doctoral Dissertation, St. John's University, 1972, 112p.

3332
Cooper, Lillie Dolores Preston. "Aspirations, Attitudes And Changing Roles of Black Women in American Society." Doctoral Dissertation, Wayne State University, 1975, 197p.

3333
Copeland, Elaine J. "Counseling Black Women With Negative Self Concepts." Personnel and Guidance Journal. Vol. 55, March, 1977, pp. 397-400.

3334
Cuffaro, Sara Todd. "A Discriminant Analysis of Sociocultural, Motivation, and Personality Differences Among Black, Anglo and Chicano Female Drug Users In A Medium Security Prison." Doctoral Dissertation, U. S. International University, 1978.

3335
Cundiff, Cynthia H. "Fear of Success, Social Class And Performance In Competive and Non-Competive Situations In Black College Women." Master's Thesis, Howard University, 1972, 79p.

3336
Dansby, Pearl Gore. "Perceptions of Role and Status of Black Females." Journal and Social And Behavioral Sciences. Vol. 21, Winter, 1975, pp. 31-38.

3337
Darity, Evangeline Royall. "A Comparison of Fear-of-Success Imagery Between Black Male and Female Undergraduates." Doctoral Dissertation, University of Massachusetts, 1978, 244p.

3338
Davis, June Bernice. "Reflex, Premotor and Reaction Times For Black and White Females to A Kinesthetic Stimulus." Doctoral Dissertation, Texas Woman's University, 1975, 106p.

3339
Davis, Maria Susanne. "Sex-Role Factors In The Career Development of Black Female High School Students." Doctoral Dissertation, University of Cincinnati, 1977, 162p.

3340
deAlmeida, Eleanor Engram, "A Descriptive And Analytical Study of The Early Adult Roles of Black and White Women." Doctoral Dissertation, Duke University, 1977, 123p.

3341
Duckro, Rose, Paul Duckro and Don Beal. "Relationship of Self-Disclosure and Mental Health in Black Females." Journal of Consulting and Clinical Psychology. Vol. 44, December, 1976, pp. 940-944.

3342
Eagleson, Oran W. and Eleanor S. Bell. "The Values of Negro Women College Students." Journal of Social Psychology, Vol. 22, November, 1945, pp. 149-154.

3343
Fitzpatrick, Virginia Briggs. "Body Image and Weight Loss In Chronically Obese and Late Onset Obese Black Lower Socioeconomic Status Adolescent Girls." Doctoral Dissertation, The Catholic University of America, 1975, 79p.

3344
Fleming, Jacqueline. "Predictive Validity of The Motive To Avoid Success In Black Women." Humanitas. Vol. 13, May, 1977, pp. 225-244.

3345
Foster, Frances S. "Changing Concepts of The Black Woman." Journal of Black Studies. Vol. 3, June, 1973, pp. 433-454.

3346
Fowler, Dale Eugene. "An Exploratory Investigation of The Relationship Between Locus-of-Control and Parenting Tasks Among Lower Socio-economic Status Black Mothers." Doctoral Dissertation, University of Florida, 1978, 114p.

3347
Frumkin, Robert M. and Mayme S. Brandyburg. "Expected Versus Actual Social Behavior of Negro Adolescent Girls In A Southern Rural Community." Journal of Negro Education. Vol. 23, Spring, 1954, pp. 197-200.

3348
Gardner-Coleman, Jacquelyn Lea. "A Comparative Study of The Assertiveness of Black and White Women At The University Level." Doctoral Dissertation, Southern Illinois University at Carbondale, 1977, 79p.

3349
Goldberg, Eugene L., Wayne A. Myers and Israel Zeifman. "Some Observations On Three Interracial Analyses." International Journal of Psycho-Analysis. Vol. 55, 1974, pp. 495-500.

3350
Goldberg, Marsha. "The Black Female Client: The White Psychotherapist: An Evaluation of Therapy Through Clients' Retrospective Reports." Doctoral Dissertation, California School of Professional Psychology, 1972, 233p.

3351
Gordon, Ruth L. Hill. "Differential Value Patterns of Black and White Women in Higher Education." Doctoral Dissertation, U. S. International University, 1974, 108p.

3352
Grant, Gwendolyn Gertrude Goldsby. "Black Female Leadership Success In Mental Health: An Exploratory of Determinants And Coping Behavior." Doctoral Dissertation, Fairleigh Dickinson University, 1978, 285p.

3353
Gray, Susan W. "Notes on The Values of Southern College Women, White and Negro." Journal of Social Psychology. Vol. 25, May, 1947, pp. 239-241.

3354
Griggs, Shirley Ann. "A Study of The Life Plans of Culturally Disadvantaged Negro Adolescent Girls With Father-Absent In the Home." Doctoral Dissertation, Columbia University, 1967, 249p.

3355
Gullatte, Alyce C. "Psychiatric Factors to Consider In Research On The Black Woman." The Journal of Afro American Issues. Vol. 2, Summer, 1974, pp. 199-203.

3356
Hannon, Charles B. "Black Female Adolescents' Self-Concept," in Perspectives On Afro American Women, edited by Willa D. Johnson and Thomas L. Green. Washington, D. C.: Educational Community Counselors Associates, Inc., 1975, 197p., pp. 126-145.

3357
Hanson, Barbara. "Black Process In Clinically Depressed Women: A Conceptual Framework For Practice." Clinical Social Work Journal. Vol. 2, Fall, 1974, pp. 163-171

3358
Harrison, Algea O. "Dilemma of Growing Up Black And Female." Journal of Social and Behavioral Sciences. Vol. 20, Spring, 1974, pp. 28-40.

3359
Henderson, Grace Gist. "The Academic Self-Concept of Black Female Children Within Differential School Settings," in Perspectives On Afro American Women, edited by Willa D. Johnson and Thomas L. Green. Washington, D. C.: Educational Community Counselors Associates, Inc., 1975, 197p., pp. 146-164.

3360
Herbert, Jill C. "Manifest and Latent Constructions Of Power in Black and White Working Class Women." Doctoral Dissertation, New School for Social Research, 1976, 240p.

3361
Howell, C. Diane. "Black Concepts of The Ideal Black Woman." Doctoral Dissertation, University of California At Berkeley, 1978, 137p.

3362
Howze, Beverly. "Suicide: Special References to Black Women." Journal of Nonwhite Concerns. Vol. 5, January, 1977, pp. 65-72.

3363
Jackson, Agnes Durham. "Militancy And Black Women's Competive Behavior In Competive vs. Non-Competive Conditions." Doctoral Dissertation, Rutgers University, 1978, 90p.

3364
Jackson, Lorraine Brannon. "The Attitudes of Black Females Towards Upper and Lower Class Black Males." Master's Thesis, Howard University, 1971, 23p.

Jackson, Lorraine Brannon. "The Attitudes of Black Females Towards Upper and Lower Class Black Males." The Journal of Black Psychology. Vol. 1, February, 1975, pp. 53-64.

3365
Jackson, Pamela R. "Self-Conceptions in Black Male and Female College Students." Doctoral Dissertation, Michigan State University, 1972, 114p.

3366
Jarman, Frances Elaine. "Need Patterns in Verbalization of Black College and Non-College Female Interviews." Doctoral Dissertation, University of North Carolina at Chapel Hill, 1972, 98p.

3367
Johnson, Bernice Dickerson. "A Comparative Study of Levels Of Emotional Maturity of Freshmen and Senior Women at Virginia State College." Master's Thesis, Virginia State University, 1949, 24p.

3368
Johnson, Dwight Lamont. "A Look At Black Female Suicides From A Socioeconomic Point of View." Master's Thesis, Atlanta University, 1974, 59p.

3369
Johnson, Leon Johanson, Sr. "A Comparative Study of The Womanhood Experiences of Black Young Adult Females and White Young Adult Females." Doctoral Dissertation, University of Southern California, 1976, 97p.

3370
Kellogg, Nina F. "Fulfillment of Psychological Deprivation Needs Through Foster Parenting By Black Women." Doctoral Dissertation, Claremont Graduate School, 1976, 202p.

3371
Knebel, Fletcher. "Identity...The Black Woman's Burden." Look. Vol. 33, September 23, 1969, pp. 77-79.

3372
Langdon, Elva M. "A Comparative Study of the Adjustment of Fifty-three Pairs of Negro and White Girls of Junior High School Age." Master's Thesis, University of Michigan, 1939, 102p.

3373
Lattimore, Caroline Louise. "The Relationship of Selected Antecedent Conditions and Locus Of Control Among Black Adolescent Females." Doctoral Dissertation, Duke University, 1978, 220p.

3374
London, Arcenia Phillips. "Determinants of Self-Acceptance of Black Female School Teachers Selected From The Syracuse Public School System and From Little Rock, Arkansas, Public School System." Doctoral Dissertation, Syracuse University, 1975, 164p.

3375
Lucas, Frances. "Miles To Go Before We Sleep." MH. Vol. 59, Spring, 1975, pp. 14-16.

3376
Lunceford, Ronald Douglas. "Self-Concept Change of Black College Females As A Result of A Weekend Black Experience Encounter Workshop." Doctoral Dissertation, U. S. International University, 1973, 83p.

3377
McEachin, Lois E. "A Study of The Social Factors Which Seem To Have Played A Part in The Readiness of 25 Negro Female Patients Readmitted To St. Elizabeth's Hospital Between July 1, 1949 to October 13, 1950." Master's Thesis, Howard University, 1951.

3378
Merkerson, John Wesley. "A Study of The Tested Differences In Personality Manifested By Twenty-five Female Non-Athletes at Price High School in Atlanta, Georgia." Master's Thesis, Atlanta University, 1959, 81p.

3379
Moore, Mordean T. "The Mental Health Problems And Treatment Of Black Women In An Urban Community Mental Health Center." Doctoral Dissertation, Brandeis University, 1979, 205p.

3380
Mosley, Martha Mae. "A Comparative Study of Certain Personality Factors of A Group of Delinquent and Non-Delinquent Negro Girls." Master's Thesis, Fisk University, 1941, 73p.

3381
Mugrauer, Bertha M. "A Cultural Study of Ten Negro Girls In An Alley." Doctoral Dissertation, The Catholic University of America, 1951, 239p.

3382
Murdock, Louis J. "Utilizing Smith's Inventory To Investigate Black Male and Female Differences In Identity Structure." Doctoral Dissertation, University of Pittsburgh, 1974, 162p.

3383
Myers, Lena Wright. "Black Women: Selectivity Among Roles And Reference Groups in The Maintenance Of Self-Esteem." Journal of Social And Behavioral Sciences. Vol. 21, Winter, 1975, pp. 39-47.

3384
________________. "A Study of The Self-Esteem Maintenance Process Among Black Women." Doctoral Dissertation, Michigan State University, 1973, 135p.

3385
"A New Face, A New Force In Mental Health.Care." Ebony. Vol. 30, September, 1975, pp. 64-66, 68.

3386
"No More Sapphires or Black Pearls: Self-Definition Is Where It Starts," in Woman In The Year 2000, by Maggie Tripp. New York: Arbor House Publishing Company, 1974, 302p., pp. 38-49.

3387
Oldham, Ernestine V. "The Socio-Economic Status and Personality of Adolescent Negro Girls." Journal of Negro Education. Vol. 4, October, 1935, pp. 514-522.

3388
Owens, Susan. "Self-Esteem of Black Women In A Comparative Perspective," in Perspectives On Afro American Women, edited by Willa D. Johnson and Thomas L. Green. Washington, D. C.: Educational Community Counselors Associates, Inc., 1975, 197p., pp. 92-102.

3389
Parsons, Patricia Fowler. "Research On Black Female Self-Concept: Origins, Issues, and Directions." Doctoral Dissertation, Claremont Graduate School, 1974, 131p.

3390
Pendergrass, Virginia E., Ellen Kimmel, Joan Joesting, Joyce Patersen and Endilee Bush. "Sex Discrimination In Counseling." American Psychologist. Vol. 31, January, 1976, pp. 36-46.

3391
Pickhardt, Carl Emile, II. "Perceptions By Self And Others of

Female Black and White Teachers Before And After A Six Week Training Institute." Doctoral Dissertation, University of Texas at Austin, 1970, 154p.

3392
Poussaint, Alvin. "Physical Abuse And The Black Woman." Essence. Vol. 1, October, 1970, pp. 5.

3393
Puryear, Gwendolyn Randall. "Fear of Success In Black College Women As It Related To Militancy And Effective Attachment." Master's Thesis, Howard University, 1971, 36p.

3394
Puryear, Gwendolyn Randall and Martha T. S. Mednick. "Race and Fear of Success In Black College Women: 1968 and 1971." Journal of Consulting and Clinical Psychology. Vol. 44, October, 1976, pp. 787-789.

3395
Redfering, David L. "Differential Effects of Group Counseling With Black and White Female Delinquent Girls: One Year Later." Journal of Negro Education. Vol. 44, Fall, 1975, pp. 530-537.

3396
Richardson, Winifred Ann. "The Self-Image of The Young Adult Negro Woman." Master's Thesis, The Ohio State University, 1967, 88p.

3397
Rosenblatt, Aaron and John E. Mayer. "Help Seeking For Family Problems: A Survey Of Utilization and Satisfaction." American Journal of Psychiatry. Vol. 128, March, 1972, pp. 1136-1140.

3398
Samuel, Nadene and Dorothy S. Laird. "The Self Concepts of Two Groups of Black Female College Students." Journal of Negro Education. Vol. 43, Spring, 1974, pp. 228-233.

3399
Sandford, May Daniels. "The Relationship Between Home Economics Teachers' Self-Awareness and Perception of Inner City Seventh-Grade and Eighth-Grade Negro Girls' Coping Behavior Related To Problems With Boys." Doctoral Dissertation, Columbia University, 1970, 198p.

3400
Schwartz, Marianne P. "The Perception of Social Class And Social Status and Its Relationship To Stereotyped Perception As Evidence of Social Distance In A Selected Group of Negro Women." Master's Thesis, University of Southern California, 1964, 88p.

3401
Scott, Jean C. "How The National Training School For Girls Uses The District of Columbia Child Guidance Clinic." Master's Thesis, Howard University, 1950, 39p.

3402
Scott, Patricia Bell. "The English Language and Black Womanhood: A Low Blow to Self-Esteem." The Journal of Afro American Issues. Vol. 2, Summer, 1964, pp. 218-225.

3403
Shansky, Carolbeth Rosner. "The Personality Correlates of Hypertension And Field Dependence In Black Women." Doctoral Dissertation, Illinois Institute of Technology, 1976, 160p.

3404
Shockley, Ann A. and Veronica E. Tucker. "Black Women Discuss Today's Problems: Men, Families, Society." Southern Voices. Vol. 1, August/September, 1974, pp. 16-19.

3405
Simpson, Wessylyne Alford. "Self-Concept And Career Choice Among Black Women." Doctoral Dissertation, Oklahoma State University, 1975, 73p.

3406
Singletary, Deborah. "Black Women - Building A New Self Image," in Woman In The Year 2000, by Maggie Tripp. New York: Arbor House Publishing Company, 1974, 302p., pp. 43-46.

3407
Sitkin, Emily Malsin. "Measurement of Prospective Fantasy And Other Factors In Pregnant Black Teen-Age Girls." Doctoral Dissertation, Columbia University, 1972, 166p.

3408
Slater, Jack. "Suicide: Growing Menance To Black Women." Ebony. Vol. 28, September, 1973, pp. 152-155.

3409
"Social Psychiatry Of Sexual Crisis Among Black Men And Women," in Coming Together: Black Power, White Hatred And Sexual Hang-ups, by Clavin C. Hernton. New York: Random House, 1971, 181p., pp. 147-181.

3410
Sterling, Dorothy H. "The Experience of Being-Me For Black Adolescent Females: A Phenomenological Investigation of Black Identity." Doctoral Dissertation, University of Pittsburgh, 1974, 292p.

3411
Stojanovic, Elisabeth J. "Morale and Its Correlates Among Aged Black And White Rural Women In Mississippi." Doctoral Dissertation, Mississippi State University, 1970, 125p.

3412
"Stresses And Strains On Black Women." Ebony. Vol. 29, June, 1974, pp. 33-36, 38, 40.

3413
"Study Shows Black Women See Whites Less Appealing." Jet. Vol. 45, March 4, 1974, pp. 16.

3414
Swanson, Doris D. "The Effects of Behavioral Group-Counseling On The Self-Concept of Pregnant Negro Teenagers Using Male and Female Counselors." Doctoral Dissertation, State University of New York at Buffalo, 1972, 172p.

3415
Taylor, Sue Perkins. "Aging In Black Women: Coping Strategies and Lifeways Within An Urban Population." Doctoral Dissertation, University of Massachusetts, 1978, 250p.

3416
Thorpe, Claiburne B. "Aspiration: An Index of Black Female Personality." Journal of Social and Behavioral Sciences. Vol. 19, Summer/Fall, 1972, pp. 8-12.

3417
Tooks, Kelly T. "Neurotic Tendency of Negro Women Of Low Socio-Economic Status Compared With The Neurotic Tendency of Negro College Women." Master's Thesis, Howard University, 1949, 17p.

3418
Towns, Grace. "Emotional Attitudes of Negro Girls In High School and College." Master's Thesis, The Ohio State University, 1929, 41p.

3419
Vail, John Paul. "The Effects of Encountertapes For Personal Growth on Centain Specific Aspects of The Intellectual, Behavioral, and Self-Concept Development Of Culturally Disadvantaged Negro Girls." Doctoral Dissertation, University of Georgia, 1959, 154p.

3420
Verinis, J. Scott. "Maternal and Child Pathology In An Urban Ghetto." Journal of Clinical Psychology. Vol. 32, January, 1976, pp. 13-15.

3421
Watson, Vernaline. "Self-Concept Formation and The Afro American Woman." The Journal of Afro American Issues. Vol. 2, Summer, 1974, pp. 226-236.

3422
White, Ruth Prather. "The Value of Part-time Work Experience To The Counselor (Former Titles "What A Counselor Can Learn From Work Experiences" and "An Analysis of Four Major

Occupations For Negro Women")." Master's Thesis, New York University, 1942, 31p.

3423
White, Vivian E. "The Social Contributions of A Welfare Center For Negro Grils In The City of Los Angeles." Master's Thesis, University of Southern California, 1947, 127p.

3424
Williams, Bertha M. "Black Women: Assertiveness vs. Aggressiveness." The Journal of Afro American Issues. Vol. 2, Summer, 1974, pp. 204-211.

3425
Williams, Lillian Augusta. "Black Women and Self-Image: A Phenomenological-Existential Case History Approach." Doctoral Dissertation, California School of Professional Psychology, 1976, 550p.

3426
Wright, Madeleine Elaine Pate. "Self-Concept And The Coping Process of Black Graduate and Undergraduate Women At A Predominantly White University." Doctoral Dissertation, University of Michigan, 1975, 139p.

3427
Yates, Charlotte. "The Influence of New York City Environment Upon The Intelligence Scores of Twelve Year Old Negro Girls." Master's Thesis, Columbia University, 1932, 22p.

RELIGION

3428
Adams, Elizabeth. Dark Symphony. New York: Sheed & Ward, 1942, 194p.

3429
African Methodist Episcopal Church Women In Action. Chicago: AME Church, 1975, 146p.

3430
Alexander, Margaret Walker. "Chief Worshipers At All World Altars." Encore. Vol. 4, June 23/July 4, 1975, pp. 67-68.

3431
"AME Women Convene In D. C. In July." Pittsburgh Courier. 25 June, 1955.

3432
"AME Women Give $18Gs For Sickle Cell Anemia." Jet. Vol. 44, July 26, 1973, pp. 44.

3433
"AMEZ Sunday-Schools Form A New Organization, Mrs. M. A. Moore, President." New York Age. 11 August, 1923, pp. 7.

3434
"America's First Black Nuns Fete 150 Years of Service." Jet. Vol. 56, August 2, 1979, pp. 30.

3435
"An Arrow From The Bent Bow of The Gospel," in Black Women In Nineteenth-Century American Life: Their Words, Their Thoughts, Their Feelings, by Bert James Loewenberg and Ruth Bogin. University Park: Pennsylvania State University Press, 1976, 355p., pp. 125-180,

3436
Andrew, John A., Jr. "Betsey Stockton: Stranger In A Strange Land." Journal of Presbyterian History. Vol. 52, 1974, pp. 157-166.

3437
"Baptist Women In Convention At Local Church." Norfolk Journal And Guide. 23 June, 1923, pp. 1.

3438
Bennett, Ambrose. Woman's Missionary Society Guide. Nashville: National Baptist Convention, n.d., 99p.

3439
"Black Madonna." Liberator. Vol. 7, June, 1967, pp. 14-15.

3440
"The Black Woman: A Christmas Perspective." Black Monitor. Vol. 1, December, 1976, pp. 6-7.

3441
"Black Woman Elected Church Moderator." Jet. Vol. 44, July 12, 1973, pp. 7.

3442
"Black Women Plan National Conference." The Wesley Foundation. January 9, 1976, pp. 1.

3443
Blackwell, W. A. "National Association of Ministers Wives." Star of Zion. Vol. 19, August, 1915.

3444
"A Brief Historical Sketch of The Woman's Home Missionary Society, The Methodist Episcopal Church In Relation To The The Freedman's Aid Society." in Two Centuries Of Methodist Concern: Bondage, Freedom and Education of Black People, by James P. Brawley. New York: Vantage Press, 1974, 606p., pp. 123-137.

3445
Burley, Dan. "Mistresses of Ministers." Jet. Vol. 5, February 4, 1954, pp. 18-20.

3446
Calhoun, Lillian S. "Woman On The Go For God." Ebony. Vol. 18, May, 1963, pp. 78-81, 84, 86, 88.

3447
Campbell, I. K. (Mrs.). "Woman's Day Address." The AME Zion Quarterly Review. Vol. 60, #4, 1950, pp. 188-191.

3448
Campbell, J. P. "The Ordination of Women: What's The Authority For It?" The AME Church Review. Vol. 2, April, 1886, pp. 351-361.

3449
"Claire Harvey To Be Cited As 'Churchwoman Of The Year'." Jet. Vol. 46, May 30, 1974, pp. 44.

3450
"Colored Women Organize First Congress In Canada." New York Age. 26 June, 1920.

3451
"Colored Women's Conference Held At Christiansbury, Va." New York Age. 10 September, 1921, pp. 1.

3452
"Composer of Unique Church History Pageant." Norfolk Journal And Guide. 26 March, 1927, pp. 2.

3453
"Conference of Church Women." The Southern Workman. Vol. 55, November, 1926, pp. 485-486.

3454
"Conference of Colored Women Held At Cambria." Norfolk Journal And Guide. 9 July, 1927, pp. 10.

3455
"Conference of Presbyterian Women Held." Norfolk Journal And Guide. 11 July, 1925, pp. 6.

3456
Crawford, Eilleen E. "A Comparative Study of The Socio-Cultural Dynamics of The Role of Women In Nationalist Religious Movements: A Case Study of The Nation of Islam In The United States and The Cherubim and Seraphim Movement In Nigeria." Master's Thesis, Howard University, 1973, 110p.

3457
DeWitt, Karen. "Rose Catchings' Saving Grace." Essence. Vol. 6, March, 1976, pp. 82-83, 129-130.

3458
"Expansion of Mission Work of AME Church." Norfolk Journal And Guide. 5 November, 1927, pp. 9.

3459
"Female Ministry Milestone." Jet. Vol. 47, October 17, 1974, pp. 52.

3460
"1st Black Woman Also 1st Southerner To Head Church Women United." Jet. Vol. 40, May 20, 1971, pp. 15.

3461
"First Black Woman Priest Ordained For Episcopalians." Jet. Vol. 51, January 27, 1977, pp. 8.

3462
"First Negro Woman Priest Holds Service In N. C." Washington Post. 25 February, 1977, pp. D-14.

3463
"First Woman Acolyte." Jet. Vol. 47, March 20, 1975, pp. 46.

3464
"First Woman Chaplain." Jet. Vol. 46, August 1, 1974, pp. 20.

3465
"First Woman To Get Doctor of Divinity Degree." Norfolk Journal And Guide. 4 July, 1925, pp. 8.

3466
Fitchett, Elijah H. "The Role of The Minister's Wive In Modern Society." The Foundation. Vol. 29, 1949.

3467
Gillard, John T. More Negro Nuns. Baltimore: Josephite Press, n.d., 48p.

3468
Guidry, Mary Gabriella. The Southern Negro Nun: An Autobiography. New York: Exposition Press, 1974, 156p.

3469
Hartvik, Allen. "Catherine Ferguson: Black Founder Of A Sunday School." The Negro History Bulletin. Vol. 35, December, 1972, pp. 176-177.

3470
Hill, Hilda Anderson. "The College Woman And The Church." Journal of The National Association of College Women. #12, 1935, pp. 5-8.

3471
Hill, Raymond George. "Social Work of The Colored Sisterhoods: A Historical Study." Master's Thesis, The Catholic University of America, 1932, 37p.

3472
"Holy War of The Rev. Trudie Trimm." Ebony. Vol. 24, September, 1969, pp. 72-74, 76-77.

3473
Hoover, Theressa. "Black Women And The Churches: Triple Jeopardy," in Sexist Religion And Women In The Church: No More Silence, edited by Alice Hageman. New York: Association Press, 1974, 221p., pp. 63-76.

3474
"How To Become A Nun." Ebony. Vol. 10, December, 1954, pp. 107-110, 113-114, 116.

3475
Jones, Deborah. "In His Image." Essence. Vol. 5, November, 1974, pp. 101.

3476
Jones, Pearl Williams. "A Minority Report: Black Pentecostal Women." Spirit: A Journal of Issues Incident To Black Pentecostalism. Vol. 1, #2, 1977, pp. 31-44.

3477
Kline, Alberta. "Women: The Guiding Light In Religion." New York Age. 29 October, 1949.

3478
"Lady Preachers." Jet. Vol. 5, February 18, 1954, pp. 26-28.

3479
Lee, Jarena. Religious Experiences And Journal of Mrs. Jarena Lee, Giving An Account of Her Call To Preach The Gospel. Philadelphia: Jarena Lee, 1849, 97p.

3480
McAfee, Sara Jane. History of The Woman's Missionary Society in The Colored Methodist Episcopal Church. Jackson, Tennessee: CME Church Publishing House, 1934, 203p.

3481
Meeks, Cathy. I Want Somebody To Know My Name. Nashville: T. Nelson, 1978, 153p.

3482
"Methodist Women Act To Lift Racial Barriers." Jet. Vol. 2, October 16, 1952, pp. 30.

3483
"Methodist Women Adopt Plans Against Bias." Jet. Vol. 1, January 31, 1952, pp. 20.

3484
Mielke, Sharon. "Women Examine Missions." The Wesley Foundation. January 9, 1976, pp. 3.

3485
"Missionary Department," in A History of The African Methodist Episcopal Church, by Charles Spencer Smith. Philadelphia: Book Concern of The AME Church, 1922, 570p., pp. 342-343.

3486
"New York Woman Goes To French Congo As Baptist Missionary." New York Age. 1 Spetember, 1923, pp. 1.

3487
"None But Women Members In This Carolina Church." Norfolk Journal And Guide. 1 August, 1925, pp. 8.

3488
Norment, Lynn. "The Miracle of Providence: The Oblate Sisters Celebrate 150 Years of Service To The Black Community." Ebony. Vol. 34, September, 1979, pp. 142-144, 146.

3489
"Nun Urges Backing Ghetto." Ebony. Vol. 23, October, 1968, pp. 48-50.

3490
Oliver, Elizabeth M. "Statue Is Dedicated To Oblate Sisters Founder." Dawn Magazine. Vol. 6, September, 1978, pp. 16-17.

3491
"The Order of Shepherds and Daughters of Bethlehem Meet." Norfolk Journal And Guide. 19 September, 1925, pp. 10.

3492
Polk, Alma A. Twelve Pioneer Women In The African Methodist Episcopal Church. n.p.: Alma A. Polk, 1947, 36p.

3493
"Presbyterians Elect Black Woman To High Office." Jet. Vol. 50, July 1, 1976, pp. 9.

3494
Schmelz, Annie M. "A Presbyterian Conference For Colored Women." The Southern Workman. Vol. 54, September, 1925, pp. 416-418.

3495
"Serving God Is Helping One Another." Black Stars. Vol. 7, November, 1977, pp. 6-10.

3496
Sharrieff, Bayyinah. "Messenger Muhammad: Reformer of The Black Woman." Muhammad Speaks. May 19, 1972, pp. 18.

3497
Sherwood, Grace. Oblates: One Hundred And One Years. New York: MacMillan, 1931, 226p.

3498
"Sister Lois Davis: Black Nun." Sacramento Observer. 1 June, 1972, pp. D-20.

3499
Smith, Vernon E. "The Perpetual Mission of Mother Waddles." Ebony. Vol. 27, May, 1972, pp. 50-52, 54, 56, 58.

3500
"They Ordain Women, But..." Washington Evening Star. 26 June, 1976, pp. B-8.

3501
"3rd Annual Southern District Meeting, Indiana Conference Branch Women's Mite Missionary Society." The Missionary Recorder. Vol. 33, April, 1941, pp. 2.

3502
"Training School For Colored Workers." Southern Churchman. 22 July, 1922.

3503
Valentine, Rachel. "Synopisis of The History of The Women's Missionary Society, A.M.E. Church." Missionary Magazine. Vol. 19, September, 1971, pp. 17.

3504
"Virginia Likely To Get New Seminary For Negro Women." Norfolk Journal And Guide. 12 September, 1925, pp. 1.

3505
"We Belong Together: The Gospel Lights, Mother-Daughter Evangelists." Pulse. Vol. 1, June, 1943, pp. 26-27.

3506
White, Joyce. "Women In The Ministry." Essence. Vol. 7, November, 1976, pp. 62-63, 104, 107-108.

3507
Willingham, Saundra. "Why I Quit The Convent." Ebony. Vol. 24, December, 1968, pp. 64-66, 68, 70, 72, 74.

3508
Winston, Ethna Beulah. "Religion in The Guidance of Women For Community Responsibility." Quarterly Review of Higher Education Among Negroes. Vol. 9, October, 1941, pp. 189-190.

3509
"Woman Chaplain Breaks Barrier." Ebony. Vol. 30, October, 1975, pp. 44-46, 48, 50-52.

3510
"Woman of God." Our World. Vol. 6, February, 1951, pp. 42-45.

3511
"Woman's Baptist State Convention Meets In Danville." Norfolk Journal And Guide. 20 June, 1925, pp. 6.

3512
"Women At The Beginning Of The Sunday School Movement." Christian Recorder, 28 October, 1909.

3513
"The Women's Baptist Home Mission Convention of North Carolina," in A History of The Negro Baptists of North Carolina, by J. A. Whitted. Raleigh: Edwards & Broughton Printing Company, 1908, 212p., pp. 112-120.

3514
"Women's Mission Body In Its Annual Session." New York Age. 13 August, 1921, pp. 7.

3515
"Women's Mite Missionary Society." Norfolk Journal And Guide. 12 May, 1917, pp. 6.

3516
"Women's Work," in History of The Negro Baptists of Tennessee, by Thomas O. Fuller. Memphis: Thomas O. Fuller, 1936, 346p., pp. 144-162.

SCIENCE

3517
Banks, Lester. "Scientific Job Opportunities." The Crisis. Vol. 63, April, 1956, pp. 205-207.

3518
"Black Contributors To Science and Energy Technology - Annie Easley: Computer Codes For Energy Technology." Soul Teen. Vol. 9, July, 1979, pp. 68.

3519
"Black Woman Named To National Science Board." Jet. Vol. 47, October 31, 1974, pp. 5.

3520
"Chicago Girl Chemist." Chicago Defender. 30 April, 1921, pp. 1.

3521
"Clinical Laboratory." The Brown American. Vol. 3, September, 1939, pp. 11-12.

3522
"Dr To Long Island Ducks (Women As Scientists)." Ebony. Vol. 19, September, 1964, pp. 76-78, 80, 82.

3523
George, Yolanda Scott. "The Status of Black Women In Science." The Black Collegian. Vol. 9, May/June, 1979, pp. 64, 68-72, 114.

3524
Malcolm, Shirley, Paula Quick-Hall and Janet Welsh Brown. The Double Bind: The Price of Being A Minority Woman In Science. Washington, D. C.: American Association For The Advancement of Science, 1976, 70p.

3525
"The Negro Female Science Doctorate," in Negroes In Science:

Natural Science Doctorates, 1876-1969, by James M. Jay. Detroit: Belamp, 1971, 87p., pp. 58-61.

3526
"New York Girl Selected To Head Chemistry Dept. at Shaw Univ., Raleigh." *New York Age*. 30 August, 1924, pp. 9.

3527
"Only One of Five." *Headlines And Pictures*. Vol. 2, December, 1945, pp. 39.

3528
"Scientist Named 'Young Woman of The Year' by Mademoiselle Magazine. *The Negro History Bulletin*. Vol. 16, March, 1953, pp. 128.

3529
"Theogood and Burton, Clinical Laboratories." *Negro Business*. Vol. 1, August, 1939, pp. 8.

3530
U. S. Department of Labor, Women's Bureau. "Negro Women," in *The Outlook For Women In Science (General Information)*. Bulletin #223-1. Washington, D. C.: G. P. O., 1952, 81p pp. 58-61.

SEX AND SEXUAL DISCRIMINATION

3531
"Are Kept Women Out of Vogue?" Jet. Vol. 6, September 9, 1954, pp. 22-24.

3532
"Are Negro Women Getting Sexier?" Jet. Vol. 1, January 31, 1952, pp. 28-31.

3533
"Bitch's Brew," in Beautiful, Also, Are The Souls Of My Black Sisters: A History of The Black Woman In America, by Jeanne Noble. New Jersey: Prentice-Hall, 1978, 353p., pp 313-346.

3534
"A Black Man Speaks Out For Black Women." Black Male/Female Relationships. Vol. 1, June/July, 1979, pp. 4, 29.

3535
"Black Women Psychiatrist Says Sex Manuals Not Intended For Blacks." Jet. Vol. 40, June 24, 1971, pp. 46.

3536
"Black Women; Double Discrimination." Sepia. Vol. 18, September, 1969, pp. 18-19.

3537
"Black Women Called Most Disadvantaged In American Society." Jet. Vol. 42, May 11, 1972, pp. 10.

3538
Bond, Julian. "Self-Defense Against Rape: The Joanne Little Case." Black Scholar. Vol. 6, March, 1975, pp. 29- 30.

3539
Bonner, Florence B. "Black Women and White Women: A Comparative Analysis of Perceptions of Sex Roles For Self, Ideal-Self And The Ideal-Male." The Journal of Afro-American Issues. Vol. 2, Summer, 1974, pp. 237-247.

3540
Brooks, Gwendolyn. "Why Negro Women Leave Home." _The Negro Digest_. Vol. 9, March, 1951, pp. 26-28.

3541
Buck, Pearl S. "Women - A Minority Group." _Opportunity_. Vol. 18, July, 1940, pp. 201-202.

3542
Chisholm, Shirley. "A Black Congresswoman Speaks Out For Women's Rights," in _Women In American Life: Selected Readings_, edited by Anne Firor Scott. New York: Houghton-Mifflin, 1970, 214p., pp. 195-197

3543
________________. "A Visiting Feminine Eye: I'd Rather Be Black Than Be Female." _McCalls_. Vol. 97, August, 1970, pp. 6.

3544
Cooper, Anna Julia. "Double Discrimination," in _Women In American Life: Selected Readings_, edited by Anne Firor Scott. New York: Houghton-Mifflin, 1970, 214p., pp. 83-87.

3545
Crawford, Charlene. "The Status of Black Women." _Ebony_. Vol. 30, March, 1975, pp. 26.

3546
"The Current Snares of Sexism: Inequality In Any Class," in _Womanhood In America: From Colonial Times To Present_, by Mary R. Ryan. New York: New Viewpoints, 1975, 496p., pp. 365-429.

3547
Cuthbert, Marion V. "Problems Facing Negro Young Women." _Opportunity_. Vol. 14, February, 1936, pp. 47-49.

3548
"The Damnation Of Women," in _Darkwater: Voices From Within The Veil_, by W. E. B DuBois. New York: Schocken Books, 1920, 276p., pp. 163-186.

3549
"Darkwater - 'The Damnation of Women'." in _The Art And Imagination of W. E. B. DuBois_, by Arnold Rampersad. Cambridge: Harvard University Press, 1976, 325p., pp. 176.

3550
De Ridder, Joyce Anna. "Sex Related Roles, Attitudes, And Orientation of Negro, Anglo and Mexican-American Women Over The Life Cycle." Doctoral Dissertation, North Texas State University, 1976, 42p.

3551
"Do Women Improve With Age?" _Jet_. Vol. 6, July 22, 1954, pp. 22-25.

3552
"Early Sex Life Is Forced On Black Women: Sociologist." Jet. Vol. 42, June 29, 1972, pp. 15.

3553
Fitzgerald, William A. "Pseudoheterosexuality In Prison And Out: A Study of The Lower Class Black Lesbian." Doctoral Dissertation, City University of New York, 1977, 357p.

3554
Fox, Loreda Lynn White. "A Comparative Analysis of Internal-External Locus-Of-Control and Sex Role Concepts In Black And White Freshmen Women." Doctoral Dissertation, East Texas State University, 1975, 79p.

3555
Gardner, Mynelle. "The Black Woman." The Afro American Journal. Vol. 1, May, 1973, pp. 4, 10.

3556
George, Felicia. "Black Woman, Black Man." Harvard Journal Of Afro-American Affairs. Vol. 2, #2, 1971, pp. 1-17.

3557
Gillespie, Marcia Ann. "Macho Myths and Michele Wallace." Essence. Vol. 10, August, 1979, pp. 76-77, 99-100, 102.

3558
Grosnenor, Verta Mae. "Is A Woman 'Over The Hill' At 40?" Ebony. Vol. 32, August, 1977, pp. 144-146, 148.

3559
Gump, Janice P. "Comparative Analysis of Black Women's and White Women's Sex Role Attitude." Journal of Consulting And Clinical Psychology. Vol. 43, December, 1975, pp. 858-863.

3560
Hackney, Mykel Ann. "Black, Beautiful and Harasses." Essence Vol. 7, May, 1976, pp. 15.

3561
Hambrick, Edith R. "Black Woman To Black Woman." Liberator. Vol. 9, February, 1969, pp. 8.

3562
Hare, Nathan. "Black Male-Female Relations." Doctoral Dissertation, California School of Professional Psychology, 1975, 173p.

3563
Harris, Mary Mitchell. "Personal Constructions of Sex-Typed Roles and Need Achievement Among Black and White Women." Doctoral Dissertation, University of Pittsburgh, 1974, 168p.

3564
Haynes, Michelle. "Black Sisterhood Discovered." Essence. Vol. 6, November, 1975, pp. 36.

3565
Hine, Darlene C. "Female Slave Resistance: The Economics of Sex." The Western Journal of Black Studies. Vol. 3, Summer, 1979, pp. 123-127.

3566
Hobson, Charles. "What Black Men Want From Black Women." Essence. Vol. 1, September, 1970, pp. 38-41.

3567
"Hollywood Beauties Rap About Sensual Side of Black Dudes." Jet. Vol. 46, July 11, 1974, pp. 54-57.

3568
Horne, Lena. "The Three-Horned 'Dilemma' Facing Negro Women." Ebony. Vol. 21, August, 1966, pp. 118-122, 124.

3569
Jackson, Jacquelyne J. "But Where Are The Men." Black Scholar. Vol. 3, December, 1971, pp. 30-41.

3570
"Joan Little Case: Biggest Civil Rights Trial of '70s." Washington Evening Star. 13 July, 1975, pp. A-1, A-5.

3571
Johnson, Linda D. "The Black Woman." The Afro-American Journal. Vol. 2, November/December, 1974, pp. 15.

3572
Johnson, Robert. "Are Women Changing Our Sex Morals?" Jet. Vol. 4, August 27, 1953, pp. 26-28.

3573
Karenga, Maulana Ron. "In Love And Struggle: Toward A Greater Togetherness." Black Scholar. Vol. 6, March, 1975, pp. 16-28.

3574
King, Mae C. "The Politics of Sexual Stereotypes." Black Scholar. Vol. 4, March/April, 1973, pp. 12-23.

3575
Kirby, Dorothy Lovette. "Suicide In The First Degree." New Lady. Vol. 4, May, 1971, pp. 9, 43-44.

3576
Labinjohn, Justin. "The Sexual Life of The Oppressed: An Examination of The Family Life of Ante-Bellum Slaves." Phylon. Vol. 35, December, 1974, pp. 375-397.

3577
"Laws Ban Wedding of Ohio Lesbians." Jet. Vol. 47, February 20, 1975, pp. 22-24.

3578
Long, Amelia. "Role of The Afro American Woman." Liberator. Vol. 6, May, 1966, pp. 20.

3579
Lyles, Barbara D. "The Black Woman: Person or Non-Person." The Crisis. Vol. 82, May, 1975, pp. 163-166.

3580
McDougald, Elsie Johnson. "The Double Task - The Struggle of Negro Women For Sex and Race Emancipation." Survey. Vol. 53, March, 1925, pp. 689-691.

3581
McDowell, Ruth Doris Angel. "Beliefs About Sex Among College Women And The Sources of Their Information." Master's Thesis, Atlanta University, 1949, 55p.

3582
Mehliner, Kermit. "The Sexual Revolution." Ebony. Vol. 21, August, 1966, pp. 57-60, 62.

3583
"Men on Women." Essence. Vol. 2, January, 1972, pp. 28-29.

3584
Moore, Louise. "Black Men vs. Black Women." Liberator. Vol. 6, August, 1966, pp. 16-17.

3585
Nemy, Enid. "Numbers of Black Women Say They Will Not Date White Men." New York Times. 23 November, 1970, pp. 44C.

3586
Norment, Lynn. "Older Women - Younger Men." Ebony. Vol. 33, May, 1978, pp. 74-76, 78, 80.

3587
Ottley, Roi. "What's Wrong With Negro Women?" The Negro Digest. Vol. 9, December, 1950, pp. 71-75.

3588
Parks, Carole A. "Today's Black Woman Examines Her Role With Black Men." Jet. Vol. 39, January 14, 1971, pp. 24-27.

3589
Parrish, Milton. "Black Woman's Guide to The Black Man." Essence. Vol. 4, April, 1974, pp. 56-57, 91, 93, 95.

3590
Poussaint, Alvin and Ann Ashmore Poussaint. "Black Women/Black Men: Has Something Gone Wrong Between Them?" Ebony. Vol. 32, August, 1977, pp. 160-162.

3591
"Prejudice and Discrimination - Black Women," in Women and Sex

Roles: A Social Psychological Perspective, by Irene H. Frieze, et. al. New York: Norton, 1978, 444p., pp. 288-289.

3592
"Professor Says Black Women Face Race, Sex Burdens." Jet. Vol. 47, October 31, 1974, pp. 24.

3593
"Psychology of Rape." Black Male/Female Relationships. Vol. 1, June/July, 1979, pp. 19-20.

3594
"Quit Hiding, Fight The Real Enemy, Woman Scholar Tells Black Men." Jet. Vol. 40, May 20, 1971, pp. 51.

3595
"Rent-A-Doll Gets Tar and Feathers From Women's Lib." Jet. Vol. 42, July 20, 1972, pp. 44-45.

3596
Russell, Michelle and Mary Jane Lupton. "Black Women And The Market," in Feminist Frameworks: Alternative Theoretical Accounts of The Relations Between Women And Men, edited by Alison J. Jagger and Paula R. Strukl. New York: McGraw-Hill, 1978, 333p., pp. 25.

3597
Scarborough, Bernice. "Constructive Stillness for Use By Soul Sisters In Solving The Problem..." New Lady. Vol. 2, December, 1969, pp. 3-4.

3598
Self, Ruthie Lee. "Black Male/White Female Relationships: Implications For Black Women." Doctoral Dissertation, U. S. International University, 1978, 176p.

3599
"Sex Discrimination: Sharon Johnson vs. The University of Pittsburgh." Encore. Vol. 5, March 8, 1976, pp. 9-10.

3600
"Sex Habits of Negro Women." Jet. Vol. 1, January 10, 1952, pp. 18-21.

3601
"Sexual Life Between Black and White." Black Male/Female Relationships. Vol. 1, June/July, 1979, pp. 15-18.

3602
"Slavery And Sex," in Roots of Bitterness: Documents of The Social History of American Women, edited by Nancy F. Cott. New York: Dutton, 1972, 373p., pp. 181-216.

3603
Staples, Robert. "The Black Prostitute In White America," in The Black Family: Essays and Studies, by Robert Staples.

Belmont, California: Wadsworth Publishing Company, 1971, 393p., pp. 366-375.

3604
Staples, Robert. "Can Black Women Go It Alone?" Black Male/Female Relationships. Vol. 1, June/July, 1979, pp. 25-26.

3605
______________. "Research on Black Sexuality: It's Implications For Family Life, Sex Education, and Public Policy." Family Coordinator. Vol. 21, April, 1972, pp. 183-188.

3606
______________. "The Sexuality of Black Women." Sexual Behavior. Vol. 2, June, 1972, pp. 4-15.

3607
Stember, Charles Herbert. Sexual Racism: The Emotional Barriers To An Integrated Society. New York: Elsevier, 1976, 234p.

3608.
Stone, Pauline Terrelonge. "Institutional Sexism and The Quest For Racial Equality." The Black Collegian. Vol. 9, May/June, 1979, pp. 39-46, 112, 114.

3609
Thompson, Era Bell. "What Weaker Sex?" Ebony. Vol. 21, August, 1966, pp. 84-86, 88.

3610
Tolbert, Janette C. "Black Women: The Silent Victims of Rape." Essence. Vol. 4, February 17, 1975, pp. 20-22.

3611
Trescott, Jacqueline. "Fighting The 'Double Whammy' of Sexism and Racism In Careers." Washington Post. 6 March, 1976, pp. B-3.

3612
Turner, Inez. "Black Women - Futuristic Definition," in Woman In The Year 2000, edited by Maggie Tripp. New York: Arbor House, 1974, 302p., pp. 39-40.

3613
Walker, Alice. "Alice Walker Talks About Black Women." Encore. Vol. 2, April, 1973, pp. 41.

3614
Wallace, Michele. Black Macho and The Myth of The Superwoman. New York: Dial Press, 1979, 182p.

3615
Watson, Bill. "Shange Strikes A Major Chord." Black Arts Review. Vol. 2, July/August, 1979, pp. 3, 11.

3616
Weaver, Charles N. "Sex Differences In Job Satisfaction." Business Horizons. Vol. 17, June, 1974, pp. 43-49.

3617
Webster, Elizabeth Carol. "Personality Correlates of Sexual Responsiveness and Patterns of Organismic Functioning In Black Women." Doctoral Dissertation, New York University, 1978, 252p.

3618
"Where Have All The Black Males Gone?" Black Male/Female Relationships. Vol. 1, June/July, 1979, pp. 5.

3619
"Why Lesbians Marry." Jet. Vol. 3, January 1, 1953, pp. 20-23.

3620
"Why Women Become Call Girls." Jet. Vol. 4, June 4, 1953, pp. 26-29.

3621
Winslow, David J. "Occupational Superstitions of Negro Prostitutes In An Upstate New York City." New York Folklore Quarterly. Vol. 24, December, 1968, pp. 294-301.

3622
"Woman Wins Sex Bias Suit Against Justice Dept. Boss." Jet. Vol. 50, June 3, 1976, pp. 12.

3623
"Women on Men." Essence. Vol. 3, January, 1973, pp. 32-33.

3624
"Women Want To Wed." Jet. Vol. 41, October 28, 1971, pp. 7.

3625
"Women Who Fall For Lesbians." Jet. Vol. 5, February 25, 1954, pp. 20-22.

3626
"The World's Sexiest Negro Women." Jet. Vol. 1, December 27, 1951, pp. 33-41.

SLAVE NARRATIVES

3627
Albert, Octavia Victoria Roger. The House of Bondage; or, Charlotte Brooks and Other Slaves. New York: Hunt & Eaton, 1890, 161p.

3628
"The Auction Block Ends A Dream." Encore. Vol. 4, June 23/ July 4, 1975, pp. 28-29.

3629
Blassingame, John W. Slave Testimony: Two Centuries of Letters, Speeches, Interviews, And Autobiographies. Baton Rouge: Louisiana State University Press, 1977, 777p., pp. 7-8, 13-15, 20-23, 72-82, 87, 90, 96, 102, 106-107, 117-119, 183-189, 213-216, 268-274, 341-346, 387-390, 408-409, 411-412, 418, 454-465, 468-470, 500, 508-509, 562-565, 572-580, 589-594, 611-614, 639-655, 697-698, 738-740.

3630
Boyd, Georgia. Fugitive Girl. Rexdale, Ontario: Identity, 1977, 27p.

3631
Brent, Linda. "Slave and Master," in Women In American Life: Selected Readings, by Anne Firor Scott. New York: Houghton Mifflin, 1970, 214p., pp. 24-26.

3632
__________. "The Treats of Girlhood," in Roots of Bitterness: Documents Of The Social History of American Women, edited by Nancy F. Cott. New York: Dutton, 1972, 373p., pp. 200-208.

3633
Brown, Clarence. "Reflections On 119 Years of Living." Jet. Vol. 46, July 4, 1974, pp. 22-25.

3634
Browne, Martha Griffiths. Autobiography of A Female Slave. New York: Redfield, 1857, 401p.

3635
Burton, Annie L. Memories Of Childhood Slavery Days. Boston: Ross Publishing Company, 1909, 97p.

3636
Edwards, J. Lloyd. The Ex-Slave Extra, The Living Voice And Autobiography of An Ex-Slave In Bicentennial History. Chattanooga: Cosmopolitan Community Church, 1976, 108p.

3637
Goodson, Martia Graham. "An Introductory Essay and Subject Index To Selected Interviews From The Slave Narrative Collection." Doctoral Dissertation, Union Graduate School, 1977.

3638
______. "The Slave Narrative Collection: A Tool For Reconstructing Afro-American Women's History." The Western Journal of Black Studies. Vol. 3, Summer, 1979, pp. 116-123.

3639
Green, Thomas L. "The Voyage of The Sable Venus - Black Women in Slave Narratives," in Perspectives On Afro American Women, edited by Willa D. Johnson and Thomas L. Green. Washington, D. C.: Educational Community Counselors Associates, Inc., 1975, 197p., pp. 11-21.

3640
Harlan, Mary B. Ellen, or The Chained Mother; And Pictures Of Kentucky Slavery. Cincinnati: Applegate & Company, 1853, 259p.

3641
Jacobs, Harriet Brent. Incidents In The Life Of A Slave Girl. Edited by L. M. Child. Boston: n.p., 1861.

3642
"Narratives From Escaped Slaves," in Roots of Bitterness: Documents of The Social History of American Women, edited by Nancy F. Cott. New York: Dutton, 1972, 373p., pp. 186-193.

3643
Pickard, Kate E. R. The Kidnapped And The Ransomed: Being The Personal Recollections of Peter Still and His Wife. "Vina," After Forty Years of Slavery. New York: W. T. Hamilton, 1856, 409p.

3644
Ray, Emma. Twice Sold, Twice Ransomed: Autobiography of Mr. And Mrs. L. P. Ray. Chicago: Free Methodist Publishing House, 1926, 320p.

3645
Truth, Sojourner. "Narrative of A Life," in Female Liberation: History And Current Politics, by Robert Solper. New York: Knopf, 1972, 256p., pp. 75-82.

3646
_______________. "The Narrative of Sojourner Truth, 1878," in The American Sisterhood: Writings of The Feminist Movement From Colonial Times To The Present, by Wendy Martin. New York: Harper & Row, 1972, 374p., pp. 101-105.

3647
Veney, Bethany. A Narrative Of Bethany Veney: A Slave Woman. Philadelphia: Bicknell Press, 1970.

SPECIAL COLLECTIONS

3648
Afro-American Women's Collection
Thomas F. Holgate Library
Bennett College
Greensboro, North Carolina 27420

3649
Arthur & Elizabeth Schlesinger Library
On The History of Women In America
Radcliffe College
3 James Street
Cambridge, Massachusetts 02138

3650
International Women's History Archive
Special Collections Library
Northwestern University
Evanston, Illinois 60201

3651
Mary McLeod Bethune Memorial Museum & National
Archives For Black Women's History
1318 Vermont Avenue, N. W.
Washington, D. C. 20005

3652
Research Center on Women
May Bonfils Station Library
Loretto Heights College
3001 S. Federal Blvd.
Denver, Colorado 80236

3653
Sophia Smith Collection
William Allan Neilson Library
Smith College
Northampton, Massachusetts 01060

SPECIAL PERIODICAL ISSUES

3654
The Aframerican Woman's Journal. Special Issue on The Negro Woman in National Defense. Vol. 2, Summer/Fall, 1941.

3655
The Aframerican Woman's Journal. Special Issue on The Negro Woman Serves America. Vol. 3, Summer, 1943.

3656
The Aframerican Woman's Journal. Special Issue On Women's Archives And Seminar Issues. Vol. 1, Summer/Fall, 1940.

3657
The Afro American Magazine. Special Issue on Black Woman's World. November 25, 1972.

3658
Black Arts Review. Special Issue on Women In Art. Vol. 2, July/August, 1979.

3659
The Black Collegian. Special Issue on Black Women. Vol.6, May/June, 1976.

3660
The Black Collegian. Special Issue on Black Women. Vol. 7, May/June, 1977.

3661
The Black Collegian. Special Issue On Black Women. Vol. 9, May/June, 1979.

3662
Black Enterprise. Special Issue on Black Women. Vol. 5, August, 1974.

3663
Black Scholar. Special Issue on The Black Woman. Vol. 1, January/February, 1970.

3664
Black Scholar. Special Issue on Black Women. Vol. 3, December, 1971.

3665
Black Scholar. Special Issue on Black Women's Liberation. Vol. 4, March/April, 1973.

3666
Black Scholar. Special Issue on The Black Woman, 1975. Vol. 6, March, 1975.

3667
Core. Special Issue on Black Women. Vol. 3, Summer, 1973.

3668
The Crisis. Special Issue on Black Women. Vol. 82, May, 1975.

3669
The Crisis. Special Issue on Votes For Women. Vol. 10, August,

3670
The Crisis. Special Issue on Woman's Suffrage. Vol. 4, September, 1912.

3671
Ebony. Special Issue on The Negro Woman. Vol. 21, August, 1966.

3672
Encore. Special Issue on Black Women. Vol. 3, Summer, 1973.

3673
Encore. Special Issue on The Black Woman. Vol. 4, June 23/July 4, 1975.

3674
The Journal of Afro-American Issues. Special Issue on Black Women in America. Vol. 2, Summer, 1974.

3675
Journal of Social and Behavioral Sciences. Special Issue on Contemporary Research on Black Women. Vol. 21, Winter, 1975.

3676
The Messenger. Special Issue on The New Negro Woman. Vol. 7, July, 1923.

3677
Monthly Labor Review. Special Issue on Women At Work. Vol. 93, June, 1970.

3678
The Negro History Bulletin. Special Issue on Emphasis on Women. Vol. 39, May, 1976.

3679
Northwest Journal of African and Black American Studies. Special Issue on Black Women. Vol. 2, Winter, 1974.

3680
Opportunity. Special Issues on Brown American Womanpower. Vol. 21, April, 1943.

3681
Opportunity. Special Issue on Negro Nurses. Vol. 15, November, 1937.

3682
Sacramento Observer. Special Issue on Black Women. 1 June, 19 1972.

3683
Social Work. Special Issue on Women. Vol. 21, November, 1976.

3684
Southern Voices. Special Issue on Black Women. Vol. 1, August/September, 1974.

3685
Voice of The Negro. Special Issue on Black Women. Vol. 1, July, 1904.

3686
The Woman's National Magazine. Special Issue On The Phillis Wheatley Department. Vol. 4, March, 1937.

SPORTS, PHYSICAL EDUCATION, AND RECREATION

3687
Abbott, Jessie Ellen. "Teacher Preparation For Physical Education Majors In Twelve Representative Accredited Negro Colleges With Special Reference To Women: (A Comparative Survey)." Master's Thesis, University of Wisconsin, 1941, 51p.

3688
Acklen, Ehrai Walker. "A Study of The Recreational Program At The Tennessee Vocational School For Colored Girls In Nashville, Tennessee, In Relation To The Interests Of The Girls Served." Master's Thesis, Atlanta University, 1948, 33p.

3689
Adams, Edward Haygood. "An Anthropometric Study of The Effect of Hard Labor During Youth As A Stimulator of Physical Growth in Young Colored Women." Master's Thesis, University of Iowa, 1936, 18p.

3690
Adkins, Vivian Bernice Lee. "The Development of Negro Female Olympic Talent." Doctoral Dissertation, Indiana University, 1967, 323p.

3691
"Andrea Whitmore Among 3 Tennis Award Winners." Jet. Vol. 56, May 10, 1979, pp. 55.

3692
Arnold, Edith Mae. "A Study of The Recreational Activities Of A Number of Negro Women Working In Industry In Atlanta, Georgia." Master's Thesis, Atlanta University, 1943, 58p.

3693
Athletics," in Black Women Makers of History: A Portrait, by George F. Jackson. Sacramento: Fong & Fong, 1977, 289p., pp. 272-278.

3694
"Back From Russia, Teen Seeks Olympic Track Berth." Jet. Vol. 50, April 1, 1976, pp. 49.

3695
"Black Girls Basketball Team Seeking New Talent." Jet. Vol. 54, February 2, 1978, pp. 49.

3696
"Black Woman Promoter Gets Pro Boxing Match." Jet. Vol. 44, July 5, 1973, pp. 52.

3697
"Black Women in Golf." Sepia. Vol. 19, January, 1970, pp. 46-49.

3698
Brandford, Pat Audrey. "Training And Opportunities For Negro Women In Physical Education." Master's Thesis, State University of Iowa, 1939, 39p.

3699
Brower, William A. "Wilberforce's Mercurial Maiden." Opportunity. Vol. 19, June, 1941, pp. 172-173, 187-188.

3700
"Champion." The Brown American. Vol. 2, January, 1937, pp. 24.

3701
"Charged Atoms: Brooklyn's Mostly Black Atoms Track Club For Women. Newsweek. Vol. 76, July 20, 1970, pp. 42.

3702
"Chicago Girl, 14, Retains Two Tennis Titles." Jet. Vol. 3, April 9, 1953, pp. 54.

3703
"Chicago Girl Makes Sweep at Three European Meets." Jet. Vol. 44, August 30, 1973, pp. 50.

3704
"Chicago Girl Wins Two Tennis Titles." Jet. Vol. 1, April 10, 1952, pp. 52.

3705
"Chicago Woman Sets New World Indoor 220 Record." Jet. Vol. 45, February 21, 1974, pp. 58.

3706
Closs, Elizabeth Lee. "Isokinetic Measurement of Strength In Black And In White University Women." Doctoral Dissertation, Texas Women's University, 1977, 156p.

3707
"Colored Woman Wins City Tennis Title In New York Tourney." New York Age. 15 September, 1923, pp. 1.

3708
"Delta State Women's Cage Coach Retires at 156-21." Jet. Vol. 56, April 19, 1979, pp. 49.

3709
Dodson, Anna Gill. "A Study of The Physical Fitness of The Girls At Ruffner Junior High School, Norfolk, Virginia." Master's Thesis, Hampton Institute, 1960, 57p.

3710
Duke, Robert Page. "A Study Of The Nature of Community Activities Engaged In By Thrity Negro Women at Lynchburg Hoisery Mill Number Two During 1945." Master's Thesis, Atlanta University, 1947, 62p.

3711
Dunham, Elizabeth D. "Physical Education of Women at Hampton Institute." The Southern Workman. Vol. 53, April, 1924, pp. 161-168.

3712
Ebert, Alan. "Women on Wheels." Essence. Vol. 3, April, 1973, pp. 49, 56-57, 66, 78.

3713
Elliott, Ottrus Murlen. "The Evaluation of The Program of Physical Education For Girls In The Negro High Schools of Logan County, West Virginia." Master's Thesis, The Ohio State University, 1952, 75p.

3714
Ellis, A. W. "The Status of Health and Physical Education For Women in Negro Colleges and Universities." Journal of Negro Education. Vol. 8, January, 1939, pp. 58-63.

Ellis, A. E. "The Status of Health and Physical Education For Women in Negro Colleges and Universities." Research Quarterly. Vol. 10, May, 1939, pp. 135-141.

3715
English, Mary W. "The Adaptation of Certain Activities In Physical Education For Girls in Schools For The Blind." Master's Thesis, Hampton Institute, 1945, 44p.

3716
"Female Joe Louis." Our World. Vol. 6, October, 1951, pp. 64-65.

3717
"Female Slugger." Jet. Vol. 46, September 19, 1974, pp. 48.

3718
"Fighting Lady." Our World. Vol. 4, June, 1949, pp. 53-56.

3719
"1st Black Woman Goes to Ga. Hall of Fame." Jet. Vol. 50, April 1, 1976, pp. 50.

3720
"First Negro Team Ever To Win The Annual Women's International Bowling Tournament In Youngstown, Ohio." Jet. Vol. 20, June 22, 1961, pp. 57.

3721
"Flying High." Jet. Vol. 50, June 3, 1976, pp. 13.

3722
"Four Black Tennis Stars "Rise" During Avon Future Tournament." Black Odyssey. Vol. 1, April, 1979, pp. 16-18.

3723
"A Fruitful Past But A Shaky Future." Ebony. Vol. 32, August, 1977, pp. 60-62, 64.

3724
"Gifted Ohio Lass Makes $10,000 Per Year In Wrestling Circuit." Jet. Vol. 3, April 23, 1953, pp. 56-57.

3725
"Girl Fencer." Ebony. Vol. 7, November, 1951, pp. 81-82, 84.

3726
"Girl on The Varsity." Ebony. Vol. 21, May, 1966, pp. 71-72, 74, 76-78.

3727
"Girl Tennis Star." Ebony. Vol. 7, June, 1952, pp. 41-45.

3728
"Girls To Have Track Team." Tuskegee Messenger. Vol. 5, March 9, 1929, pp. 7.

3729
Henderson, Edwin B. "Negro Women In Sports." The Negro History Bulletin. Vol. 15, December, 1951, pp. 55.

3730
"Indianapolis Clowns Sign Woman Infielder." Jet. Vol. 3, March 5, 1953, pp. 51.

3731
Jacobs, Karen Folger. "Earlene Brown: Down From Olympia." Essence. Vol. 10, May, 1979, pp. 12, 14.

3732
Jacobs, Mary G. "An Evaluation of The Physical Education Service Programs For Women In Certain Selected Colleges." Doctoral Dissertation, New York University, 1957.

3733
"Jet's Cover Girl Gets Her Jockey License." Jet. Vol. 40, August 5, 1971, pp. 51.

3734
"Jet's Cover Girl Wins Her First Horse Race Riding Victorious." Jet. Vol. 40, September 23, 1971, pp. 52.

3735
"Jogging Not Harmful To Black Women; It's Dangerous To White Women, Says Expert." Jet. Vol. 56, July 26, 1979, pp. 54.

3736
"Judo Black Belt Queen." Ebony. Vol. 22, April, 1967, pp. 107-108, 110.

3737
"Lady Boxer." Ebony. Vol. 4, March, 1949, pp. 30.

3738
"Lady Boxing Boss." Ebony. Vol. 2, May, 1947, pp. 31-35.

3739
"Lady Horse Trainer." Ebony. Vol. 17, December, 1961, pp. 101-104.

3740
"Lady Pros Seek Golf Glory." Ebony. Vol. 26, July, 1971, pp. 16-18.

3741
"Lady Wrestlers." Jet. Vol. 1, February 21, 1952, pp. 56-58.

3742
"Lorraine Williams Loses in Western Tennis Tourney." Jet. Vol. 6, August 5, 1954, pp. 53.

3743
"Lorraine Williams Named Top Girl Tennis Star." Jet. Vol. 4, December 17, 1953, pp. 56.

3744
"Lorraine Williams Wins, Althea Gibson Loses." Jet. Vol. 8, August 4, 1955, pp. 51.

3745
"Lucy Hits The Ice." Headlines And Pictures. Vol. 3, August, 1946, pp. 25-26.

3746
"Lucienne Collins...Destination: 1980 Olympics." Soul Teen. Vol. 9, July, 1979, pp. 26-27.

3747
Miller, Carrie. "Afro-Women In American Sports." The African. Vol. 6, February/March, 1948, pp. 13.

3748
"Negro Girls In Sports," in The Negro In Sports, by Edwin B. Henderson. Washington, D. C.: The Associated Publishers, 1949, 507p., pp. 230-242.

3749
"Negro Women's Bowling Team, The Termites, From Chicago, Win Rich WHIO Radio and TV Annual Ladies Handicap Tournament, Dayton, Ohio; $1,200 Prize." Jet. Vol. 20, June 8, 1961, pp. 54.

3750
"Nets of Cleveland Sign Black Women To Team." Jet. Vol. 48, May 1, 1975, pp. 50.

3751
"New Upsurge in Women's Track." Ebony. Vol. 18, June, 1963, pp. 115-117.

3752
"Nine Negro Girls Named on U. S. Olympic Team." Chicago Defender. 24 July, 1948.

3753
Norrell, Sondra L. "A Study To Determine The Success of Black Women In Beginning Swimming At Howard University As Related To Opportunity, Exposure And Instruction." Master's Thesis, Howard University, 1973.

3754
"Olympian Quintessence." Life. Vol. 49, September 19, 1960, pp. 115.

3755
Ott, Dwight. "World Trampoline Champ In Air About Her Future." Jet. Vol. 44, August 23, 1973, pp. 44-48.

3756
Pinkney, Ron. "Taking A Sporting Chance." Encore. Vol. 4, June 3/July 4, 1975, pp. 58, 62-63.

3757
"Queen of Kingpins." Ebony. Vol. 3, March, 1948, pp. 52-53.

3758
"Queen of The Courts." Our World. Vol. 6, September, 1951, pp. 46-49.

3759
"Ride On." Jet. Vol. 40, July 8, 1971, pp. 49.

3760
Robinson, Lawrence D. "From Tomboys To Girl Athletes." Essence. Vol. 5, September, 1974, pp. 16.

3761
"Roller Derby Demon." Ebony. Vol. 14, January, 1959, pp. 60, 62-63.

3762
Shoup, Richard Frank. "Anthropometric and Physique Characteris-

tics of Black, Mexican American And White Female High School Athletes in Three Sports." Master's Thesis, University of Texas at Austin, 1978, 59p.

3763
Simmons, Winnie Allen. "A Comparative Study of The Rhythmic Ability of White and Negro Girls In The Ninth Grade." Master's Thesis, University of Texas at Austin, 1940, 64p.

3764
"Sonya Dalton's Coach Says 'She Can Do Anything'." Encore. Vol. 8, April 2, 1979, pp. 46-47.

3765
"A Striking 102." Ebony. Vol. 28, June, 1973, pp. 58-60, 62.

3766
"Table Tennis Champion At Eight." Ebony. Vol. 14, April, 1959, pp. 64-66, 68-69.

3767
"Teen-Aged Girl Cracks Barrier On Race Track." Jet. Vol. 40, July 29, 1971, pp. 46-48.

3768
"Tennessee State Sprinter Named 'Female Athlete of The Year'." Jet. Vol. 39, March 18, 1971, pp. 51.

3769
"340 Pound Mat Queen Tussles With The Law." Jet. Vol. 50, July 1, 1976, pp. 17.

3770
"Tramp Champ." Ebony. Vol. 27, June, 1972, pp. 57-58, 60, 62.

3771
"Two Teams of The 230 Women's Bowling Teams In The Georgia State Women's Bowling Tournament Will Be Negro: This Year for The First Time." Interracial Review. Vol. 35, April, 1962, pp. 106.

3772
"Two Women Set Records in Olympic Trials." Jet. Vol. 2, July 17, 1952, pp. 56.

3773
"Virginia Girl, 15, Sets Record 52 Points In Basketball." Jet. Vol. 50, May 4, 1976, pp. 52.

3774
"Water Whiz." Headlines And Pictures. Vol. 2, October, 1945, pp. 43.

3775
"Weaker Sex? - My Foot." Ebony. Vol. 29, November, 1973, pp. 182-184, 186, 188-190.

3776
Wilkinson, Lula Love. "The Present Status of Physical Education For Women In Negro Colleges and Universities." Master's Thesis, New York University, 1932, 60p.

3777
Williams, Ophelia Clemintine. "A Study of The Leisure Activities of Negro Women In Orangeburg County, South Carolina." Master's Thesis, Pennsylvania State University, 1939, 168p.

3778
"Winning Her Point In A Man's Arena." Ebony. Vol. 30, June, 1975, pp. 44-46, 48, 50, 52.

3779
"Woman Recruiter Looks At Thrills, Spills Of Position." Jet. Vol. 46, July 11, 1974, pp. 50.

3780
"Women In The Ring." Ebony. Vol. 31, April, 1976, pp. 83-84, 86, 88.

3781
"Women May Box, Wrestle in State of Pennsylvania." Jet. Vol. 44, June 28, 1973, pp. 49.

SUFFRAGE

3782
Adams, Mildred. The Right To Be People. Philadelphia: Lippincott, 1966, 248p.

3783
"Agility." The Crisis. Vol. 9, January, 1915, pp. 133.

3784
Baldwin, Maria L. "Votes For Teachers." The Crisis. Vol. 10, August, 1915, pp. 189.

3785
Braithwaite, William Stanley. "Democracy And Art." The Crisis. Vol. 10, August, 1915, pp. 186-187.

3786
Brawley, Benjamin. "Politics and Womanliness." The Crisis. Vol. 10, August, 1915, pp. 179.

3787
Bruce, Blanche K. (Mrs.). "Colored Women's Clubs." The Crisis. Vol. 10, August, 1915, pp. 190.

3788
Burroughs, Nannie H. "Black Women and Reform." The Crisis. Vol. 10, August, 1915, pp. 187.

3789
Chesnutt, Charles W. "Women's Rights." The Crisis. Vol. 10, August, 1915, pp. 182-183.

3790
Clifford, Carrie W. "Votes For Children." The Crisis. Vol. 10, August, 1915, pp. 185.

3791
"Colored Women And Suffrage." New York Globe. 27 September, 1917.

3792
Cook, Coralie Franklin. "Votes For Mothers." *The Crisis*. Vol. 10, August, 1915, pp. 184-185.

3793
Crogman, W. H. "Woman in The Ancient State." *The Crisis*. Vol. 10, August, 1915, pp. 181-182.

3794
Davis, Elizabeth L. "Votes For Philanthropy." *The Crisis*. Vol. 10, August, 1915, pp. 191.

3795
De Priest, Oscar. "Chicago and Woman's Suffrage." *The Crisis*. Vol. 10, August, 1915, pp. 179.

3796
Du Bois, W. E. B. "The Ballot." *The Crisis*. Vol. 17, December, 1918, pp. 62.

3797
______________. "Decent Into Hell." *The Crisis*. Vol. 18, June, 1919, pp. 6.

3798
______________. "Get Ready." *The Crisis*. Vol. 20, May, 1920, pp. 5-6.

3799
______________. "Suffrage." *The Crisis*. Vol. 21, November, 1920, pp. 7-8.

3800
______________. "Triumph." *The Crisis*. Vol. 20, October, 1920, pp. 261.

3801
______________. "Votes." *The Crisis*. Vol. 19, December, 1919, pp. 44.

3802
______________. "Votes For Women." *The Crisis*. Vol. 4, September, 1912, pp. 234.

3803
______________. "The Woman Voter." *The Crisis*. Vol. 21, March, 1921, pp. 200.

3804
Dunbar, Paul Lawrence (Mrs.). "Votes And Literature." *The Crisis*. Vol. 10, August, 1915, pp. 184.

3805
Flexner, Eleanor. *Century of Struggle: The Woman's Rights Movement in The United States*. Cambridge: Belknap Press, 1959, 384p.

3806
Foner, Philip S. Frederick Douglass On Women's Rights. Connecticut: Greenwood Press, 1976, 190.

3807
"Forward, Backward." The Crisis. Vol. 2, October, 1911, pp. 243-244.

3808
Garland, Phyl. "Builders Of A New South." Ebony. Vol. 21, August, 1966, pp. 27-30, 34, 36, 37.

3809
Greuning, Martha. "Two Suffrage Movements." The Crisis. Vol. 4, September, 1912, pp. 245-247.

3810
Grimke, Francis J. "The Logic of Woman Suffrage." The Crisis. Vol. 10, August, 1915, pp. 178-179.

3811
"Hail Columbia." The Crisis. Vol. 5, April, 1913, pp. 289-290.

3812
Hershaw, L. M. "Disfranchisement in The District of Columbia." The Crisis. Vol. 10, August, 1915, pp. 183.

3813
Hunton, A. W. "Y.W.C.A." The Crisis. Vol. 10, August, 1915, pp. 188-189.

3814
Hurst, John. "Christianity And Women." The Crisis. Vol. 10, August, 1915, pp. 179-180.

3815
Jackson, M. E. "The Self-Supporting Woman And The Ballot." The Crisis. Vol. 10, August, 1915, pp. 187-188.

3816
Johnson, J. W. "About Aunties." The Crisis. Vol. 10, August, 1915, pp. 180-181.

3817
Jonas, Rosalie. "Brother Baptis' On Woman Suffrage." The Crisis. Vol. 4, September, 1912, pp. 247.

3818
Jones, Anna H. "Woman Suffrage And Social Reform." The Crisis. Vol. 10, August, 1915, pp. 189-190.

3819
Kitchelt, Florence L. C. "Chapters in History of Human Rights." Journal of Human Relations. Vol. 4, Winter, 1956, pp. 61-76.

3820
Logan, Adella H. "Colored Women As Voters." The Crisis. Vol. 4, September, 1912, pp. 242-243.

3821
Lynch, John R. "States' Rights and The Suffrage." The Crisis. Vol. 10, August, 1915, pp. 183.

3822
Mayo, A. D. "The Woman's Movement in The South." New England Magazine. Vol. 5, October, 1891, pp. 249-260.

3823
Miller, Kelly. "The Risk of Woman Suffrage." The Crisis. Vol. 11, November, 1915, pp. 37-38.

3824
"Most Rigid Tests Applied to Afro-American Women." Norfolk Journal And Guide. 2 October, 1920.

3825
"Mrs. Ida B. Wells and Her Crusaders Criticized," in The Philosophy of Negro Suffrage, by Jerome R. Riley. Hartford: Connecticut: American Publishing Company, 1895, 110p., pp. 46-51

3826
Murray, Ella Rush. "The Woman's Party and The Violation of The 19th Amendment." The Crisis. Vol. 21, April, 1921, pp. 259-261.

3827
"Negro Suffragettes To Meet." New York Tribune. 19 January, 1910.

3828
"The Negro Woman and Suffrage." Baltimore Commonwealth. 11 October, 1918.

3829
The Negro Woman And Suffrage. Newspaper Clippings, 1910-1918. Clipping #182. Hampton, Virginia: Hampton Institute, Peabody Collection.

3830
"Negro Women Ask Fair Play." New York Globe. 10 October, 1917.

3831
"New Citizen And Her Vote." The Crisis. Vol. 20, October, 1920, pp. 278-282.

3832
"Ohio." The Crisis. Vol. 4, August, 1912, pp. 181-182.

3833
"Organize Negro Women." Philadelphia Record. 5 October, 1915.

3834
"Our Colored Sisters, The North Star, November 16, 1849," in Frederick Douglass On Women's Rights, by Philip S. Foner. Connecticut: Greenwood Press, 1976, 190p., pp. 52-53.

3835
Pickens, William. "The Woman Voter Hits The Color Line," in A Documentary History of The Negro People In The United States, 1910-1932, edited by Herbert Aptheker. New Jersey: Citadel Press, 1973, 754p., pp. 305-309.

3836
Ruffin, Josephine St. Pierre. "Trust The Women." The Crisis. Vol. 10, August, 1915, pp. 188.

3837
"Says Negro Women With Ballot Would Aid Race." Philadelphia North American. 26 July, 1915.

3838
Scott, Minnie M. "Views on Women and The Franchise." Norfolk Journal And Guide. 25 November, 1916, pp. 3.

3839
"Senators' Records." The Crisis. Vol. 8, June, 1914, pp. 77-78.

3840
"Some Political Echoes." The Crisis. Vol. 7, April, 1914, pp. 277-278.

3841
"Some Southern Logic." The Crisis. Vol. 7, December, 1913, pp. pp. 76-77.

3842
"South Strongly Opposes Negro Women As Voters." Brooklyn Eagle. 1 October, 1918.

3843
Straker, Davis A. Citizenship, Its Rights and Duties - Woman Suffrage. Washington, D. C. New National Era Printers, 1874, 22p.

3844
"Suffering Suffragettes." The Crisis. Vol. 4, June, 1912, pp. 76-77.

3845
"Suffrage Again." Newport News Star. 12 July, 1918.

3846
Talbert, Mary B. "Women And Colored Women." The Crisis. Vol. 10, August, 1915, pp. 184.

3847
Terborg-Penn, Rosalyn. "Afro Americans In The Struggle For Woman Suffrage." Doctoral Dissertation, Howard University, 1978.

3848
______. "Nineteenth Century Black Women And Woman Suffrage." The Potomac Review. Vol. 7, Spring/Summer, 1977, pp. 13-24.

3849
Terrell, Mary C. "The Justice of Woman Suffrage." The Crisis. Vol. 4, September, 1912, pp. 243-245.

3850
______. "Use The Franchise! An Appeal To Colored Women To Vote." The Aframerican Woman's Journal. Fall, 1946, pp. 5, 12-13.

3851
______. "Woman Suffrage and The 15th Amendment." The Crisis. Vol. 10, August, 1915, pp. 191

3852
Terrell, Robert H. "Our Debt To Suffragists." The Crisis. Vol. 10, August, 1915, pp. 181.

3853
Thurman, Sue Bailey and Lucy Schulte. "On This We Stand." Radio Script, WWDC, Washington, D. C., June 29, 1946, 8p.

3854
Truth, Sojourner. "Ain't I A Woman?" in Feminism: The Essential Historical Writings, by Miriam Schneir. New York: Random House, 1972, 360p., pp. 93-95.

3855
______. "Keeping The Thing Going While Things Are Stirring," in Feminism: The Essential Historical Writings, by Miriam Schneir. New York: Random House, 1972, 360p., pp. 128-131.

3856
______. "What Time of Night Is It," in Feminism: The Essential Historical Writings, by Miriam Schneir. New York: Random House, 1972, 360p., pp. 96-98.

3857
"Trying To Vote - Letters From Hampton, Va., October 28, 1920," in A Documentary History of The Negro People In The United States, 1910-1932, edited by Herbert Aptheker. New Jersey: Citadel Press, 1973, 754p., pp. 315.

3858
Turner, Lillian A. "Votes For Housewives." The Crisis. Vol. 10, August, 1915, pp. 192.

3859
"Two Black Women Discuss Frederick Douglass As A Champion Of The Woman Suffrage Movement," in Frederick Douglass On Women's Rights, by Philip S. Foner. Connecticut: Greenwood Press, 1976, 190p., pp. 170-181.

3860
Villard, Fanny G. "Garrison And Woman's Suffrage." The Crisis. Vol. 4, September, 1912, pp. 240-242.

3861
"Votes For All - A Symposium." The Crisis. Vol. 15, November, 1912, pp. 19-21.

3862
"Votes For Women." The Crisis. Vol. 8, August, 1914, pp. 179-180.

3863
"Votes For Women." The Crisis. Vol. 15, November, 1917, pp. 8.

3864
"Votes For Women, Symposium by Leading Thinkers of Colored Americans." The Crisis. Vol. 10, August, 1915, pp. 178-192.

3865
Walker, S. Jay. "Frederick Douglass and Woman Suffrage." Black Scholar. Vol. 4, March/April, 1973, pp. 24-31.

3866
Waring, Mary F. "Training and The Ballot." The Crisis. Vol. 10, August, 1915, pp. 185-186.

3867
"What Women May Do - Suffragists Talk of The Work Which Is Open To Them." Wasington Post. 10 February, 1900.

3868
"White Suffragettes Ask Colored Women To Help." Washington Afro American. 3 June, 1916.

3869
"Woman Suffrage." The Crisis. Vol. 9, April, 1915, pp. 285.

3870
"Woman Suffrage." The Crisis. Vol. 11, November, 1915, pp. 29-30.

3871
"Woman Suffrage." The Crisis. Vol. 19, March, 1920, pp. 234.

3872
"A Woman's Suffrage Symposium." The Crisis. Vol. 4, September, 1912, pp. 240-247.

3873
"Woman's Vote And The Negro." New York Post. 16 October, 1917.

3874
"Women With The Vote," in The Southern Lady: From Pedestal To Politics, 1830-1930, by Anne Firor Scott. Chicago: The University of Chicago Press, 1970, 247p., pp. 197-198.

3875
"Women's Brains." Opportunity. Vol. 1, April, 1923, pp. 4.

3876
"Women's Citizenship Classes." The Crisis. Vol. 21, November, 1920, pp. 23-25.

3877
"Women's Suffrage." Chicago Defender. 12 October, 1918.

THEATER AND FILM INDUSTRY

3878
Armstead-Johnson, Helen. "Some Late Information on Some Early People." Encore. Vol. 4, June 23/July 4, 1975, pp. 48, 52-53.

3879
"The Black Woman As A Sex Image In Films." Black Stars. Vol. 21, December, 1972, pp. 32-39.

3880
"The Black Woman In 1972...A Retrospective." Black Stars. Vol. 28, November, 1978, pp. 26.

3881
"Black Women Stars Behind Scenes In New York Drama." Ebony. Vol. 28, April, 1973, pp. 106-108.

3882
"Bloody Mary Makes Good." Our World. Vol. 6, November, 1951, pp. 23-26.

3883
Bond, Jean Carey. "The Media Image of Black Women." Freedomways. Vol. 15, #1, 1975, pp. 34-37.

Bond, Jean Carey. "The Media Image of Black Women," in A Freedomways Reader: Afro Americans In The Seventies, edited by Ernest Kaiser. New York: International Publishers, 1977, 432p., pp. 230-234.

3884
"Broadway 'Oriental'." Ebony. Vol. 14, March, 1959, pp. 128-130.

3885
"Claudine: A Movie That Blacks Can Relate To." Jet. Vol. 46, July 4, 1974, pp. 56-59.

3886
"Colored Woman Is Big Film Producer." Norfolk Journal And Guide. 5 May, 1923, pp. 1.

3887
"First Black Woman Chosen For Director's Program." Jet. Vol. 44, August 9, 1973, pp. 54.

3888
Gant, Liz. "Ain't Beulah Dead Yet? Or Images of The Black Woman In Film." Essence. Vol. 4, May, 1973, pp. 61, 72-73, 75.

3889
Gent, George. "Black Women Take Roles As Directors." New York Times. 17 November, 1971, pp. 40-C.

3890
Greene, Laura. "Bad Black Image In Film." Essence. Vol. 4, May, 1973, pp. 70.

3891
"Hilda Sims: First Negro Lady of The Theater." Our World. Vol. 2, April, 1947, pp. 31.

3892
Horton, Luci. "Battle Among The Beauties: Black Actresses Vie For Top Movie Roles." Ebony. Vol. 29, November, 1973, pp. 144-146, 148, 150.

3893
"Iridescent Fredi: Black Girl In Search Of A Black Role," in Toms, Coons, Mulattoes, Mammies, And Bucks, by Donald Bogle, New York: Viking Press, 1973, 260p., pp. 60-62.

3894
"Judy Pace Wants Better Roles for Black Women." Jet. Vol. 45, October 4, 1973, pp. 86.

3895
Kisner, Ronald E. "What Films Are Doing To The Image of Black Women." Jet. Vol. 42, June 29, 1972, pp. 56-61.

3896
"The Mammy," in Toms, Coons, Mulattoes, Mammies, And Bucks, by Donald Bogle. New York: Viking Press, 1973, 260p., pp. 9.

3897
Mapp, Edward. "Black Women in Films." Black Scholar. Vol. 5, March/April, 1973, pp. 42-46.

3898
Martin, Sharon Stockard. "The Invisible Reflection: Images And Self-Images of Black Women On State And Screen." The Black Collegian. Vol. 9, May/June, 1979, pp. 74-81.

3899
"Movie Director; Marie Bryant Teaches Dancing Routines To Hollywood Stars." Ebony. Vol. 5, April, 1950, pp. 22-26.

3900
"Pinky's Tragic Mulatto And Its Strong Black Woman," in Toms, Coons, Mulattoes, Mammies And Bucks, by Donald Bogle. New York: Viking Press, 1973, 260p., pp. 150-154.

3901
Pollard, Gayle. "Black Women In The Movies - Where Is Reality?" Miami Herald. 11 August, 1974, pp. 8-G.

3902
Reid, Hazel. "First Lady of The Theatre: Anita Bush." Essence. Vol. 3, June, 1972, pp. 36-37, 79.

3903
Smallwood, William. "They Made Good In The Movie Capital." Opportunity. Vol. 19, March, 1941, pp. 76-77.

3904
Smith, Barbara. "Reader's Forum: Black Women In Film Symposium." Freedomway. Vol. 14, #3, 1974, pp. 266-269.

3905
"Sue Shapiro: Lady Movie Producer." Sepia. Vol. 19, August, 1970, pp. 32-36.

3906
Symposium On Black Images In Films. Stereotypes And Self Perception As Viewed By Black Actresses. Boston: Boston University, 1974, 69p.

3907
Taylor, Clyde. "The Screen Scene: A Review Of The Movies." The Black Collegian. Vol. 9, May/June, 1979, pp. 94-96.

3908
Thompson, Cordell S. "Black History: Anita Bush Called 'Mother' of Black Theatre." Jet. Vol. 39, February 18, 1971, pp. 60-61.

3909
"The Tragic Mulatto," in Toms, Coons, Mulattoes, Mammies, And Bucks, by Donald Bogle. New York: Viking Press, 1973, 260p. pp. 9.

3910
"Why Brownskin Girls Get The Best Movie Roles." Jet. Vol. 2, Ocotber 16, 1952, pp. 56-61.

WOMEN'S RIGHTS AND FEMINIST MOVEMENT

3911
Athey, Louis L. "Florence Kelley and The Quest for Negro Equality." Journal of Negro History. Vol. 56, October, 1971, pp. 249-261.

3912
Ballard, Audreen. "Feminism: A Way for Black Women to Survive." Washington Post. 4 December, 1973.

3913
Beal, Frances. "Double Jeopardy: To Be Black And Female," in Female Liberation: History and Current Politics, by Roberta Salper. New York: Knopf, 1972, 246p., pp. 208-218.

Beal. Frances. "Double Jeopardy: To Be Black And Female," in Sisterhood Powerful, by Robin Morgan. New York: Vantage Books, 1970, 577p., pp. 340-352.

Beal, Frances. "Double Jeopardy: To Be Black And Female," in The New Women, edited by Joanne Cooke, Charlotte Bunch-Weeks, and Robin Morgan. New York: Bobbs-Merrill, 1970, 196p., pp. 44-57.

3914
"Black Feminism: A New Mandate." Ms. Vol. 2, May, 1974, pp. 97-100.

3915
"Black Feminists Announce Nationwide Organization." Jet. Vol. 44, August 30, 1973, pp. 5.

3916
"Black Panther Women Speak," in The Black Panthers Speak, edited by Philip Foner. Philadelphia: Lippincott, 1970, 274p., pp. 145-165.

3917
"The Black Struggle, Affirmative Action, and Women's Liberat-

ion: Establishing Priorities," in Perspectives On Afro American Women, edited by Willa D. Johnson and Thomas L. Green. Washington, D. C.: Educational Community Counselors Associates, Inc., 1975, 197p., pp. 1-10.

3918
"Black Women: Internationalizing The Struggle." Freedomways. Vol. 15, #1, 1975, pp. 5-6.

3919
"Black Women in Revolt," in Feminist Frameworks: Alternative Theoretical Accounts of The Relations Between Women And Men, edited by Alison M. Jagger and Paul R. Struhl. New York: McGraw Hill, 1978, 333p., pp. 45-51.

3920
"Black Women's Group Starts Feminism School." Jet. Vol. 56, April 26, 1979, pp. 51.

3921
"Blacks vs. Feminists." Time. Vol. 101. March 26, 1973, pp. 64.

3922
Bradley, Valeria Jo. "Feminist Likens Sexism to Racism Against Blacks." Jet. Vol. 38, June 4, 1970, pp. 46-50.

3923
"Brenda Verner Examines Liberated Sisters." Encore. Vol. 3, April, 1974, pp. 22-24.

3924
Burke, Ruth. "Why Black Women Control The Future." The Black Collegian. Vol. 6, May/June, 1976, pp. 18, 67.

3925
Chambers, Eddie. "Black Perspectives on the Women's Liberation Movement." Master's Thesis, Atlanta University, 1973.

3926
Chisholm, Shirley. "The 51% Minority, 1970," in The American Sisterhood: Writings of The Feminist Movement From Colonial Times To The Present, by Wendy Martin. New York: Harper & Row, 1972, 374p., pp. 144-151.

3927
________________. "Racism and Anti-Feminism." Black Scholar. Vol. 1, January/February, 1970, pp. 40-45.

3928
________________. "Women Must Rebel," in Voices of The New Feminism, by Mary Lou Thompson. Boston: Beacon Press, 1970, 246p., pp. 207-216.

3929
Cole, Dorothy. "A Typological Study of The Women's Rights

Movement: Implications For Black Women And Education." Doctoral Dissertation, Rutgers University, 1976, 383p.

3930
Conely, Madelyn. "Do Black Women Need the Women's Lib?" Essence. Vol. 1, August, 1970, pp. 29-34.

3931
Cummings, Gwenna. "Black Women - Often Discussed But Never Understood," in The Black Power Revolt, by Floyd B. Barbour. Massachusetts: Porter Sargent Publishers, 1968, 287p., pp. 235-239.

3932
DeJoie, Carolyn M. "The Black Woman In Alienation In White Academia." The Negro Educational Review. Vol. 28, January, 1977, pp. 4-12.

3933
Dennison, Mary. "Total Liberation Before New Roles." Sacramento Observer. 1 June, 1972, pp. D-4.

3934
Dreyfuss, Joel. "Civil Rights And The Women's Movement." Black Enterprise. Vol. 8, September, 1977, pp. 35-37.

3935
"Feminism: The Black Nuance." Newsweek. Vol. 82, December 17, 1973, pp. 89.

3936
"Feminist Movements Through The Ages - Remarks: Sojourner Truth," in Women Out of History: A Herstory Anthology, edited by Ann Forfreedom. Los Angeles: Ann Forfreedom, 1972, 255p., pp. 228.

3937
Gillespie, Marcia A. "Getting Down: A Black Woman's View of Women's Liberation." Essence. Vol. 2, February, 1972, pp. 25-27.

3938
__________. "Jackson on Male/Female Roles." Sacramento Observer. 1 June, 1972, pp. D-5.

3939
Giovanni, Nikki. "Why Weren't Our 'Sisters In Liberation' In Boston?" Encore. Vol. 4, January 6, 1975, pp. 20.

3940
Golden, Bernett. "Black Women's Liberation." Essence. Vol. 4, February, 1974, pp. 36-37, 75-76, 86.

3941
Gordon, L. "Radical Academic Guide, Women And History." Liberation. Vol. 15, January, 1971, pp. 45-47.

3942
Guswiler, Mert. "The Black Woman and The Women's Liberation Movement." Sepia. Vol. 19, October, 1970, pp. 63, 65.

3943
Hall, Richard. "Do Women Want To Be Free?" Essence. Vol. 1, July, 1970, pp. 7.

3944
Hare, Nathan. "What Happened To The Black Movement." Black World. Vol. 25, January, 1976, pp. 20-32.

3945
Hemmons, Willa Mae. "Towards An Understanding of Attitudes Held By The Black Women On The Women's Liberation Movement." Doctoral Dissertation, Case Western Reserve University, 1973, 173p.

3946
Howard, Odette M. "Black Woman - Find Yourself." Essence. Vol. 3, May, 1972, pp. 12.

3947
Hunter, Charlayne. "Black Women and the Liberation Movement." Black Politician. Vol. 2, January, 1971, pp. 15, 39.

3948
Jackson, Larry R. "Welfare Mothers and Black Liberation. Black Scholar. Vol. 1, April, 1970, pp. 31-37.

3949
Jeffers, Trellie. "The Black Black Woman and The Black Middle Class." Black Scholar. Vol. 4, March/April, 1973, pp. 37-41.

3950
Jefferson, Margo and Margaret Sloane. "In Defense of Black Feminism." Encore. Vol. 3, July, 1974, pp. 46-47.

3951
Johnson, Patrice. "Black Women's Rights: A Bread and Butter Issue." Encore. Vol. 6, November 21, 1977, pp. 10-12.

3952
Jordan, June. "Second Thoughts Of A Black Feminist." Ms. Vol. 5, February, 1977, pp. 113-115.

3953
King, Helen. "The Black Woman And Women's Lib." Ebony. Vol. 26, March, 1971, pp. 68-76.

3954
Kolmer, Elizabeth. "Nineteenth Century Woman's Rights Movement: Black and White." The Negro History Bulletin. Vol. 35, December, 1972, pp. 178-180.

3955
Koontz, Elizabeth Duncan. "Women As A Minority," in Voices Of The New Feminism, by Mary Lou Thompson. Boston: Beacon Press, 1970, 246p., pp. 77-86.

3956
Ladner, Joyce. "Redefining Black Womanhood." Sacramento Observer. 1 June, 1972, pp. D-4.

3957
LaRue, Linda. "Black Liberation and Women's Lib." Transaction. Vol. 8, November/December, 1970, pp. 59-64.

3958
__________. "The Black Movement and Women's Liberation." Black Scholar. Vol. 1, May, 1970, pp. 36-42.

3959
Lewis, Helen Matthews. The Woman Movement And The Negro Movement, Parallel Struggles For Rights. Charlottesville: University of Virginia, 1949, 89p.

3960
Lewis, Ida. "I Am A Woman." Essence. Vol. 1, January, 1971, pp. 21.

3961
Lomax, Alena. "Women's Lib Reductio ad Absurdum." Ebony. Vol. 28, July, 1973, pp. 122.

3962
Lomax, Betty Frank. "Afro-American Woman: Growth Deferred." Liberator. Vol. 6, May, 1966, pp. 18.

3963
Lomax, Pearl. "Black Women's Lib?" Essence. Vol. 3, August, 1972, pp. 68.

3964
Lucas, Emily Diedre. "A Study of Black People's Perception Of The Liberation of The Black Woman." Master's Thesis, Atlanta University, 1973, 58p.

3965
Mayo, Julia. "The New Black Feminism: A Minority Report," in Contemporary Sexual Behavior: Critical Issues In The 1970's, edited by Joseph Zubin and John Money. Baltimore: The Johns Hopkins University Press, 1973, 468p., pp. 175-186.

3966
McCluskey, Aurdry. "Is There Only One Role For The Black Woman?" Essence. Vol. 1, March, 1971, pp. 11.

3967
Mitchell, J. "Out From Under...Excerpt." Liberation. Vol. 16, December, 1971, pp. 6-13.

3968
Morris, Linda G. "More Power To You, Ms. Ann." The Crisis. Vol. 84, August/September, 1977, pp. 374-375.

3969
Morrison, Toni. "Black Women and Women's Lib." Sacramento Observer. 1 June, 1972, pp. D-6.

3970
____________. "What The Black Woman Thinks of Women's Lib." New York Times Magazine. August 22, 1971, pp. 14-15.

3971
Murphy, Sara. "Women's Lib In The South." New South. Vol. 27, Spring, 1972,pp. 42-46.

3972
Murray, Pauli. "The Liberation of Black Women," in Voices Of The New Feminism, by Mary Lou Thompson. Boston: Beacon Press, 1970, 246p., pp. 87-102.

Murray, Pauli. "The Liberation of Black Women," in Women: A Feminist Perspective, edited by Jo Freeman. Palo Alto, California: Mayfield Publishing Company, 1975, 487p., pp. 351-363.

3973
"A Negro Woman On Women's Rights, 1827," in A Documentary History of The Negro People In The United States, Vol. 1, New York: Citadel Press, 1951, 942p., pp. 89.

3974
Newman, Pamela. "Take A Good Look At Our Problem. The Militant. October 30, 1970, pp. 12-15.

Newman, Pamela. "Take A Good Look At Our Problem," in The American Sisterhood: Writings of The Feminist Movement From Colonial Times To The Present, edited by Wendy Martin. New York: Harper & Row, 1972, 374p., pp. 179-182.

3975
Norton, Eleanor Holmes. "For Sadie And Maude," in Sisterhood Powerful, by Robin Morgan. New York: Vantage Books, 1970, 577p., pp. 353-359.

3976
Peterson, Franklynn. "Fannie Lou Hamer: Mother of 'Black Women's Lib'." Sepia. Vol. 21, December, 1972, pp. 16-24.

3977
Poussaint, Alvin. "Black Women Are Double Subjegated." Essence. Vol. 1, May, 1970, pp. 75.

3978
Prettyman, Julia. "Black Feminity." Sacramento Observer. 1 June, 1972, pp. D-4.

3979
Quarles, Benjamin. "Frederick Douglass and The Women's Rights Movement." Journal of Negro History. Vol. 25, January, 1940, pp. 35-44.

3980
"Rep. Chisholm Criticizes Women's Lib Convention." Jet. Vol. 43, March 1, 1973, pp. 25.

3981
Rickman, Geraldine. "A Natural Alliance: The New Role For Black Women." The Civil Rights Digest. Vol. 6, Spring, 1974, pp. 57-65

3982
Rodgers, Evelyn. "Sisters - Stop Castrating The Black Man!" Liberator. Vol. 6, May, 1966, pp. 21.

3983
Rogers, C. "Blacks and The Feminists." Christian Century. Vol. 91, February 13, 1974, pp. 172-173.

3984
"The Role of The Black Woman in A White Society." Liberator. Vol. 5, August, 1965, pp. 4-5.

3985
"The Role of Women in The Liberation Struggle. Voice of Women. 1st quarter, 1978, pp. 6-7.

3986
Shockley, Ann Allen. "The New Black Feminists." Northwest Journal of African and Black American Studies. Vol. 2, Winter, 1974, pp. 1-5.

3987
Sloan, Margaret. "Keeping The Black Woman In Her Place." Ms. Vol. 11, January, 1974, pp. 30-31.

3988
Sloan, Margaret and Gloria Steinem. "Ms -- Today and Tomorrow." The Civil Rights Digest. Vol. 5, Spring, 1973, pp. 34-42.

3989
Smythe, Mabel M. "Feminism And Black Liberation," in Women In Higher Education, edited by W. Todd Furniss and Patricia A. Graham. Washington, D. C.: American Council on Education, 1974, 336p., pp. 279-281.

3990
Staples, Robert. "Some Comments on Black Women And Women's Liberation." Black Scholar. Vol. 1, June, 1970, pp. 53-54.

3991
Stiles, Thelma. "Later For The Feminists." New Lady. Vol. 4, July/August, 1971, pp. 18-20, 33.

3992
Stimpson, Catharine R. "Conflict, Probable; Coalition, Possible: Feminism And The Black Movement," in *Women In Higher Education*, edited by W. Todd Furniss and Patricia A. Graham. Washington, D. C.: American Council on Education, 1974, 336p., pp. 261-278.

3993
Stokes, Gail. "Black Woman To Black Man." *Liberator*. Vol. 8, December, 1968, pp. 17.

3994
Stone, M. "Liberation Struggle Generated Tension on Race, Sex Issues." *Christian Century*. Vol. 87, June, 1970, pp. 736-739.

3995
Trescott, Jacqueline. "Focus - Black Women." *Washington Evening Star*. 28 December, 1970.

3996
U. S. President's Task Force on Women's Rights and Responsibilities. *A Matter of Simple Justice*. Washington, D. C.: G. P. O., 1970, 33p.

3997
Washington, Jackie. "Appeal To Black Women - 'Lib' Strike Boycott Urged." *Washington Sunday Star*. 23 August, 1970.

3998
Welsing, Frances. C. "Black Women Moving Toward The 21st Century." *Essence*. Vol. 6, December, 1975, pp. 50-51, 98, 100, 103.

3999
Welsing, Frances and Imamu Baraka. "The Woman Question." *Blacknews*. Vol. 2, October 30, 1974, pp. 5-8.

4000
"What Women Want." *Encore*. Vol. 4, June 23/July 4, 1975, pp. 17.

4001
Whyte, Annette. "The Afro American Woman. " *African Woman*. Vol. 1, October/November, 1975, pp. 43.

4002
Williams, Maxine. "Why Women's Liberation Is Important To Black Women." *The Militant*. July 3, 1970, pp. 3-11.

Williams, Maxine. "Why Women's Liberation Is Important To Black Women, 1970," in *The American Sisterhood: Writings of The Feminist Movement From Colonial Times To The Present*, by Wendy Martin. New York: Harper & Row, 1972, 374p., pp. 171-178.

4003
Williams, Valena M. "Aileen Hernandez, Women's Lib." Urban West. Vol. 3, July/August, 1970, pp. 12-13, 31-35.

4004
"The Woman Movement and The War," in Everyone Was Brave: The Rise and Fall of Feminism In America. Chicago: Quandrangle Books, 1969, 369p., pp. 197-198.

4005
"Women In The Black Liberation Movement: Three Views," in Sisterhood Powerful, by Robin Morgan. New York: Vantage Books, 1970, 577p., pp. 340-361.

4006
Women's International Democratic Federation. For Their Rights As Mothers, Workers, Citizens. Berlin: WIDF, n.d., 62p.

4007
Wright, Charles. "On My Mind: Progress Can't Make Black Women Hard or Cold." Vogue. Vol. 162, July, 1973, pp. 66.

4008
Yellin, Jean Fegan. "DuBois' Crisis and Woman's Suffrage. The Massachusetts Review. Vol. 14, Spring, 1973, pp. 365-375.

INDEX

About the Compiler

JANET L. SIMS is reference librarian at the Moorland-Spingarn Research Center at Howard University, Washington, D.C. She is the compiler of the bibliography *Black Women in the Employment Sector* and assisted Lenwood G. Davis in compiling *The Black Family in the United States* (Greenwood Press, 1978).